Adobe®
Type Library *OpenType® Edition*

Reference Book

Adobe

Notes:

➻ ℮ indicates an Adobe Originals typeface. For more information, refer to pages 7–10.

➻ For a complete listing of symbol and ornament faces, refer to pages 47–48.

Remarques :

➻ ℮ asignale les polices Adobe Originals. Pour plus d'informations, reportez-vous aux pages 7–10.

➻ Pour obtenir la liste complète des polices de symboles et ornementales, reportez-vous aux pages 47–48.

Hinweise:

➻ ℮ kennzeichnet eine Adobe Originals-Schrift. Weitere Informationen hierzu finden Sie auf den Seiten 7–10.

➻ Eine vollständige Liste der Symbol- und Ornamentschriften finden Sie auf den Seiten 47–48.

www.adobe.com/type

Vast Selection With more than 2,200 typefaces from internationally renowned foundries, such as Adobe, Agfa Monotype, ITC, and Linotype, as well as award-winning individual type designers and distinguished design studios, the Adobe Type Library offers one of the largest collections of high-quality type in the world. In addition, all typefaces in the Adobe Type Library are now delivered in OpenType format, a true cross-platform font format for the Macintosh and Windows® platforms that works with most popular applications. More details about the OpenType format are given on page 11.

World-Class Quality Adobe's expert typographic staff thoroughly analyzes every aspect of a typeface before it is allowed to join the Adobe Type Library. Specially designed, Adobe software tools assure that licensed typefaces remain true to their original foundry designs and that exclusive Adobe Originals capture the designer's intent with unparalleled digital precision. All typefaces in the Adobe Type Library undergo extensive testing to guarantee that the fonts live up to Adobe's unrivaled standard of excellence.

Immediate Availability Adobe type is easily accessible over the Web, 24 hours a day, 7 days a week. Visit Adobe's Web site, *www.adobe.com/ type* (or your local Adobe web site), and discover the amazing depth and power of the Adobe Type Browser. Use it to learn more about the history of type and type designers. View type by the many classifications shown on pages 32–49 and even more that are unique to the Type Browser. In addition to the Type Browser, *www.adobe. com/type* offers up-to-the-minute information about special offers, new releases, and tips & techniques. Whenever you have questions about typography, *www.adobe.com/type* has answers.

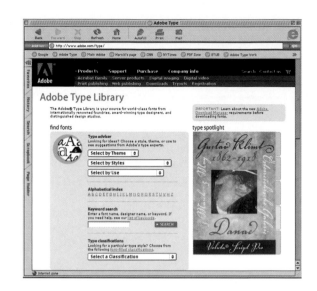

Visit www.adobe.com/type *for the latest news about the Adobe Type Library, including Current Pricing, New Releases, Special Offers, Tips and Techniques, Designer Biographies, and much more.*

Consultez le site www.adobe.com/type *pour connaître les nouvelles de dernière minute sur Adobe Type Library. Il vous renseigne sur les prix, les nouvelles versions et les offres spéciales, tout en vous proposant des conseils et des astuces, la biographie des créateurs d'Adobe Type Library et une foule d'autres informations.*

Besuchen Sie unsere Website www.adobe.com/type *und erfahren Sie die neuesten Nachrichten über Adobe Type Library sowie aktuelle Preise, neue Produkte, Sonderangebote, Tipps und Techniken, Biographien der Designer und vieles mehr.*

L'embarras du choix La typothèque Adobe constitue sans aucun doute l'une des plus importantes collections de polices de qualité au monde. Elle rassemble plus de 2 200 polices créées par des fondeurs de renommée mondiale comme Adobe, Agfa Monotype, ITC, et Linotype, des dessinateurs indépendants et des studios spécialisés.

De plus, toutes les polices de caractères de la Typothèque Adobe sont désormais fournies au format OpenType, un format de police commun aux plates-formes Windows et Macintosh et qui fonctionne avec la plupart des applications courantes. Pour plus de détails sur le format OpenType, reportez-vous à la page 11.

Une qualité optimale Les experts en typographie employés par Adobe examinent en détail chaque caractère d'une police avant de l'inclure à la typothèque Adobe. Grâce aux outils logiciels Adobe spécialement développés à cet effet, vous avez l'assurance que les polices concédées sous licence sont conformes au dessin original des fondeurs et que les polices exclusives Adobe Originals reproduisent avec une extrême fidélité l'idée de leur concepteur. De plus, toutes les polices de la typothèque Adobe sont soumises à des contrôles de qualité très stricts pour garantir qu'elles répondent aux critères d'excellence qui font la renommée d'Adobe.

Une disponibilité immédiate Vous pouvez vous procurer les polices Adobe très facilement en passant commande sur le Web, 24 heures sur 24, 7 jours sur 7. Consultez le site Web Adobe, *www.adobe.com/type* (ou votre site Web Adobe local) et découvrez la richesse et la puissance d'Adobe Type Browser. Servez-vous de cet utilitaire pour vous informer sur l'histoire de la typographie et sur ses créateurs. Visualisez les polices par les classes répertoriées aux pages 32–49 et bien d'autres spécifiques à cc logiciel. Outre l'utilitaire Type Browser, le site *www.adobe.com/type* propose des informations de dernière minute sur les offres spéciales, les nouvelles versions ainsi qu'une foule de conseils et astuces. Le site *www.adobe.com/type* a toutes les réponses aux questions que vous vous posez sur la typographie.

Große Auswahl Mit mehr als 2.200 Schriften von international anerkannten Herstellern wie Adobe, Agfa Monotype, ITC und Linotype, renommierten Schriftdesignern und Designstudios, bietet die Adobe-Schriftenbibliothek eine der größten Sammlungen hochwertiger Schriften weltweit. Außerdem werden alle Schriften in der Adobe-Schriftenbibliothek jetzt im OpenType-Format geliefert, einem plattformübergreifendem Schriftformat, das sowohl in Windows- als auch in Macintosh-Versionen verfügbar ist und nahtlos mit den meisten gängigen Anwendungen funktioniert. Weitere Einzelheiten zum OpenType-Format erfahren Sie auf Seite 12.

Qualität der Weltklasse Adobes Typographie-experten analysieren jedes Zeichen einer Schrift gründlich, bevor sie in die Adobe-Schriften-bibliothek aufgenommen wird. Spezielle Adobe Softwaretools gewährleisten, daß lizenzierte Schriften den Originaldesigns treu bleiben und daß exklusive Adobe Originals der Absicht des Designers mit unvergleichlicher digitaler Präzision gerecht werden. Zusätzlich werden alle Schriften in der Adobe-Schriftenbibliothek ausführlichen Qualitätstests unterzogen, damit die Schriften garantiert dem exzellenten Standard von Adobe entsprechen.

Sofortige Verfügbarkeit Der Zugriff auf Adobe-Schriften über das Internet ist einfach und jeden Tag rund um die Uhr möglich. Besuchen Sie die Adobe-Website *www.adobe. com/type* (oder die lokale Adobe-Website) und entdecken Sie den erstaunlichen Umfang und die Leistung des Adobe Type Browsers. Lernen Sie mehr über die Geschichte von Schriften und deren Designer. Lassen Sie sich Schriften nach den Kategorien anzeigen, die auf den Seiten 32–49 aufgeführt werden, sowie zusätzlich nach einigen speziellen Kategorien des Type Browsers. Neben dem Type Browser bietet *www.adobe.com/type* stets aktuelle Informationen zu besonderen Angeboten, Neuheiten und Tipps und Techniken. Wenn Sie Fragen zur Typographie haben, hat *www.adobe.com/type* die Antworten.

Glyph Complement PDF files are available online for all Adobe typefaces.

Le jeux de glyphes de chaque police est disponible en PDF sur le Web.

Kompletter Zeichensatz aller Adobe Schriften als PDF-Dokument online verfügbar.

To Order on the Web *www.adobe.com/type* 24 hours a day, 7 days a week—the fastest, easiest, most economical way to buy Adobe type in the United States and Canada.

downloadcentre.adobe.com 24 hours a day, 7 days a week—the fastest, easiest, most economical way to buy Adobe type in western Europe, Australia, New Zealand, Hong Kong and Singapore.

For font availability in other regions, please check your local Adobe web site.

Licensing For information about licensing, license extensions and volume purchases, call 800-682-3623 (in North America) or check your local Adobe web site.

Typefaces may be withdrawn from the library without notice.

Commandes sur le web Connectez-vous sur notre site *www.adobe.com/type*, 24 heures sur 24, 7 jours sur 7 : le moyen le plus rapide, le plus facile et le plus économique d'acheter des polices Adobe aux États-Unis et au Canada.

Connectez-vous sur notre site *downloadcentre. adobe.com*, 24 heures sur 24, 7 jours sur 7 : le moyen le plus rapide, le plus facile et le plus économique d'acheter des polices Adobe en Europe occidentale, Australie, Nouvelle-Zélande, Hong-Kong et Singapour.

Veuillez consulter votre site Web local pour plus d'informations sur la disponibilité des polices dans d'autres régions.

Licence Pour plus de détails sur l'octroi ou la prorogation de licences, et sur les achats en gros, contactez votre revendeur de polices Adobe ou consultez votre site Web Adobe local.

Adobe se réserve le droit de retirer des polices de la typothèque sans préavis.

Bestellen über das Internet *www.adobe.com/ type* Jeden Tag, rund um die Uhr, der schnellste, einfachste und günstigste Weg, in den USA und Kanada Adobe-Schriften zu kaufen.

downloadcentre.adobe.com Jeden Tag, rund um die Uhr, der schnellste, einfachste und günstigste Weg, in Westeuropa, Australien, Neuseeland, Hongkong und Singapur Adobe-Schriften zu kaufen.

Sehen Sie bitte auf der lokalen Adobe-Website nach, welche Schriften in anderen Regionen erhältlich sind.

Lizenzen Falls Sie an weiteren Informationen zu Lizenzen, Lizenzerweiterungen und Großeinkäufen interessiert sind, wenden Sie sich bitte an Ihren Adobe-Händler oder informieren Sie sich auf der lokalen Adobe-Website.

Schriften können ohne Ankündigung aus der Bibliothek genommen werden.

Technical Support Please contact the appropriate number from the following list to receive prompt and courteous assistance.

PERSON-TO-PERSON
Macintosh   206-675-6206
Windows   206-675-6306

WORLD WIDE WEB
www.adobe.com/support/products/type.html

OUTSIDE THE U.S. AND CANADA Please consult your local Adobe web site for the appropriate phone numbers, fax numbers, and web support information.

Service Bureau Support Service bureaus, imaging centers, color film shops, full-service printers, photo labs, and media centers are eligible to become Adobe Authorized Service Providers. For details, in the U.S. and Canada, call 800-685-3510 or visit *partners.adobe.com*. Elsewhere, please consult your local Adobe web site for more information.

Support Technique Composez le numéro adéquat ci-dessous pour obtenir une assistance rapide et de qualité.

ÉTATS-UNIS ET CANADA
Macintosh   206-675-6206
Windows   206-675-6306

WORLD WIDE WEB
www.adobe.com/support/products/type.html

EN DEHORS DES ÉTATS-UNIS ET DU CANADA
Veuillez consulter votre site Web Adobe local pour obtenir les informations d'assistance Web et les numéros de téléphone et de facsimilé de notre support technique.

Assistance pour les sociétés de services Les ateliers de photocomposition et d'impression de films couleur, les studios de retouche d'images, les imprimeurs, les laboratoires photo et les magasins multimédia peuvent prétendre au statut de prestataires de services agréés Adobe (Adobe Authorized Service Providers). Pour plus d'informations, composez le 800-685-3510 ou visitez le site *partners.adobe.com* si vous résidez aux Etats-Unis ou au Canada. Sinon, veuillez consulter votre site Web Adobe local.

Technischer Support Bitte rufen Sie die jeweilige Nummer aus der folgenden Liste an, um schnelle und freundliche Unterstützung zu erhalten.

PERSÖNLICH
Macintosh   206-675-6206
Windows   206-675-6306

WORLD WIDE WEB
www.adobe.com/support/products/type.html

AUSSERHALB DER USA UND KANADA Sehen Sie bitte auf der lokalen Adobe-Website nach, welche Telefon- und Faxnummern für Sie gelten und welche Unterstützung Ihnen per Internet zugänglich ist.

Unterstützung von Druckdienstleistern
Druckdienstleister, Belichtungszentren, Farbfilmgeschäfte, Druckereien, Fotolabore und Medienzentren können „Adobe Authorized Service Providers" werden. In den USA und Kanada erfahren Sie Einzelheiten unter 800-685-3510 oder besuchen Sie *partners.adobe. com*. In anderen Ländern können Sie der lokalen Adobe-Website weitere Informationen entnehmen.

Adobe Originals Typefaces Created exclusively for Adobe by award-winning type designers worldwide, Adobe Originals typefaces include new designs as well as revivals of classics from typographic history. They uniquely combine the power of Adobe's unrivaled imaging technologies with the spirit of craftsmanship that has inspired type design for more than 500 years. Ranging in style from fully featured text composition families with Optical sizes to individual typefaces of uncommon character, Adobe Originals always live up to their name.

Classical Revivals Some Adobe Originals are revivals of typefaces that are considered classic historical designs, such as Adobe Caslon, Adobe Garamond, and Adobe Jenson. To create classical revivals, Adobe's designers work from impressions of the original type, usually found on rare specimen sheets preserved in libraries, foundries, and private collections throughout the world. During the design process, designers visually compare the original type with Adobe's digital version. Their revivals capture the form and feel of classical typeface designs with outstanding accuracy in the digital format.

New Text and Display Typefaces Original text and display typefaces of remarkable beauty and digital integrity make up a large part of the Adobe Originals collection. Text families such as Minion, Kepler and Warnock include a full complement of weights, characters, and kerning pairs, while beautiful script and display types such as Caflisch Script, Bickham Script, Lithos, Charlemagne, and Trajan offer some of the most exciting designs in the Adobe Type Library.

Glyph and Character Sets Text families in the Adobe Originals collection in OpenType format often include a full range of expert typographic glyphs to meet the exacting demands of professional typesetters and designers. These glyphs include some or all of the following: old style figures, small capitals, ligatures, fractions, superior and inferior figures, and swashes. Several Adobe Originals typefaces also offer extended multilingual character sets to support additional languages, such a Polish, Turkish, Czech, Greek, and Cyrillic. For more information on the glyphs and character sets in OpenType fonts, refer to page 17.

▾ *Calcite Pro, Warnock Pro*

EXTREME Racing in Spain

11th Mountain Bike World Championships

Racers from around the world converged this week near the city of Granada, in southern Spain for the Mountain Bike World championships.

The long 12 kilometer course with its numerous challenging technical descents, higher altitudes than almost any venue, and the hot weather promise to make this one of the most exciting and grueling events of the year. Although the sky was azure and cloudless, the air was an extremely hot 92°F and dry combined with the rugged terrain of the Sierra Nevada mountains and a roster of fiercely competitive men and women means anything can happen during this mid-season competition.

The schedule includes cross country, downhill, and dual events over the next four days. The line-up includes seasoned veterans of the mountain biking world, like Alison Dunlap, (USA), Gunn-Rita Dahle, (Norway), Steve Peat, (Great Britain), Myles Rockwell (USA), Alison Sydor (Canada), Nicolas Vouilloz (France) along with a heavy dose of strong, hungry newcomers, like Jeff Warin (USA), François Pullet (France), Tolly Maslen (Spain), Jalil Samavarchian, (USA), Gunther Kloth (Germany), Barbara Victorino (Portugal), Pietro Bembo, (Italy).

Sadly Freida Byrd (Yugoslavia) will not be competing, after sustaining serious injuries in a fall during a practise run on Sunday. A large crowd gathered to watch as the national cross country team from Spain won the team relay race for the second consecutive

The Adobe Type Staff At Adobe, type is developed by a staff of designers, each of whom has the specialized skills required to produce world-class digital type. In addition, Adobe's in-house staff works with other distinguished designers and type experts throughout the world to make sure that the Adobe Type Library offers a wide variety of the highest quality type to creative professionals.

To easily spot the Adobe Originals typefaces in the typeface listings, look for this logo: **€**°

Polices Adobe Originals Dessinées exclusive-ment pour Adobe par des concepteurs de renom, les polices Adobe Originals sont des créations originales ou des reproductions de polices classiques appartenant à l'histoire de la typogra-phie. Cette collection reflète à la fois le moder-nisme et la puissance des technologies d'imagerie employées par Adobe et le caractère artisanal qui reste attaché à la création typographique depuis plus de 500 ans. Fidèle à son image, la collection Adobe Originals propose des polices de styles très variés, des familles avec des tailles « Optiques » pour la composition de texte avec jeux de caractères étendus, aux polices fantaisie les plus inattendues.

Reproductions de polices classiques

Certaines des polices Adobe Originals sont des reproductions de polices considérées comme des classiques de l'histoire de la typographie. Adobe Caslon, Adobe Garamond et Adobe Jenson appartiennent à cette catégorie. Pour créer ces polices, les experts typographes d'Adobe travaillent à partir d'impressions des polices originales, généralement sur des documents rares précieusement conservés dans des bibliothèques, des fonderies ou des

collections privées. A chaque phase de la conception, ils comparent la police originale et la police numérique Adobe. Les polices ainsi obtenues sont des reproductions très fidèles du dessin des polices classiques adaptées aux supports numériques.

Nouvelles polices de texte et d'enseigne

La collection Adobe Originals compte un grand nombre de polices de texte et d'enseigne très esthétiques et de qualité irréprochable. Les familles de polices de texte, telles que Minion, Kepler et Warnock, offrent une gamme complète de graisses, de caractères et de paires de crénage. Quant aux polices cursives et d'enseigne (par exemple, Caflisch Script, Bickham Script, Poetica, Lithos, Charlemagne et Trajan) proposées dans la typothèque Adobe, leur dessin ne peut que vous séduire.

Jeux de glyphes et de caractères

Les familles de polices de texte de la collection Adobe Originals au format OpenType incluent souvent un éventail complet de glyphes typographiques spécialisés conçus pour répondre aux besoins des compositeurs et graphistes professionnels. Ces glyphes proposent certains ou tous les caractères classiques suivants : chiffres en bas de casse, petites capitales, ligatures, fractions, chiffres en exposant et en indice et lettres en exposant. Plusieurs caractères de la collection Adobe Originals offrent également des jeux de caractères multilingues qui permettent la prise en charge de langues supplémentaires telles que le polonais, le turc, le tchèque, le grec et le cyrillique. Pour plus d'informations sur les jeux de glyphes et de caractères dans les polices OpenType, reportez-vous à la page 18.

^ *Nueva Std*

Les spécialistes typographiques Adobe Pour créer ces polices, Adobe emploie une équipe de dessinateurs qui ont tous les qualifications et le talent requis pour concevoir des polices numériques impeccables. De plus, le personnel Adobe travaille en collaboration avec des créateurs et experts typographes renommés du monde entier. La typothèque Adobe Type Library offre ainsi un choix inégalé de polices d'excellente qualité aux professionnels de la création.

Les polices Adobe Originals proposées dans la typothèque Adobe sont identifiées par le logo Ⓐ dans la liste.

Adobe Originals-Schriften Von ausgezeichneten Designern in der ganzen Welt exklusiv für Adobe erstellt, enthalten Adobe Originals-Schriften neue Designs und Neuauflagen von Klassikern aus der Geschichte der Typographie. Eine einzigartige Kombination der hervorragenden Belichtungstechnik von Adobe und der Handwerkskunst, die Schriftdesign seit mehr als 500 Jahren inspiriert. Stilistisch reichen Adobe Originals von voll ausgestalteten Textkompositionsfamilien mit optischen Größen bis zu einzelnen ungewöhnlichen Schriften.

Klassiker Einige Adobe Originals sind Neuauflagen klassischer historischer Designs, wie Adobe Caslon, Adobe Garamond und Adobe Jenson. Um die Klassiker neu aufzulegen, arbeiten Adobes Designer mit Drucken der Originalschrift auf seltenen Musterbögen, die in Bibliotheken, Setzereien und Privatsammlungen in der ganzen Welt erhalten sind. Während des gesamten Designprozesses werden visuelle Vergleiche zwischen der Originalschrift und Adobes digitaler Version angestellt. Die resultierenden Schriften erfassen den Charakter klassischer Schriftdesigns mit hervorragender Präzision und sind gleichzeitig an das digitale Medium angepaßt worden.

Neue Text- und Auszeichnungsschriften
Originaltext- und Auszeichnungsschriften von erstaunlicher Schönheit und digitaler Integrität bilden einen großen Teil der Adobe Originals Collection. Textschriftfamilien wie Minion, Kepler und Warnock umfassen eine vollständige Palette von Schriftstärken, -typen und Unterschneidungspaaren; während schöne Schreibschriften und Auszeichnungsschriften wie Caflisch Script, Bickham Script, Poetica, Lithos, Charlemagne und Trajan zu den interessantesten Designs in der Adobe Type Library gehören.

Expert Collections Textschriftfamilien in der Adobe Originals Collection werden oft von Expertenschriften begleitet. Diese Spezialschrifttypen werden den hohen Ansprüchen professioneller Setzer und Designer gerecht. Expert Collections enthalten einige oder alle der folgenden Elemente: Minuskel- oder Mediävalziffern, Kapitälchen, f-Ligaturen, Bruchziffern, hoch- und tiefgestellte Ziffern und hochgestellte Buchstaben. Weitere Informationen zu Expert Collections finden Sie auf Seite 23.

Glyphen- und Zeichensätze Textschriftfamilien in der Adobe Originals Collection im OpenType-Format werden oft von einem umfassenden Sortiment an ausgefeilten typographischen Glyphen begleitet. Diese Spezialschrifttypen werden den hohen Ansprüchen professioneller Setzer und Designer gerecht. Diese Glyphen enthalten einige oder alle der folgenden Elemente: Mediävalziffern, Kapitälchen, Ligaturen, Frakturen, hoch- und tiefgestellte Ziffern und Schwungbuchstaben. Eine Reihe der Schriften von Adobe Originals bieten außerdem erweiterte mehrsprachige Zeichensätze zur Unterstützung zusätzlicher Sprachen wie Polnisch, Türkisch, Tschechisch, Griechisch und Kyrillisch. Weitere Informationen zu den Glyphen- und Zeichensätzen in OpenType-Schriften finden Sie auf Seite 19.

Das Adobe-Schriftteam Bei Adobe werden Schriften von einem Team von Designern entwickelt, in dem jeder einzelne über die Spezialkenntnisse verfügt, die für die Produktion von digitalen Schriften der Weltklasse erforderlich sind. Zusätzlich arbeitet Adobes internes Team mit anderen renommierten Designern und Typographieexperten in der ganzen Welt zusammen, damit die Adobe-Schriftenbibliothek ein breites Spektrum an Schriften höchster Qualität für kreative professionelle Designer und Desktop-Publisher bietet.

Adobe Originals-Schriften in der Adobe-Schriftenbibliothek erkennen Sie an diesem Logo: 𝘦

OpenType Fonts OpenType is a cross-platform font file format developed by Adobe and Microsoft. The OpenType format is an extension of the TrueType SFNT format that can support PostScript® font data and new typographic features. OpenType fonts may include an expanded character set and layout features to provide richer linguistic support and advanced typographic control. They can also be installed and used alongside PostScript Type 1 and TrueType fonts.

One Cross-Platform Font File Any OpenType font uses a single font file for all of its outline, metric, and bitmap data, making file management simpler. In addition, the same font file works on Macintosh and Windows computers. As a result, OpenType lets you move font files back and forth between platforms with noticeable improvement in cross-platform portability for any documents that use type.

Better Language Support Based on Unicode, an international character encoding that covers virtually all of the world's languages, OpenType fonts can make multilingual typography easier by including multiple language character sets in one font. All OpenType Pro fonts from Adobe include the standard range of Latin characters used in the Western world and several international characters, including the estimated, litre, and euro currency symbols. OpenType Pro fonts from Adobe add a full range of accented characters to support central and eastern European languages, such as Turkish and Polish. Many of the Pro fonts also contain Cyrillic and Greek character extensions in the same font.

▲ *Silentium Pro*

Polices OpenType OpenType est un format développé par Adobe et Microsoft pour être compatible avec toutes les plates-formes.
Le format OpenType est une extension du format TrueType SFNT qui prend en charge les nouvelles données et les fonctions typographiques des polices PostScript. Les polices OpenType peuvent comporter un jeu de caractères étendu et des fonctions de mise en page destinées à permettre la prise en charge d'un plus grand nombre de langues et un meilleur contrôle typographique. Elles peuvent également être utilisées conjointement avec les polices de type PostScript et TrueType.

Un fichier de polices unique pour toutes les plates-formes Les polices OpenType utilisent un fichier de polices unique pour leurs données vectorielles, métriques et en mode point, ce qui simplifie grandement leur gestion. En outre, le même fichier de polices fonctionne aussi bien sous Macintosh que sous Windows, ce qui vous permet de transférer vos fichiers de polices d'une plate-forme à une autre et d'améliorer ainsi la portabilité de vos documents.

Meilleure prise en charge linguistique Les polices OpenType utilisent la norme Unicode, un système d'encodage de caractères qui couvre virtuellement toutes les langues du monde. Elles simplifient la typographie multilingue en permettant la réunion dans une même police de caractères de plusieurs alphabets. Toutes les polices Adobe OpenType incluent les caractères latins normalement utilisés dans le monde occidental et plusieurs caractères internationaux, parmi lesquels les symboles « environ », litre et euro. Les polices Adobe OpenType Pro comprennent également une gamme complète de caractères accentués pour la prise en charge des langues d'Europe Centrale et Orientale, telles le turc et le polonais. De nombreuses polices Pro reprennent en outre les caractères cyrilliques et grecs.

Time Will Tell
HOROLOGICAL BOOKSELLERS

▲ *Warnock Pro*

OpenType-Fonts OpenType ist ein plattform-übergreifendes Font-Dateiformat, das gemeinsam von Adobe und Microsoft entwickelt wurde. Das OpenType-Format ist eine Erweiterung des TrueType-Formats sfnt und unterstützt Postscript-Fontdaten und neue typografische Features. OpenType-Fonts bieten erweiterte Zeichensätze und Layoutmerkmale zur Unter-stützung einer größeren Sprachenvielfalt und weit reichender typografischer Gestaltungs-möglichkeiten. Sie können OpenType-Fonts außerdem zusammen mit Postscript Type 1- und TrueType-Fonts installieren und verwenden.

Eine Plattformübergreifende Fontdatei

Jeder OpenType-Font verwendet eine einzige Fontdatei für sämtliche Outline-, Maß- und Bitmapdaten und vereinfacht so die Dateiverwal-tung. Darüber hinaus kann dieselbe Fontdatei sowohl auf Windows- als auch auf Macintosh-Rechnern verwendet werden. So können Sie Fontdateien problemlos von einer Plattform zur anderen verschieben und damit die Portabilität aller Schriftdokumente deutlich verbessern.

Verbesserte Sprachunterstützung OpenType-Fonts basieren auf Unicode, einem internationa-len Multibyte-Kodierungssystem, das praktisch sämtliche Weltsprachen abdeckt. Das vereinfacht typografisches Arbeiten in mehreren Sprachen, da multilinguale Zeichensätze in einem Font enthalten sind. Alle Adobe OpenType-Fonts umfassen den in der westlichen Welt gebräuchli-chen Standardumfang an lateinischen Zeichen-sätzen sowie mehrere international gebräuchliche Zeichen wie die Symbole für „geschätzt", Liter und Euro. Die Adobe OpenType Pro-Fonts ergänzen die Palette um einen vollen Satz akzen-tuierter Zeichen zur Unterstützung mittel- und osteuropäischer Sprachen wie z. B. Türkisch und

Polnisch. Viele der Pro-Fonts enthalten darüber hinaus Erweiterungen in Form von kyrillischen und griechischen Zeichen.

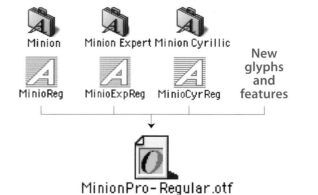

MinionPro-Regular.otf

Previous font technologies required separate font files for expert character sets and multiple languages. OpenType fonts combine base character sets, expert sets, and extensive additional glyphs into one file.

Les technologies précédentes en matière de polices faisaient appel à des fichiers de polices séparés pour les jeux de caractères experts et les différentes langues. Avec les polices OpenType, les jeux de caractères de base, les jeux experts ainsi que les glyphes supplémentaires largement répandus sont regroupés dans un seul et même fichier.

Früher verwendete Schriftart-Techniken erforderten getrennte Schriftart-Dateien für Profi-Zeichensätze und mehrere Sprachen. OpenType-Schriftarten verbinden Basis-Zeichensätze, Profisätze und umfangreiche, zusätzliche Glyphen und führen sie in einer Datei zusammen.

Advanced Typography OpenType fonts may contain more than 65,000 glyphs, unleashing exciting typographic capabilities. Many non-standard glyphs, such as oldstyle figures, true small capitals, fractions, swashes, superiors, inferiors, titling letters, contextual and stylistic alternates, beginning and ending letterforms, and a full range of ligatures may also be included in a single font. In the past, a typical Western PostScript font was limited to 256 glyphs, forcing you to install and manage two or more style-related fonts in order to access "expert set" characters. OpenType significantly simplifies font management and the publishing workflow by ensuring that all of the required glyphs for a document are contained in one cross-platform font file throughout the workflow.

Historically, some of the highest-quality typefaces have had different designs for different print sizes. Several OpenType fonts from Adobe include four optical size variations: caption, regular, subhead, and display. Called Opticals, these variations have been optimized for use at specific point sizes. Although the exact intended sizes vary by family, the general size ranges include caption (6–8 point), regular (9–13 point), subhead (14–24 point), and display (25–72 point).

OpenType Feature Support To access alternate glyphs in an OpenType font, an application must understand OpenType features and present a user interface that allows end users to select and apply different layout features to text. Applications that don't provide support for Unicode or advanced OpenType layout features can still access and print the basic glyph sets of OpenType fonts, which are analogous to the glyph sets in PostScript Type 1 fonts.

OpenType and Adobe Applications InDesign,® Adobe's flagship page layout program, was the first Adobe application to provide advanced OpenType feature support. With InDesign and other OpenType savvy applications, you can turn on OpenType layout features that automatically substitute alternate glyphs in an OpenType font.

Further Information Overall, OpenType provides richer support for the world's languages, more powerful typographic capabilities, better cross-platform compatibility, as well as simplified font management. For more information on OpenType, please refer to the Adobe Web site at *www.adobe.com/type.*

Unbelievable
Display

Unbelievable
Subhead

Unbelievable
Regular

Unbelievable
Caption

Several OpenType fonts from Adobe include four optical size variations.

Plusieurs polices OpenType disposent de quatre variantes de taille optique.

Mehrere der Adobe OpenType-Fonts enthalten vier optische Größenvarianten.

Typographie avancée Les polices OpenType peuvent contenir plus de 65 000 glyphes, un véritable gisement de possibilités typographiques. De nombreux glyphes spéciaux, tels les chiffres en bas de casse, petites capitales, fractions, exposants, caractères de titres, autres caractères de style et de contexte, les dessins de début et de fin de mot, et une gamme étendue de liaisons peuvent également être repris dans une même police. Par le passé, une police PostScript occidentale était en général limitée à 256 caractères, ce qui vous obligeait à installer et à gérer deux, voire plusieurs polices de style apparenté pour accéder aux caractères « experts ». Le format OpenType simplifie considérablement la gestion des polices et les circuits de production en regroupant, dans un seul fichier de polices compatible avec toutes les plates-formes, tous les glyphes qui seront nécessaires à un document.

Historiquement, certains caractères de haute qualité ont bénéficié de dessins différents selon leur taille. Plusieurs polices OpenType d'Adobe disposent de quatre variantes de taille optique : légende, normale, sous-titre et affiche. Appelées « Optiques », ces variantes ont été optimisées pour permettre leur utilisation dans plusieurs corps de caractères. Bien que les forces de corps diffèrent en fonction de la famille de caractère, elles sont en général de 6–8 points (légende), 9–13 points (normal), 14–24 points (sous-titre) et 25–72 points (affiche).

Prise en charge des fonctions OpenType

Pour accéder aux glyphes alternatifs d'une police OpenType, une application doit être en mesure de comprendre les fonctions OpenType et de présenter à l'utilisateur une interface lui permettant de sélectionner et d'appliquer différentes fonctions de mise en page. Les applications qui ne prennent pas en charge la norme Unicode ou les fonctions de mises en page OpenType avancées ont toujours la possibilité d'accéder et d'imprimer les jeux de glyphes de base des polices OpenType, analogues aux jeux de glyphes actuels des polices PostScript Type 1.

OpenType et Applications Adobe

InDesign, le fleuron des programmes de mise en page d'Adobe, a été la première application de la marque à proposer la prise en charge des fonctionnalités avancées OpenType. Grâce à InDesign et à d'autres applications intelligentes, il vous est possible d'activer des fonctions OpenType de mise en page capables de remplacer automatiquement certains glyphes par d'autres puisés dans une police de caractères OpenType.

Informations complémentaires

Dans l'ensemble, le format OpenType, permet la prise en charge d'un plus grand nombre de langues, propose des fonctionnalités typographiques plus évoluées, une meilleure compatibilité entre plates-formes et une gestion simplifiée des polices de caractères. Pour plus d'informations à propos du format OpenType, consultez le site Web d'Adobe à l'adresse *www.adobe.com/type*.

*The lowercase **a** character can be represented by multiple glyphs in an OpenType font.*

*Dans une police OpenType, le **a** minuscule peut être représenté par plusieurs glyphes.*

*Der Kleinbuchstabe **a** lässt sich bei einem OpenType-Font mit mehreren Glyphen darstellen.*

Erweiterte Typografische Möglichkeiten

OpenType-Fonts können über 65.000 Glyphen umfassen. Der typografischen Gestaltungsmöglichkeit sind damit kaum noch Grenzen gesetzt. Viele Nichtstandard-Glyphen wie Mediävalziffern, echte Kapitälchen, Frakturen, Schwungbuchstaben, Hoch- und Tiefstellung, Versalschrift für Titel, kontextuelle und stilistische Alternativen, Anfangs- und Endbuchstaben sowie eine ganze Palette von Ligaturen können ebenfalls in einem einzigen Font enthalten sein. Früher war ein typischer westlicher Postscript-Font auf ganze 256 Glyphen beschränkt, so daß man gezwungen war, mindestens zwei weitere stilverwandte Fonts zu installieren und zu verwalten, wenn man Zugriff auf einen „Experten-Satz" haben wollte. OpenType vereinfacht das Font-Management und den DTP-Workflow beträchtlich, da alle für ein Dokument benötigten Glyphen in einer plattformübergreifenden Fontdatei während des gesamten Arbeitsablaufs zur Verfügung stehen.

Früher gab es bei manchen der hochwertigsten Schriften unterschiedliche Designs für die unterschiedlichen Druckgrößen. Mehrere der Adobe OpenType-Fonts enthalten vier optische Größenvarianten: Bildüber-/Bildunterschrift, Standard, Zwischenüberschrift und Display. Diese „Opticals" genannten Varianten sind zur Verwendung in bestimmten Punktgrößen optimiert. Obwohl die exakt vorgesehenen Größen nach Schriftfamilie variieren, umfassen die generellen Größenbereiche Bildüber-/Bildunterschrift (6–8 Pt), Standard (9–13 Pt), Zwischenüberschrift (14–24 Pt) und Display (25–72 Pt).

Unterstützung des OpenType-Merkmals

Um auf alternative Glyphen in einem OpenType-Font zugreifen zu können, muß eine Anwendung OpenType-Anweisungen „verstehen" und über eine Benutzeroberfläche verfügen, mit der Endnutzer einem Text unterschiedliche Format-merkmale zuweisen können. Anwendungen, die Unicode bzw. weitergehende OpenType-Formatmerkmale nicht unterstützen, können dennoch auf die Basis-Zeichensätze von OpenType-Fonts zugreifen und sie auch drucken, da diese den Zeichensätze der heutigen Post-Script Type 1-Fonts entsprechen.

OpenType und Adobe-Anwendungen

InDesign, das erfolgreiche Seitengestaltungs-programm von Adobe, ist die erste Adobe-Anwendung, die eine weitgehende Unterstützung des OpenType-Merkmals bietet. Mit InDesign und anderen OpenType-fähigen Anwendungen können Sie OpenType-Formatmerkmale aktivieren, durch die alternative Glyphen in einem OpenType Font automatisch ersetzt werden.

Weitere Informationen Insgesamt gesehen, bietet OpenType neben einem vereinfachten Font-Management eine umfassendere Unterstützung der Weltsprachen, weitreichen-dere typografische Gestaltungsmöglichkeiten sowie eine bessere plattformübergreifende Kompatibilität. Weitere Informationen über OpenType erhalten Sie auf der Adobe-Website unter *www.adobe.com/type.*

Languages Supported OpenType fonts from Adobe contain a variety of character sets that support different languages around the world. The exact level of character support for each font family is listed on *www.adobe.com/type*. All alphanumeric OpenType fonts contain a minimum character set known as an Adobe Western 2 character set. Some OpenType Pro fonts may also contain one or more of the additional character extensions listed below. Japanese OpenType fonts from Adobe contain their own unique character sets (also listed below).

ADOBE WESTERN 2 Fonts with an Adobe Western 2 character set support most western languages including: Afrikaans, Basque, Breton, Catalan, Danish, Dutch, English, Finnish, French, Gaelic, German, Icelandic, Indonesian, Irish, Italian, Norwegian, Portuguese, Sami, Spanish, Swahili, and Swedish.

ADOBE CE Fonts with an Adobe CE character set extension include the characters necessary to support the following central European languages: Croatian, Czech, Estonian, Hungarian, Latvian, Lithuanian, Polish, Romanian, Serbian (Latin), Slovak, Slovenian, and Turkish.

GREEK The Greek alphabet is one of the oldest known writing systems, having been adapted from the Phoenician alphabet about 3,000 years ago. Fonts with a Greek character set include the characters and punctuation required to support the modern Greek language.

POLYTONIC GREEK Fonts that support Polytonic Greek support the basic Greek characters and also include additional archaic Greek characters that are useful when setting historical or Biblical texts in the Greek language.

CYRILLIC The Cyrillic alphabet was reformed by Peter the Great in Russia in the early eighteenth century. Fonts that include a Cyrillic character set support the following languages: Russian, Adyg, Avarish, Balkarian, Belorussian, Bulgarian, Chechen, Darginish, Ingushian, Kabardino-Cherkesian, Kumykish, Lakish, Lesginian, Macedonian, Mordovsko-Ersatian, Mordovsko-Mokshanian, Nanaish, Nenish, Nivkh, Nogaian, Selkup, Serbian, Tabasaranish, and Ukrainian.

LATIN EXTENDED Fonts with a Latin Extended character set include additional Latin characters beyond the combined Adobe Western and Adobe CE character sets to support languages such as Welsh, archaic Danish and Esperanto.

SYMBOL/PI Certain fonts contain additional non-alphabetic characters not in standard character sets, such as bullets, ornaments, symbols, flourishes, icons, and border elements.

CUSTOM These fonts may contain a subset of the entire standard Adobe Western 2 character range and may support a limited number of languages.

ADOBE JAPAN 1–4 The Adobe-Japan 1–4 character collection contains 15,444 glyphs, including thousands of kanji and kana variants to provide rich typographic support.

ADOBE JAPAN 1–3 The Adobe-Japan 1–3 character collection contains 9,354 glyphs, including some glyph variants. It provides complete JIS X 0208 support, along with JIS78 (JIS C 6226-1978) variants and IBM Selected Kanji.

KANA Kana fonts contain a subset of the Adobe-Japan 1–3 character collection and include a set of 471 hiragana and katakana glyphs.

Langues Prises en Charge Les polices OpenType d'Adobe contiennent divers jeux de caractères qui prennent en charge un grand nombre de langues. Pour toute information sur le niveau exact de prise en charge des caractères pour chacune des familles de polices, veuillez consulter le site *www.adobe.com/type*. Toutes les polices alphanumériques OpenType contiennent un jeu de caractères minimum appelé Adobe Western 2. Certaines polices OpenType Pro peuvent également contenir une ou plusieurs extensions de caractères supplémentaires de la liste ci-dessous. Les polices OpenType japonaises d'Adobe contiennent leurs propres jeux de caractères uniques (voir également ci-dessous).

ADOBE WESTERN 2 Les polices possédant un jeu de caractères Adobe Western 2 prennent en charge la plupart des langues occidentales y compris les langues suivantes : afrikaans, basque, breton, catalan, danois, néerlandais, anglais, finnois, français, gaélique, allemand, islandais, indonésien, irlandais, italien, norvégien, portugais, sami, espagnol, swahili et suédois.

ADOBE EUROPE CENTRALE Les polices possédant l'extension de jeu de caractères Adobe Europe centrale contiennent les caractères nécessaires à la prise en charge des langues d'Europe centrale suivantes : croate, tchèque, estonien, hongrois, polonais, letton, lithuanien, serbe (latin), slovaque, slovène, roumain et turc.

GREC L'alphabet grec est l'un des plus anciens systèmes d'écriture connus. Il a été adapté de l'alphabet phénicien il y a près de 3 000 ans. Les polices possédant un jeu de caractères grec contiennent les caractères et la ponctuation nécessaires à la prise en charge du grec moderne.

GREC POLYTONIQUE Les polices qui prennent en charge le grec polytonique prennent aussi en charge les caractères grecs de base et incluent également les caractères grecs archaïques qui peuvent s'avérer utiles pour les textes historiques et bibliques.

CYRILLIQUE L'alphabet cyrillique fut réformé par Pierre le Grand au début du dix-huitième siècle en Russie. Les polices qui contiennent un jeu de caractères cyrillique prennent en charge les langues suivantes : russe, adyg, avare, balkare, bélarussien, bulgare, tchétchène, darguine, ingouche, kabardien-circassien, koumyk, lak, lesghien, tabassaran, macédonien, mordve-mokcha, nanai, nenets, nivkh, nogaï, selkoup, serbe et ukrainien.

LATIN ÉTENDU Les polices qui contiennent un jeu de caractères Latin étendu possèdent des caractères latins supplémentaires s'ajoutant aux jeux de caractères d'Europe centrale d'Adobe et Adobe Western 2 qui permettent de prendre en charge des langues telles que le gallois, le danois archaïque et l'espéranto.

SYMBOLE/PI Certaines polices contiennent des caractères non-alphabétiques que l'on ne trouve pas dans les jeux de caractères standard, tels que les puces, les ornements, les symboles, les fioritures, les icônes et les bordures.

PERSONNALISÉ Ces polices peuvent contenir un sous-ensemble de l'éventail complet des caractères Adobe Western 2 standard et prennent éventuellement en charge un nombre limité de langues.

ADOBE JAPAN 1–4 La collection de caractères Adobe-Japan 1–4 contient 15 444 glyphes, y compris des milliers de variantes des caractères kanji et kana qui vous permettent d'accéder à une sélection typographique très riche.

ADOBE JAPAN 1–3 La collection de caractères Adobe-Japan 1–3 contient 9 354 glyphes, y compris certaines variantes de glyphes. Elle offre une prise en charge JIS X 0208 totale, ainsi que celle des variantes JIS78 (JIS C 6226-1978) et des caractères IBM Selected Kanji.

KANA Les polices Kana contiennent un sous-enscmble de la collection de caractères Adobe-Japan 1–3 et comprennent un jeu de 471 glyphes hiragana et katakana.

Unterstützte Sprachen OpenType-Fonts von Adobe umfassen eine Vielfalt von Zeichensätzen, mit denen verschiedene Sprachen rund um die Welt unterstützt werden. Informationen darüber, auf genau welcher Stufe die Zeichenunter-stützung für jede Schriftartenfamilie erhältlich ist, finden Sie unter *www.adobe.com/type*. Alle alphanumerischen OpenType-Fonts enthalten einen Mindestzeichensatz namens Adobe Western 2. Einige OpenType Pro-Fonts können auch eine oder mehrere der nachstehend aufge-führten Zeichenerweiterungen umfassen. Japani-sche OpenType-Fonts von Adobe enthalten ihre eigenen, eindeutigen Zeichensätze (ebenfalls nachstehend aufgeführt).

ADOBE WESTERN 2 Schriften mit einem Zei-chensatz vom Typ Adobe Western 2 unterstützen die meisten westlichen Sprachen, einschließlich folgender: Afrikaans, Baskisch, Bretonisch, Kata-lanisch, Dänisch, Niederländisch, Englisch, Finnisch, Französisch, Gälisch, Deutsch, Islän-disch, Indonesisch, Irisch, Italienisch, Norwe-gisch, Portugiesisch, Sami, Spanisch, Suaheli und Schwedisch.

ADOBE CE Schriftsätze mit einer Schriftsatzer-weiterung Adobe CE enthalten die Zeichen, die zur Unterstützung folgender mitteleuropäi-scher Sprachen erforderlich sind: Kroatisch, Tschechisch, Estnisch, Ungarisch, Lettisch, Litauisch, Polnisch, Rumänisch, Serbisch (Latein), Slowakisch, Slowenisch und Türkisch.

GRIECHISCH Das griechische Alphabet ist eines der ältesten bekannten Schriftsysteme, das vor rund 3000 Jahren aus dem phönizischen Alphabet gebildet wurde. Schriftarten mit einem griechischen Zeichensatz umfassen die Zeichen und Interpunktion, die zur Unterstützung der modernen griechischen Sprache benötigt werden.

POLYTONISCHES GRIECHISCH Schriftarten, die polytonisches Griechisch unterstützen, bieten auch eine Unterstützung der grundlegenden griechischen Zeichen und beinhalten außerdem zusätzliche altgriechische Zeichen, die beim Setzen historischer oder biblischer Texte in der griechischen Sprache nützlich sind.

KYRILLISCH Peter der Große hat das kyrillische Alphabet Anfang des achtzehnten Jahrhunderts in Rußland reformiert. Mit den Schriftarten, die einen kyrillischen Zeichensatz beinhalten, werden folgende Sprachen unterstützt: Russisch, Adyg, Avarisch, Balkarisch, Belarussisch, Bulgarisch, Tschetschenisch, Darginisch, Ingu-schetisch, Kabardino-Tscherkessisch, Kumü-ckisch, Lakisch, Lesginisch, Makedonisch, Mordowisch-Erzanisch, Mordowisch-Moksha-nisch, Nanaisch, Nenzisch, Nivchisch, Nogaisch, Selkup, Serbisch, Tabasaranisch und Ukrainisch.

ERWEITERTES LATEIN Schriftarten mit dem Zeichensatz erweitertes Latein enthalten zusätzlich zu den kombinierten Zeichensätzen Adobe Western 2 und Adobe CE noch weitere lateinische Zeichen, um Sprachen wie Walisisch, Altdänisch und Esperanto zu unterstützen.

SYMBOL/PI Bestimmte Schriftarten enthalten zusätzliche nichtalphabetische Zeichen, die nicht in Standardzeichensätzen zu finden sind, wie z. B. Aufzählungszeichen, Verzierungen, Marken, Schnörkel, Symbole und Fugenelemente.

EIGENE ZEICHEN Diese Schriftarten können eine Untergruppe des gesamten Standardzeichensortiments vom Typ Adobe Western 2 umfassen und eine begrenzte Anzahl an Sprachen unterstützen.

ADOBE JAPAN 1–4 Die Zeichenkollektion Adobe-Japan 1–4 enthält 15.444 Glyphen, einschließlich tausenden von Kanji- und Kana-Variationen zur Unterstützung einer größeren typografischen Vielfalt.

ADOBE JAPAN 1–3 Die Zeichenkollektion Adobe-Japan 1–3 enthält 9.354 Glyphen, einschließlich einer Reihe von Glyphenvariationen. Sie bietet eine komplette JIS X 0208-Unterstützung und enthält JIS78 (JIS C 6226-1978)-Varianten und IBM Selected Kanji.

KANA Kana-Schriften umfassen eine Untergruppe der Zeichenkollektion Adobe-Japan 1–3 und beinhalten einen Satz mit 471 Hiragana- und Katakana-Glyphen.

Character and Glyph Sets Supported

OpenType fonts from Adobe may also contain an expanded glyph set for enhanced linguistic support and advanced typographic control. The distinction between characters and glyphs is important in understanding OpenType. Characters are the code points assigned by the Unicode standard, which represent the smallest semantic units of language, such as letters. Glyphs are the specific forms or shapes that those characters or letters can take in a font.

When a font has a specific character set, it has a glyph complement that offers default glyph shapes for those characters, and it may have additional glyphs that are stylistic or linguistic variations of the characters. A key point is that one character may be represented by any of several different glyphs. For example, lowercase a, small cap A and an alternate swash lowercase a are all the same character—namely the lowercase a—but they are three separate glyphs. Additionally, although the relationship between glyphs and characters is often one-to-one, it may be many-to-one, one-to-many, or many-to-many. For example, sometimes several characters may be represented by one glyph, as in the case of the ffi ligature, which corresponds to a sequence of three characters: f, f, and i.

For every character, there is a default glyph and positioning behavior. Applying OpenType layout features to one or more characters may change the default positioning or substitute a different glyph. For example, the application of the small capitals feature to the a would substitute the small cap A glyph for the usual lowercase a glyph.

The icons below are used in this guide and on the Adobe web site to identify the specific glyphs that are included in each OpenType font. For more information, please refer to *www.adobe.com/type*. Also, please refer to the Adobe web site for more information on the exact glyph complements in Japanese OpenType fonts from Adobe.

BASIC A-Z These fonts include a basic glyph complement containing uppercase letterforms, lowercase letterforms, figures, accented characters, and punctuation. These fonts also contain currency symbols, standard ligatures, common fractions, common mathematics operators, superscript numerals, common delimiters and conjoiners, and other symbols. These basic glyphs are shown in the Adobe Western 2 sample below.

ABCDEFGHIJKLMNOPQRSTUVWXYZ
abcdefghijklmnopqrstuvwxyz
–& 0123456789$¢£¥ƒ¤€
ÆÁÂÃÄÀÅÇÉÊÈÍÎÏÌŁÑŒÓÔÖÒÕØŠÚÛÜ
ÙÝŸŽÐÞ
æáâãäàåçéêèíîïìłñœúóôöòõøšßúûüùýÿžðþ
™©®ℓ℮@ªº†‡§¶*!¡?¿.,:;'"''""„,…‹›«»
()[]{}¦|/_\•·`´ˆ˜¯˘˙˚˝¸˛ˇ #^¼½¾ /º0123
%‰-+÷×±=~<>¬≈≠≤≥∆Ωπµ∂∏∑√∞∫◊

EURO € These fonts include the new euro currency symbol, which represents the standard currency in European Union member countries. Most OpenType fonts from Adobe also include symbols for cent, dollar, florin, pound sterling, and yen. Some OpenType fonts may also include the symbols for the colon, franc, lira, peseta, and rupiah. Some OpenType fonts from Adobe also include oldstyle versions of most of the monetary symbols which are designed to be compatible with the oldstyle figures.

LIGATURES ffi Ligatures are designed to correct awkward combinations where letters may collide. These fonts contain an extended set of ligatures beyond the basic fi and fl ligatures found in most fonts. These special ligatures usually include ff, ffi, and ffl, and they can also include Th, tt, and other special letter combinations. Some fonts, such as Silentium Pro, also include a unique set of uppercase ligatures that impart a liveliness to the letterforms.

SMALL CAPS BB These letterforms are smaller versions of the normal capitals and are designed to be visually compatible with the lowercase characters of a typeface. They can be used to introduce the first few words at the beginning of a story, or to highlight key words within text. They are also commonly used when setting acronyms or abbreviations, such as IBM, PDF, or ISBN,in text.

OLDSTYLE FIGURES 619 These figures are designed with ascenders and descenders and have features and proportions compatible with the lowercase characters of the typeface. Oldstyle figures, also known as hanging figures, are typically used for text settings because they blend in well with the optical flow and rhythm of the lowercase alphabet. Fonts with oldstyle figures include both proportional (0123456789) and tabular (0123456789) versions.

PROPORTIONAL LINING FIGURES 123 Most fonts include lining figures that are designed to be compatible with the capital letters. They are usually capital height or slightly smaller and are typically designed with the same widths, also known as tabular widths. Tabular lining figures (0123456789) are especially useful when setting columns of number, such as in financial reports.

Fonts with proportional lining figures (0123456789) also include a set of lining figures that have unique widths that are determined by the shape of the figure. Proportional lining figures are preferred when setting certain text, such as an all-capital headline.

DIAGONAL FRACTIONS ⅞ These fonts include an expanded set of the most commonly used diagonal fractions beyond ¼, ½, and ¾ and may include additional fractions such as ⅛, ⅜, ⅝, ⅞, ⅓, and ⅔. Some OpenType fonts from Adobe also support the creation of arbitrary fractions.

SUPERSCRIPT/SUBSCRIPT H_2 Superior and inferior figures, also known as superscript and subscript letterforms, are used for footnote references, chemical compounds, and as mathematical exponents.

ORDINALS AND SUPERIOR LETTERS 1st These fonts contain superior letterforms that are used when creating ordinals, which specify position in a numbered series, and in certain English, French, and Spanish abbreviations, such as Madame, compagnie, and segundo. The extent of the glyph coverage varies, but usually includes the figures 0123456789 and abdeilmnorst.

SWASHES A Swash capitals, which originated in the italic handwriting of the Italian Renaissance, were adapted as letterforms during the early sixteenth century. Since then, swash letters have evolved along with new handwriting and typeface styles. Swash capitals can be used effectively for expressive passages of text, or for titles and signage when an elegant touch is called for.

ALTERNATES e Some fonts include alternate ligatured forms, alternate lowercase letters, or lowercase within uppercase combined forms. The alternate forms were designed to give words a slightly more animated and informal appearance and to lend more interest to type composition. Because of their decorative quality, they are best used in moderation.

TITLING CAPITALS A Titling capitals are specially designed letterforms, such as ornate, inline, white-stroked or refined versions of regular capitals, designed for use in all-capital settings or as initial capitals. Titling capitals also have specific letterspacing that lends itself to all-capital settings. Fonts with titling capitals may also include specially designed figures, monetary symbols, related punctuation, and accented characters for use with the titling capitals. Reversed titling capitals can be used as initial forms in book chapters or related paragraphs.

ORNAMENTS ❧ Throughout history, type designers have created printer's ornaments to accompany their typefaces. These ornaments add a personal signature to the type family and can be used as title page decoration, paragraph markers, dividers for blocks of text, or as repeated bands and borders. Common ornaments include flowers, leaves, bullets, brackets, and contemporary graphic decorations.

CASE FORMS aA These fonts contain special alternate letterforms and punctuation with a distinct design and spacing for use in all-capital text settings.

HISTORIC BLACKLETTER ẞ These fonts contain special historic glyphs that allow users to follow the conventions for German or blackletter text setting.

Jeux de Caractères et de Glyphes Pris en Charge Les polices OpenType d'Adobe peuvent également contenir un jeu de glyphes étendu qui améliore le soutien linguistique et permet un contrôle typographique avancé. Il est important de faire la distinction entre caractères et glyphes si l'on veut comprendre les polices OpenType. Les caractères sont les points de code attribués par la norme Unicode, et représentent les plus petites unités sémantiques de la langue écrite, telles que les lettres. Les glyphes sont les formes particulières que prennent ces caractères ou lettres dans une police.

Lorsqu'une police possède un jeu de caractères spécifique, elle contient un jeu de glyphes complémentaire qui offre des formes de glyphe par défaut pour ces caractères et, le cas échéant, des glyphes représentant des variantes stylistiques ou linguistiques des caractères. Il est important de noter que plusieurs glyphes différents peuvent représenter un caractère. Par exemple, le « a » miniscule, la petite capitale « A » et le « a » orné minuscule représentent tous le même caractère, c'est-à-dire « a » minuscule, mais ce sont trois glyphes séparés. D'autre part, bien que la relation entre les glyphes et les caractères est souvent un glyphe par caractère, elle peut être de plusieurs glyphes pour un caractère, un glyphe pour plusieurs caractères ou encore plusieurs glyphes pour plusieurs caractères. Par exemple, un glyphe peut parfois représenter plusieurs caractères, comme dans le cas de la ligature « ffi », qui correspond à une série de trois caractères : f, f et i.

À chaque caractère correspondent un glyphe et un comportement de positionnement par défaut. L'application de fonctions de mise en page OpenType à un ou plusieurs caractères peut donc modifier leur positionnement ou substituer un glyphe différent. Par exemple, l'application de la fonction petites capitales à un « a » substitue le glyphe petite capitale « A » au glyphe bas de casse habituel « a ».

Les icônes ci-dessous sont utilisées dans ce manuel et sur le site Web d'Adobe afin d'identifier les glyphes qui sont inclus dans chacune des polices OpenType. Veuillez consulter le site Web *www.adobe.com/type* pour plus d'informations. Pour en savoir plus sur les glyphes supplémentaires des polices OpenType japonaises d'Adobe, consultez le site Web d'Adobe.

DE BASE `A-z` Ces polices contiennent des glyphes de base comprenant des dessins de lettres bas de casse et haut de casse, des figures, des caractères avec accent et la ponctuation. Ces polices contiennent également les symboles monétaires, les ligatures standard, les fractions et les opérateurs mathématiques courants, des chiffres en exposant, des séparateurs et des conjoncteurs communs, et autres symboles. Ces glyphes essentiels sont illustrés dans l'échantillon Adobe Western 2 ci-dessous.

ABCDEFGHIJKLMNOPQRSTUVWXYZ
abcdefghijklmnopqrstuvwxyz
–&—0123456789$¢£¥ƒ¤€
ÆÁÂÄÀÅÃÇÉÊÈÍÎÏÌŁÑŒÓÔÖÒÕØŠÚÛÜ
ÙÝŸŽÐÞæáâäàåãçéêèëfiflíîïìłñœóôöòõøšßúû
üùýÿžðþ
™©®℮@ªº†‡§¶*!¡?¿.,:;""''""„,…‹›«»
()[]{}¦|/_\•·`´^˜¯˘˙˚˝"˝#^¼½¾/º0123
%‰-+÷×±=~<>¬≈≠≥≤∆Ωπμ∂∏∑√∞∫◊

EURO `€` Ces polices comprennent le nouveau symbole monétaire de l'euro, monnaie standard adoptée par les pays membres de l'Union Européenne. La plupart des polices OpenType d'Adobe contiennent également des symboles pour le centime, le dollar, le florin, la livre sterling et le yen. Certaines polices OpenType contiennent aussi les symboles pour le colon, le franc, la lire, la peseta et la roupie. Enfin, certaines polices OpenType comprennent des versions bas de casse de la plupart des symboles monétaires conçus pour être compatibles avec les chiffres en bas de casse.

LIGATURES ffi Les ligatures sont conçues pour corriger les associations de lettres délicates. Ces polices contiennent un jeu étendu de ligatures qui vont au-delà des ligatures « fi » et « fl » courantes que l'on trouve dans la plupart des polices. Ces ligatures spéciales contiennent généralement « ff », « ffi » et « ffl » et éventuellement « Th », « tt » et d'autres combinaisons de lettres particulières. Certaines polices, telle que Silentium Pro, contiennent également un jeu unique de ligatures haut de casse qui permet d'animer les dessins de lettres.

PETITES CAPITALES Bʙ Ces dessins de lettre sont des versions plus petites des capitales normales et sont conçus pour être visuellement compatibles avec les caractères bas de casse d'une police. Vous pouvez les utiliser pour introduire les tous premiers mots d'une histoire, ou pour mettre en valeur des mots-clés dans un texte. Elles sont également couramment utilisées pour insérer des acronymes ou des abréviations (IBM, PDF ou ISBN) dans un texte.

CHIFFRES EN BAS DE CASSE 619 Ces chiffres sont conçus avec des ascendantes et des descendantes et possèdent des caractéristiques et des proportions qui sont compatibles avec les caractères bas de casse de la police. Les chiffres bas de casse, également connus sous le nom de lettrines en retrait, sont généralement utilisés

pour la composition de texte car ils se fondent dans le flot visuel et le rythme de l'alphabet bas de casse. Les polices comprenant des chiffres bas de casse contiennent une version proportionnelle (0123456789) et une version tabulaire (0123456789).

CHIFFRES MODERNES PROPORTIONNELS 123 La plupart des polices contiennent des chiffres modernes conçus pour être compatibles avec les lettres capitales. Ces chiffres sont généralement de la même taille que les lettres capitales ou légèrement plus petits et possèdent typiquement les mêmes largeurs, ou largeurs tabulaires. Les chiffres modernes tabulaires (0123456789) sont particulièrement utiles pour la création de colonnes de chiffres, dans les rapports financiers par exemple. Les polices possédant des chiffres modernes proportionnels (0123456789) contiennent également un jeu de chiffres modernes dont les largeurs uniques sont déterminées par la forme du chiffre. Les chiffres modernes proportionnels sont idéals pour la création de certains textes, tel que les titres en lettres capitales.

FRACTIONS DIAGONALES ⅞ Ces polices contiennent un jeu étendu des fractions diagonales les plus courantes, en plus de ¼, ½ et ¾, et peuvent posséder des fractions supplémentaires telles que ⅛, ⅜, ⅝, ⅞, ⅓ et ⅔. Certaines polices OpenType d'Adobe prennent également en charge la création de fractions arbitraires.

INDICES INFÉRIEURS/INDICES SUPÉRIEURS H₂ Les indices supérieurs et inférieurs, également appelés lettres supérieures et inférieures, sont utilisés pour les notes en bas de page, les composants chimiques et les exposants mathématiques.

ORDINAUX ET LETTRES SUPÉRIEURES [1st] Ces polices contiennent des dessins de lettre supérieurs utilisés pour la création d'ordinaux, qui indiquent la position dans une série numérotée ainsi que dans certaines abréviations en français, anglais et espagnol telles que Madame, compagnie et segundo. L'étendue de la couverture de glyphe varie, mais elle inclut généralement les chiffres 0123456789 et les lettres abdeilmnorst.

LETTRES ORNÉES [𝒜] Les lettres ornées capitales, dont l'origine remonte à l'écriture italique de la Renaissance italienne, furent adoptées comme dessins de lettre au début du seizième siècle. Elles ont évolué depuis, tout comme la nouvelle écriture et les styles de police. Les lettres ornées capitales peuvent être utilisées de manière efficace dans les passages expressifs d'un texte, ou encore dans les titres et les annonces publicitaires auxquels elles ajoutent une note élégante.

CARACTÈRES SECONDAIRES [ĕ] Certaines polices contiennent des formes ligaturées secondaires, des lettres bas de casse secondaires ou encore des associations de formes minuscules à l'intérieur de formes majuscules. Les formes secondaires ont été conçues pour animer légèrement les mots et leur donner une apparence plus informelle, et pour relancer l'intérêt dans la composition typographique. A cause de leur qualité décorative, il est préférable de les utiliser avec modération.

LETTRES CAPITALES DE TITRE [A] Les lettres majuscules de titre sont des dessins de lettre – lettres ornées, lignes, surlignés ou versions raffinées de capitales normales – spécialement conçus pour être utilisés dans les textes exclusivement en lettres capitales ou comme capitales initiales. L'interlettrage des lettres capitales de titre est très spécifique et se prête aux compositions entièrement en lettres capitales. Les polices contenant des lettres capitales de titre peuvent également posséder des figures spécialement conçues, des symboles monétaires, de la ponctuation et des caractères avec accents. Vous pouvez utiliser les lettres capitales de titre renversées comme lettres d'introduction dans les chapitres de livre ou pour les paragraphes.

ORNEMENTS [❦] A travers l'histoire, les dessinateurs de polices de caractères ont créé des ornements d'impression pour agrémenter leurs polices. Ces ornements ajoutent une signature personnelle à la famille des caractères et peuvent être utilisés pour décorer la page de titre, marquer les paragraphes, séparer les blocs de texte ou comme bandes et bordures en répétition. Parmi les ornements courants on compte les fleurs, les feuilles, les puces, les crochets et les décorations graphiques contemporaines.

DESSINS DE CASSE [aA] Ces polices contiennent des dessins de lettre et des caractères de ponctuation secondaires spéciaux dont la conception et l'espacement uniques sont destinés aux textes entièrement en lettres capitales.

BLACKLETTER HISTORIQUE [ß] Ces polices contiennent des glyphes historiques spéciaux qui permettent à l'utilisateur de respecter les conventions pour Allemande ou blackletter textes entièrement.

Unterstütze Zeichen- und Glyphensätze

OpenType-Fonts von Adobe können zur Unterstützung einer größeren Sprachenvielfalt und weit reichender typografischer Gestaltungsmöglichkeiten auch einen erweiterten Glyphensatz umfassen. Zum besseren Verständnis von

OpenType ist es wichtig, den Unterschied zwischen Zeichen und Glyphen zu verstehen. Bei Zeichen handelt es sich um die Codepunkte, die vom Unicode-Standard zugeordnet werden und die kleinsten semantischen Spracheinheiten darstellen, wie z. B. Buchstaben. Bei Glyphen handelt es sich um spezifische Formen oder Figuren, die diese Zeichen oder Buchstaben in einer Schriftart annehmen können.

Wenn eine Schriftart einen spezifischen Zeichensatz beinhaltet, verfügt sie über eine Glyphenergänzung, das vorgegebene Glyphenfiguren für diese Zeichen bietet, und außerdem können zusätzliche Glyphen für stilistische oder linguistische Variationen der Zeichen vorhanden sein. Es ist zu beachten, daß ein Zeichen durch eine von mehreren verschiedenen Glyphen dargestellt werden kann. Zum Beispiel handelt es sich bei **a**, in Kleinbuchstaben, **A**, in Kapitälchen und einem alternativen Schwungbuchstaben **a** um das gleiche Zeichen, ein **a**, in Kleinbuchstaben, aber dies sind drei separate Glyphen. Des weiteren kann das Verhältnis zwischen Glyphe und Zeichen, das oft eins zu eins ist, auch viele zu eins, eins zu vielen oder viele zu vielen sein. Manchmal können mehrere Zeichen z. B. von einer Glyphe dargestellt werden, wie beispielsweise bei der **ffi**-Ligatur, die einer Folge von drei Zeichen entspricht: **f**, **f** und **i**.

Es gibt für jedes Zeichen eine standardmäßige Glyphe und ein Standardpositionsverhalten. Wenn die Formatmerkmale von OpenType auf ein oder mehrere Zeichen angewendet wird, kann die Standardposition geändert oder eine andere Glyphe als Ersatz verwendet werden. Durch Anwendung der Kapitälchen auf **a** würde die Kapitälchen-Glyphe **A** beispielsweise die gebräuchliche Glyphe **a** in Kleinbuchstaben ersetzen.

Die nachstehend aufgeführten Symbole werden in diesem Handbuch und auf der Adobe-Website dazu verwendet, die spezifischen Glyphen zu identifizieren, die jeder OpenType-Font enthält. Weitere Informationen finden Sie unter *www.adobe.com/type*. Konsultieren Sie die Adobe-Website bitte auch, um mehr Informationen zu den exakten Glyphenergänzungen in den japanischen OpenType-Fonts von Adobe zu erhalten.

BASIS-ZEICHENSÄTZE A-z Diese Schriftarten enthalten einen Glyphen-Basiszeichensatz, der Buchstaben in Großformat, Buchstaben in Kleinformat, Ziffern, akzentuierte Zeichen und Interpunktion beinhaltet. Außerdem enthalten diese Schriftarten Währungssymbole, Standardligaturen, gebräuchliche Frakturen, gebräuchliche mathematische Vorzeichen, hochgestellte Zahlen, gebräuchliche Trennsymbole und Verbindungszeichen und andere Symbole. Dieser Glyphen-Basiszeichensatz ist im Beispiel für Adobe Western 2 unten abgebildet.

ABCDEFGHIJKLMNOPQRSTUVWXYZ
abcdefghijklmnopqrstuvwxyz
–&—0123456789$¢£¥ƒ¤€
ÆÁÂÄÀÅÃÇÉÊËÈÍÎÏÌŁÑŒÓÔÖÒÕØŠÚÛÜ
ÙÝŸŽÐÞæáâäàåãçéêëèfiflıíîïìłñœóôöòõøšßúû
üùýÿžðþ
™©®ℓ℮@ªº†‡§¶*!¡?¿.,:;'"‘’“”‚„…‹›«»
()[]{}¦|/_\•·`´ˆ˜¯˘˙¨˚˝ˇ¸˛#^¼½¾⁄°¹²³
%‰-+÷×±=~<>¬≈≠≤≥∆Ωπµ∂∏∑√∞∫◊

EURO € Diese Schriftarten beinhalten das neue Euro-Währungssymbol, mit dem die Standardwährung in EU-Ländern dargestellt wird. Die meisten OpenType-Fonts von Adobe schließen außerdem Symbole für Cent, Dollar, Florin, Pfund Sterling und Yen mit ein. Einige OpenType-Fonts können auch die Symbole für

Colon, Franc, Lira, Peseta und Rupie umfassen. Manche OpenType-Fonts von Adobe beinhalten außerdem Mediävalversionen der meisten Währungssymbole, die für eine Kompatibilität mit den Mediävalziffern sorgen.

LIGATUREN [ffi] Ligaturen sind dazu gedacht, ungünstige Kombinationen, bei denen Buchstaben eventuell kollidieren, zu korrigieren. Diese Schriften beinhalten außer den grundlegenden Ligaturen fi and fl, die in den meisten Schriftarten zu finden sind, einen erweiterten Satz an Ligaturen. Diese besonderen Ligaturen schließen normalerweise ff, ffi und ffl, mit ein, und können auch Th, tt und anderen besondere Buchstabenkombinationen beinhalten. Manche Schriftarten wie z. B. Silentium Pro umfassen außerdem einen einmaligen Satz an Ligaturen in Großbuchstaben, die den Buchstaben Lebendigkeit verleihen.

KAPITÄLCHEN [Bb] Bei diesen Buchstaben handelt es sich um kleinere Versionen der normalen Großbuchstaben, die dazu gedacht sind, optisch für eine Kompatibilität mit den Kleinbuchstaben einer Schriftart zu sorgen. Sie können für die ersten paar Wörter zur Einleitung eines Artikels oder zum Hervorheben bedeutender Wörter im Text verwendet werden. Sie werden normalerweise auch beim Setzen von Akronymen oder Abkürzungen wie beispielsweise IBM, PDF oder ISBN im Text benutzt.

MEDIÄVALZIFFERN [619] Diese Ziffern wurden mit Oberlängen und Unterlängen entworfen und verfügen über Eigenschaften und Proportionen, die mit den Kleinbuchstaben der Schriftart kompatibel sind. Mediävalziffern, die auch hängende Ziffern genannt werden, werden normalerweise beim Setzen von Text verwendet, weil sie sich gut in den optischen Fluß und Rhythmus des Alphabets in Kleinbuchstaben einfügen. Schriftarten mit Mediävalziffern schließen sowohl proportionale (0123456789) als auch tabellarische (0123456789) Versionen mit ein.

PROPORTIONALE VERSALZIFFERN [123] Die meisten Schriftarten beinhalten Versalziffern, die so konzipiert wurden, daß sie mit den Großbuchstaben kompatibel sind. Sie sind normalerweise genau so hoch wie Großbuchstaben oder geringfügig kleiner, und haben die gleichen Breiten, die auch tabellarische Breiten genannt werden. Tabellarische Versalziffern (0123456789) sind beim Setzen von Spalten mit Zahlen, wie beispielsweise Finanzberichten, besonders nützlich. Schriftarten mit proportionalen Versalziffern beinhalten außerdem einen Satz Versalziffern mit spezifischen Breiten, die von der Form der Ziffer festgelegt werden. Proportionale Versalziffern (0123456789) werden beim Setzen von bestimmten Texten wie beispielsweise einer gänzlich in Großbuchstaben gehaltenen Überschrift bevorzugt.

DIAGONALE FRAKTUREN [⅞] Diese Schriftarten beinhalten neben ¼, ½ und ¾ einen erweiterten Satz mit den am häufigsten benutzen diagonalen Frakturen, und können zusätzliche Frakturen wie ⅛, ⅜, ⅝, ⅞, ⅓ und ⅔ umfassen. Einige OpenType-Fonts von Adobe unterstützen außerdem die Erstellung frei wählbarer Frakturen.

HOCHGESTELLT/TIEFGESTELLT [H₂] Hoch- und tiefgestellte Ziffern, auch hochgestellte und tiefgestellte Buchstaben genannt, werden für Verweise in Fußnoten, chemische Verbindungen und als mathematische Exponenten verwendet.

ORDINALZAHLEN UND HOCHGESTELLTE BUCHSTABEN 1st Diese Schriftarten enthalten hochgestellte Buchstaben, die bei der Erstellung von Ordinalzahlen verwendet werden, die eine Position in einer nummerierten Reihenfolge angeben und in bestimmten englischen, französischen und spanischen Abkürzungen wie beispielsweise für Madame, compagnie bzw. segundo benutzt werden. Welche Glyphen für diese Buchstaben erhältlich sind, ist unterschiedlich, schließt aber normalerweise die Zahlen 0123456789 und die Buchstaben abdeilmnorst mit ein.

SCHWUNGBUCHSTABEN A Schwungbuchstaben in Großbuchstaben, die auf die kursive Handschrift der italienischen Renaissance zurückzuführen sind, wurden Anfang des sechzehnten Jahrhunderts als Formen von Buchstaben übernommen. Inzwischen haben sich Schwungbuchstaben mit den neuen Hand- und Typenschriften weiterentwickelt. Schwungbuchstaben in Großbuchstaben können in ausdrucksvollen Textpassagen oder für Titel und Unterschriften, die elegant aussehen sollen, effektiv eingesetzt werden.

ALTERNATIVEN & Einige Schriftarten beinhalten alternative Ligaturformen, alternative Kleinbuchstaben oder Kombinationen von Kleinbuchstaben innerhalb von Großbuchstaben. Alternative Formen dienen dazu, Wörtern ein lebhafteres und informelleres Erscheinungsbild zu verleihen und die Typenkomposition interessanter zu gestalten. Aufgrund ihrer dekorativen Eigenschaft sollten sie nur in Maßen verwendet werden.

VERSALSCHRIFT FÜR TITEL A Bei der Versalschrift für Titel handelt es sich um speziell entworfene Buchstaben wie z. B. verzierte, flachliegende, weißgestrichelte oder verfeinerte Versionen regulärer Großbuchstaben, die für die Verwendung im nur Großbuchstaben enthaltenden Satz oder als Anfangsgroßbuchstaben gedacht sind. Die Versalschriften für Titel besitzen außerdem einen spezifischen Zeichenabstand, der gut für einen nur Großbuchstaben enthaltenden Satz geeignet ist und können speziell entworfene Ziffern, Währungssymbole, verwandte Interpunktion und akzentuierte Zeichen zur Verwendung mit der Versalschrift umfassen. Die umgekehrte Versalschrift kann für Anfangsbuchstaben in Buchkapiteln oder verwandte Absätze genutzt werden.

VERZIERUNGEN Designer von Schriften haben schon immer Druckerverzierungen erstellt, die ihre Schriften begleiten. Diese Verzierungen verleihen der Schriftartfamilie eine persönliche Note und können als Ausschmückungen auf der Titelseite, Absatzmarkierungen, Aufteilungen für Textblöcke oder als sich wiederholende Streifen und Rahmen verwendet werden. Zu den gebräuchlichen Verzierungen gehören Blumen, Blätter, Hervorhebungspunkte, eckige Klammern und zeitgenössische grafische Dekorationen.

GROSS/KLEINSCHREIBUNGSFORMEN aA Diese Schriftarten enthalten spezielle alternative Buchstaben und Interpunktionszeichen mit klar ausgeprägtem Design und Zeichenabstand, die beim Setzen von nur Großbuchstaben enthaltendem Text verwendet werden.

HISTORISCHE GOTISCHE SCHRIFTEN ß Diese Schriftarten enthalten spezielle, historische deutsche Frakturglyphen, die es dem Benutzer ermöglichen, Text getreu den Konventionen für deutsche gotische Schriften zu setzen.

Adobe Font Folio OpenType Edition

The complete type solution for creative professionals, Adobe Font Folio OpenType Edition contains more than 2,200 typefaces from the Adobe Type Library in OpenType format on CD-ROM. With these high-quality typefaces unlocked and ready to use, you'll always find the right face for your print, web, and digital video projects. *For Macintosh and Windows*

For more information, please visit *www.adobe. com/type* (or your local Adobe web site) or contact your local Adobe software distributor.

Adobe Font Folio OpenType Edition

Pour garantir une solution typographique complète aux professionnels de la composition créatifs, Adobe Font Folio OpenType Edition regroupe 2 200 polices au format OpenType de la Typothèque Adobe sur CD-ROM. Grâce à ces polices non codées immédiatement disponibles, vous trouverez toujours le caractère adéquat pour vos projets Web, vidéo numérique et d'impression. *Pour Macintosh et Windows*

Pour plus d'informations, veuillez consulter le site Web suivant : *www.adobe.com/type* (ou votre site Web Adobe local) ou contactez votre revendeur de logiciels Adobe.

Adobe Font Folio OpenType Edition

Als vollständige Schriftlösung für kreative professionelle Designer enthält Adobe Font Folio OpenType Edition 2.200 Schriften aus der Adobe Schriftenbibliothek im OpenType-Format auf CD-ROM. Mit diesen hochwertigen Schriften, freigeschaltet und gebrauchsfertig, haben Sie immer die richtige Schrift für ihre Druck-, Internet- und digitalen Videoprojekte zur Hand. *Für Macintosh und Windows*

Weitere Informationen finden Sie unter *www.adobe.com/type* (oder auf der lokalen Adobe-Website), oder wenden Sie sich an Ihren Adobe-Händler.

Today, designers and desktop publishers have thousands of typefaces in the Adobe Type Library to choose from, with new designs added on a regular basis. To help make the job of selecting type easier, we've organized the library according to a simplified classification system based on type styles. Most of the categories are drawn from the internationally recognized system adopted by the Association Typographique Internationale (ATypI). However, many typefaces fit into more than one category, and even the experts can't agree. In addition, we've added categories unique to the Adobe Type Library, such as Opticals.

La typothèque Adobe Type Library offre aux professionnels de la composition et de la mise en page un vaste choix de polices très variées. Cette typothèque, riche de plusieurs milliers de polices, est en outre complétée régulièrement. Pour faciliter la sélection des polices, nous les avons classées par style dans la typothèque. Ces catégories respectent pour la plupart le système de classification officiel de l'Association Typographique Internationale (ATypI). De nombreuses polices entrent dans plusieurs catégories (même les experts ne parviennent pas à se mettre d'accord). Nous avons également ajouté des catégories propres à la typothèque Adobe Type Library, par exemple, Polices Optiques.

Heutzutage können Designer und Desktop-Publisher unter Tausenden von Schriften in der Adobe-Schriftenbibliothek wählen, und regelmäßig kommen neue Designs hinzu. Um Ihnen das Wählen einer Schrift zu erleichtern, haben wir die Bibliothek nach einem vereinfachten Schriftklassifizierungssystems angeordnet. Die meisten Kategorien sind an das international anerkannte System der Association Typographique Internationale (ATypI) angelehnt. Viele Schriften passen in mehr als eine Kategorie (selbst die Experten sind sich nicht einig). Außerdem haben wir spezielle Kategorien für die Adobe-Schriftenbibliothek hinzugefügt, wie etwa Opticals-Schriften.

Serif The serif, or cross-line at the end of a stroke, probably dates from early Rome. Father Edward Catich proposed in his seminal work, *The Origin of the Serif,* that the serif is an artifact of brushing letters onto stone before cutting them. Serif, or roman, types are useful in text because the serifs help distinguish individual letters and lead the eye along a line of type. Serif typefaces fall into four main categories: Venetian, Garalde, Transitional, and Didone (Modern), as described next.

Polices à empattements L'empattement, ou serif, est la ligne perpendiculaire marquant l'extrémité d'un trait. Son origine remonte probablement à l'antiquité romaine. Dans son essai « The Origin of the Serif », le père Edward Catich supposait que les empattements étaient apparus parce que les lettres étaient alors peintes sur la pierre avant d'être gravées. Les polices à empattements, dites de style normal, sont utiles dans les textes, car les empattements aident à distinguer les caractères et guident l'œil du lecteur. Il existe quatre grandes catégories de polices à empattements : Vénitiennes, Garaldes, Transitionnelles et Didones (Modernes).

Serifenschriften Die Serifen, oder Endstriche, an den Zeichen gehen wahrscheinlich auf die frühe Römerzeit zurück. Father Edward Catich stellt in seiner Schrift „The Origin of the Serif" die These auf, daß die Serifen ihren Ursprung darin haben, daß Zeichen zunächst auf den Stein gepinselt und dann gemeißelt wurden. Serifen- oder Roman-Schriften sind für den Fließtext nützlich, da die Serifen das Erkennen der einzelnen Zeichen erleichtern und das Auge an der Textzeile entlang führen. Serifenschriften werden wie im folgenden beschrieben in vier Hauptkategorien unterteilt: Venezianische Renaissance-Antiqua, Französische Renaissance-Antiqua, Barock-Antiqua und Klassizistische Antiqua.

VENETIAN OLDSTYLE Named after the first roman typefaces that appeared in Venice in 1470, Venetian typefaces were initially designed to imitate the handwriting of Italian Renaissance scholars. These typefaces originated as book type and still serve that function well because of their clarity and legibility.

VÉNITIENNES Nommées ainsi en raison des premières polices romaines créées à Venise en 1470, les polices vénitiennes étaient initialement destinées à imiter l'écriture courante des lettrés de la Renaissance italienne. A l'origine, ces polices servaient essentiellement à la composition de livres et elles sont toujours appréciées dans ce contexte grâce à leur clarté et à leur lisibilité.

VENEZIANISCHE RENAISSANCE-ANTIQUA Benannt nach den ersten 1470 in Venedig erschienenen Serifenschriften, imitierten diese Schriften ursprünglich die Handschriften der Gelehrten in der italienischen Renaissance. Diese Schriften haben ihren Ursprung in der Buchschrift und erfüllen aufgrund ihrer Klarheit und Lesbarkeit diesen Zweck immer noch sehr gut.

W o r e
A B C D

A *Moderate contrast between thick and thin strokes*
B *Axis curves inclined to the left* C *Irregular or lightly bracketed serifs* D *Diagonal bar on* e

ITC Berkeley Oldstyle Std
Brioso PRO
Centaur STD
Guardi Std
Hadriano
Italia Std
Monotype Italian Old Style Std
Adobe Jenson PRO
ITC Legacy Serif Std
Raleigh Std
Stempel Schneidler Std
ITC Weidemann Std

GARALDE OLDSTYLE Garalde typefaces include some of the most popular serif types in use today. They were first designed during the 16th and 17th centuries by such masters as the French printer Claude Garamond and the Venetian printer Aldus Manutius. The distinguishing features of Garalde typefaces are apparent in Adobe Garamond, which has a horizontal bar on the lowercase e, a slightly greater contrast between thick and thin strokes than Venetian types, axis curves that are inclined to the left, and bracketed serifs.

GARALDES La famille des garaldes regroupe un grand nombre de polices à empattements très couramment employées de nos jours. Ces polices ont été dessinées au cours des 16ème et 17ème siècles par des autorités reconnues comme l'imprimeur français Claude Garamond et l'imprimeur vénitien Alde Manuce. Les caractéristiques des garaldes sont évidentes dans la police Adobe Garamond, qui présente un trait horizontal sur le e minuscule, un contraste légèrement plus marqué que dans les polices vénitiennes entre les traits épais et fins, des courbes dont l'axe est incliné vers la gauche et des empattements avec arrondis.

FRANZÖSISCHE RENAISSANCE-ANTIQUA Zu diesen Schriften gehören manche der heute beliebtesten Serifenschriften. Sie wurden im 16. und 17. Jahrhundert von Druckmeistern wie dem Franzosen Claude Garamond und dem Venezianer Aldus Manutius gestaltet. Die Merkmale der französischen Renaissance-Antiqua-Schriften sind in der Adobe Garamond erkennbar, die einen horizontalen Strich im Kleinbuchstaben e hat, einen etwas größeren Kontrast zwischen dicken und dünnen Strichen als die venezianischen Schriften und nach links geneigte Achsenkurven und Kehlung der Serifen.

W o r e

A *More contrast between thick and thin strokes* B *Axis curves inclined to the left* C *Bracketed serifs* D *Horizontal bar on e*

Aldus STD
New Aster Std
Bembo STD
Berling Std
Caxton Std
MVB Celestia Antiqua STD
Dante STD
ITC Esprit Std
ITC Galliard Std
Adobe Garamond PRO
Garamond 3 STD
ITC Garamond Std
Simoncini Garamond Std
Stempel Garamond STD
ITC Giovanni Std
Goudy STD
Granjon STD
Hiroshige Std
Horley Old Style Std
ITC Leawood Std

Lucida Std
ITC Mendoza Roman Std
Minion PRO
Minister Std
Octavian STD
Old Claude STD
Palatino STD
Plantin Std
Sabon STD
Spectrum STD
ITC Tiepolo Std
Trump Mediäval STD
ITC Usherwood Std
Weiss Std

TRANSITIONAL In typography, the 18th century was a time of transition. Containing elements of both Garalde and Didone (Modern) typefaces, Transitional typefaces such as ITC New Baskerville and Caslon are beautifully suited for text because of their regularity and precision. The axis of the round characters is vertical or barely inclined, the contrast between hairlines and main strokes is slightly pronounced, and serifs are thin, flat, and bracketed.

TRANSITIONNELLES En typographie, le 18ème siècle fut une période de transition. Les polices transitionnelles comme ITC New Baskerville et Caslon reprennent des éléments des garaldes et des didones (Modernes) et conviennent particulièrement bien au texte en raison de leur régularité et de leur précision. L'axe des caractères arrondis est vertical ou à peine incliné, le contraste entre les pleins et les déliés est légèrement marqué et les empattements sont fins, plats et avec arrondis.

BAROCK-ANTIQUA In der Typographie war das 18. Jahrhundert eine Übergangszeit. Schriften dieser Gruppe enthalten Elemente der Französischen Renaissance-Antiqua und Elemente der Klassizistischen Antiqua. Barock Antiqua-Schriften wie ITC New Baskerville und Caslon sind wegen ihrer Gleichmäßigkeit und Präzision sehr schön im Fließtext. Die Achse der runden Zeichen ist vertikal oder kaum geneigt, der Kontrast zwischen Haarlinien und anderen Strichen ist recht stark und die Serifen sind dünn, flach und gekehlt.

w o r

A *Slight contrast* B *Curved strokes on a vertical axis or barely inclined* C *Thin, flat, and bracketed serifs*

Americana Std
Apollo STD
ITC New Baskerville STD
Bell STD
ITC Bookman Std
Bulmer STD
Adobe Caslon PRO
Caslon 3 STD
Caslon 540 STD
ITC Caslon 224 Std
Century Old Style Std
ITC Clearface Std
Cochin Std
Corona Std
ITC Cushing Std
Ehrhardt Std
Fournier STD
Gazette Std
Monotype Goudy Modern Std
Impressum Std
Janson Text STD

Joanna Std
ITC Korinna Std
Life Std
Maximus Std
Meridien Std
Old Style 7 STD
Olympian Std
Perpetua STD
Photina Std
Rotation Std
Rotis Semi Serif
Rotis Serif
ITC Slimbach Std
ITC Stone Serif Std
ITC Tiffany Std
Times STD
Times Europa Std
Times New Roman Std
Times Ten STD
Utopia STD
ITC Veljovic Std
Versailles Std
Warnock PRO
Wilke Std

DIDONE (MODERN) Improvements in paper production, composition, printing, and binding in the late 18th century profoundly affected the course typography would take. It was possible to develop a type style with strong vertical emphasis and fine hairlines; this is what the French family Didot did, and what the Italian printer Bodoni perfected. It is for these designers that the Didone type category is named. Characteristics of Didone types include strong contrast between thick and thin strokes, curved strokes on a vertical axis, and often serifs with no brackets.

DIDONES (MODERNES) Vers la fin du 18ème siècle, les progrès réalisés en matière de qualité du papier, de composition, d'impression et de reliure ont profondément influencé l'évolution de la typographie. Il était désormais possible d'utiliser une écriture avec des traits verticaux très marqués et des déliés très fins. La dynastie d'imprimeurs français Didot a donc créé ces nouveaux caractères et l'imprimeur italien Bodoni les a perfectionnés. D'où le nom de cette catégorie de polices. Les polices de la famille des didones ont les caractéristiques suivantes : un fort contraste entre les traits épais et fins, des courbes suivant un axe vertical et, souvent, des empattements sans arrondis.

KLASSIZISTISCHE ANTIQUA Verbesserungen in der Papierproduktion, beim Setzen, Drucken und Binden Ende des 18. Jahrhunderts haben die Entwicklung der Typographie stark beeinflußt. Es war nun möglich einen Schriftstil mit starker Betonung der vertikalen Linien und feinen Haarlinien zu entwickeln, wie es die französische Familie Didot zeigt und der italienische Drucker Bodoni perfektionierte. Diese Designer gaben dieser Gruppe ihren englischen Namen: Didone. Merkmale Klassizistischer Antiqua-Schriften sind

u. a. ein starker Kontrast zwischen dicken und dünnen Linien, gebogene Linien auf einer vertikalen Achse und häufig Serifen ohne Kehlung.

A Strong contrast between thick and thin strokes
B Curved strokes on a vertical axis C Serifs without brackets

Bodoni Std
Bauer Bodoni STD
New Caledonia STD
Linotype Centennial STD
Century Expanded Std
ITC Century Std
New Century Schoolbook Std
Linotype Didot STD
Electra STD
Ellington Std
Else NPL Std
Fairfield STD
ITC Fenice Std
Kepler STD
Monotype Modern Std
Monotype Scotch Roman Std

SLAB SERIF The Industrial Revolution of the early 19th century encouraged the development of very bold printing types that could be used for a new vehicle of communication: advertising. Posters, flyers, and broadsides competed for attention. They were often created using slab serif typefaces, which, with their strong, square finishing strokes, proved extremely effective for commanding the reader's attention.

There are actually three kinds of slab serif typefaces: slab serifs, Clarendons, and typewriter types. Slab serifs have a square, unbracketed serif; Clarendons have a square, bracketed serif; and typewriter types feature stems and serifs of similar weight as well as constant character widths.

POLICES À EMPATTEMENTS RECTANGULAIRES
Au tout début du 19ème siècle, la Révolution industrielle a encouragé le développement de polices de caractères très grasses appliquées à un nouveau mode de communication : la publicité. Affiches, dépliants et prospectus se disputaient l'attention. Ces documents publicitaires étaient souvent créés à l'aide de polices à empattements rectangulaires (traits horizontaux épais et aux extrémités carrées) qui se sont avérées très efficaces pour attirer l'attention du lecteur.

Il existe, en fait, trois types de polices à empattements rectangulaires : les polices à empattements rectangulaires bruts (égyptiennes), les polices de la famille Clarendon et les polices de machine à écrire. Les polices à empattements rectangulaires bruts se terminent par un trait horizontal rectangulaire sans arrondis, les polices de la famille Clarendon ont des empattements rectangulaires avec arrondis et les polices de machine à écrire se distinguent par des fûts et des empattements de graisse similaire et par une chasse constante.

SERIFENBETONTE LINEAR-ANTIQUA Die Industrielle Revolution Anfang des 19. Jahrhunderts förderte die Entwicklung sehr fetter Druckbuchstaben, denn sie konnten in einem neuen Kommunikationsmittel verwendet werden: Werbung. Um die Aufmerksamkeit der Betrachter rangen Poster, Flugblätter und Plakate. Diese wurden oft mit serifenbetonten Antiqua-Schriften erstellt, die mit ihren starken, eckigen Abschlußstrichen leicht die Aufmerksamkeit der Leser erregen.

Es gibt drei Untergruppen: Serifenbetonte Antiqua, Clarendons und Schreibmaschinenschriften. Linear-Antiqua mit eckigen Serifen ohne Kehlung; Clarendons mit eckigen Serifen mit Kehlung und Schreibmaschinenschriften, deren Grundstriche und Serifen ähnliche Strichstärken und konstante Dickten der Zeichen aufweisen.

A *Slab serifs have square, unbracketed serifs* B *Clarendons have square, bracketed serifs* C *Typewriter typefaces have similar weights of stems and serifs*

ITC American Typewriter Std
PMN Cæcilia STD
Calvert Std
Candida Std
℮ Chaparral PRO
ITC Cheltenham Std
Clarendon Std
Egyptienne F Std
Excelsior Std

Glypha Std
LinoLetter STD
ITC Lubalin Graph Std
Memphis Std
ITC Officina Serif Std
℮ **Postino Std**
Rockwell Std
Serifa Std
ITC Stone Informal Std

Sans Serif Though the first sans serif (without serif) typeface was issued in 1816, another hundred years passed before this style gained popularity. Then, in the 1920's, when typography was heavily influenced by the "less is more" philosophy of Germany's Bauhaus school of design, designers began creating typefaces without serifs. Ornamentation almost vanished. These typefaces are highly legible as display types and may also be used successfully in text. They generally fall into one of four categories: Grotesque, Neo-Grotesque, Geometric, and Humanist, as described next.

Polices sans empattements La première police sans empattements a été créée en 1816, mais il a fallu attendre près d'un siècle pour que ce style devienne populaire. En effet, dans les années 1920, sous l'influence très nette du dépouillement qui caractérise le Bauhaus allemand, les stylistes et dessinateurs se sont mis à créer des polices sans empattements. Toute ornementation fut pratiquement bannie. Ces polices sont très lisibles lorsqu'elles sont utilisées comme polices d'enseigne, mais elles peuvent aussi très bien convenir au texte. Elles sont généralement classées en quatre catégories : Grotesques, Néo-grotesques, Géométriques et Humanistes.

Serifenlose Schriften Obwohl die erste serifenlose Schrift (Sans Serif) 1816 veröffentlicht wurde, ist ein weiteres Jahrhundert vergangen, bis diese Schriften an Beliebtheit gewannen. In den zwanziger Jahren dann, als die Typographie stark von der Philosophie „weniger ist mehr" der deutschen Designerschule Bauhaus beeinflußt wurde, fingen Designer an, serifenlose Schriften zu entwickeln. Verzierungen verschwanden fast völlig. Diese Schriften sind als Auszeichnungsschriften sehr gut lesbar und können auch im Fließtext erfolgreich eingesetzt werden. Sie fallen in eine von vier Kategorien: Grotesk, Neo-Grotesk, Geometrisch und Humanistisch, wie im folgenden beschrieben.

A *Serif—a stroke added to the beginning or end of the letter's main strokes* B *Sans serif—without serifs*

GROTESQUE Early sans serif designs such as News Gothic are called Grotesque, a name coined by the English, who considered the first of these typefaces awkward and unappealing because they lacked the traditional serif.

GROTESQUES Les premières polices sans empattements (News Gothic, par exemple) furent qualifiées de grotesques par les Anglais qui les considéraient maladroites et sans attrait du fait de l'absence de l'empattement traditionnel.

GROTESK Frühe serifenlose Designs wie News Gothic werden Grotesk genannt. Der Name kam in England auf, wo die ersten dieser Schriften als ungeschickt und unansprechend empfunden wurden, weil ihnen die traditionellen Serifen fehlten.

Doric Std

Franklin Gothic Std

ITC Franklin Gothic Std

Gothic 13 Std

Monotype Grotesque Std

News Gothic Std

Tempo Std

Trade Gothic Std

NEO-GROTESQUE More recent sans serif Swiss-style designs are called Neo-Grotesque because they are more graceful versions of the earlier Grotesques.

NÉO-GROTESQUES Cette catégorie regroupe des polices plus récentes (Swiss, par exemple) qui sont des versions plus raffinées des premières grotesques.

NEO-GROTESK Neuere serifenlose Designs im Schweizer Stil werden Neo-Grotesk genannt, da sie grazilere Versionen der frühen Grotesken sind.

Antique Olive Std

Bell Centennial Std

Bell Gothic Std

DIN Schriften Std

Helvetica Std

Helvetica Neue Std

Neuzeit S Std

VAG Rounded Std

GEOMETRIC Geometric sans serif typefaces were heavily influenced by the Bauhaus movement and are characterized by circular or otherwise geometric- or mechanical-looking o's and other "bowl" and "arch" shapes. (Bowls are the round parts of **a**, **b**, **c**, **d**, **e**, **g**, **p**, and **q**. Arches are created where curves join the stems of **h**, **m**, **n**, and **u**.) Geometrics often have a one-story **a** and **g**, and very little modulation of stroke contrast.

GÉOMÉTRIQUES Les polices géométriques sans empattements ont subi la très nette influence du mouvement Bauhaus et se caractérisent par des lettres aux arrondis et panses de forme circulaire ou géométrique (ou mécanique). On appelle panse l'arrondi des lettres **a**, **b**, **c**, **d**, **e**, **g**, **p**, et **q**, et arrondi l'intersection de la courbe et du fût des lettres **h**, **m**, **n**, et **u**. Dans ces polices, le **a** et le **g** n'ont souvent qu'un seul niveau et la force des traits présente très peu de contraste.

GEOMETRISCH Geometrische serifenlose Schriften wurden stark von der Bauhaus-Bewegung beeinflußt und zeichnen sich durch kreisrunde oder anderweitig geometrisch oder mechanisch anmutende **o**'s und andere Bogen- und Schulterformen aus. (Bogen sind die runden Teile von **a**, **b**, **c**, **d**, **e**, **g**, **p** und **q**. Schultern entstehen dort, wo die Kurven an die geraden Linien von **h**, **m**, **n** und **u** stoßen.) Geometrische Schriften haben oft einstöckige Kleinbuchstaben für **a** und **g** sowie wenig Modulation der Strichstärke.

A *Circular or otherwise geometric- or mechanical-looking o's*
B *One-story a and g* C *Little modulation of stroke contrast*

ITC Avant Garde Gothic Std

Avenir Std

ITC Bauhaus Std

Briem Akademi Std

Eurostile Std

Folio Std

Futura Std

Kabel Std

ITC Kabel Std

PENUMBRA SANS STD

ITC Serif Gothic Std

Serpentine

Verve Std

HUMANIST Humanist sans serifs are characterized by noncircular, organic-looking bowl and arch shapes. They often exhibit widely varying letter widths and at least some modulation in stroke contrast. The **a** and **g** are usually two-story.

HUMANISTES Les polices sans empattements de cette catégorie se distinguent par des panses et arrondis non circulaires. La chasse des caractères présente souvent de grandes variations et la force des traits est généralement plus contrastée que dans les polices géométriques. En outre, les lettres **a** et **g** comportent habituellement deux niveaux.

HUMANISTISCH Humanistische serifenlose Schriften zeichnen sich durch nicht-kreisrunde, organisch anmutende Bogen- und Schulterformen aus. Die Dickten variieren oft sehr stark und es gibt zumindest etwas Modulation bei der Strich-stärke. Die Kleinbuchstaben **a** und **g** sind in der Regel zweistöckig.

o a m

A Noncircular, organic-looking bowl and arch shapes
B *The a and g are usually two-story* C *Widely varying letter widths and at least some modulation in stroke contrast*

Cronos PRO
ITC Eras Std
ITC Flora Std
Frutiger Std
Gill Sans Std
ITC Goudy Sans Std
ITC Highlander Std
ITC Legacy Sans Std
Lucida Sans Std
Club Type Mercurius Std
Myriad Pro
Ocean Sans Std
ITC Officina Sans Std
Optima Std
Rotis Sans Serif
Rotis Semi Serif
Shannon
ITC Stone Sans Std
Strayhorn STD
ITC Symbol Std
Syntax Std

Script and Hand-Lettered Since a Parisian printer created the first one in 1643, script typefaces have become almost as numerous as the handwriting instruments—brush, broad-edged pen, and pointed pen—that they were designed to imitate. Script typefaces often mimic handwriting techniques by joining letters with connecting lines. The variety of these freeform typefaces makes them appropriate for anything from casual grocery store advertisements to formal wedding invitations.

Polices cursives et manuelles Depuis l'apparition de la première police de ce genre, créée par un imprimeur parisien en 1643, de très nombreuses autres ont vu le jour. Elles reproduisent le dessin des lettres obtenues à l'aide de tous les types d'outils d'écriture manuelle (pinceau, plume large ou fine, etc.) Les polices cursives imitent souvent les techniques d'écriture manuelle en reliant les lettres. Il existe un vaste choix de polices cursives qui se prêtent à pratiquement tous les types de compositions, du panneau publicitaire au carton d'invitation le plus formel.

Schreibschriften und Handschriftliche Antiqua
Seit ein Drucker in Paris 1643 die erste derartige Schrift schuf, sind Schreibschriften fast genauso zahlreich wie die handschriftlichen Schreibgeräte Pinsel, Breitfeder und spitze Feder, die sie imitieren sollen. Schreibschriften ahmen Handschriften oft nach, indem die Buchstaben miteinander verbunden werden. Aufgrund der Vielfalt dieser Freiformschriften können sie für so unterschiedliche Zwecke wie formlose Sonderange botsschilder und formelle Hochzeitseinladungen verwendet werden.

Arcana Std
Ariadne Std (with Diotima Std)
Bickham Script Std
MVB Bossa Nova Std
Carolina Std
Coronet Std
Delphin Std
Diskus Std
Dorchester Script Std
Ex Ponto Pro
Florens Std
ITC Isadora Std
Kaufmann Std
Künstler Script Std
Linoscript Std
Medici Script Std
Nuptial Script Std
Oxford
Palace Script Std
Park Avenue Std
Poetica STD
Monotype Script Std
Shelley Script Std
Snell Roundhand Std
Voluta Script Pro
ITC Zapf Chancery Std

CASUAL SCRIPT   CURSIVES INFORMELLES
INFORMELLE SKRIPTEN

Alexa Std
Ashley Script Std
Balzano Std
Banshee Std
New Berolina Std
Biffo Std
Briem Script STD
Bruno Std
Brush Script Std
Caflisch
Script Pro
Caliban Std
Cascade
Script Std
Charme Std
Dom Casual Std
MVB
Emmascript Std
FLOOD STD
Forte Std
Freestyle Script Std
Giddyup Std
Graphite Std
MVB
Greymantle Std
Immi 505 Std
Legault Std

Marigold
Matura Std
Mercurius Std
Mistral Std
Monoline
Script Std
Pelican
Pepita Std
Present Std
Reporter Std
Ruling
Script Std
Russell Oblique Std
Ruzicka Freehand STD
Sanvito Pro
Silentium Pro
Spring Std
Tekton PRO
Visigoth
Wendy Std
Wiesbaden
Swing Std
Zipty Do Std

Display   While typefaces in this group incorporate elements from many different styles, they all have one thing in common: they are usually more effective when used at large sizes for display purposes, such as headlines and titles.

Polices ornementales et d'enseigne   Les polices proposées dans cette catégorie sont de styles très divers, mais elles ont toutes un point commun : elles sont plus particulièrement destinées à être utilisées comme polices d'enseigne (pour des titres, par exemple) et en gros corps de caractères.

Zier- und Auszeichnungsschriften   Die Schriften in dieser Gruppe enthalten Elemente von vielen verschiedenen Stilen, sie haben aber eines gemeinsam: Sie sind am effektvollsten in großen Größen und für Auszeichnungszwecke wie Überschriften und Titel.

DECORATED ORNÉES ZIERSCHRIFTEN

ANDREAS STD

BERMUDA STD

Caslon Open Face Std

CASTELLAR STD

ITC Century Handtooled Std

ITC Cheltenham Handtooled Std

Cloister Open Face Std

Conga Brava Std Stencil

COPAL STD

CORIANDER STD

ITC Garamond Handtooled Std

GILL FLORIATED CAPITALS STD

GILL SANS STD

Helvetica Neue Std

Industria Std

MOONGLOW STD

Myriad Std Sketch

NYX STD

Monotype Old Style Std

PEPPERWOOD STD

Pompeia Std

ROSEWOOD STD

Sassafras Std

SMARAGD STD

STENCIL STD

Strumpf Std

STAOZ STD

UMBRA STD

Viva Std

ZEBRAWOOD STD

OTHER DISPLAY AUTRES POLICES D'ENSEIGNE SONSTIGE AUSZEICHNUNGSSCHRIFTEN

Aachen Std

Albertus Std

Amigo

ITC ANNA STD

Arcadia Std

Arnold Böcklin Std

Auriol Std

BANCO STD

ITC Bauhaus Std

ITC BEE/KNEE/ /TD

Belwe Std

ITC Benguiat Std

ITC Benguiat Gothic Std

BERMUDA STD

Bernhard Std

Bernhard Modern Std

Birch Std

Blackoak Std

Blue Island Std

Briem Akademi Std

Calcite Pro

Cantoria Std

ITC Cerigo Std

CHARLEMAGNE STD

Clearface Gothic Std

Cooper Black Std

COTTONWOOD STD

CRITTER STD

CUTOUT STD

Diotima STD

ECCENTRIC STD

ENGRAVERS STD

Falstaff Std

Flyer Std

FUSAKA Std

Neue Hammer Unziale Std

Hardwood Std

Helvetica Inserat Std

Helvetica Rounded Std

Hobo Std

Impact Std

Industria Std

Inflex Std

Insignia Std

⋲ IRONWOOD STD

Isabella Std

⋲ **Jimbo Std**

⋲ **JUNIPER STD**

Khaki Std

Kino Std

Klang Std

Koch Antiqua Std

KOLO STD

Kompakt Std

ITC Korinna Std

Latin Std

ITC MACHINE STD

⋲**Madrone Std**

MVB MAGNESIUM STD

MVB MAGNOLIA STD

MANITO STD

⋲ MESQUITE STD

⋲ MOJO STD

ITC Mona Lisa Std

MONTARA STD

ITC Motter Corpus Std

⋲ Myriad Std Tilt

⋲ MYTHOS STD

NEULAND STD

Notre Dame Std

⋲ Nueva Std

Old Claude STD

OMNIA STD

Ondine Std

Onyx Std

Orgánica Std

⋲ OUCH! STD

ITC Ozwald Std

Parisian Std

Peignot Std

⋲ PENUMBRA SANS STD

⋲ PENUMBRA FLARE STD

⋲ PENUMBRA HALFSERIF STD

⋲ PENUMBRA SERIF STD

POMPEIJANA STD

⋲ PONDEROSA STD

⋲ **Poplar Std**

⋲ **Postino Std**

⋲ Quake Std

ITC Quorum Std

⋲ RAD STD

Raphael Std

Reliq Std

Revue Std

Romic Std

Runic Std

Russell Square

RUSTICANA STD

ITC Serif Gothic Std

SERLIO STD

Serpentine

Sho Std

⋲ **Shuriken Boy Std**

Spumoni Std

⋲ TOOLBOX STD

University Std

⋲ Viva Std

⋲ WATERS TITLING PRO

⋲ Willow Std

Glyphic Unlike most typefaces, which are based on forms created with pen or brush, glyphic designs are based on letters resembling those carved or chiselled in stone. Since most inscribed letters are capitals, glyphic typefaces also tend to have only capitals. Some can be used effectively for text, but most are better suited to display applications such as posters, packaging, and book titles.

Polices glyptiques A l'inverse de la plupart des autres polices qui reproduisent les caractères obtenus à l'aide d'une plume ou d'un pinceau, les polices glyptiques imitent les lettres gravées dans la pierre. Dans la majeure partie des cas, il s'agissait de lettres capitales. C'est pourquoi de nombreuses polices de cette catégorie ne proposent que des capitales. Certaines d'entre elles peuvent convenir à la composition de texte, mais elles sont généralement utilisées comme polices d'enseigne pour les titres de livres ou les affiches.

Inzisen Anders als die meisten Schriften, die auf mit Feder oder Pinsel gemalten Formen beruhen, basieren die Inzisen auf in Stein geritzten oder gemeißelten Zeichen. Da die meisten gemeißelten Zeichen Großbuchstaben sind, enthalten Inzisen oft nur Großbuchstaben. Einige dieser Schriften können effizient für Fließtext eingesetzt werden, aber die meisten eignen sich besser für Zwecke wie Poster, Verpackungen und Buchtitel.

Albertus Std
Conga Brava Std
COPPERPLATE GOTHIC STD
Friz Quadrata Std
HERCULANUM STD
Kigali Std
Kinesis STD
LITHOS PRO
MANITO STD
Mezz Std
ITC Novarese Std
NYX STD
Origami Std
Pompeia Std Inline
Reliq Std
Strayhorn STD
TRAJAN PRO

Blackletter When Gutenberg produced his movable type, the letterforms mimicked contemporary manuscript handwriting, which was written with a wide, flat pen. This hand developed in the middle ages in Europe and remains popular around the world today. Blackletter typefaces—sometimes referred to as Old English or Gothic—were used for text in Germany until World War II but now are primarily used as display types.

Polices gothiques Les lettres utilisées par Gutenberg, lorsqu'il mit au point sa technique de composition à l'aide de caractères mobiles, avaient une forme qui imitait le dessin de l'écriture manuelle de l'époque, c'est-à-dire des lettres tracées avec une plume large et à bout plat. Cette écriture, très répandue au Moyen-Age en Europe, est encore populaire aujourd'hui dans le monde entier. En Allemagne, les polices gothiques ont servi à la composition du texte jusqu'à la deuxième guerre mondiale, mais, de nos jours, elles sont principalement utilisées comme polices d'enseigne.

Gebrochene Schriften Als Gutenberg die beweglichen Lettern entwickelte, orientierten sich die Zeichenformen an zeitgenössischen Manuskripthandschriften, die mit einer breiten, flachen Feder geschrieben wurden. Diese Handschriften wurden im Mittelalter in Europa entwickelt und sind weiterhin rund um den Globus beliebt. Gebrochene Schriften werden auch als Frakturen oder gotische Schriften bezeichnet und wurden in Deutschland bis zum 2. Weltkrieg für Fließtext verwendet. Sie werden jetzt in erster Linie als Auszeichnungsschriften eingesetzt.

Clairvaux Std

Duc De Berry Std

Fette Fraktur Std

Goudy Text Std

Linotext Std

San Marco Std

Wilhelm Klingspor Gotisch Std

Wittenberger Fraktur Std

Monospaced Also known as fixed-pitch, monospaced type was popularized by the invention of the typewriter, which required all characters to use the same width. In fact, many monospaced designs aim to capture the familiar informality of typewritten text. They can be especially useful wherever it helps to have the letters align vertically, such as in some computer code listings.

Polices à chasse constante Ces polices ont vu le jour avec l'avènement de la machine à écrire qui exige des caractères de largeur identique. En fait, le but de la plupart des polices à chasse constante est de reproduire le caractère informel du texte tapé à la machine. Elles sont particulièrement utiles dans des contextes où il est nécessaire d'aligner les lettres dans le sens vertical, comme dans certains listings de code informatique.

Dicktengleiche Die dicktengleichen Schriften, auch nicht-proportional genannt, wurden mit der Erfindung der Schreibmaschine beliebt, wo es erforderlich war, daß alle Zeichen gleich viel Platz in Anpruch nehmen. Viele dicktengleiche Designs versuchen, die gewohnte Formlosigkeit des maschinengeschriebenen Texts einzufangen. Sie sind besonders nützlich, wenn die Zeichen vertikal ausgerichtet sein sollen, wie etwa bei Computercode-Listings.

```
Courier Std
Letter Gothic Std
Lucida Typewriter Std
Lucida Sans Typewriter Std
OCR-A Std
OCR-B Std
ORATOR STD
Prestige Elite Std
```

Cyrillic Cyrillic typefaces are specifically designed to provide the special characters and accents required by Russian, Belarusian, Ukrainian, Serbo-Croatian, Bulgarian, and Macedonian.

Cyrillique Ces polices particulières proposent tous les caractères spéciaux utilisés dans les langues slaves (russe, bélarussien, ukrainien, serbo-croate, bulgare et macédonien).

Kyrillisch Kyrillische Schriften wurden speziell für die Zeichen und Akzente entwickelt, die für die Sprachen Russisch, Belarussisch, Ukrainisch, Serbokroatisch, Bulgarisch und Mazedonisch erforderlich sind.

Баскервиль Кириллица Ст
Baskerville Cyrillic Std

Эксцельсиор Ст
Excelsior Std

Гельветика Ст
Helvetica Std

Гельветика Инзерат Ст
Helvetica Inserat Std

Миньон Про
Minion PRO

Мириад Про
Myriad Pro

Таймс Тен Ст
Times Ten STD

Уорнок Про
Warnock PRO

Greek Greek typefaces are specifically designed to provide the characters used in the Greek language.

Grec Les polices grecques sont conçues spécifiquement pour fournir les caractères utilisés dans la langue grecque.

Griechisch Griechische Schriftarten dienen vor allem dazu, die in der griechischen Sprache verwendeten Zeichen bereitzustellen.

ΛΊΘΟΣ ΠΡΟ
LITHOS PRO

Μινιόν Προ
Minion PRO

Μύριαντ Προ
Myriad Pro

Γουόρνοκ Προ
Warnock PRO

Ornament and Symbol These typefaces have been created for a variety of nontext uses: musical notation, map making, mathematics, newspaper and commercial publishing, and even desktop publishing. These packages can put the finishing touch on a project or help with specialized tasks.

Polices d'ornements et de symboles Ces polices ont été créées spécialement pour des applications exigeant des symboles et non des caractères alpha-numériques : notation musicale, cartographie, mathématiques, publication de journaux et de documents publicitaires et PAO. Elles permettent de donner une touche finale à un document ou d'effectuer des tâches spécialisées.

Ornamente und Symbole Diese Schriften wurden für eine Reihe von Nicht-Textverwendungen entwickelt: Musiknotendruck, Landkartenerstellung, Mathematik, Zeitungs- und

Ornament and Symbol

kommerzieller Druck, sogar Desktop-Publishing.
Diese Pakete können einem Projekt den letzten
Schliff geben oder bei Spezialaufgaben helfen.

ORNAMENT POLICES D'ORNEMENTS ORNAMENTE

Bickham Script STD
Caravan Borders STD
Adobe Caslon PRO
MVB Celestia Antiqua STD
Chaparral PRO
Cronos PRO
Linotype Decoration Pi STD
Linotype Didot STD
Adobe Garamond PRO
Giddyup STD
MVB Greymantle STD
Adobe Jenson PRO
Kepler STD
Minion PRO
Notre Dame STD
Poetica STD
Pompeijana STD
Rusticana STD
Silentium PRO
Utopia STD
Warnock PRO
Wiesbaden Swing STD
Adobe Wood Type Ornaments STD
ITC Zapf Dingbats STD

SYMBOL POLICES DE SYMBOLES SYMBOL

Linotype Astrology Pi STD
Linotype Audio Pi STD
Border Pi STD
Bundesbahn Pi STD
Carta STD
MVB Celestia Antiqua STD
New Century Schoolbook STD Fractions
Cheq STD
European Pi STD
Fournier STD
Linotype Game Pi STD
Helvetica STD Fractions
Linotype Holiday Pi STD
Lucida Math STD
Mathematical Pi STD
MICR STD
National Codes Pi STD
Sonata STD
ITC Stone Sans STD Phonetic
ITC Stone Serif STD Phonetic
Times STD Phonetic
Universal STD Greek with Math Pi
Universal STD News with Commercial Pi
Utopia STD
Warning Pi STD
Adobe Wood Type Ornaments STD
ITC Zapf Dingbats STD

Opticals Beginning in the 16th century, type designers often cut a series of point sizes for a particular type style. For every size that was hand-sculpted in metal, subtle adjustments were made to letter proportion, weight, contrast, and spacing so that the type would be comfortable to read. However, most type manufacturers abandoned the design of optical masters, because it was economically more viable to produce a single master which was then scaled photographically or algorithmically for a given point size. Several OpenType families aim to revive this typographic refinement by including four optical size variations: caption, regular, subhead, and display. Called Opticals, these variations have been optimized for use at specific point sizes and are designed for maximum legibility. The general size ranges include caption (6–8 point), regular (9–13 point), subhead (14–24 point), and display (25–72 point).

Optiques Dès le début du seizième siècle, les concepteurs de caractères créaient souvent une série de corps pour un style de caractères particulier. Pour chaque corps sculpté à la main dans le métal, le concepteur devait effectuer d'infimes modifications et ajuster la proportion, le poids, le contraste et l'espacement des lettres afin que le caractère se lise aisément. Cependant la plupart des fabricants de caractères ont abandonné la création de caractères optiques pour des raisons économiques, optant pour la création d'une matrice unique qui était ensuite mise à l'échelle pour une taille de caractère donnée à l'aide de la photographie ou des algorithmes. Plusieurs familles OpenType ont pour but de raviver ce raffinement typographique en incluant quatre variations de taille optique : légende, régulier, sous-titre et affichage. Appelées « Optiques », ces variations ont été optimisées pour être utilisées à des tailles de caractère spécifiques et conçues pour offrir une lisibilité maximum. Les plages de tailles courantes incluent Légende (6–8 points), Régulier (9–13 points), Sous-titre (14–24 points) et Affichage (25–72 points).

Opticals Schriftdesigner schneiden schon seit dem 16. Jahrhundert oftmals eine Reihe von Punktgrößen für einen bestimmten Stil zurecht. Für jede Größe, die von Hand aus Metall geformt wurde, wurden feine Anpassungen von Buchstabenproportion, Gewicht, Kontrast und Abstand vorgenommen, damit die Schrift bequem leserlich war. Die meisten Schriftenhersteller haben das Design optischer Mustervorlagen jedoch aufgegeben, weil es rationeller ist, eine einzelne Mustervorlage zu erstellen, die dann fotografisch oder algorithmisch auf eine bestimmte Punktgröße skaliert wird. Mehrere Schriftfamilien von OpenType bieten jetzt anhand vier optischer Größenvariationen eine Neuauflage dieser typographischen Feinheiten an: Bildüber-/Bildunterschrift, Standard, Zwischenüberschrift und Display. Diese Variationen mit dem Namen „Opticals" wurden für die Verwendung mit spezifischen Punktgrößen optimiert und für eine maximale Leserlichkeit konzipiert. Die generellen Größenbereiche schließen Bildüber-/Bildunterschrift (6–8 Punkt), Standard (9–13 Punkt), Zwischenüberschrift (14–24 Punkt) und Display (25–72 Punkt) mit ein.

Brioso PRO Opticals

Chaparral PRO Opticals

Cronos PRO Opticals

Adobe Jenson PRO Opticals

Kepler STD Opticals

Minion PRO Opticals

Minion PRO Condensed Opticals

Sanvito Pro Opticals

Utopia STD Opticals

Warnock PRO Opticals

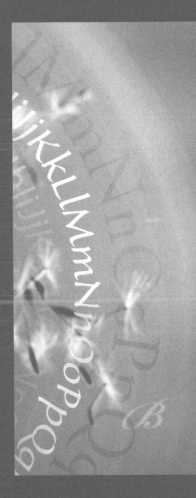

 Typeface Family Name STD

Designer, Trademark Owner

A-z **€**

1   2   3

KEY TO LISTING

Typeface families are listed alphabetically.

1 Adobe Originals logo. See pages 7–10 for more information.

2 OpenType fonts may contain an expanded glyph set for enhanced linguistic support and advanced typographic control. Below are descriptions of the different kinds of glyphs that may be found in the western OpenType fonts from Adobe. The exact glyph coverage may vary from font to font, and for each listing in this guide we have included a representative sample of the glyphs in each font. Please see pages 20–28 for a complete description of each category of glyphs. Complete glyph complement PDFs can be viewed or downloaded from the Adobe web site at *www.adobe.com/type*.

   A-z Basic

   € Euro

   ffi Ligatures

   BB Small Capitals

   619 Oldstyle Figures

   123 Proportional Lining Figures

   7/8 Diagonal Fractions

   H₂ Superscript/Subscript

   1st Ordinals and Superior Letters

   A Swashes

   ě Alternates

   A Titling Capitals

   ⟩⟨ Ornaments

   aA Case Forms

   ʧ Historic Blackletter

3 Standard character complement or Pro character complement. See page 17 for details.

Aachen STD

Colin Brignall, Esselte Pendaflex, Letraset, Esselte Letraset

A-z **€**

Typography

ABCDEFGHIJKLMN OPQRSTUVWXYZ abcdefghijklnopqrs tuvwxyz&0123456 789$€!?.;:, ""{½}

Letterforms have tone, timbre, character, just

BOLD

Albertus STD

Berthold Wolpe, Monotype Corp.

A-z **€**

Typography

ABCDEFGHIJKLMNOPQRSTU
VWXYZabcdefghijklmnopqrstuv
wxyz&0123456789$€!?.;:,""{½}

Letterforms have tone, timbre, character, just as words and sentences do. The mo ment a text and typeface are chosen, two

LIGHT

Letterforms have tone, timbre, character, just as words and sentences do. The mo ment a text and typeface are chosen, two

REGULAR

Letterforms have tone, timbre, character, just as words and sentences do. The moment a text and typeface are chosen, two streams of thought, two

ITALIC

Aldus STD

Hermann Zapf, Linotype Library GmbH

A-z € BB 619

Typography

ABCDEFGHIJKLMNOPQRSTU
VWXYZabcdefghijklmnopqrstuv
wxyz&0123456789$€!?.,;:,""{½}

ABCDEFGHIJKLMNOPQRSTUVWXYZ&
0123456789

*ABCDEFGHIJKLMNOPQRSTU
VWXYZabcdefghijklmnopqrstuv
wxyz&0123456789$€!?.,;:,""{½}
0123456789*

LETTERFORMS HAVE TONE, timbre, character, just as words and 567 sentences do. The moment a text and typeface are chosen,

ROMAN

Letterforms have tone, timbre, character, just as words and 567 sentences do. The moment a text and typeface are chosen,

ITALIC

Alexa STD

John Benson, Adobe Systems

A-z €

Typography

*ABCDEFGHIJKLMNOPQ
RSTUVWXYZabcdefghijkl
mnopqrstuvwxyz&012345
6789$€!?.,;:, ""{½}*

Letterforms have tone, timbre, char acter, just as words and sentences

REGULAR

ITC American Typewriter STD

Joel Kaden and Tony Stan, ITC

A-z € e/e

Typography

ABCDEFGHIJKLMNOPQRS
TUVWXYZabcdefghijklmnop
qrstuvwxyz&0123456789
$€!?.,;:,""{½}

Re&$

Alternates

Letterforms have tone, timbre, char acter, just as words and sentences do. The moment a text and typefac

LIGHT

Letterforms have tone, timbre, character, just as words and sen tences do. The moment a text and
MEDIUM

Letterforms have tone, timbre, character, just as words and sen tences do. The moment a text and
BOLD

Letterforms have tone, timbre, character, just as words and sentences do. The moment a text and typeface are chosen, two streams of
LIGHT CONDENSED

Letterforms have tone, timbre, character, just as words and sentences do. The moment a text and typeface are chosen, two streams
CONDENSED

Letterforms have tone, timbre, character, just as words and sentences do. The mo ment a text and typeface are chosen, two
BOLD CONDENSED

Americana STD

Richard Isbell, Kingsley/ATF

A-z €

Typography

ABCDEFGHIJKLMNOPQRS TUVWXYZabcdefghijklmn opqrstuvwxyz&012345678 9$€!?.;:,""{½}

ABCDEFGHIJKLMNOPQRS TUVWXYZabcdefghijklmn opqrstuvwxyz&01234567 89$€!?.;:,""{½}

Letterforms have tone, timbre, character, just as words and sen tences do. The moment a text
REGULAR

Letterforms have tone, timbre, char acter, just as words and sentences do. The moment a text and type
ITALIC

Letterforms have tone, timbre, character, just as words and sen tences do. The moment a text
BOLD

Letterforms have tone, timbre, character, just as words and sen tences do. The moment a text
EXTRA BOLD

Amigo

Arthur Baker, AlphaOmega Typography

Typography

ABCDEFGHIJKLMNOPQ RSTUVWXYZabcdefghijkl mnopqrstuvwxyz&012345 6789$!?.;:,""{½}

Letterforms have tone, timbre, character, just as words and sen
REGULAR

Andreas STD

Michael Harvey, Adobe Systems

`A-z` `€`

TYPOGRAPHY

ABCDEFGHIJKLMNOPQR
STUVWXYZ&0123456789
$€!? ·· "" {½}

LETTERFORMS HAVE TONE, TIM
BRE, CHARACTER, JUST AS WORD

REGULAR

ITC Anna STD

Daniel Pelavin, ITC

`A-z` `€`

TYPOGRAPHY

ABCDEFGHIJKLMNOPQRSTUVWX
YZ&0123456789$€!?.;:, ""{½}

LETTERFORMS HAVE TONE, TIMBRE,
CHARACTER, JUST AS WORDS AND SENT

REGULAR

Antique Olive STD

Roger Excoffon, M. Olive

`A-z` `€` `123`

Typography

ABCDEFGHIJKLMNOPQRSTUVWX
YZabcdefghijklmnopqrstuvwxy
z&0123456789$€!?.;:, ""{½}

*ABCDEFGHIJKLMNOPQRSTUVWX
YZabcdefghijklmnopqrstuvwxy
z&0123456789$€!?.;:, ""{½}*

Letterforms have tone, timbre, character,
just as words and sentences do. The
moment a text and typeface are chosen,
LIGHT

Letterforms have tone, timbre, char
acter, just as words and sentences
do. The moment a text and typeface
ROMAN

*Letterforms have tone, timbre, char
acter, just as words and sentences do.
The moment a text and typeface are*
ITALIC

**Letterforms have tone, timbre, char
acter, just as words and sentences
do. The moment a text and typeface**
BOLD

**Letterforms have tone, timbre, char
acter, just as words and sentences
do. The moment a text and typeface**
BLACK

**Letterforms have tone, timbre,
character, just as words and sen**
BOLD CONDENSED

Letterforms have tone, timbre, char
COMPACT

Letterforms ha ve tone, timbre,
NORD

Letterforms have tone, timbre, cha
NORD ITALIC

Apollo STD

Adrian Frutiger, Monotype Corp.

A-z € ffi BB 619 123 ⅞ H₂ 1st

Typography

ABCDEFGHIJKLMNOPQRSTUVW
XYZabcdefghijklmnopqrstuvwxyz
&0123456789$€!?.;:,"" { ½ }

ABCDEFGHIJKLMNOPQRSTUVWXYZ&
0123456789$¢ ffi ⅛ 0123456789

*ABCDEFGHIJKLMNOPQRSTUV
WXYZabcdefghijklmnopqrstuvwxyz
&0123456789$€!?.;:,"" { ½ }
0123456789$¢ ffi ⅛ 0123456789*

LETTERFORMS HAVE TONE, timbre, character,
just as words and 567 sentences do. The
moment a text and typeface are chosen,
REGULAR

*Letterforms have tone, timbre, character,
just as words and 567 sentences do. The
moment a text and typeface are chosen, two*
ITALIC

Letterforms have tone, timbre, charac
ter, just as words and 567 sentences do.
The moment text and typeface are cho
SEMI BOLD

Arcadia STD

Neville Brody, Linotype Library GmbH

A-z € 123 é

Typography

ABCDEFGHIJKLMNOPQRSTUVWXYZ
abcdefghijklmnopqrstuvwxyz&0123
456789$¢!?.;:, ""{½}

bdhpq
Alternates

Letterforms have tone, timbre,
character, just as words and sen
REGULAR

Arcana STD

Gabriel Martínez Meave, Gabriel Martínez Meave

A-z € ffi 619 A ε ✿

Typography

Aa Bb Cc Dd Ee Ff Gg Hh Ii
Jj Kk Ll Mm Nn Oo Pp Qq
Rr Ss Tt Uu Vv Ww Xx Yy Zz
& 0123456789$€!?.;:,""{½}

A G H K M N R S
U V X Y Ჟ Ჟ Ჟ 8

Swash

α ł ჟ fi fl fs tt

Alternates and Ligatures

⌒ ⌒ ⌒ ⌒ ⌒ ⌒

Ornaments

Letterforms have tone, timbre, charac-
ter, Just as words and sentences do.

MANUSCRIPT

The moment a text and typeface
are chosen, two streams of thought,
two rhythmical systems,
two sets of habits, or if you like,
two personalities, intersect.

⌒

Ariadne STD

Gudrun Zapf von Hesse, Linotype Library GmbH

A-z €

Typography

A B C D E F G H I J K L
M N O P Q R S T U V W
X Y Z & ! ? . ; : , ""

Letterforms Have Tone, Tim-
bre, Character, Just as Words

ARIADNE WITH DIOTIMA ITALIC

Arnold Böcklin STD

O. Weisert

A-z €

Typography

ABCDEFGHIJKLMNOP
QRSTUVWXYZabcdefg
hijklmnopqrstuvwxyz&
0123456789$€!?.;:,""{½}

Letterforms have tone,
timbre, character, just as

REGULAR

Ashley Script STD

Ashley Havindon, Monotype Corp.

A-z €

Typography

ABCDEFGHIJKLMNOPQRS
TUVWXYZabcdefghijklmnop
qrstuvwxyz&0123456789
$€!?.;:, ""{½}

Letterforms have tone, timbre, char
acter, just as words and sentences do.
REGULAR

New Aster STD

Francesco Simoncini, Simoncini S.A.

A-z €

Typography

ABCDEFGHIJKLMNOPQRSTU
VWXYZabcdefghijklmnopqrstuv
wxyz&0123456789$€!? .;:,""{½}

*ABCDEFGHIJKLMNOPQRSTUV
WXYZabcdefghijklmnopqrstuvwx
yz&0123456789$€!?.;:, ""{½}*

Letterforms have tone, timbre, char
acter, just as words and sentences do.
The moment a text and typeface are
REGULAR

*Letterforms have tone, timbre, char
acter, just as words and sentences do.
The moment a text and typeface are*
ITALIC

Letterforms have tone, timbre, char
acter, just as words and sentences
do. The moment a text and typeface
SEMI BOLD

*Letterforms have tone, timbre, char
acter, just as words and sentences do.
The moment a text and typeface are*
SEMI BOLD ITALIC

**Letterforms have tone, timbre,
character, just as words and sen
tences do. The moment a text and**
BOLD

***Letterforms have tone, timbre, char
acter, just as words and sentences
do. The moment a text and typeface***
BOLD ITALIC

**Letterforms have tone, timbre,
character, just as words and sen
tences do. The moment a text**
BLACK

***Letterforms have tone, timbre,
character, just as words and sen
tences do. The moment a text***
BLACK ITALIC

Linotype Astrology Pi STD

Linotype Staff

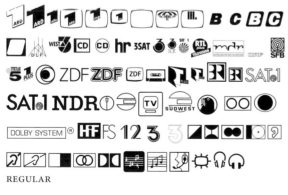

1

2

Linotype Audio Pi STD

Linotype Staff

REGULAR

Auriol STD

Georges Auriol, Linotype Library GmbH

A-Z €

Typography

ABCDEFGHIJKLMNOP
QRSTUVWXYZabcdefghij
klmnopqrstuvwxyz012345
6789$€!?.,:,""{½}

ABCDEFGHIJKLMNOPQ
RSTUVWXYZabcdefghijklm
nopqrstuvwxyz&0123456789
$€!?.,:,""{½}

Letterforms have tone, timbre,
character, just as words and
ROMAN

Letterforms have tone, timbre, char
acter, just as words and sentences
ITALIC

Letterforms have tone, tim
bre, character, just as word
BOLD

Letterforms have tone, timbre,
character, just as words and
BOLD ITALIC

Letterforms have tone, tim
bre, character, just as wor
BLACK

Letterforms have tone, tim
bre, character, just as wor
BLACK ITALIC

ITC Avant Garde Gothic STD

Ed Benguiat, Herb Lubalin, and Tom Carnase, ITC

A-z €

Typography

ABCDEFGHIJKLMNOPQRSTUV
WXYZabcdefghijklmnopqrstuv
wxyz&0123456789$€!?.;:, ""{½}

ABCDEFGHIJKLMNOPQRSTUV
WXYZabcdefghijklmnopqrstuv
wxyz&0123456789$€!?.;:, ""{½}

Letterforms have tone, timbre, chara
cter, just as words and sentences
do. The moment a text and typeface
EXTRA LIGHT

Letterforms have tone, timbre, chara
cter, just as words and sentences
do. The moment a text and typeface
EXTRA LIGHT OBLIQUE

Letterforms have tone, timbre, char
acter, just as words and sentences
do. The moment a text and type
BOOK

Letterforms have tone, timbre, char
acter, just as words and sentences
do. The moment a text and type
BOOK OBLIQUE

Letterforms have tone, timbre, char
acter, just as words and sentences
do. The moment a text and type
MEDIUM

Letterforms have tone, timbre, char
acter, just as words and sentences
do. The moment a text and type
MEDIUM OBLIQUE

Letterforms have tone, timbre, char
acter, just as words and sentences
do. The moment a text and type
DEMI

Letterforms have tone, timbre, char
acter, just as words and sentences
do. The moment a text and type
DEMI OBLIQUE

Letterforms have tone, timbre,
character, just as words and sen
tences do. The moment a text
BOLD

Letterforms have tone, timbre,
character, just as words and sen
tences do. The moment a text
BOLD OBLIQUE

ITC Avant Garde Gothic STD Condensed

Ed Benguiat, Herb Lubalin, and Tom Carnase, ITC

A-z €

Typography

ABCDEFGHIJKLMNOPQRSTUVWXYZ
abcdefghijklmnopqrstuvwxyz&0123
456789$€!?.;:, ""{½}

ABCDEFGHIJKLMNOPQRSTUVWXYZ
abcdefghijklmnopqrstuvwxyz&0123
456789$€!?.;:, ""{½}

Letterforms have tone, timbre, character, just
as words and sentences do. The moment a
text and typeface are chosen, two streams of
EXTRA LIGHT CONDENSED

Letterforms have tone, timbre, character, just as words and sentences do. The moment a text and typeface are chosen, two streams of
EXTRA LIGHT CONDENSED OBLIQUE

Letterforms have tone, timbre, character, just as words and sentences do. The moment a text and typeface are chosen, two streams of
BOOK CONDENSED

Letterforms have tone, timbre, character, just as words and sentences do. The moment a text and typeface are chosen, two streams of
BOOK CONDENSED OBLIQUE

Letterforms have tone, timbre, character, just as words and sentences do. The moment a text and typeface are chosen, two streams of
MEDIUM CONDENSED

Letterforms have tone, timbre, character, just as words and sentences do. The moment a text and typeface are chosen, two streams of
MEDIUM CONDENSED OBLIQUE

Letterforms have tone, timbre, character, just as words and sentences do. The mo ment a text and typeface are chosen, two
DEMI CONDENSED

Letterforms have tone, timbre, character, just as words and sentences do. The mo ment a text and typeface are chosen, two
DEMI CONDENSED OBLIQUE

Letterforms have tone, timbre, character, just as words and sentences do. The mo ment a text and typeface are chosen, two
BOLD CONDENSED

Letterforms have tone, timbre, character, just as words and sentences do. The mo ment a text and typeface are chosen, two
BOLD CONDENSED OBLIQUE

Adrian Frutiger, Linotype Library GmbH

A-z €

Typography

ABCDEFGHIJKLMNOPQRSTU
VWXYZabcdefghijklmnopqrstuv
wxyz&0123456789$€!?.;:," "{½}

*ABCDEFGHIJKLMNOPQRSTU
VWXYZabcdefghijklmnopqrstuv
wxyz&0123456789$€!?.;:," "{½}*

Letterforms have tone, timbre, charac ter, just as words and sentences do. The moment a text and typeface are
35 LIGHT

Letterforms have tone, timbre, charac ter, just as words and sentences do. The moment a text and typeface are
35 LIGHT OBLIQUE

Letterforms have tone, timbre, charac ter, just as words and sentences do. The moment a text and typeface are
45 BOOK

Letterforms have tone, timbre, charac ter, just as words and sentences do. The moment a text and typeface are
45 BOOK OBLIQUE

Letterforms have tone, timbre, charac ter, just as words and sentences do. The moment a text and typeface are
55 ROMAN

Letterforms have tone, timbre, charac ter, just as words and sentences do. The moment a text and typeface are
55 OBLIQUE

Letterforms have tone, timbre, charac
ter, just as words and sentences do.
The moment a text and typeface are

65 MEDIUM

*Letterforms have tone, timbre, charac
ter, just as words and sentences do.
The moment a text and typeface are*

65 MEDIUM OBLIQUE

**Letterforms have tone, timbre, char
acter, just as words and sentences
do. The moment a text and typeface**

85 HEAVY

***Letterforms have tone, timbre, char
acter, just as words and sentences
do. The moment a text and typeface***

85 HEAVY OBLIQUE

**Letterforms have tone, timbre, char
acter, just as words and sentences
do. The moment a text and typeface**

95 BLACK

***Letterforms have tone, timbre, char
acter, just as words and sentences
do. The moment a text and typeface***

95 BLACK OBLIQUE

Baker Signet

Arthur Baker, Visual Graphics Corp.

Typography

ABCDEFGHIJKLMNOPQRSTU
VWXYZabcdefghijklmnopqrstu
vwxyz&0123456789$!?.;:,""{½}

Letterforms have tone, timbre,
character, just as words and sen

REGULAR

Balzano STD

John Benson, Adobe Systems

A-z €

Typography

ABCDEFGHIJKLMNOPQRSTU
VWXYZabcdefghijklmnopqrstuv
wxyz&0123456789$€!?.;:,""{½}

*Letterforms have tone, timbre, char
acter, just as words and sentences*

REGULAR

Banco STD

Roger Excoffon, M. Olive

A-z € 123

TYPOGRAPHY

ABCDEFGHIJKLMNOPQR
STUVWXYZ&0123456789
$€!?.;:,""{½}

LETTERFORMS HAVE TONE,
TIMBRE, CHARACTER, JUST

REGULAR

Banshee STD

Tim Donaldson, Adobe Systems

A-z €

Typography

*ABCDEFGHIJKLMN
OPQRSTUVWXYZabc
defghijklmnopqrstuvwxyz
&0123456789$€!?.,:;""{½}*

*Letterforms have tone, tim
bre, character, just as words*

REGULAR

Baskerville Cyrillic STD

Linotype Staff

A-z €

Typography

ABCDEFGHIJKLMNOPQRS
TUVWXYZabcdefghijklmnop
qrstuvwxyz$€!?.,:;""{½}

Типографика

АБВГЃГДЂЕЁЄЖЗЅИЙІЇЈК
ЌЛЉМНЊОПРСТЋУЎФХЦ
ЏЧШЩЪЫЬЭЮЯабвгѓгдђеё

єжзѕийіїјкќлљмнњопрстћуўфх
цџчшщъыьэюя

ABCDEFGHIJKLMNOPQRST
UVWXYZabcdefghijklmnopqrstuv
wxyz$€!?.,:;""{½}

АБВГЃГДЂЕЁЄЖЗЅИЙІЇЈКЌ
ЛЉМНЊОПРСТЋУЎФХЦЏІЧ
ШЩЪЫЬЭЮЯабвгѓгдђеёєжзѕи
йіїјкќлљмнњопрстћуўфхцџчшщ
ъыьэюя

Letterforms have tone, timbre, charac
ter, just as words and sentences do.
The moment a text and typeface are

Точно найденные слова достойны
точности в подборе шрифтов; те, в
свою очередь, заслуживают чутко

UPRIGHT

*Letterforms have tone, timbre, character, just
as words and sentences do. The moment a
text and typeface are chosen, two streams of*

*Точно найденные слова достойны точ
ности в подборе шрифтов; те, в свою
очередь, заслуживают чуткого, осмы*

INCLINED

**Letterforms have tone, timbre, charac
ter, just as words and sentences do.
The moment a text and typeface are**

**Точно найденные слова достойны
точности в подборе шрифтов; те, в
свою очередь, заслуживают чутко**

BOLD

ITC New Baskerville STD

George W. Jones, ITC

A-z € BB 619

Typography

ABCDEFGHIJKLMNOPQRSTU
VWXYZabcdefghijklmnopqrstuv
wxyz&0123456789$€!?.;:,""{½}

ABCDEFGHIJKLMNOPQRSTUVWXY
z&0123456789

ABCDEFGHIJKLMNOPQRSTUV
WXYZabcdefghijklmnopqrstuvwxyz
&0123456789$€!?.;:, ""{½}

0123456789

LETTERFORMS HAVE TONE, timbre, char
acter, just as words 567 and sentences
do. The moment a text and typeface are
ROMAN

Letterforms have tone, timbre, character, just
as words and 567 sentences do. The moment
a text and typeface are chosen, two streams of
ITALIC

LETTERFORMS HAVE TONE, timbre, char
acter, just as words 567 and sentences
do. The moment a text and typeface are
BOLD

Letterforms have tone, timbre, character,
just as words 567 and sentences do. The
moment a text and typeface are chosen, two
BOLD ITALIC

ITC Bauhaus STD

Ed Benguiat, Herb Lubalin, and Tom Carnase, ITC

A-z €

Typography

ABCDEFGHIJKLMNOPQRSTUVWX
YZabcdefghijklmnopqrstuvwxyz&
0123456789$€!?.;:, ""{½}

Letterforms have tone, timbre, character,
just as words and sentences do. The mo
ment a text and typeface are chosen,
LIGHT

Letterforms have tone, timbre, character,
just as words and sentences do. The mo
ment a text and typeface are chosen,
MEDIUM

Letterforms have tone, timbre, character,
just as words and sentences do. The mo
ment a text and typeface are chosen,
DEMI

Letterforms have tone, timbre, charac
ter, just as words and sentences do. The
moment a text and typeface are chos
BOLD

Letterforms have tone, timbre, char
acter, just as words and sentences
do. The moment a text and typeface
HEAVY

ITC Beesknees STD

David Farey, ITC

TYPOGRAPHY
ABCDEFGHIJKLMNOPQ RSTUVWXYZ&012345 6789¿€!?.;:,""{½}

LETTERFORMS HAVE TONE, TIMBRE, CHARA

REGULAR

Bell STD

Richard Austin, Monotype Corp.

Typography

ABCDEFGHIJKLMNOPQRST UVWXYZabcdefghijklmnopqrstu vwxyz&0123456789$€!?.;:,""{½}

ABCDEFGHIJKLMNOPQRSTUVWXYZ& ffi ⅛ 0123456789

ABCDEFGHIJKLMNOPQRSTU VWXYZabcdefghijklmnopqrstuvwxy z&0123456789$€!?.;:,""{½}

ffi ⅛ 0123456789

JKQRkjkqr.AFJKNQRTVYbk
Alternates

LETTERFORMS HAVE TONE, timbre, character, just as words and sentences do. The mo ment a text and typeface are chosen, two
REGULAR

Letterforms have tone, timbre, character, just as words and sentences do. The moment a text and typeface are chosen, two streams of thought
ITALIC

LETTERFORMS HAVE TONE, timbre, character, just as words and sentences do. The mo ment a text and typeface are chosen, two
SEMI BOLD

Letterforms have tone, timbre, character, just as words and sentences do. The moment a text and typeface are chosen, two streams
SEMI BOLD ITALIC

Letterforms have tone, timbre, charac ter, just as words and sentences do. The moment a text and typeface are chosen,
BOLD

Letterforms have tone, timbre, character, just as words and sentences do. The mo ment a text and typeface are chosen, two
BOLD ITALIC

Bell Centennial STD

Matthew Carter

Typography

ABCDEFGHIJKLMNOPQRSTUVWXYZ abcdefghijklmnopqrstuvwxyz&0123456 789$€!?.;:,""{1₂}

Letterforms have tone, timbre, character, just as words and sentences do. The moment a text and typeface are chosen, two streams of thought,
ADDRESS

Letterforms have tone, timbre, character, just as words and sentences do. The mo ment a text and typeface are chosen, two
SUB CAPTION

Letterforms have tone, timbre, charac ter, just as words and sentences do. The moment a text and typeface are
NAME & NUMBER

LETTERFORMS HAVE TONE, TIMBRE, CHARACTER, JUST AS WORDS AND SENTENCES DO. THE MOMENT A TEXT
BOLD LISTING, BOLD LISTING ALTERNATE (BASE FONT SITS BELOW BASELINE, ALTERNATE FONT SITS ON BASELINE)

Bell Gothic STD

Chauncey H. Griffith

Typography

ABCDEFGHIJKLMNOPQRSTU VWXYZabcdefghijklmnopqrstuvw xyz&0123456789$€!?.;:,‘’“”{½}

Letterforms have tone, timbre, character, just as words and sentences do. The mo ment a text and typeface are chosen, two
LIGHT

Letterforms have tone, timbre, character, just as words and sentences do. The mo ment a text and typeface are chosen, two
BOLD

Letterforms have tone, timbre, charac ter, just as words and sentences do. The moment a text and typeface are
BLACK

Belwe STD

Georg Belwe, Esselte Pendaflex, Letraset, Esselte Letraset

Typography

ABCDEFGHIJKLMNOPQRSTU VWXYZabcdefghijklmnopqrst uvwxyz&0123456789$€!?.;:,“”{½}

Letterforms have tone, timbre, charac ter, just as words and sentences do. The moment a text and typeface are chosen,
LIGHT

Letterforms have tone, timbre, charac ter, just as words and sentences do. The moment a text and typeface are
MEDIUM

Letterforms have tone, timbre, char acter, just as words and sentences do. The moment a text and typeface
BOLD

Letterforms have tone, timbre, character, just as words and sentences do. The moment a text and typeface are chosen, two streams
CONDENSED

Bembo STD

Monotype Staff and Stanley Morison, Monotype Corp.

Typography

ABCDEFGHIJKLMNOPQRSTU VWXYZabcdefghijklmnopqrstuvw xyz&0123456789$€!?.;:,“”{½}

ABCDEFGHIJKLMNOPQRSTUVWXYZ&
0123456789$¢ ffi ⅛ 0123456789

ABCDEFGHIJKLMNOPQRSTU
VWXYZabcdefghijklmnopqrstuvwxyz
&0123456789$€!?.;:,""{½}

0123456789$¢ ffi ⅛ 0123456789

LETTERFORMS HAVE TONE, timbre, character,
just as words and 567 sentences do. The mo
ment a text and typeface are chosen, two
REGULAR

Letterforms have tone, timbre, character, just as
words and 567 sentences do. The moment a text
and typeface are chosen, two streams of thought,
ITALIC

Letterforms have tone, timbre, character,
just as words and 567 sentences do. The
moment a text and typeface are chosen,
SEMIBOLD

Letterforms have tone, timbre, character, just
as words and 567 sentences do. The moment a
text and typeface are chosen, two streams of
SEMIBOLD ITALIC

Letterforms have tone, timbre, charac
ter, just as words and 567 sentences do.
The moment a text and typeface are
BOLD

Letterforms have tone, timbre, character, just
as words and 567 sentences do. The moment
a text and typeface are chosen, two streams
BOLD ITALIC

Letterforms have tone, timbre, char
acter, just as words and 567 sentenc
es do. The moment a text and type
EXTRA BOLD

Letterforms have tone, timbre, character,
just as words and 567 sentences do. The
moment a text and typeface are chosen,
EXTRA BOLD ITALIC

Ed Benguiat, ITC

`A-z` `€`

Typography

ABCDEFGHIJKLMNOPQRSTUVW
XYZabcdefghijklmnopqrstuvwxy
z&0123456789$€!?.;:,""{½}

ABCDEFGHIJKLMNOPQRSTUVW
XYZabcdefghijklmnopqrstuvwx
yz&0123456789$€ !?.;:,""{½}

Letterforms have tone, timbre, charac
ter, just as words and sentences do.
The moment a text and typeface are
BOOK

Letterforms have tone, timbre, charac
ter, just as words and sentences do.
The moment a text and typeface are
BOOK ITALIC

Letterforms have tone, timbre, char
acter, just as words and sentences
do. The moment a text and typeface
MEDIUM

Letterforms have tone, timbre, char
acter, just as words and sentences
do. The moment a text and typeface
MEDIUM ITALIC

Letterforms have tone, timbre, char
acter, just as words and sentences
do. The moment a text and typeface
BOLD

Letterforms have tone, timbre,
character, just as words and sen
tences do. The moment a text and
BOLD ITALIC

B

ITC Benguiat Gothic STD

Ed Benguiat, ITC

A-z **€**

Typography

ABCDEFGHIJKLMNOPQRSTUVW
XYZabcdefghijklmnopqrstuvwxy
z&0123456789$€!?.;:,'"{½}

*ABCDEFGHIJKLMNOPQRSTUVW
XYZabcdefghijklmnopqrstuvwxy
z&0123456789$€!?.;:,'"{½}*

Letterforms have tone, timbre, charac
ter, just as words and sentences do.
The moment a text and typeface are
BOOK

*Letterforms have tone, timbre, charac
ter, just as words and sentences do.
The moment a text and typeface are*
BOOK OBLIQUE

Letterforms have tone, timbre, charac
ter, just as words and sentences do.
The moment a text and typeface are
MEDIUM

*Letterforms have tone, timbre, charac
ter, just as words and sentences do.
The moment a text and typeface are*
MEDIUM OBLIQUE

**Letterforms have tone, timbre, charac
ter, just as words and sentences do.
The moment a text and typeface are**
BOLD

***Letterforms have tone, timbre, charac
ter, just as words and sentences do.
The moment a text and typeface are***
BOLD OBLIQUE

**Letterforms have tone, timbre, char
acter, just as words and sentences
do. The moment a text and typeface**
HEAVY

***Letterforms have tone, timbre, char
acter, just as words and sentences
do. The moment a text and typeface***
HEAVY OBLIQUE

ITC Berkeley Oldstyle STD

Frederic W. Goudy, ITC

A-z **€**

Typography

ABCDEFGHIJKLMNOPQRSTUV
WXYZabcdefghijklmnopqrstuvwx
yz&0123456789$€!?.;:,""{½}

*ABCDEFGHIJKLMNOPQRSTUV
WXYZabcdefghijklmnopqrstuvwxyz
&0123456789$€!?.;:,""{½}*

Letterforms have tone, timbre, character,
just as words and sentences do. The mo
ment a text and typeface are chosen, two
BOOK

*Letterforms have tone, timbre, character, just
as words and sentences do. The moment a text
and typeface are chosen, two streams of thou*
BOOK ITALIC

Letterforms have tone, timbre, character,
just as words and sentences do. The mo
ment a text and typeface are chosen, two
REGULAR

*Letterforms have tone, timbre, character,
just as words and sentences do. The moment
a text and typeface are chosen, two streams*
ITALIC

Letterforms have tone, timbre, character, just as words and sentences do. The mo ment a text and typeface are chosen,
BOLD

Letterforms have tone, timbre, character, just as words and sentences do. The mo ment a text and typeface are chosen, two
BOLD ITALIC

Letterforms have tone, timbre, charac ter, just as words and sentences do. The moment a text and typeface are
BLACK

Letterforms have tone, timbre, character, just as words and sentences do. The mo ment a text and typeface are chosen, two
BLACK ITALIC

Berling STD

Karl-Erik Forsberg, Verbum AB

A-z €

Typography

ABCDEFGHIJKLMNOPQRSTU
VWXYZabcdefghijklmnopqrstu
vwxyz&0123456789$€!?.;:,""{½}

*ABCDEFGHIJKLMNOPQRST
UVWXYZabcdefghijklmnopqrstuv
wxyz&0123456789$€!?.;:,""{½}*

Letterforms have tone, timbre, character, just as words and sentences do. The mo ment a text and typeface are chosen,
ROMAN

Letterforms have tone, timbre, character, just as words and sentences do. The mo ment a text and typeface are chosen, two
ITALIC

Letterforms have tone, timbre, charac ter, just as words and sentences do. The moment a text and typeface are chosen,
BOLD

Letterforms have tone, timbre, charac ter, just as words and sentences do. The moment a text and typeface are chosen,
BOLD ITALIC

Bermuda STD

Garrett Boge and Paul Shaw, LetterPerfect

A-z € Bb 123

TYPOGRAPH

ABCDEFGHIJKLM
NOPQRSTUVWXYZ
ABCDEFGHIJKLMN
OPQRSTUVWXYZ
0123456789$€!?.,, 6699{½}

LETTERFORMS HAVE TO NE, TIMBRE, CHARACTER
SOLID

LETTERFORMS HAVE TO NE, TIMBRE, CHARACTER
OPEN

LETTERFORMS HAVE TO NE, TIMBRE, CHARACTER
DOTS

LETTERFORMS HAVE TO NE, TIMBRE, CHARACTER
SQUIGGLE

Bernhard STD

Lucian Bernhard

A-z €

Typography

ABCDEFGHIJKLMNOPQRSTUV
WXYZabcdefghijklmnopqrst
uvwxyz&0123456789$€!?.;:,
""{½}

Letterforms have tone, timbre, character, just as words and
BOLD CONDENSED

Bernhard Modern STD

Lucian Bernhard

A-z €

Typography

ABCDEFGHIJKLMNOPQRSTUV
WXYZabcdefghijklmnopqrstuvwxyz&
0123456789$€!?.;:,""{½}

*ABCDEFGHIJKLMNOPQRSTUV
WXYZabcdefghijklmnopqrstuvwxyz&01
23456789$€!?.;:,""{ ½}*

Letterforms have tone, timbre, character,
just as words and sentences do. The mo
ment a text and typeface are chosen, two
ROMAN

*Letterforms have tone, timbre, character, just
as words and sentences do. The moment a text
and typeface are chosen, two streams of thou*
ITALIC

Letterforms have tone, timbre, character,
just as words and sentences do. The mo
ment a text and typeface are chosen, two
BOLD

*Letterforms have tone, timbre, character,
just as words and sentences do. The mo
ment a text and typeface are chosen, two*
BOLD ITALIC

New Berolina STD

Martin Wilke, Monotype Corp.

A-z €

Typography

ABCDEFGHIJKL
MNOPQRSTUVW
XYZabcdefghijklmnopqrst
uvwxyz&0123456789$€!?.;:,
""{½}

*Letterforms have tone, timbre, char
acter, just as words and sentences*
REGULAR

Richard Lipton, Adobe Systems

Typography

Aa Bb Cc Dd Ee Ff Gg Hh Ii Jj Kk Ll Mm Nn Oo Pp Qq Rr Ss Tt Uu Vv Ww Xx Yy Zz & 0123456789$€ !?.;:, ""{½}

Swash Capitals

acdee fgi ilmno o pqrrs ttu urwy y

Beginnings

Endings

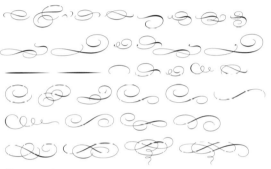

Alternates

Ligatures

Ornaments

Letterforms have tone, timbre, character, just as words and sentences do. The moment a
REGULAR

Letterforms have tone, timbre, character, just as words and sentences do. The mo
SEMIBOLD

Letterforms have tone, timbre, character, just as words and sentences do. The mo
BOLD

The moment a text and typeface are chosen, two streams of thought, two rhythmical systems, two sets of habits, or if you like, two personalities, intersect.

Biffo STD

Monotype Staff, Monotype Corp.

A-z **€**

Typography

ABCDEFGHIJKLMNOPQRST
UVWXYZabcdefghijklmnopq
rstuvwxyz&0123456789$€
.:; ""{½}

*Letterforms have tone, timbre,
character, just as words and sen*

REGULAR

Birch STD

Kim Buker Chansler, Adobe Systems

A-z **€**

Typography

ABCDEFGHIJKLMNOPQRSTUVWXYZ
abcdefghijklmnopqrstuvwxyz&012345
6789$€!?.:;,'"" {½}

Letterforms have tone, timbre, character,
just as words and sentences do. The moment

REGULAR

Blackoak STD

Joy Redick, Adobe Systems

A-z **€**

Typogra

ABCDEFGHIJ
KLMNOPQRST
UVWXYZabcdef
ghijklmnopqrs
tuvwxyz&01234
56789$€.;:,!?'"" {½}

Letterforms
have tone, tim

REGULAR

Blue Island STD

Jeremy Tankard, Adobe Systems

A-z **€**

Typography

ABCDEFGHIJKLMNO
PQRSTUVWXYZabcdef
ghijklmnopqrstuvwxyz
&0123456789$€!?.;:,'"" {½}

Letterforms have tone,
timbre, character, just as

REGULAR

Bodoni STD

Morris Fuller Benton

A-Z €

Typography

ABCDEFGHIJKLMNOPQRSTU
VWXYZabcdefghijklmnopqrstuv
wxyz&0123456789$€!?.;:,""{½}

*ABCDEFGHIJKLMNOPQRSTU
VWXYZabcdefghijklmnopqrstuv
wxyz&0123456789$€!?.;:,""{½}*

Letterforms have tone, timbre, character,
just as words and sentences do. The moment
a text and typeface are chosen, two streams
BOOK

*Letterforms have tone, timbre, character, just
as words and sentences do. The moment a
text and typeface are chosen, two streams of*
BOOK ITALIC

Letterforms have tone, timbre, charac
ter, just as words and sentences do. The
moment a text and typeface are chosen,
ROMAN

*Letterforms have tone, timbre, charac
ter, just as words and sentences do. The
moment a text and typeface are chosen,*
ITALIC

**Letterforms have tone, timbre, charac
ter, just as words and sentences do.
The moment a text and typeface are**
BOLD

***Letterforms have tone, timbre, charac
ter, just as words and sentences do.
The moment a text and typeface are***
BOLD ITALIC

**Letterforms have tone
timbre, character, jus**
POSTER

***Letterforms have ton
timbre, character, jus***
POSTER ITALIC

**Letterforms have tone, timbre, char
acter, just as words and sentences do**
BOLD CONDENSED

**Letterforms have tone, timbre, character,
just as words and sentences do. The moment**
POSTER COMPRESSED

Bauer Bodoni STD

Heinrich Jost and Louis Höll, Bauer Types, S.A.

A-Z € BB 619

Typography

ABCDEFGHIJKLMNOPQRSTU
VWXYZabcdefghijklmnopqrstuv
wxyz&0123456789$€!?.;:,""{½}

ABCDEFGHIJKLMNOPQRSTUVWXYZ&
0123456789

*ABCDEFGHIJKLMNOPQRSTU
VWXYZabcdefghijklmnopqrstuvw
xyz&0123456789$€!?.;:,""{½}
0123456789*

LETTERFORMS HAVE TONE, timbre, charac
ter, just as words and 567 sentences do.
The moment a text and typeface are
ROMAN

Letterforms have tone, timbre, character, just as words and 567 sentences do. The moment a text and typeface are chosen,
ITALIC

Letterforms have tone, timbre, charac ter, just as words and 567 sentences do. The moment a text and typeface
BOLD

Letterforms have tone, timbre, charac ter, just as words and 567 sentences do. The moment a text and typeface are
BOLD ITALIC

Letterforms have tone, timbre, character, just
BLACK

Letterforms have tone, timbre, character, just
BLACK ITALIC

Letterforms have tone, timbre, character, just as words and
BOLD CONDENSED

Letterforms have tone, timbre, character, just as words and
BLACK CONDENSED

ITC Bookman STD

Ed Benguiat, ITC

A-z €

Typography

ABCDEFGHIJKLMNOPQRSTU
VWXYZabcdefghijklmnopqrstu
vwxyz0123456789$€!?.;:,""{½}

*ABCDEFGHIJKLMNOPQRSTU
VWXYZabcdefghijklmnopqrstu
vwxyz&0123456789$€!?.;:,""
{½}*

Letterforms have tone, timbre, char acter, just as words and sentences do. The moment a text and typeface
LIGHT

Letterforms have tone, timbre, char acter, just as words and sentences do. The moment a text and typeface
LIGHT ITALIC

Letterforms have tone, timbre, character, just as words and sen tences do. The moment a text
MEDIUM

Letterforms have tone, timbre, character, just as words and sen tences do. The moment a text
MEDIUM ITALIC

Letterforms have tone, timbre, character, just as words and sen tences do. The moment a text
DEMI

Letterforms have tone, timbre, character, just as words and sen tences do. The moment a text
DEMI ITALIC

Letterforms have tone, timbre, character, just as words and sen tences do. The moment a text
BOLD

Letterforms have tone, timbre, character, just as words and sentences do. The moment a
BOLD ITALIC

Border Pi STD

Linotype Staff

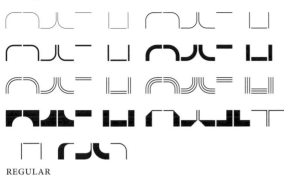

REGULAR

MVB Bossa Nova STD

Holly Goldsmith, MVB Fonts

A-z € ffi é

Typography

ABCDEFGHIJKLMNOPQ
RSTUVWXYZabcdefghijklm
nopqrstuvwxyz&0123456789$€
!?.,;:,""{½}

Tbdꝥhklɽꞃ Th ff ffi ffl H
Alternates and Ligatures

Letterforms have tone, timbre, char
acter, just as words and sentences do.
REGULAR

Briem Akademi STD

Gunnlaugur SE Briem, Gunnlaugur SE Briem

A-z €

Typography

ABCDEFGHIJKLMNOPQRS
TUVWXYZabcdefghijkl
mnopqrstuvwxyz&012
3456789$€.,;:,""{12}

Letterforms have tone,
timbre, character, just as
REGULAR

Letterforms have tone,
timbre, character, just as
SEMIBOLD

Letterforms have tone, tim
bre, character, just as wor
BOLD

Letterforms have tone, tim
bre, character, just as word
BLACK

Briem Akademi STD Compressed

Gunnlaugur SE Briem, Gunnlaugur SE Briem

A-z €

Typography

ABCDEFGHIJKLMNOPQRSTUVWXYZabcdefghijk
lmnopqrstuvwxyzð 123456789$€.,;, ""''{12}

Letterforms have tone, timbre, character, just

REGULAR COMPRESSED

Letterforms have tone, timbre, character, just as

SEMIBOLD COMPRESSED

Letterforms have tone, timbre, character, just as

BOLD COMPRESSED

Letterforms have tone, timbre, character, just as

BLACK COMPRESSED

Briem Akademi STD Condensed

Gunnlaugur SE Briem, Gunnlaugur SE Briem

A-z €

Typography

ABCDEFGHIJKLMNOPQRSTUVWXYZ
abcdefghijklmnopqrstuvwxyzð
0123456789$€.,;, ""''{12}

Letterforms have tone, timbre, character,
just as words and sentences do. The mo

REGULAR CONDENSED

Letterforms have tone, timbre, character,
just as words and sentences do. The mo

SEMIBOLD CONDENSED

Letterforms have tone, timbre, character, just
as words and sentences do. The moment a

BOLD CONDENSED

Letterforms have tone, timbre, character, just
as words and sentences do. The moment a text

BLACK CONDENSED

Briem Script STD

Gunnlaugur SE Briem, Gunnlaugur SE Briem

A-z € ffi BB 619 123 ⅞ H₂ 1ˢᵗ

Typography

ABCDEFGHIJKLMNOPQRSTUW
XYZabcdefghijklmnopqrstuvw
xyz&0123456789$€!?.,;:,""''{¹₂}

ABCDEFGHIJKLMNOPQRSTUVW
XYZ&0123456789 ffi ¹₈ 0123456
789

LETTERFORMS HAVE TONE, timbre, char
acter, just as words and 567 sentences
do. The moment a text and typeface

LIGHT

LETTERFORMS HAVE TONE, timbre, char
acter, just as words and 567 sentences
do. The moment a text and typeface

REGULAR

LETTERFORMS HAVE TONE, timbre,
character, just as words and 567 sen
tences do. The moment a text and

MEDIUM

LETTERFORMS HAVE TONE, timbre,
character, just as words and 567 sen
tences do. The moment a text and

BOLD

Letterforms have tone, timbre, character, just
as words and sentences do. The moment a

BOLD CONDENSED

Letterforms have tone, timbre, character, just
as words and sentences do. The moment a text

BLACK CONDENSED

LETTERFORMS HAVE TONE, timbre, character, just as words and 567 sentences do. The moment a text
BLACK

LETTERFORMS HAVE TONE, timbre, character, just as words and 567 sentences do. The moment a text
ULTRA BLACK

Brioso PRO

Robert Slimbach, Adobe Systems

Typography

ABCDEFGHIJKLMNOPQRSTU
VWXYZabcdefghijklmnopqrstuvw
xyz&ABCDEFGHIJKLMNOPQRSTU
VWXYZ&

ABCDEFGHIJKLMNOPQRSTUV
WXYZabcdefghijklmnopqrstuvwxyz&

ABCDEFGHIJKLMNOPQRS
TUVWXYZThbbdddddffggghhh
hjjkkklll pppqqryy
Swash

0123456789
0123456789 0123456789
0123456789
0123456789 0123456789
Proportional and Tabular Figures

KQRdgkl prſQ efijmnprtuvw
adeghlmnortuz ctfifjflftffffi
ffjfflfftspsttt Th abdehilmnorst
Alternates, Ligatures & Superiors

KQRdfghklmnprvy ae mn r ctfifjflft
ffffiffifflfftspstTh abdehilmnorst
Italic Alternates, Ligatures & Superiors

Ø$¢£¥ƒF£₽€₡#¤%‰Rp$¢£¥ƒ¢€#%‰
0123456789($¢-.,)0123456789($¢-.,) / 0123456789($
¢-.,)0123456789($¢-.,) ¼½¾⅛⅜⅝⅞⅓⅔^~·+
±<=>-|¦×÷∂μπΔ∏∑Ω√∞∫≈≤≥◊¬№℮
ℓ°ao _———-— ' " " ' ' „ ' ' «»«» ‹›‹›,.:; … ..
.. ·!?¡¿¡¿!?¡¿()()[][]{}{}/*•§†‡¶©℗™@@
Currency, Punctuation, and Related Forms

Ø$¢£¥ƒF£₽€₡#¤%‰Rp$¢£¥ƒ¢€#%‰⁰¹
²³456789($¢-.,)0123456789($¢-.,) / 0123456789($¢-
·,)0123456789($¢-.,) ¼½¾⅛⅜⅝⅞⅓⅔^~·+
<=>-|¦×÷∂μπΔ∏∑Ω√∞∫≈≤≥◊¬№℮ℓ°
ao _———-— ' " " ' ' „ ' ' «»«» ‹›‹›,.:; …
.. ·!?¡¿¡¿()()[][]{}{}/*•§|+¶©℗™@@
Italic Currency, Punctuation, and Related Forms

ÆŁØŒÞÐÁÂÄÀÅÃÇÉÊËÈÍÎÏÌ
ÑÓÔÖÒÕŠÚÛÜÙÝŸŽĂĀĄĆČ
ĎĐĚĖĘĒĞĢĪĮĶĹĽĻŃŇŅŐŌŔŘ
ŖŚŞŠŢŤŲŰÛŲŮŹŻŊĦ IJ Ŧæıłœß
þðáâäàåãéêëèíîïìñóôöòõšúûüùýÿžă
āąćčďđěėęēğģīįķĺľļńňņőōŕřŗśşšťűūų
ůźżŋ ij ŧĸÆŁØŒÞÐÁÂÄÀÅÃÇÉÊ
ÈÍÎÏÌÑÓÔÖÒÕŠÚÛÜÙÝŸŽĂĀĄĆČ

ĎĐĚĖĒĘĞĠĪĮĶĹĽĻŃŇŅŊŐŌŔŘŖŚŞŠŤ
ŢŰŨŲŮŹŻ
Accented Characters

ÆŁØŒÞÐÁÂÄÀÅÃÇÉÊËÈÍÎÏÌÑ
ÓÔÖÒÕŠÚÛÜÙÝŸŽĂĀĄĆĆČĎĐĚ
ĖĒĘĞĠĪĮĶĹĽĻŃŇŅŊŐŌŔŘŖŚŞŠŤŢ
ŰŨŲŮŹŻŊH IJ Ŀ Ŧ æ ı ł ø œ ß þ ð á â ä à å ã ç
é ê ë è í î ï ì ñ ó ô ö ò õ š ú û ü ù ý ÿ ž ă ā ą ć ć č ď đ ě ė ē ę ğ ġ ī į
ķ ĺ ľ ļ ń ň ņ ŋ ő ō ŕ ř ŗ ś ş š ţ ŧ ű ũ ų ů ź ż ẑ ŋ ħ ij ŀ ŧ κ
Italic Accented Characters

Ornaments

LETTERFORMS HAVE TONE, timbre, charac
ter, just as words and 567 sentences do. The
moment a text and typeface are chosen, two
LIGHT

*Letterforms have tone, timbre, character, just as
words and 567 sentences do. The moment a text
and typeface are chosen, two streams of thought,*
LIGHT ITALIC

LETTERFORMS HAVE TONE, timbre, charac
ter, just as words and 567 sentences do. The
moment a text and typeface are chosen, two
REGULAR

*Letterforms have tone, timbre, character, just as
words and 567 sentences do. The moment a text
and typeface are chosen, two streams of thought,*
ITALIC

LETTERFORMS HAVE TONE, timbre, charac
ter, just as words and 567 sentences do. The
moment a text and typeface are chosen, two
MEDIUM

*Letterforms have tone, timbre, character, just as
words and 567 sentences do. The moment a text
and typeface are chosen, two streams of thought,*
MEDIUM ITALIC

**LETTERFORMS HAVE TONE, timbre, char
acter, just as words and 567 sentences do.
The moment a text and typeface are chosen,**
SEMIBOLD

*Letterforms have tone, timbre, character, just
as words and 567 sentences do. The moment a
text and typeface are chosen, two streams of*
SEMIBOLD ITALIC

**LETTERFORMS HAVE TONE, timbre, char
acter, just as words and 567 sentences do.
The moment a text and typeface are cho**
BOLD

***Letterforms have tone, timbre, character, just
as words and 567 sentences do. The moment a
text and typeface are chosen, two streams of***
BOLD ITALIC

*To download a complete glyph complement PDF, please visit
www.adobe.com/type.*

Brioso PRO Opticals

Robert Slimbach, Adobe Systems

A-Z € ffi Bb 619 7/8 H₂ 1st A e A

LETTERFORMS HAVE TONE, timbre, character, just as words and
567 sentences do. The moment a text and typeface are chosen,

LETTERFORMS HAVE TONE, timbre, charac
ter, just as words and 567 sentences do. The

LETTERFORMS have tone, tim
bre, character, just as words and

LETTERFORMS have
tone, timbre, character,
LIGHT: CAPTION, REGULAR, SUBHEAD, DISPLAY

Letterforms have tone, timbre, character, just as words and 567 sentenc
es do. The moment a text and typeface are chosen, two streams of

Letterforms have tone, timbre, character, just as words and 567 sentences do. The moment a text

Letterforms have tone, timbre, character, just as words and 567 sentenc

Letterforms have tone, timbre character, just as

LIGHT ITALIC: CAPTION, REGULAR, SUBHEAD, DISPLAY

LETTERFORMS HAVE TONE, timbre, character, just as words and 567 sentences do. The moment a text and typeface are cho

LETTERFORMS HAVE TONE, timbre, character, just as words and 567 sentences do. The

LETTERFORMS have tone, timbre, character, just as words and

LETTERFORMS have tone, timbre, character,

CAPTION, REGULAR, SUBHEAD, DISPLAY

Letterforms have tone, timbre, character, just as words and 567 sen
tences do. The moment a text and typeface are chosen, two streams of

Letterforms have tone, timbre, character, just as words and 567 sentences do. The moment a text

Letterforms have tone, timbre, char acter, just as words and 567 senten

Letterforms have tone, timbre character, just as

ITALIC: CAPTION, REGULAR, SUBHEAD, DISPLAY

LETTERFORMS HAVE TONE, timbre, character, just as words and 567 sentences do. The moment a text and typeface are cho

LETTERFORMS HAVE TONE, character, just as words and 567 sentences do. The

LETTERFORMS have tone, tim bre, character, just as words and

LETTERFORMS have tone, timbre, character,

MEDIUM: CAPTION, REGULAR, SUBHEAD, DISPLAY

Letterforms have tone, timbre, character, just as words and 567 sen tences do. The moment a text and typeface are chosen, two streams of

Letterforms have tone, timbre, character, just as words and 567 sentences do. The moment a text

Letterforms have tone, timbre, char acter, just as words and 567 senten

Letterforms have tone, timbre character, just as

MEDIUM ITALIC: CAPTION, REGULAR, SUBHEAD, DISPLAY

LETTERFORMS HAVE TONE, timbre, character, just as words and 567 sentences do. The moment a text and typeface are cho

LETTERFORMS HAVE TONE, timbre, char acter, just as words and 567 sentences do.

LETTERFORMS have tone, tim bre, character, just as words and

LETTERFORMS have tone, timbre, character,

SEMIBOLD: CAPTION, REGULAR, SUBHEAD, DISPLAY

Letterforms have tone, timbre, character, just as words and 567 sen tences do. The moment a text and typeface are chosen, two streams

Letterforms have tone, timbre, character, just as words and 567 sentences do. The moment a

Letterforms have tone, timbre, character, just as words and 567

Letterforms have tone, timbre, character, just as

SEMIBOLD ITALIC: CAPTION, REGULAR, SUBHEAD, DISPLAY

Letterforms have tone, timbre, character, just as words and 567 sentences do. The moment a text and typeface are

Letterforms have tone, timbre, char acter, just as words and 567 sentences do.

Letterforms have tone, timbre, character, just as words

Letterforms have tone, timbre, character

BOLD: CAPTION, REGULAR, SUBHEAD, DISPLAY

Letterforms have tone, timbre, character, just as words and 567 sentences do. The moment a text and typeface are chosen, two

Letterforms have tone, timbre, character, just as words and 567 sentences do. The moment

Letterforms have tone, timbre, character, just as words and 567

Letterforms have tone, timbre, character, just as

BOLD: ITALIC CAPTION, REGULAR, SUBHEAD, DISPLAY

To download a complete glyph complement PDF, please visit www.adobe.com/type.

Brioso PRO Poster

Robert Slimbach, Adobe Systems

Typography

LETTERFORMS have tone, tim bre, character, just as words and

LIGHT POSTER

Letterforms have tone, timbre, character, just as words and sen

LIGHT POSTER ITALIC

To download a complete glyph complement PDF, please visit www.adobe.com/type.

Bruno STD

Jill Bell

Typography

ABCDEFGHIJKLMNOPQ
RSTUVWXYZabcdefghijklm
nopqrstuvwxyz&0123456789
$€!?.;:,!?"''{½}

Letterforms have tone, timbre, char acter, just as words and sentences

REGULAR

Letterforms have tone, timbre, character, just as words and

BOLD

Brush Script STD

Robert E. Smith

Typography

*ABCDEFGHIJKLMN
OPQRSTUVWXYZabcd
efghijklmnopqrstuvwxyz&0
123456789$€.,:.,!?""''{½}*

*Letterforms have tone, timbre,
character, just as words and*
REGULAR

Bulmer STD

William Martin, Monotype Corp.

A-z € ffi BB 619 123 ⅞ H₂ 1st è

Typography

ABCDEFGHIJKLMNOPQRSTUV
WXYZabcdefghijklmnopqrstuvwxyz
&0123456789$€!?.;:,""''{½}

ABCDEFGHIJKLMNOPQRSTUVWXYZ&
0123456789 ffi ⅛ 0123456789

ABCDEFGHIJKLMNOPQRSTUV
WXYZabcdefghijklmnopqrstuvwxyz&
0123456789$€!?.;:,""''{½}

0123456789 ffi ⅛ 0123456789

LETTERFORMS HAVE TONE, timbre, character,
just as words and 567 sentences do. The
moment a text and typeface are chosen, two
REGULAR

*Letterforms have tone, timbre, character, just
as words and 567 sentences do. The moment
a text and typeface are chosen, two streams of*
ITALIC

**LETTERFORMS HAVE TONE, timbre, character,
just as words and 567 sentences do. The
moment a text and typeface are chosen, two**
SEMIBOLD

***Letterforms have tone, timbre, character, just
as words and 567 sentences do. The moment
a text and typeface are chosen, two streams of***
SEMIBOLD ITALIC

**Letterforms have tone, timbre, character,
just as words and 567 sentences do. The mo
ment a text and typeface are chosen, two**
BOLD

***Letterforms have tone, timbre, character,
just as words and 567 sentences do. The mo
ment a text and typeface are chosen, two***
BOLD ITALIC

Letterforms have tone, timbre, charac
ter, just as words and 567 sentences
REGULAR DISPLAY

*Letterforms have tone, timbre, charac
ter, just as words and 567 sentences*
ITALIC DISPLAY

Letterforms have tone, timbre, character, just as words and 567
BOLD DISPLAY

Letterforms have tone, timbre, character, just as words and 567
BOLD ITALIC DISPLAY

Bundesbahn Pi STD

Linotype Staff

1

2

3

PMN Cæcilia STD

Peter Matthias Noordzij, Linotype Library GmbH

A-Z € BB 619

Typography

ABCDEFGHIJKLMNOPQRSTUV
WXYZabcdefghijklmnopqrstuv
wxyz&0123456789$€!?.;:,""{½}

ABCDEFGHIJKLMNOPQRSTUVWXYZ
&0123456789

ABCDEFGHIJKLMNOPQRSTUVW
XYZabcdefghijklmnopqrstuvwxyz
&0123456789$€!?.;:,""{½}

ABCDEFGHIJKLMNOPQRSTUVWXYZ&
0123456789

LETTERFORMS HAVE TONE, timbre,
character, just as words and 567 sen
tences do. The moment a text and
45 LIGHT

*LETTERFORMS HAVE TONE, timbre, char
acter, just as words and 567 sentences
do. The moment a text and typeface are*
46 LIGHT ITALIC

LETTERFORMS HAVE TONE, timbre,
character, just as words and 567
sentences do. The moment a text
55 ROMAN

*LETTERFORMS HAVE TONE, timbre, char
acter, just as words and 567 sentences
do. The moment a text and typeface are*
56 ITALIC

LETTERFORMS HAVE TONE, timbre, character, just as words and 567 sentences do. The moment a text
75 BOLD

LETTERFORMS HAVE TONE, timbre, char acter, just as words and 567 sentenc es do. The moment a text and type
76 BOLD ITALIC

LETTERFORMS HAVE TONE, timbre, character, just as words and 567 sentences do. The moment a text
85 HEAVY

LETTERFORMS HAVE TONE, timbre, char acter, just as words and 567 sentenc es do. The moment a text and type
86 HEAVY ITALIC

Caflisch Script PRO

Robert Slimbach, Adobe Systems

A-z € ffi 619 123 A e

Typography

ABCDEFGHIJKLMNOPQRSTUVWX
YZabcdefghijklmnopqrstuvwxyz&
ABCDEFGHIJKLMNPQRST
UVWXYZ

0123456789 0123456789
0123456789 0123456789
Proportional and Tabular Figures

aaabbbccddddeeeefgghh
hiiviiiiljkkkkllmmmmn
nnnooooopppppppppp
ppQgrrssttuuuuvvvv
wwwwwxyyzzz&
Alternates

Th ass bj ch ck ct ec es ess et ett ex
ext ey ff ffi ffj fi fi fi fi fj fj fl fl fr
ft gg gg iss of off offi ofi oft ot ott oy
pp pst rr ss ss ss ss st sy tt wh xt
Ligatures

Ø$¢£¥ƒ¤€#%‰$¢£¥ƒ€#% 1234/
¼ ½ ¾ ^~·+±<=>−|¦×÷∂μπΔΠΣ
Ω√∞∫≈≠≤≥◊¬№ℓℓ°ao_——
''"""„'‚«»‹›,.;…!?¿¡()[]{}/*·§†‡
¶©®™@
Currency, Punctuation, and Related Forms

ÆŁØŒÞÐÁÂÄÀÅÃÇÉÊËÈÍÎÏÌÑÓ
ÔÖÒÕŠÚÛÜÙÝŸŽĂĀĄĆČĎĐĚĖĘ
ĞĠĪĮĶĹĽĻŃŇŅŐŌŎŘŔŖŚŞŠŤŢŰŮŲ
ŮŹŻæłøœßþðáâäàåãçéêëèíîïìñóô
öòõšúûüùýÿžăāąćčďěėęğġįķĺľļń
ňņőōŏŕřŗśşšťţűůųůźż
Accented Characters

Letterforms have tone, timbre, charac ter, just as words and sentences do.
LIGHT

Letterforms have tone, timbre, char acter, just as words and sentences
REGULAR

Letterforms have tone, timbre, char acter, just as words and sentences
SEMI BOLD

Letterforms have tone, timbre, char acter, just as words and sentences
BOLD

The moment a text and typeface are chosen, two streams of thought, two rhythmical systems, two sets of habits, or if you like, two personalities, intersect.

To download a complete glyph complement PDF, *please visit www.adobe.com/type.*

Calcite PRO

Akira Kobayashi, Adobe Systems

A-z € ffi 619 123 𝐴 ᵉₑ aA

Typography

ABCDEFGHIJKLMNOPQRSTUVWXYZ
abcdefghijklmnopqrstuvwxyz&

0123456789 0123456789
0123456789 0123456789
Proportional and Tabular Figures

ABDEEFGHIJKLMNPQRTUVWXYZ
agkyzeʒ
Alternates

Ca Ca Ce Ci Co Cr Cu Ex Th Et fi fj fl fr ff
ffi ffj ffl ffr gy Sp st ta tz zz
Ligatures

0$₵£¥f€$₵£¥f€¤#%‰¹²³⁴/¼½¾^~
·+±<=>-|¦×÷∂μπΔΠΣΩ√∞∫≈≠
≤≥◊¬ℓ°ªº_――----'''""„",«»‹›⟨⟩
⟨⟩,.:;...·!?¡¿()()[][]{}{}/*•§†‡₡©®™@
Currency, Punctuation, and Related Forms

ÆŁØŒÞÐÁÂÄÀÅÃÇÉÊËÈÍÎÏÌÑÓÔÖÒÕ
ÚÛÜÙÝŸŽĀĄĆČĎĐĚĖĘĢĢĪĮĶĹĽĻŃŇ
ŅŐŌŔŘŖŚŞŠŢŤŲŰŪŲŮŽŻœ ıłøœßþðáâ
äàåãçéêëèíîïìñóôöòõšúûüùýÿžāąćč
ďđěėęģ ğ ĝ ıįķĺľļ ń ňņ ő ōŕř ŗ ś ş š ţ ť ų ű ū ų ů ż
Accented Characters

Letterforms have tone, timbre, character, just as words and 567 sentences do. The
REGULAR

Letterforms have tone, timbre, char acter, just as words and 567 senten
BOLD

Letterforms have tone, timbre, character, just as words and 567
BLACK

To download a complete glyph complement PDF, please visit www.adobe.com/type.

New Caledonia STD

William A. Dwiggins, Linotype Library GmbH

A-z € BB 619

Typography

ABCDEFGHIJKLMNOPQRST
UVWXYZabcdefghijklmnopqrstuv
wxyz&0123456789$€!?.;:,""{½}

ABCDEFGHIJKLMNOPQRSTUVWXY
Z&0123456789

*ABCDEFGHIJKLMNOPQRSTU
VWXYZabcdefghijklmnopqrstuvw
xyz&0123456789$€!?.;:,""{½}
0123456789*

LETTERFORMS HAVE TONE, timbre, char
acter, just as words and 567 sentences do.
The moment a text and typeface are cho
REGULAR

*Letterforms have tone, timbre, character,
just as words and 567 sentences do. The
moment a text and typeface are chosen,*
ITALIC

Letterforms have tone, timbre, charac
ter, just as words and sentences do. The
moment a text and typeface are chosen,
SEMIBOLD

*Letterforms have tone, timbre, character,
just as words and sentences do. The mo
ment a text and typeface are chosen, two*
SEMIBOLD ITALIC

LETTERFORMS HAVE TONE, timbre,
character, just as words and 567 sen
tences do. The moment a text and
BOLD

*Letterforms have tone, timbre, char
acter, just as words and 567 sentences
do. The moment a text and typeface*
BOLD ITALIC

**Letterforms have tone, timbre,
character, just as words and sen
tences do. The moment a text and**
BLACK

***Letterforms have tone, timbre, char
acter, just as words and sentences
do. The moment a text and typeface***
BLACK ITALIC

Caliban STD

John Benson, Adobe Systems

A-z €

Typography

ABCDEFGHIJKLMNOPQRSTU
VWXYZabcdefghijklmnopqrstuv
wxyz&0123456789$€!?.;:, ""{½}

Letterforms have tone, timbre, charac
ter, just as words and sentences do.
REGULAR

Calvert STD

Margaret Calvert, Monotype Corp.

A-z €

Typography

ABCDEFGHIJKLMNOPQRSTUV
WXYZabcdefghijklmnopqrstuv
wxyz&0123456789$€!?.;:,""{½}

Letterforms have tone, timbre, char
acter, just as words and sentences
do. The moment a text and typeface
LIGHT

Letterforms have tone, timbre, char
acter, just as words and sentences
do. The moment a text and typeface
REGULAR

**Letterforms have tone, timbre, char
acter, just as words and sentences
do. The moment a text and typeface**
BOLD

Candida STD

J. Erbar, Bauer Types, S.A.

A-z €

Typography

ABCDEFGHIJKLMNOPQRSTU
VWXYZabcdefghijklmnopqrstu
vwxyz&0123456789$€!?.;:," "{½}

*ABCDEFGHIJKLMNOPQRSTU
VWXYZabcdefghijklmnopqrstu
vwxyz&0123456789$€!?.;:," "{½}*

Letterforms have tone, timbre, char
acter, just as words and sentences do.
The moment a text and typeface are
ROMAN

*Letterforms have tone, timbre, char
acter, just as words and sentences do.
The moment a text and typeface are*
ITALIC

**Letterforms have tone, timbre, char
acter, just as words and sentences
do. The moment a text and typeface**
BOLD

Cantoria STD

Ron Carpenter, Monotype Corp.

A-z €

Typography

ABCDEFGHIJKLMNOPQRST
UVWXYZabcdefghijklmnopqrstu
vwxyz&0123456789$€!?.;:,""{½}

*ABCDEFGHIJKLMNOPQRSTU
VWXYZabcdefghijklmnopqrstuvwx
yz&0123456789$€!?.;:, ""{½}*

Letterforms have tone, timbre, character,
just as words and sentences do. The mo
ment a text and typeface are chosen, two
LIGHT

*Letterforms have tone, timbre, character, just
as words and sentences do. The moment a
text and typeface are chosen, two streams of*
LIGHT ITALIC

Letterforms have tone, timbre, charac
ter, just as words and sentences do. The
moment a text and typeface are chosen,
REGULAR

Letterforms have tone, timbre, character, just as words and sentences do. The mo ment a text and typeface are chosen, two
ITALIC

Letterforms have tone, timbre, charac ter, just as words and sentences do. The moment a text and typeface are
SEMI BOLD

Letterforms have tone, timbre, character, just as words and sentences do. The mo ment a text and typeface are chosen, two
SEMI BOLD ITALIC

Letterforms have tone, timbre, char acter, just as words and sentences do. The moment a text and typeface
BOLD

Letterforms have tone, timbre, charac ter, just as words and sentences do. The moment a text and typeface are
BOLD ITALIC

Letterforms have tone, timbre, character, just as words and sen tences do. The moment a text and
EXTRA BOLD

Letterforms have tone, timbre, char acter, just as words and sentences do. The moment a text and typeface
EXTRA BOLD ITALIC

Caravan Borders STD

Linotype Staff, Linotype Library GmbH

1

2

3

4

Carolina STD

Gottfried Pott, Linotype Library GmbH

Typography

ABCDEFGHIJKLMNOPQRSTUV WXYZabcdefghijklmnopqrstuv wxyz&0123456789$€!?.,;,""{½}

ch ck ff fi fl ft ll ſ ſi ſſ ß ſt tz
Historic Blackletter

Letterforms have tone, timbre, charac ter, just as words and sentences do. The moment a text and typeface are
REGULAR

Carta STD

Lynne Garell, Adobe Systems

MEDIUM

Cascade Script STD

Matthew Carter, Linotype Library GmbH

A-z €

Typography

ABCDEFGHIJKLMNOPQR
STUVWXYZabcdefghijklm
nopqrstuvwxyz&0123456
789$€!?.;:, ""{½}

Letterforms have tone, timbre, character, just as words and

REGULAR

Adobe Caslon PRO

Carol Twombly, Adobe Systems

A-z € ffi BB 619 123 ⅞ H₂ 1st A e a aA

Typography

ABCDEFGHIJKLMNOPQRST
UVWXYZabcdefghijklmnopqrstu
vwxyz&ABCDEFGHIJKLMNOPQRSTU
VWXYZ&

*ABCDEFGHIJKLMNOPQRSTU
VWXYZabcdefghijklmnopqrstuvwxy
z&*

*ABCDEFGHIJKLMNO
PQRSTUVWXYZkyw*
Swash

0123456789 0123456789
0123456789 0123456789
0123456789 0123456789
0123456789 0123456789
Proportional and Tabular Figures

ſ Th & ff fi fj fl ffi ffj ffl st fh fi fl ff ft
abdehilmnorst

Alternates, Ligatures & Superiors

ſ Th Th & fi fj fl ff ffi ffi ffl st fh fi fl ff ft
abdehilmnorst

Italic Alternates, Ligatures & Superiors

Ø$¢£¥ƒ₡¤€#Rp%‰₀0$¢£¥ƒ₡€#$¢%
‰₀0123456789($¢-.,)0123456789($¢-.,)01234567
89($¢-.,)0123456789($¢-.,)¼½¾⅛⅜⅝⅞⅓⅔
^~·+±<=>−|¦×÷∂μπΔΠΣΩ√∞∫≈≠≤≥
◊¬℮ℓ°ªº_——————–––'"""‚'«»«»‹›
‹›,.:; . . . .·!?¡¿¿()()[][]§§/ *•§†‡
¶©®™@@

Currency, Punctuation, and Related Forms

Ø$¢£¥ƒ₡¤€#Rp%‰₀0$¢£¥ƒ₡€#$¢%
‰₀0123456789($¢-.,)0123456789($¢-.,)0123456789
($¢-.,)0123456789($¢-.,)¼½¾⅛⅜⅝⅞⅓⅔
^~·+±<=>−|¦×÷∂μπΔΠΣΩ√∞∫≈≠≤≥
◊¬℮ℓ°ªº_——————–––'"""‚'«»«»‹›‹›
,.:; . . . .·!?¡¿¿()()[][]§§/ *•§†‡
¶©®™@@

Italic Currency, Punctuation, and Related Forms

ÆŁØŒÞÐÁÂÄÀÅÃÇÉÊËÈÍÎ
ÏÌÑÓÔÖÒÕŠÚÛÜÙÝŸŽĂĀĄ
ĆČĎĐĚĖĒĘĞĠĪĮĶĹĽĿŃŇ
ŐŌŔŘŖŚŞŠŢŤŰŪŲŮŹŻÆɪŁøœ
ßþðáâäàåãçéêëèíîïìñóôöòõšúûüùýÿž
ăāąćčďděėēęğġīįķĺľŀńňņőōŕřŗśşşţťű
ūųůźżÆŁØŒÞÐÁÂÄÀÅÃÇÉÊËÈÍÎÏÌÑ
ÓÔÖÒÕŠÚÛÜÙÝŸŽĂĀĄĆČĐĎĚĖĒĘĞĠĪ
ĮĶĹĽĿŃŇŅŐŌŔŘŖŚŞŞŤŢŰŪŲŮŹŻ

Accented Characters

ÆŁØŒÞÐÁÂÄÀÅÃÇÉÊËÈÍÎÏÌ
ÑÓÔÖÒÕŠÚÛÜÙÝŸŽĂĀĄĆČĎ
ĐĚĖĒĘĞĠĪĮĶĹĽĿŃŇŅŐŌŔŘŖ
ŚŞŞŤŢŰŪŲŮŹŻÆɪłøœßþðáâäàåãçé

êëèíîïìñóôöòõšúûüùýÿžăāąćčďděėēęğġįį
ķĺľŀńňņőōŕřŗśşşţťűūųůźż

Italic Accented Characters

Ornaments

LETTERFORMS HAVE TONE, timbre, charac
ter, just as words and 567 sentences do. The
moment a text and typeface are chosen,
REGULAR

Letterforms have tone, timbre, character, just
as words and 567 sentences do. The moment
a text and typeface are chosen, two streams of
ITALIC

LETTERFORMS HAVE TONE, timbre, charac
ter, just as words and 567 sentences do. The
moment a text and typeface are chosen,
SEMIBOLD

Letterforms have tone, timbre, character, just
as words and 567 sentences do. The moment
a text and typeface are chosen, two streams of
SEMIBOLD ITALIC

Letterforms have tone, timbre, character,
just as words and 567 sentences do. The
moment a text and typeface are chosen,
BOLD

Letterforms have tone, timbre, character, just
as words and 567 sentences do. The moment
a text and typeface are chosen, two streams of
BOLD ITALIC

To download a complete glyph complement PDF, please visit
www.adobe.com/type.

Caslon 3 STD

American Type Founders Staff

A-z € BB 619 123

Typography

ABCDEFGHIJKLMNOPQRS
TUVWXYZabcdefghijklmnopq
rstuvwxyz&0123456789$€!?.;:,
""{½}

ABCDEFGHIJKLMNOPQRSTUVWX
YZ&0123456789 0123456789

*ABCDEFGHIJKLMNOPQRST
UVWXYZabcdefghijklmnopqrstuv
wxyz&0123456789$€!?.;:,""{½}*

0123456789 0123456789

LETTERFORMS HAVE TONE, timbre,
character, just as words and 567 sen
tences do. The moment a text and
3 ROMAN

*Letterforms have tone, timbre, character,
just as words and 567 sentences do. The
moment a text and typeface are chosen,*
3 ITALIC

Caslon 540 STD

American Type Founders Staff

A-z € BB 619 123

Typography

ABCDEFGHIJKLMNOPQRSTU
VWXYZabcdefghijklmnopqrstuvw
xyz&0123456789$€!?.;:,""{½}

ABCDEFGHIJKLMNOPQRSTUVWXYZ&
0123456789 0123456789

*ABCDEFGHIJKLMNOPQRSTUVW
XYZabcdefghijklmnopqrstuvwxyz&012
3456789$€!?.;:,""{½}*

0123456789 0123456789

LETTERFORMS HAVE TONE, timbre, charac
ter, just as words and 567 sentences do.
The moment a text and typeface are
540 ROMAN

*Letterforms have tone, timbre, character, just
as words and 567 sentences do. The moment
a text and typeface are chosen, two streams of*
540 ITALIC

Caslon Open Face STD

BB&S Staff

A-z €

Typography

ABCDEFGHIJKLMNOP
QRSTUVWXYZabcdefghijkl

mnopqrstuvwxyz&0123456789
$€!?.,;:,""{½}

Letterforms have tone, timbre,
character, just as words and sen
REGULAR

ITC Caslon 224 STD

Ed Benguiat, ITC

`A-z` `€`

Typography

ABCDEFGHIJKLMNOPQRSTUV
WXYZabcdefghijklmnopqrstuvw
xyz&0123456789$€!?.,;:,""{½}

ABCDEFGHIJKLMNOPQRSTUV
WXYZabcdefghijklmnopqrstuv
wxyz&0123456789$€!?.,;:,""{½}

Letterforms have tone, timbre, char
acter, just as words and sentences do.
The moment a text and typeface are
BOOK

Letterforms have tone, timbre, char
acter, just as words and sentences do.
The moment a text and typeface are
BOOK ITALIC

Letterforms have tone, timbre, char
acter, just as words and sentences do.
The moment a text and typeface are
MEDIUM

Letterforms have tone, timbre, char
acter, just as words and sentences do.
The moment a text and typeface are
MEDIUM ITALIC

Letterforms have tone, timbre, char
acter, just as words and sentences do.
The moment a text and typeface are
BOLD

Letterforms have tone, timbre, char
acter, just as words and sentences
do. The moment a text and typeface
BOLD ITALIC

Letterforms have tone, timbre, char
acter, just as words and sentences
do. The moment a text and typeface
BLACK

Letterforms have tone, timbre, char
acter, just as words and sentences
do. The moment a text and typeface
BLACK ITALIC

Castellar STD

John Peters, Monotype Corp.

`A-z` `€`

TYPOGRAPH

ABCDEFGHIJKLMN
OPQRSTUVWXYZ&
0123456789$€!?.,;:,""{½}

LETTERFORMS HAVE
TONE, TIMBRE, CHAR
REGULAR

Caxton STD

Leslie Usherwood, Esselte Pendaflex, Letraset, Esselte Letraset

[A-z] [€]

Typography

ABCDEFGHIJKLMNOPQRSTUVW
XYZabcdefghijklmnopqrstuvwxy
z&0123456789$€!?.;:, ""{½}

*ABCDEFGHIJKLMNOPQRSTUVW
XYZabcdefghijklmnopqrstuvwxy
z&0123456789$€!?.;:, ""{½}*

Letterforms have tone, timbre, char
acter, just as words and sentences do.
The moment a text and typeface are
LIGHT

*Letterforms have tone, timbre, char
acter, just as words and sentences do.
The moment a text and typeface are*
LIGHT ITALIC

Letterforms have tone, timbre, char
acter, just as words and sentences do.
The moment a text and typeface are
BOOK

*Letterforms have tone, timbre, char
acter, just as words and sentences do.
The moment a text and typeface are*
BOOK ITALIC

**Letterforms have tone, timbre, char
acter, just as words and sentences
do. The moment a text and typefac**
BOLD

***Letterforms have tone, timbre,
character, just as words and sen
tences do. The moment a text and***
BOLD ITALIC

MVB Celestia Antiqua STD

Mark van Bronkhorst, MVB Fonts

[A-z] [€] [ffi] [Bb] [619] [🐍]

Typography

ABCDEFGHIJKLMNOPQRSTUV
WXYZabcdefghijklmnopqrstuvwxy
z&$€!?.;:, ""{½}

ABCDEFGHIJKLMNOPQRSTUVWXY
Z&0123456789 ffi

ABCDEFGHIJKLMNOPQRSTUVW
XYZ*abcdefghijklmnopqrstuvwxyz&*$€
!?.;:, ""{½}

&0123456789 ffi

LETTERFORMS HAVE TONE, timbre, charac
ter, just as words and 567 sentences do. The
moment a text and typeface are chosen, two
REGULAR

*Letterforms have tone, timbre, character, just as
words and 567 sentences do. The moment a text
and typeface are chosen, two streams of thought,*
ITALIC

**Letterforms have tone, timbre, character,
just as words and 567 sentences do. The
moment a text and typeface are chosen,**
SEMIBOLD

Letterforms have tone, timbre, char acter, just as words and 567 sen tences do. The moment a text and
BOLD

Centaur STD

Bruce Rogers and Frederic Warde, Monotype Corp.

A-Z € ffi BB 619 123 ⅞ H₂ 1ˢᵗ 𝒜

Typography

ABCDEFGHIJKLMNOPQRSTUV
WXYZabcdefghijklmnopqrstuvwxyz&
0123456789$€!?.;:,"" {½}

ABCDEFGHIJKLMNOPQRSTUVWXYZ&012345
6789$¢ ffi ⅛ 0123456789

ABCDEFGHIJKLMNOPQRSTUVWXY
Zabcdefghijklmnopqrstuvwxyz&01234567
89$€!?.;:,""{½}

0123456789$¢ ffi ⅛ 0123456789

ABCD E F G H IJ K L M N O P Q R
S T U V W X Y Z ae'k r¯t¯v w z
Swash

Alternates

LETTERFORMS HAVE TONE, timbre, character, just
as words and 567 sentences do. The moment
a text and typeface are chosen, two streams of
REGULAR

Letterforms have tone, timbre, character, just as words and
567 sentences do. The moment a text and typeface are cho
sen, two streams of thought, two rhythmical systems, two
ITALIC

Letterforms have tone, timbre, character, just
as words and 567 sentences do. The moment
a text and typeface are chosen, two streams of
BOLD

Letterforms have tone, timbre, character, just as words
and 567 sentences do. The moment a text and typeface
are chosen, two streams of thought, two rhythmical sys
BOLD ITALIC

Linotype Centennial STD

Adrian Frutiger, Linotype Library GmbH

A-Z € BB 619

Typography

ABCDEFGHIJKLMNOPQRSTUV
WXYZabcdefghijklmnopqrstuv
wxyz&0123456789$€!?.;:,""{½}

ABCDEFGHIJKLMNOPQRSTUVWXYZ
&0123456789

ABCDEFGHIJKLMNOPQRSTUV
WXYZabcdefghijklmnopqrstuvw
xyz&0123456789$¢.,:,!?""{½}

0123456789

LETTERFORMS HAVE TONE, timbre, char
acter, just as words and 567 sentenc
es do. The moment a text and type
45 LIGHT

Letterforms have tone, timbre, char
acter, just as words and 567 sentenc
es do. The moment a text and type
46 LIGHT ITALIC

LETTERFORMS HAVE TONE, timbre, char acter, just as words and 567 sentenc es do. The moment a text and type
55 ROMAN

Letterforms have tone, timbre, char acter, just as words and 567 sentenc es do. The moment a text and type
56 ITALIC

Letterforms have tone, timbre, char acter, just as words and 567 sen tences do. The moment a text and
75 BOLD

Letterforms have tone, timbre, char acter, just as words and 567 sen tences do. The moment a text and
76 BOLD ITALIC

Letterforms have tone, timbre, character, just as words and 567 sentences do. The moment a text
95 BLACK

Letterforms have tone, timbre, character, just as words and 567 sentences do. The moment a text
96 BLACK ITALIC

Century Expanded STD

Linn Boyd Benton

A-Z €

Typography

ABCDEFGHIJKLMNOPQRST
UVWXYZabcdefghijklmnopqrst
uvwxyz&0123456789$€!?.;:, ""{½}

*ABCDEFGHIJKLMNOPQRST
UVWXYZabcdefghijklmnopqrst
uvwxyz&0123456789$€!?.;:, ""{½}*

Letterforms have tone, timbre, charac ter, just as words and sentences do. The moment a text and typeface are
REGULAR

Letterforms have tone, timbre, charac ter, just as words and sentences do. The moment a text and typeface are chosen
ITALIC

Century Old Style STD

Morris Fuller Benton

A-Z €

Typography

ABCDEFGHIJKLMNOPQRSTU
VWXYZabcdefghijklmnopqrstuv
wxyz&0123456789$€!?.;:, ""{½}

*ABCDEFGHIJKLMNOPQRSTU
VWXYZabcdefghijklmnopqrstuvw
xyz&0123456789$€!?.;:, {½}*

Letterforms have tone, timbre, charac ter, just as words and sentences do. The moment a text and typeface are chosen,
REGULAR

Letterforms have tone, timbre, character, just as words and sentences do. The mo ment a text and typeface are chosen, two
ITALIC

Letterforms have tone, timbre, char acter, just as words and sentences do. The moment a text and typeface
BOLD

Tony Stan, ITC

A-Z €

Typography

ABCDEFGHIJKLMNOPQRSTU
VWXYZabcdefghijklmnopqrstuv
wxyz&0123456789$€!?.;:,""{½}

*ABCDEFGHIJKLMNOPQRSTU
VWXYZabcdefghijklmnopqrstuv
wxyz&0123456789$€!?.;:,""{½}*

Letterforms have tone, timbre, charac
ter, just as words and sentences do. The
moment a text and typeface are chosen,
LIGHT

*Letterforms have tone, timbre, charac
ter, just as words and sentences do.
The moment a text and typeface are*
LIGHT ITALIC

Letterforms have tone, timbre, charac
ter, just as words and sentences do. The
moment a text and typeface are chosen
BOOK

*Letterforms have tone, timbre, charac
ter, just as words and sentences do.
The moment a text and typeface are*
BOOK ITALIC

**Letterforms have tone, timbre, char
acter, just as words and sentences
do. The moment a text and typeface**
BOLD

***Letterforms have tone, timbre, char
acter, just as words and sentences
do. The moment a text and typeface***
BOLD ITALIC

**Letterforms have tone, timbre,
character, just as words and
sentences do. The moment a**
ULTRA

***Letterforms have tone, timbre,
character, just as words and
sentences do. The moment a***
ULTRA ITALIC

ITC Century STD Condensed

Tony Stan, ITC

A-Z €

Typography

ABCDEFGHIJKLMNOPQRSTUVW
XYZabcdefghijklmnopqrstuvwxyz&
0123456789$€!?.;:,""{½}

*ABCDEFGHIJKLMNOPQRSTUVW
XYZabcdefghijklmnopqrstuvwxyz&
0123456789$€!?.;:,""{½}*

Letterforms have tone, timbre, character,
just as words and sentences do. The moment
a text and typeface are chosen, two streams
LIGHT

*Letterforms have tone, timbre, character,
just as words and sentences do. The moment
a text and typeface are chosen, two streams*
LIGHT ITALIC

Letterforms have tone, timbre, character,
just as words and sentences do. The moment
a text and typeface are chosen, two streams
BOOK

Letterforms have tone, timbre, character, just as words and sentences do. The moment a text and typeface are chosen, two streams
BOOK ITALIC

Letterforms have tone, timbre, character, just as words and sentences do. The mo ment a text and typeface are chosen, two
BOLD

Letterforms have tone, timbre, character, just as words and sentences do. The mo ment a text and typeface are chosen, two
BOLD ITALIC

Letterforms have tone, timbre, char acter, just as words and sentences do. The moment a text and typeface
ULTRA

Letterforms have tone, timbre, character, just as words and sen tences do. The moment a text and
ULTRA ITALIC

ITC Century Handtooled STD

Ed Benguiat, ITC

Typography

ABCDEFGHIJKLMNOPQ
RSTUVWXYZabcdefghijkl
mnopqrstuvwxyz&012345
6789$€!?.;:,""{½}

ABCDEFGHIJKLMNOPQ
RSTUVWXYZabcdefghijkl
mnopqrstuvwxyz&012345
6789$€!?.;:, ""{½}

Letterforms have tone, timbre, character, just as
BOLD

Letterforms have tone, timbre, character, just as
BOLD ITALIC

New Century Schoolbook STD

Morris Fuller Benton

Typography

ABCDEFGHIJKLMNOPQRST
UVWXYZabcdefghijklmnopqrstu
vwxyz&0123456789$€!?.;:,""{½}

ABCDEFGHIJKLMNOPQRST
UVWXYZabcdefghijklmnopqrstu
vwxyz&0123456789$€!?.;:,""{½}

Letterforms have tone, timbre, char acter, just as words and sentences do. The moment a text and typeface are
ROMAN

Letterforms have tone, timbre, char acter, just as words and sentences do. The moment a text and typeface are
ITALIC

Letterforms have tone, timbre, character, just as words and sen tences do. The moment a text and
BOLD

Letterforms have tone, timbre, character, just as words and sen tences do. The moment a text and
BOLD ITALIC

New Century Schoolbook STD Fractions

Morris Fuller Benton

0123456789/0123456789

0123456789 0123456789 0123456789

½ ⁷⁄₁₆ ⁶³⁄₆₄ 1⅓ ²⁄₇₇ ⁴⁴⁄₁₀₀ ½ ⁷⁄₁₆ ⁶³⁄₆₄ 1⅓ ²²⁄₇ ⁴⁴⁄₁₀₀

REGULAR

½ ⁷⁄₁₆ ⁶³⁄₆₄ 1⅓ ²⁄₇₇ ⁴⁴⁄₁₀₀ ½ ⁷⁄₁₆ ⁶³⁄₆₄ 1⅓ ²²⁄₇ ⁴⁴⁄₁₀₀

BOLD

ITC Cerigo STD

Jean-Renaud Cuaz, ITC

[A-z] [€]

Typography

ABCDEFGHIJKLMNOPQRSTUV
WXYZabcdefghijklmnopqrstuvw
xyz&0123456789$€!?.;:,""{½}

*ABCDEFGHIJKLMNOPQRSTUV
WXYZabcdefghijklmnopqrstuvw
yz&0123456789$€!?.;:,""{½}*

Letterforms have tone, timbre, charac
ter, just as words and sentences do. The
moment a text and typeface are chosen,
BOOK

*Letterforms have tone, timbre, character,
just as words and sentences do. The mo
ment a text and typeface are chosen, two*
BOOK ITALIC

**Letterforms have tone, timbre, char
acter, just as words and sentences do.
The moment a text and typeface are**
MEDIUM

*Letterforms have tone, timbre, charac
ter, just as words and sentences do. The
moment a text and typeface are chosen,*
MEDIUM ITALIC

**Letterforms have tone, timbre, char
acter, just as words and sentences
do. The moment a text and typeface**
BOLD

***Letterforms have tone, timbre, char
acter, just as words and sentences do.
The moment a text and typeface are***
BOLD ITALIC

Chaparral PRO

Carol Twombly, Adobe Systems

[A-z] [€] [ffi] [BB] [619] [123] [⅞] [H₂] [1st] [℮] [↘] [aA]

Typography

ABCDEFGHIJKLMNOPQRSTUV
WXYZabcdefghijklmnopqrstuvwx
yz&ABCDEFGHIJKLMNOPQRSTUV
WXYZ&

*ABCDEFGHIJKLMNOPQRSTUVW
XYZabcdefghijklmnopqrstuvwxyz&
ABCDEFGHIJKLMNOPQRSTUVWXYZ&*

0123456789 0123456789
0123456789 0123456789
0123456789 *0123456789*
0123456789 *0123456789*

Proportional and Tabular Figures

Th ff ffi ffj ffl fi fj fl abdehilmnorst

Th ff ffi ffj ffl fi fj fl abdehilmnorst

Ligatures and Superiors

Ø$¢£¥ƒ₡¤€#$¢£¥ƒ€Rp%‰$¢£¥ƒ
€#$¢£¥ƒ€#°%‰0123456789($¢-.,)012345
6789($¢-.,)/0123456789($¢-.,)0123456789($¢-.,)
¼½¾⅛⅜⅝⅞⅓⅔^~·+±<=>-|¦×÷∂μ
π∆∏∑Ω√∞∫≈≠≤≥◊¬℮ℓ°ªº_——–--–
——'"""„",«»«»‹›‹›,.:;……··!?¡¿¡¿!?¡¿()

○[][]{}∕∖*•§†‡¶©®™@@

Currency, Punctuation, and Related Forms

*Ø$¢£¥ƒ₡¤€#$¢£¥ƒ€Rp%‰$¢£¥ƒ€
#$¢£¥ƒ€#°%‰0123456789($¢-.,)0123456789
(¢$-.,)/0123456789($¢-.,)0123456789($¢-.,)¼½¾
⅛⅜⅝⅞⅓⅔^~·+±<=>-|¦×÷∂μπ∆∏∑
Ω√∞∫≈≠≤≥◊¬℮ℓ°ªº_——–--––'"
""„",«»«»‹›‹›,.:;……··!?¡¿¡¿!?¡¿()()[][]
{}∕∖*•§†‡¶©®™@@*

Italic Currency, Punctuation, and Related Forms

ÆŁØŒÞÐÁÂÄÀÅÃÇÉÊËÈÍÎÏÌÑÓ
ÔÖÒÕŠÚÛÜÙÝŸŽĂĀĄĆČĎĐĚĖĒ
ĘĞĠĪĮĶĹĽĻŃŇŅŐŌŔŘŖŚŞŞŤŢŰŨ
ŲŮŹŻæ ıłøœßþðáâäàåãçéêëíîïñóô
öòõšúûüùýÿžăāąćčďđěėēęğġīįķĺľļń
ňņőōŕřŗśşşť űūųůźżÆŁØŒÞÐÁÂÄ
ÅÃÇÉÊËÈÍÎÏÌÑÓÔÖÒÕŠÚÛÜÙÝŸŽĂĀ
ĄĆČĎĐĚĖĒĘĞĠĪĮĶĹĽĻŃŇŅŐŌŔŘŖŚ
ŞŤŢŰŨŲŮŹŻ

Accented Characters

*ÆŁØŒÞÐÁÂÄÀÅÃÇÉÊËÈÍÎÏÌÑÓ
ÔÖÒÕŠÚÛÜÙÝŸŽĂĀĄĆČĎĐĚĖĒĘ
ĞĠĪĮĶĹĽĻŃŇŅŐŌŔŘŖŚŞŞŤŢŰŨŲ
ŮŽŻæ ıłøœßþðáâäàåãçéêëíîïñóôöò
šúûüùýÿžāāąćčďđěėēęğġīįķĺľļńňņőōŕř
ŗśşşť űūųůźżÆŁØŒÞÐÁÂÄÀÅÃÇÉÊË
ÍÎÏÌÑÓÔÖÒÕŠÚÛÜÙÝŸŽĂĀĄĆČĎĐĚĖ
ĘĞĠĪĮĶĹĽĻŃŇŅŐŌŔŘŖŚŞŞŤŢŰŨŲŮŹŻ*

Italic Accented Characters

Ornaments

LETTERFORMS HAVE TONE, timbre, charac
ter, just as words and 567 sentences do. The
moment a text and typeface are chosen, two
LIGHT

*LETTERFORMS HAVE TONE, timbre, character,
just as words and 567 sentences do. The mo
ment a text and typeface are chosen, two
LIGHT ITALIC*

LETTERFORMS HAVE TONE, timbre, charac
ter, just as words and 567 sentences do.
The mo ment a text and typeface are cho
REGULAR

*LETTERFORMS HAVE TONE, timbre, charac
ter, just as words and 567 sentences do. The
moment a text and typeface are chosen, two
ITALIC*

**LETTERFORMS HAVE TONE, timbre, char
acter, just as words and 567 sentences
do. The moment a text and typeface are**
SEMIBOLD

***LETTERFORMS HAVE TONE, timbre, char
acter, just as words and 567 sentences do.
The moment a text and typeface are cho***
SEMIBOLD ITALIC

LETTERFORMS HAVE TONE, timbre, character, just as words and 567 sen tences do. The moment a text and

BOLD

LETTERFORMS HAVE TONE, timbre, char acter, just as words and 567 sentences do. The moment a text and typeface are

BOLD ITALIC

To download a complete glyph complement PDF, please visit www.adobe.com/type.

ⓒ Chaparral PRO Opticals

Carol Twombly, Adobe Systems

LETTERFORMS HAVE TONE, timbre, character, just as words and 567 sentences do. The moment a text and typeface are chosen,

LETTERFORMS HAVE TONE, timbre, charac ter, just as words and 567 sentences do. The

LETTERFORMS have tone, timbre, character, just as words and 567

LETTERFORMS have tone, timbre, character, just as

LIGHT: CAPTION, REGULAR, SUBHEAD, DISPLAY

LETTERFORMS HAVE TONE, timbre, character, just as words and 567 sentences do. The moment a text and typeface are chosen, two stream

LETTERFORMS HAVE TONE, timbre, character, just as words and 567 sentences do. The mo

LETTERFORMS have tone, timbre, character, just as words and 567 sen

LETTERFORMS have tone, timbre, character, just as

LIGHT ITALIC: CAPTION, REGULAR, SUBHEAD, DISPLAY

LETTERFORMS HAVE TONE, timbre, character, just as words and 567 sentences do. The moment a text and typeface are chosen,

LETTERFORMS HAVE TONE, timbre, charac ter, just as words and 567 sentences do.

LETTERFORMS have tone, tim bre, character, just as words and

LETTERFORMS have tone, timbre, character,

CAPTION, REGULAR, SUBHEAD, DISPLAY

LETTERFORMS HAVE TONE, timbre, character, just as words and 567 sentences do. The moment a text and typeface are chosen,

LETTERFORMS HAVE TONE, timbre, character, just as words and 567 sentences do. The mo

LETTERFORMS have tone, timbre, character, just as words and 567 sen

LETTERFORMS have tone, timbre, character, just as

ITALIC: CAPTION, REGULAR, SUBHEAD, DISPLAY

LETTERFORMS HAVE TONE, timbre, character, just as words and 567 sentences do. The moment a text and typeface are

LETTERFORMS HAVE TONE, timbre, char acter, just as words and 567 sentences

LETTERFORMS have tone, tim bre, character, just as words

LETTERFORMS have tone, timbre, character

SEMIBOLD: CAPTION, REGULAR, SUBHEAD, DISPLAY

LETTERFORMS HAVE TONE, timbre, character, just as words and 567 sentences do. The moment a text and typeface are chosen,

LETTERFORMS HAVE TONE, timbre, character, just as words and 567 sentences do. The

LETTERFORMS have tone, timbre, character, just as words and 567

LETTERFORMS have tone, timbre, character,

SEMIBOLD ITALIC: CAPTION, REGULAR, SUBHEAD, DISPLAY

LETTERFORMS HAVE TONE, timbre, character, just as words and 567 sentences do. The moment a text and

LETTERFORMS HAVE TONE, timbre, character, just as words and 567 sen

LETTERFORMS have tone, timbre, character, just as words

LETTERFORMS have tone, timbre, charac

BOLD: CAPTION, REGULAR, SUBHEAD, DISPLAY

LETTERFORMS HAVE TONE, timbre, character, just as words and 567 sentences do. The moment a text and typeface are

LETTERFORMS HAVE TONE, timbre, character, just as words and 567 sentences

LETTERFORMS have tone, timbre, character, just as words

LETTERFORMS have tone, timbre, charac

BOLD ITALIC: CAPTION, REGULAR, SUBHEAD, DISPLAY

To download a complete glyph complement PDF, please visit www.adobe.com/type.

Charlemagne STD

Carol Twombly, Adobe Systems

[A-z] [€]

TYPOGRAPH

ABCDEFGHIJKLMN
OPQRSTUVWXYZ&0
123456789$€!?.;:,""{½}

LETTERFORMS HAVE
TONE, TIMBRE, CHAR

REGULAR

LETTERFORMS HAVE
TONE, TIMBRE, CHAR

BOLD

Charme STD

Helmut Matheis, Bauer Types, S.A.

[A-z] [€]

Typography

Aa Bb Cc Dd Ee Ff Gg
Hh Ii Jj Kk Ll Mm Nn
Oo Pp Qq Rr Ss Tt Uu
Vv Ww Xx Yy Zz &0123456
789$€!?.;:,""{½}

Letterforms have tone, timbre, character, just as words and sentences do

REGULAR

ITC Cheltenham STD

Tony Stan, ITC

A-z €

Typography

ABCDEFGHIJKLMNOPQRSTUV
WXYZabcdefghijklmnopqrstuv
wxyz&0123456789$€!?.;:,""{½}

*ABCDEFGHIJKLMNOPQRSTUV
WXYZabcdefghijklmnopqrstuvw
xyz&0123456789$€!?.;:, ""{½}*

Letterforms have tone, timbre, character,
just as words and sentences do. The mo
ment a text and typeface are chosen, two
LIGHT

*Letterforms have tone, timbre, character,
just as words and sentences do. The mo
ment a text and typeface are chosen, two*
LIGHT ITALIC

Letterforms have tone, timbre, charac
ter, just as words and sentences do.
The moment a text and typeface are
BOOK

*Letterforms have tone, timbre, charac
ter, just as words and sentences do. The
moment a text and typeface are chosen*
BOOK ITALIC

**Letterforms have tone, timbre, char
acter, just as words and sentences
do. The moment a text and typeface**
BOLD

***Letterforms have tone, timbre, char
acter, just as words and sentences
do. The moment a text and typeface***
BOLD ITALIC

**Letterforms have tone, timbre,
character, just as words and sen
tences do. The moment a text**
ULTRA

***Letterforms have tone, timbre,
character, just as words and sen
tences do. The moment a text and***
ULTRA ITALIC

ITC Cheltenham STD Condensed

Tony Stan, ITC

A-z €

Typography

ABCDEFGHIJKLMNOPQRSTUVWXYZ
abcdefghijklmnopqrstuvwxyz&012345
6789$€!?.;:,""{½}

*ABCDEFGHIJKLMNOPQRSTUVWXYZ
abcdefghijklmnopqrstuvwxyz&012345
6789$€!?.;:,""{½}*

Letterforms have tone, timbre, character,
just as words and sentences do. The moment
a text and typeface are chosen, two streams
LIGHT

*Letterforms have tone, timbre, character,
just as words and sentences do. The moment
a text and typeface are chosen, two streams*
LIGHT ITALIC

Letterforms have tone, timbre, character,
just as words and sentences do. The moment
a text and typeface are chosen, two streams
BOOK

Letterforms have tone, timbre, character, just as words and sentences do. The moment a text and typeface are chosen, two streams
BOOK ITALIC

Letterforms have tone, timbre, character, just as words and sentences do. The mo ment a text and typeface are chosen, two
BOLD

Letterforms have tone, timbre, character, just as words and sentences do. The mo ment a text and typeface are chosen, two
BOLD ITALIC

Letterforms have tone, timbre, char acter, just as words and sentences do. The moment a text and typeface
ULTRA

Letterforms have tone, timbre, character, just as words and sen tences do. The moment a text and
ULTRA ITALIC

ITC Cheltenham Handtooled STD

Ed Benguiat, ITC

A-z €

Typography

ABCDEFGHIJKLMNOP
QRSTUVWXYZabcdefgh
ijklmnopqrstuvwxyz&0
123456789$€!?.;:,""{½}

*ABCDEFGHIJKLMNOP
QRSTUVWXYZabcdefgh*

*ijklmnopqrstuvwxyz&0
123456789$€!?.;:,""{½}*

**Letterforms have tone,
timbre, character, just as**
BOLD

***Letterforms have tone,
timbre, character, just as***
BOLD ITALIC

Cheq STD

John Renner, Adobe Systems

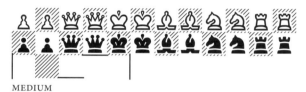

MEDIUM

Clairvaux STD

Herbert Maring, Linotype Library GmbH

A-z € ħ

Typography

ABCDEFGHIJKLMNOPQRS
TUVWXYZabcdefghijklmno
pqrstuvwxyz&0123456789$€!?
.;:,""{½}

ch ck ff ft ll ſ ſi ſſ ſt ß tz
Historic Blackletter

Letterforms have tone, timbre, char acter, just as words and sentences
REGULAR

Clarendon STD

Unknown, Linotype Library GmbH

A-z €

Typography

ABCDEFGHIJKLMNOPQRS
TUVWXYZabcdefghijklmno
pqrstuvwxyz&0123456789$
€!?.;:,""{½}

Letterforms have tone, timbre, char
acter, just as words and sentences
do. The moment a text and typefac
LIGHT

Letterforms have tone, timbre, char
acter, just as words and sentences
do. The moment a text and typefac
REGULAR

**Letterforms have tone, timbre,
character, just as words and sen
tences do. The moment a text**
BOLD

Clearface Gothic STD

Morris Fuller Benton, Linotype Library GmbH

A-z €

Typography

ABCDEFGHIJKLMNOPQRSTUVWXYZ
abcdefghijklmnopqrstuvwxyz&01234
56789$€!?.;:,""{½}

Letterforms have tone, timbre, character, just as
words and sentences do. The moment a text and
typeface are chosen, two streams of thought, two
45 LIGHT

Letterforms have tone, timbre, character, just
as words and sentences do. The moment a text
and typeface are chosen, two streams of thoug
55 ROMAN

**Letterforms have tone, timbre, character,
just as words and sentences do. The moment
a text and typeface are chosen, two streams**
65 MEDIUM

**Letterforms have tone, timbre, character,
just as words and sentences do. The mo
ment a text and typeface are chosen, two**
75 BOLD

**Letterforms have tone, timbre, charac
ter, just as words and sentences do. The
moment a text and typeface are chosen,**
95 BLACK

ITC Clearface STD

Vic Caruso, ITC

A-z €

Typography

ABCDEFGHIJKLMNOPQRSTUVW
XYZabcdefghijklmnopqrstuvwxyz
&0123456789$€!?.;:,""{½}

*ABCDEFGHIJKLMNOPQRSTUVW
XYZabcdefghijklmnopqrstuvwxyz
&0123456789$€!?.;:,""{½}*

Letterforms have tone, timbre, character, just as words and sentences do. The mo ment a text and typeface are chosen, two

REGULAR

Letterforms have tone, timbre, character, just as words and sentences do. The mo ment a text and typeface are chosen, two

REGULAR ITALIC

Letterforms have tone, timbre, character, just as words and sentences do. The mo ment a text and typeface are chosen, two

BOLD

Letterforms have tone, timbre, character, just as words and sentences do. The mo ment a text and typeface are chosen, two

BOLD ITALIC

Letterforms have tone, timbre, character, just as words and sentences do. The mo ment a text and typeface are chosen, two

HEAVY

Letterforms have tone, timbre, character, just as words and sentences do. The mo ment a text and typeface are chosen, two

HEAVY ITALIC

Letterforms have tone, timbre, char acter, just as words and sentences do. The moment a text and typeface

BLACK

Letterforms have tone, timbre, char acter, just as words and sentences do. The moment a text and typeface

BLACK ITALIC

Cloister Open Face STD

R. Hunter Middleton

Typography

ABCDEFGHIJKLMNO
PQRSTUVWXYZabcdef
ghijklmnopqrstuvwxyz&
0123456789$€!?.;:,""""{½}

Letterforms have tone, timbre, character, just as words and

REGULAR

Cochin STD

Matthew Carter, Linotype Library GmbH

Typography

ABCDEFGHIJKLMNOPQRST
UVWXYZabcdefghijklmnopqrstu
vwxyz&0123456789$€!?.;:,""{½}

*ABCDEFGHIJKLMNOPQRSTUV
WXYZabcdefghijklmnopqrstuvwxyz
&0123456789$€!?.;:,""{½}*

Letterforms have tone, timbre, character, just as words and sentences do. The mo ment a text and typeface are chosen, two

REGULAR

Letterforms have tone, timbre, character, just as words and sentences do. The moment a text and typeface are chosen, two streams of thought, two
ITALIC

Letterforms have tone, timbre, charac ter, just as words and sentences do. The moment a text and typeface are chosen,
BOLD

Letterforms have tone, timbre, character, just as words and sentences do. The mo ment a text and typeface are chosen, two
BOLD ITALIC

Conga Brava STD

Michael Harvey, Adobe Systems

`A-z` `€`

Typography

ABCDEFGHIJKLMNOPQRSTU
VWXYZabcdefghijklmnopqrstu
vwxyz&0123456789$€!?.,;:""{½}

Letterforms have tone, timbre, charac ter, just as words and sentences do. The
LIGHT

Letterforms have tone, timbre, char acter, just as words and sentences
REGULAR

Letterforms have tone, timbre, character, just as words and sen
SEMIBOLD

Letterforms have tone, timbre, character, just as words and
BOLD

Letterforms have tone, tim bre, character, just as words
BLACK

Conga Brava STD Stencil

Michael Harvey, Adobe Systems

`A-z` `€`

Typography

ABCDEFGHIJKLMNOPQRSTU
VWXYZabcdefghijklmnopqrstu
vwxyz&0123456789$€!?.,;:""{½}

Letterforms have tone, timbre, char acter, just as words and sentences
REGULAR

Letterforms have tone, timbre, character, just as words and sen
SEMIBOLD

Letterforms have tone, tim bre, character, just as words
BOLD

Letterforms have tone, tim bre, character, just as word
BLACK

C

Cooper Black STD

Oswald Bruce Cooper

Typography

ABCDEFGHIJKLMNOPQR
STUVWXYZabcdefghijkl
mnopqrstuvwxyz&01234
56789$€!?.;:,""{½}

*ABCDEFGHIJKLMNOPQRS
TUVWXYZabcdefghijklmn
opqrstuvwxyz&0123456789
$€!?.;:,""{½}*

**Letterforms have tone,
timbre, character, just as**

REGULAR

*Letterforms have tone,
timbre, character, just as*

ITALIC

Copal STD

David Lemon, Adobe Systems

Copperplate Gothic STD

Frederic W. Goudy

Use each typeface as is or overlap and color them.

DECORATED

OUTLINE

SOLID

TYPOGRAPHY

ABCDEFGHIJKLMNOPQ
RSTUVWXYZABCDEFGHIJ
KLMNOPQRSTUVWXYZ&01
23456789$€!?.;:, ""{½}

LETTERFORMS HAVE TONE,
TIMBRE, CHARACTER, JUST AS

29 AB

LETTERFORMS HAVE TONE, TIMBRE,
CHARACTER, JUST AS WORDS AND SEN

29 BC

LETTERFORMS HAVE TONE, TIMBRE, CHARACTER, JUST AS
30 AB

LETTERFORMS HAVE TONE, TIMBRE, CHARACTER, JUST AS WORDS AND SEN
30 BC

LETTERFORMS HAVE TONE, TIMBRE, CHARAC
31 AB

LETTERFORMS HAVE TONE, TIMBRE, CHARACTER, JUST AS WORDS AND SEN
31 BC

LETTERFORMS HAVE TONE, TIMBRE, CHARACTER, JUST AS
32 AB

LETTERFORMS HAVE TONE, TIMBRE, CHARACTER, JUST AS
32 BC

LETTERFORMS HAVE TONE, TIMBRE, CHARACTER, JUST AS
33 BC

Coriander STD

Tim Donaldson, Adobe Systems

A-z €

Corona STD

Chauncey H. Griffith, Linotype Library GmbH

A-z €

Typography

ABCDEFGHIJKLMNOPQR
STUVWXYZabcdefghijklm
nopqrstuvwxyz&0123456789
$€!?.;:,""{½}

*ABCDEFGHIJKLMNOPQRS
TUVWXYZabcdefghijklmnop
qrstuvwxyz&0123456789$€!?
.;:,""{½}*

Letterforms have tone, timbre, character, just as words and sen tences do. The moment a text
REGULAR

Letterforms have tone, timbre, char acter, just as words and sentences do. The moment a text and typeface
ITALIC

Letterforms have tone, timbre, character, just as words and sen tences do. The moment a text
BOLD NO. 2

REGULAR

Coronet STD

R. Hunter Middleton, Ludlow Type Foundry

A-Z **€**

Typography

Aa Bb Cc Dd Ee Ff Gg Hh Ii Jj Kk Ll Mm Nn Oo Pp Qq Rr Ss Tt Uu Vv Ww Xx Yy Zz & 012345678 9$€!?.,;:, ""{½}

Letterforms have tone, timbre, character, just as words and sentences do. The moment a text
REGULAR

Letterforms have tone, timbre, character, just as words and sentences do. The mo
BOLD

Cottonwood STD

Barbara Lind, Joy Redick, and Kim Buker Chansler, Adobe Systems

A-Z **€**

TYPOGRAPHY

ABCDEFGHIJKLMNOP QRSTUVWXYZ&01234 56789$€!?.,;:, ""{½}

LETTERFORMS HAVE TONE, TIMBE, CHARAC
MEDIUM

Courier STD

Howard Kettler, IBM

A-Z **€**

Typography

ABCDEFGHIJKLMNOPQRSTUVWXYZ
abcdefghijklmnopqrstuvwxyz
&0123456789$€!?.;:, ""{½}

ABCDEFGHIJKLMNOPQRSTUVWXYZ
abcdefghijklmnopqrstuvwxyz
&0123456789$€!?.;:, ""{½}

Letterforms have tone, timbre, character, just as words and sentences do. The moment a
MEDIUM

Letterforms have tone, timbre, character, just as words and sentences do. The moment a
MEDIUM OBLIQUE

Letterforms have tone, tim bre, character, just as words and sentences do. The moment
BOLD

Letterforms have tone, timbre, character, just as words and sentences do. The moment a
BOLD OBLIQUE

Critter STD

Craig Frazier, Adobe Systems

A-Z €

**ABCDEFGHIJKLMN
OPQRSTUVWXYZ&
0123456789$€!?.;:,""''{½}**

**LETTERFORMS HAVE
TONE, TIMBRE, CHARAC**

REGULAR

Cronos PRO

Robert Slimbach, Adobe Systems

A-Z € ffi BB 619 123 ⅞ H₂ 1st 𝒜 ê ↝ aA

Typography

ABCDEFGHIJKLMNOPQRSTUVW
XYZabcdefghijklmnopqrstuvwxyz&
ABCDEFGHIJKLMNOPQRSTUVWXYZ&

*ABCDEFGHIJKLMNOPQRSTUVWXYZ
abcdefghijklmnopqrstuvwxyz&ABC
DEFGHIJKLMNOPQRSTUVWXYZ&ABCDE
FGHIJKLMNOPQRSTUVWXYZg*

0123456789 0123456789
0123456789 0123456789

0123456789 0123456789
0123456789 0123456789
Proportional and Tabular Figures

Qℚ ſ a d e h l m n o r t u ᵃᵇᵈᵉᵍʰⁱˡᵐⁿᵒʳˢᵗ
Th ct ff ffi ffj fj ffl fi fj fl sp st
Alternates, Ligatures & Superiors

*Qℚ ſ a d e h l m n o r t u ᵃᵇᵈᵉᵍʰⁱˡᵐⁿᵒʳˢᵗ
Th ct fi fj fl ff ffi ffj ffl sp st*
Italic Alternates, Ligatures & Superiors

Ø$¢£¥ƒ₡¤€#Rp%‰$¢£¥ƒ₡€#$¢%‰⁰¹
₂₃₄₅₆₇₈₉($¢-.,)₀₁₂₃₄₅₆₇₈₉($¢-.,)/₀₁₂₃₄₅₆₇₈₉($¢-.,)₀₁₂₃
₄₅₆₇₈₉($¢-.,) ¼ ½ ¾ ⅛ ⅜ ⅝ ⅞ ⅓ ⅔ ^ ~ · + ± < = > –
| ¦ × ÷ ∂ μ π Δ Π Σ Ω √ ∞ ∫ ≈ ≠ ≤ ≥ ◊ ¬ № ℮ ℓ º ao
_ ‒ – — ‐ – — ' " " " „ ' « » ‹ › ‹ › ›, ‥; … ‥
‥ ·¹?¡¿¡?¡¿ ( ) ( ) [ ] [ ] { } { } / \ * • § † ‡ ¶ © ©™ @ @
Currency, Punctuation, and Related Forms

*Ø$¢£¥ƒ₡¤€#Rp%‰$¢£¥ƒ₡€#$¢%‰ ⁰¹²³
₄₅₆₇₈₉($¢-.,)₀₁₂₃₄₅₆₇₈₉($¢-.,)/₀₁₂₃₄₅₆₇₈₉($¢-.,)₀₁₂₃₄₅
₆₇₈₉($¢-.,) ¼ ½ ¾ ⅛ ⅜ ⅝ ⅞ ⅓ ⅔ ^ ~ · + ± < = > – | ¦
× ÷ ∂ μ π Δ Π Σ Ω √ ∞ ∫ ≈ ≠ ≤ ≥ ◊ ¬ № ℮ ℓ º ao _
‒ – — ‐ – — ' " " " „ ' « » ‹ › ‹ › ›, ‥; … ‥ ‥ ·
!?¡¿¡?¡¿ ( ) ( ) [ ] [ ] { } { } / \ * • § † ‡ ¶ © ©™ @ @*
Italic Currency, Punctuation, and Related Forms

ÆŁØŒÞÐÁÂÄÀÅÃÇÉÊËÈÍÎÏÌÑÓÔ
ÖÒÕŠÚÛÜÙÝŸŽĂĀĄĆČĎĐĚĖĒĘĞ
ĢĪĮĶĹĽĻŃŇŅŐŌŔŘŖŚŞŠŢŤŰŪŲŮŹ
ŻÆĆĈČĚŊĜĠĦĤĨ IJ ĨJĿĂŎŐŜŦŨŬŴŴ
ŴÛŴŶŶÆɪŁØŒßÞðáâäàåãçéêëèíîïìñó
ôöòõšúûüùýÿžăāąćčďðěėēęğğīįĶĺľļń
ňņőōŕřŗśşşŧťűūųůźźæĉĉěŋĝĝħĥĩ ij ĩĵ ĺⁿ

ŏøŝţũũẃŵẅẁŷỳķÆŁØŒÞÐÁÂÄÀÅÃÇÉ
ÊËÈÍÎÏÌÑÓÔÖÒÕŠÚÛÜÙÝŸŽĂĀĄĆĈČĎĐĚĒ
ĘĞĢĪĮĶĹĽĻŃŇŅŐŌŔŘŖŚŞŠŢŤŲŰŪŲŮŹŻÆ
ĈČĚŊĜĞĦĤĬ IJ ĨĴĿŎŐŚŤŲŨŴŴŴẀŶỲ
Accented Characters

ÆŁØŒÞÐÁÂÄÀÅÃÇÉÊËÈÍÎÏÌÑÓÔÖ
ÒÕŠÚÛÜÙÝŸŽĂĀĄĆĈČĎĐĚĒĘĞĢĪĶ
ĹĽĻŃŇŅŐŌŔŘŖŚŞŠŢŤŲŰŪŲŮŹŻÆĈ
ĚŊĜĞĦĤĬ IJ ĨĴĿŎØŜŤŲŨẂŴẄẀŶỲ
æıłøœßþðáâäàåãçéêëèíîïìñóôöòõšúûü
ùýÿžăāąćĉčďđěėēęğ ġ ĩĶ ĺľļ ńňņ ŏōŕřŗśşšţ
űūųůźżæĉčěŋĝ ġ ĥ ĥ ij ĩ ĵ ľ ńŏøŝţũũẃŵẅẁ
ŷỳ ķ ÆŁØŒÞÐÁÂÄÀÅÃÇÉÊËÈÍÎÏÌ ÑÓÔÖÒÕ
ŠÚÛÜÙÝŸŽĂĀĄĆĈČĎĐĚĖĒĘĞĢĪĶĹĽĻŃŇŅŐ
ŌŔŘŖŚŞŠŢŤŲŰŪŲŮŹŻÆĈČĚŊĜĞĦĤĬ IJ ĨĴĿŎŐ
ŜŤŲŨẂŴẄẀŶỲ
Italic Accented Characters

🍃🎋 🌿🎍🎏🌱🌾 ➳ ➤ ～ 〰 ✤ 🐚 🥨🐌💀
Ornaments

LETTERFORMS HAVE TONE, timbre, character, just
as words and 567 sentences do. The moment
a text and typeface are chosen, two streams of
LIGHT

LETTERFORMS HAVE TONE, timbre, character, just
as words and 567 sentences do. The moment
a text and typeface are chosen, two streams of
LIGHT ITALIC

LETTERFORMS HAVE TONE, timbre, character,
just as words and 567 sentences do. The mo
ment a text and typeface are chosen, two
REGULAR

LETTERFORMS HAVE TONE, timbre, character, just
as words and 567 sentences do. The moment
a text and typeface are chosen, two streams of
ITALIC

LETTERFORMS HAVE TONE, timbre, character,
just as words and 567 sentences do. The mo
ment a text and typeface are chosen, two
SEMIBOLD

LETTERFORMS HAVE TONE, timbre, character,
just as words and 567 sentences do. The mo
ment a text and typeface are chosen, two
SEMIBOLD ITALIC

LETTERFORMS HAVE TONE, timbre, charac
ter, just as words and 567 sentences do. The
moment a text and typeface are chosen,
BOLD

LETTERFORMS HAVE TONE, timbre, character,
just as words and 567 sentences do. The mo
ment a text and typeface are chosen, two
BOLD ITALIC

€ Cronos PRO Opticals

Robert Slimbach, Adobe Systems

| A-Z | € | ffi | BB | 619 | 123 | 7⁄8 | H₂ | 1st | 𝒜 | ę̃ | 🐚 | aA |

LETTERFORMS HAVE TONE, timbre, character, just as words and 567 sen
tences do. The moment a text and typeface are chosen, two streams

LETTERFORMS HAVE TONE, timbre, character, just
as words and 567 sentences do. The moment a

LETTERFORMS have tone, timbre,
character, just as words and 567

LETTERFORMS have tone,
timbre, character, just as
LIGHT: CAPTION, REGULAR, SUBHEAD, DISPLAY

Letterforms have tone, timbre, character, just as words and 567 sentences do. The moment a text and typeface are chosen, two streams

Letterforms have tone, timbre, character, just as words and 567 sentences do. The moment a

Letterforms have tone, timbre, character, just as words and 567

Letterforms have tone, timbre, character, just as

LIGHT ITALIC: CAPTION, REGULAR, SUBHEAD, DISPLAY

Letterforms have tone, timbre, character, just as words and 567 sentences do. The moment a text and typeface are chosen, two

Letterforms have tone, timbre, character, just as words and 567 sentences do. The mo

Letterforms have tone, timbre, character, just as words and 567

Letterforms have tone, timbre, character, just

CAPTION, REGULAR, SUBHEAD, DISPLAY

Letterforms have tone, timbre, character, just as words and 567 sentences do. The moment a text and typeface are chosen, two streams

Letterforms have tone, timbre, character, just as words and 567 sentences do. The moment a

Letterforms have tone, timbre, character, just as words and 567

Letterforms have tone, timbre, character, just as

ITALIC: CAPTION, REGULAR, SUBHEAD, DISPLAY

Letterforms have tone, timbre, character, just as words and 567 sentences do. The moment a text and typeface are chosen,

Letterforms have tone, timbre, character, just as words and 567 sentences do. The mo

Letterforms have tone, timbre, character, just as words

Letterforms have tone, timbre, character,

SEMIBOLD: CAPTION, REGULAR, SUBHEAD, DISPLAY

Letterforms have tone, timbre, character, just as words and 567 sentences do. The moment a text and typeface are chosen, two

Letterforms have tone, timbre, character, just as words and 567 sentences do. The mo

Letterforms have tone, timbre, character, just as words and sen

Letterforms have tone, timbre, character,

SEMIBOLD ITALIC: CAPTION, REGULAR, SUBHEAD, DISPLAY

Letterforms have tone, timbre, character, just as words and 567 sentences do. The moment a text and typeface are chosen,

Letterforms have tone, timbre, character, just as words and 567 sentences do.

Letterforms have tone, timbre, character, just as words

Letterforms have tone, timbre, character,

BOLD: CAPTION, REGULAR, SUBHEAD, DISPLAY

LETTERFORMS HAVE TONE, timbre, character, just as words and 567 sentences do. The moment a text and typeface are chosen, two

LETTERFORMS HAVE TONE, timbre, character, just as words and 567 sentences do. The mo

LETTERFORMS have tone, timbre, character, just as words and

LETTERFORMS have to ne, timbre, character,

BOLD ITALIC: CAPTION, REGULAR, SUBHEAD, DISPLAY

ITC Cushing STD

Vincent Pacella, ITC

A-z €

Typography

ABCDEFGHIJKLMNOPQRSTUVW
XYZabcdefghijklmnopqrstuvwxyz
&0123456789$€!?.;:,""{½}

*ABCDEFGHIJKLMNOPQRSTUVW
XYZabcdefghijklmnopqrstuvwxyz&
0123456789$€!?.;:,""{½}*

Letterforms have tone, timbre, character, just as words and sentences do. The mo ment a text and typeface are chosen, two
BOOK

Letterforms have tone, timbre, character, just as words and sentences do. The moment a text and typeface are chosen, two streams of
BOOK ITALIC

Letterforms have tone, timbre, character, just as words and sentences do. The mo ment a text and typeface are chosen, two
MEDIUM

Letterforms have tone, timbre, character, just as words and sentences do. The moment a text and typeface are chosen, two streams
MEDIUM ITALIC

Letterforms have tone, timbre, charac ter, just as words and sentences do. The moment a text and typeface are chosen,
BOLD

Letterforms have tone, timbre, character, just as words and sentences do. The mo ment a text and typeface are chosen, two
BOLD ITALIC

Letterforms have tone, timbre, charac ter, just as words and sentences do. The moment a text and typeface are
HEAVY

Letterforms have tone, timbre, character, just as words and sentences do. The mo ment a text and typeface are chosen, two
HEAVY ITALIC

Cutout STD

Gail Blumberg, Adobe Systems

A-z €

TYPOGRAPHY

ABCDEFGHIJKLMN
OPQRSTUVWXYZ&01
23456789$€!?.;:,""{½}

LETTERFORMS HAVE
TONE, TIMBRE, CHAR
REGULAR

Dante STD

Giovanni Mardersteig, Monotype Corp.

A-z € ffi BB 619 123 ⅞ H₂ 1st ℰ Ⓐ

Typography

ABCDEFGHIJKLMNOPQRSTUV
WXYZabcdefghijklmnopqrstuvwxy
z&0123456789$€!?.;:,""{½}

ABCDEFGHIJKLMNOPQRSTUVWXYZ&0123
456789 ffi ⅛ 0123456789

ABCDEFGHIJKLMNOPQRST
UVWXYZ&0123456789
Titling

*ABCDEFGHIJKLMNOPQRSTUVWX
YZabcdefghijklmnopqrstuvwxyz&0123
456789$€!?.;:,""{½}*

0123456789 ffi ⅛ 0123456789

g ʒ gg ʒy
Alternates and Ligatures

LETTERFORMS HAVE TONE, timbre, character,
just as words and 567 sentences do. The mo
ment a text and typeface are chosen, two
REGULAR

*Letterforms have tone, timbre, character, just as
words and 567 sentences do. The moment a text
and typeface are chosen, two streams of thought,*
ITALIC

Letterforms have tone, timbre, character,
just as words and 567 sentences do. The mo
ment a text and typeface are chosen, two
MEDIUM

*Letterforms have tone, timbre, character, just as
words and 567 sentences do. The moment a text
and typeface are chosen, two streams of thought*
MEDIUM ITALIC

**Letterforms have tone, timbre, character,
just as words and 567 sentences do. The
moment a text and typeface are chosen,**
BOLD

***Letterforms have tone, timbre, character, just
as words and 567 sentences do. The moment a
text and typeface are chosen, two streams of***
BOLD ITALIC

Linotype Decoration Pi STD

Linotype Staff

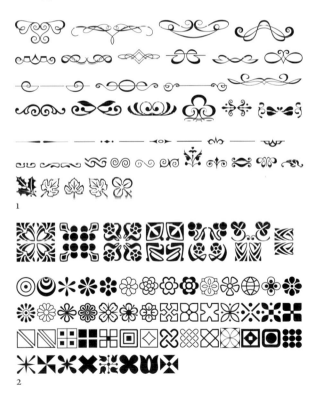

1

2

Delphin STD

Georg Trump, Linotype Library GmbH

A-z € 619 ç̆

Typography

ABCDEFGHIJKLMNOPQRS
TUVWXYZabcdefghijklmnopq
rstuvwxyz&0123456789$€
!?.;:,""{½}

dgs
Alternates

Letterforms have tone, timbre, char
acter, just as words and sentences do.
I

Letterforms have tone, timbre, char
acter, just as words and sentences
II

Linotype Didot STD

Adrian Frutiger, Linotype Library GmbH

A-z € BB 619 123 A ✎

Typography

ABCDEFGHIJKLMNOPQRST
UVWXYZabcdefghijklmnopqrst
uvwxyz&0123456789$€!?.;:,""{½}

*ABCDEFGHIJKLMNOPQRSTU
VWXYZabcdefghijklmnopqrstuvw
xyz&0123456789$€!?.;:, ""{½}*

LETTERFORMS HAVE TONE, timbre, char
acter, just as words and 567 sentences
do. The moment a text and typeface
ROMAN

*Letterforms have tone, timbre, character,
just as words and 567 sentences do. The
moment a text and typeface are chosen,*
ITALIC

**Letterforms have tone, timbre, char
acter, just as words and 567 sentences
do. The moment a text and typeface**
BOLD

Letterforms have tone, tim
bre, character, just as words
HEADLINE

ORNAMENTS

DIN Schriften STD

Linotype Staff

A-z € 123 ç̆

Typography

ABCDEFGHIJKLMNOPQRSTUVW
XYZabcdefghijklmnopqrstuvwxyz
&0123456789$€!?.;:,""{½}

69
Alternates

Letterforms have tone, timbre, character,
just as words and sentences do. The mo
ment a text and typeface are chosen, two
MITTELSCHRIFT

Letterforms have tone, timbre, character, just as words and sentences do. The moment a text and typeface are chosen, two streams of thought, two rhythmical systems
ENGSCHRIFT

Typography

ABCDEFGHIJKLMNOPQRSTUV
WXYZabcdefghijklmnopqrstu
vwxyz&0123456789$€!?.;:,""{½}

Letterforms have tone, timbre, charac ter, just as words and sentences do. The moment a text and typeface are
NEUZEIT GROTESK LIGHT

Letterforms have tone, timbre, character, just as words and sentences do. The moment a text and typeface are chosen, two streams of thought, two
NEUZEIT GROTESK BOLD CONDENSED

Diotima STD

Gudrun Zapf von Hesse, Linotype Library GmbH

A-z € BB 619

Typography

ABCDEFGHIJKLMNOPQ
RSTUVWXYZabcdefghij
klmnopqrstuvwxyz&012
3456789$€!?.;:, ""{½}

ABCDEFGHIJKLMNOPQRSTUV
WXYZ&0123456789

ABCDEFGHIJKLMNOPQR
STUVWXYZabcdefghijklm
nopqrstuvwxyz&01234567
89$€!?.;:, ""{½}

0123456789

LETTERFORMS HAVE TONE, tim bre, character, just as words
ROMAN

Letterforms have tone, timbre, char acter, just as words and 567 sen
ITALIC

Diskus STD

Martin Wilke, Linotype Library GmbH

A-z €

Typography

Aa Bb Cc Dd Ee Ff Gg
Hh Ii Jj Kk Ll Mm
Nn Oo Pp Qq Rr Ss Tt
Uu Vv Ww Xx Yy Zz
&0123456789$€!?.;:, ""{½}

Letterforms have tone, timbre, character, just as words and sentences do. The mo
REGULAR

Letterforms have tone, timbre, char acter, just as words and sentences do.
BOLD

Dom Casual STD

Peter Dombrezian

A-z €

Typography

ABCDEFGHIJKLMNOPQRSTUV
WXYZabcdefghijklmnopqrstuvwx
yz&0123456789$€!?.;:,""{½}

Letterforms have tone, timbre, char
acter, just as words and sentences
REGULAR

**Letterforms have tone, timbre,
character, just as words and sen**
BOLD

Dorchester Script STD

Unknown, Monotype Corp.

A-z €

Typography

ABCDEFGHIJKLMNOPQ
RSTUVWXYZabcdefghijklmnopqr
stuvwxyz&0123456789$€!?.;:,""{½}

Letterforms have tone, timbre, character,
just as words and sentences do. The mo
REGULAR

Doric STD

Unknown

A-z €

Typography
ABCDEFGHIJKLM
NOPQRSTUVWXY
Zabcdefghijklmnop
qrstuvwxyz&01234
56789$€!?.;:,{½}

**Letterforms have
tone, timbre, charac**
BOLD

Duc De Berry STD

Gottfried Pott, Linotype Library GmbH

A-z € ﬅ

Typography

ABCDEFGHIJKLMN
OPQRSTUVWXYZ
abcdefghijklmnopqrstuvwxyz
&0123456789$€!?.;:,""{½}

ch ck ff ft tz ſ ſi ſſ ſt ll
Historic Blackletter

Letterforms have tone, timbre,
character, just as words and sen
REGULAR

Eccentric STD

Gustav F. Schroeder

`A-z` `€`

TYPOGRAPHY

ABCDEFGHIJKLMNOPQRSTUVWXYZ&
0123456789$€!?.;:,""{½}

LETTERFORMS HAVE TONE, TIMBRE, CHAR
ACTER, JUST AS WORDS AND SENTENCES
REGULAR

Egyptienne F STD

Adrian Frutiger, Linotype Library GmbH

`A-z` `€`

Typography

ABCDEFGHIJKLMNOPQRSTU
VWXYZabcdefghijklmnopqrstu
vwxyz&0123456789$€!?.;:,""{½}

ABCDEFGHIJKLMNOPQRSTUV
WXYZabcdefghijklmnopqrstuv
wxyz&0123456789$€!?.;:,""{½}

Letterforms have tone, timbre, char
acter, just as words and sentences
do. The moment a text and typeface
55 ROMAN

Letterforms have tone, timbre, char
acter, just as words and sentences
do. The moment a text and typeface
56 ITALIC

Letterforms have tone, timbre, char
acter, just as words and sentences
do. The moment a text and typeface
65 BOLD

Letterforms have tone, timbre,
character, just as words and sen
tences do. The moment a text and
75 BLACK

Ehrhardt STD

Unknown, Monotype Corp.

`A-z` `€`

Typography

ABCDEFGHIJKLMNOPQRSTU
VWXYZabcdefghijklmnopqrstuvw
xyz&0123456789$€!?.;:,""{½}

ABCDEFGHIJKLMNOPQRSTU
VWXYZabcdefghijklmnopqrstuvwxy
z&0123456789$€!?.;:,""{½}

Letterforms have tone, timbre, character,
just as words and sentences do. The moment
a text and typeface are chosen, two streams
REGULAR

Letterforms have tone, timbre, character, just as
words and sentences do. The moment a text and
typeface are chosen, two streams of thought,
ITALIC

Letterforms have tone, timbre, charac
ter, just as words and sentences do. The
moment a text and typeface are chosen,
SEMI BOLD

Letterforms have tone, timbre, character,
just as words and sentences do. The mo
ment a text and typeface are chosen, two
SEMI BOLD ITALIC

Electra STD

William A. Dwiggins, Linotype Library GmbH

A-z € BB 619

Typography

ABCDEFGHIJKLMNOPQRSTU
VWXYZabcdefghijklmnopqrstuvw
xyz&0123456789$€!?.,;:,""{½}

ABCDEFGHIJKLMNOPQRSTUVWXYZ&
0123456789

*ABCDEFGHIJKLMNOPQRSTU
VWXYZabcdefghijklmnopqrstuvwx
yz&0123456789$€!?.,;:,""{½}*
0123456789

LETTERFORMS HAVE TONE, timbre, charac
ter, just as words and 567 sentences do.
The moment a text and typeface are cho
REGULAR

*Letterforms have tone, timbre, character,
just as words and 567 sentences do. The mo
ment a text and typeface are chosen, two*
CURSIVE

**LETTERFORMS HAVE TONE, timbre, charac
ter, just as words and 567 sentences do.
The moment a text and typeface are cho**
BOLD

***Letterforms have tone, timbre, character,
just as words and 567 sentences do. The
moment a text and typeface are chosen,***
BOLD CURSIVE

Letterforms have tone, timbre, char
acter, just as words and sentences do
DISPLAY

*Letterforms have tone, timbre, charac
ter, just as words and sentences do.*
CURSIVE DISPLAY

**Letterforms have tone, timbre, cha
racter, just as words and sentences**
BOLD DISPLAY

***Letterforms have tone, timbre, char
acter, just as words and sentences***
BOLD CURSIVE DISPLAY

Ellington STD

Michael Harvey, Monotype Corp.

A-z €

Typography

ABCDEFGHIJKLMNOPQRSTUVW
XYZabcdefghijklmnopqrstuvwxyz
&0123456789$€!?.,;:,""{½}

*ABCDEFGHIJKLMNOPQRSTUVW
XYZabcdefghijklmnopqrstuvwxyz
&0123456789$€!?.,;:,""{½}*

Letterforms have tone, timbre, character, just
as words and sentences do. The moment a text
and typeface are chosen, two streams of thoug
LIGHT

*Letterforms have tone, timbre, character, just as
words and sentences do. The moment a text and
typeface are chosen, two streams of thought, two*
LIGHT ITALIC

Letterforms have tone, timbre, character,
just as words and sentences do. The moment
a text and typeface are chosen, two streams
REGULAR

Letterforms have tone, timbre, character, just
as words and sentences do. The moment a text
and typeface are chosen, two streams of thoug
ITALIC

Letterforms have tone, timbre, character,
just as words and sentences do. The mo
ment a text and typeface are chosen, two
BOLD

Letterforms have tone, timbre, character,
just as words and sentences do. The mo
ment a text and typeface are chosen, two
BOLD ITALIC

Letterforms have tone, timbre, char
acter, just as words and sentences do.
The moment a text and typeface are
EXTRA BOLD

Letterforms have tone, timbre, char
acter, just as words and sentences do.
The moment a text and typeface are
EXTRA BOLD ITALIC

Else NPL STD

Robert Norton, Norton Photosetting Ltd.

A-z €

Typography

ABCDEFGHIJKLMNOPQRSTU
VWXYZabcdefghijklmnopqrstuv
wxyz&0123456789$€!?.;:,""{½}

Letterforms have tone, timbre, character,
just as words and sentences do. The mo
ment a text and typeface are chosen, two
LIGHT

Letterforms have tone, timbre, character,
just as words and sentences do. The mo
ment a text and typeface are chosen, two
MEDIUM

Letterforms have tone, timbre, character,
just as words and sentences do. The mo
ment a text and typeface are chosen, two
SEMI BOLD

Letterforms have tone, timbre, character,
just as words and sentences do. The mo
ment a text and typeface are chosen, two
BOLD

MVB Emmascript STD

Kanna Aoki, MVB Fonts

A-z € 123

Typography

ABCDEFGHIJKLMNOPQRSTU
VWXYZabcdefghijklmnopqr
stuvwxyz&0123456789$€!?
.;:,""{½}

Letterforms have tone, timbre, char
acter, just as words and sentences
REGULAR

Engravers STD

Linotype Staff

A-z €

TYPOGRAPH

ABCDEFGHIJKLMNO
PQRSTUVWXYZABCD
EFGHIJKLMNOPQRSTU
VWXYZ&0123456789
$€!?.;:,""{½}

LETTERFORMS HAVE TONE,
TIMBRE, CHARACTER, JUST
BOLD FACE

ITC Eras STD

Albert Boton and Albert Hollenstein, ITC

A-z €

Typography

ABCDEFGHIJKLMNOPQRSTUVW
XYZabcdefghijklmnopqrstuvwxyz
&0123456789$€!?.;:,""{½}

Letterforms have tone, timbre, character,
just as words and sentences do. The mo
ment a text and typeface are chosen, two
LIGHT

Letterforms have tone, timbre, character,
just as words and sentences do. The mo
ment a text and typeface are chosen,
BOOK

Letterforms have tone, timbre, charac
ter, just as words and sentences do.
The moment a text and typeface are
MEDIUM

Letterforms have tone, timbre, char
acter, just as words and sentences
do. The moment a text and typefa
DEMI

Letterforms have tone, timbre,
character, just as words and sen
tences do. The moment a text
BOLD

Letterforms have tone, timbre,
character, just as words and
sentences do. The moment a
ULTRA

ITC Esprit STD

Jovica Veljovic, ITC

A-z €

Typography

ABCDEFGHIJKLMNOPQRSTU
VWXYZabcdefghijklmnopqrstuv
wxyz&0123456789$€!?.;:,""{ ½ }

*ABCDEFGHIJKLMNOPQRSTU
VWXYZabcdefghijklmnopqrstuvw
xyz&0123456789$€!?.;:,""{ ½ }*

Letterforms have tone, timbre, character,
just as words and sentences do. The mo
ment a text and typeface are chosen, two
BOOK

*Letterforms have tone, timbre, character,
just as words and sentences do. The mo
ment a text and typeface are chosen, two*
BOOK ITALIC

Letterforms have tone, timbre, charac
ter, just as words and sentences do.
The moment a text and typeface are
MEDIUM

Letterforms have tone, timbre, character,
just as words and sentences do. The mo
ment a text and typeface are chosen, two
MEDIUM ITALIC

Letterforms have tone, timbre, char
acter, just as words and sentences
do. The moment a text and typeface
BOLD

Letterforms have tone, timbre, charac
ter, just as words and sentences do.
The moment a text and typeface are
BOLD ITALIC

Letterforms have tone, timbre, cha
racter, just as words and sentences
do. The moment a text and typefa
BLACK

Letterforms have tone, timbre, cha
racter, just as words and sentences
do. The moment a text and typeface
BLACK ITALIC

European Pi STD

Linotype Staff

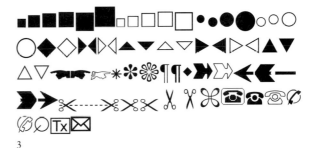

1

2

3

4

Eurostile STD

Aldo Novarese and A. Butti, Nebiolo

A-z €

Typography

ABCDEFGHIJKLMNOPQRSTU
VWXYZabcdefghijklmnopqrst
uvwxyz&0123456789$€!?.;
:,""{½}

ABCDEFGHIJKLMNOPQRSTU
VWXYZabcdefghijklmnopqrst
uvwxyz&0123456789$€!?.;
:,""{½}

Letterforms have tone, timbre, char
acter, just as words and sentences
do. The moment a text and typeface

REGULAR

*Letterforms have tone, timbre, char
acter, just as words and sentences
do. The moment a text and typeface*

OBLIQUE

**Letterforms have tone, timbre,
character, just as words and sen
tences do. The moment a text and**

DEMI

*Letterforms have tone, timbre,
character, just as words and sen
tences do. The moment a text and*

DEMI OBLIQUE

**Letterforms have tone, timbre,
character, just as words and sen
tences do. The moment a text**

BOLD

***Letterforms have tone, timbre,
character, just as words and sen
tences do. The moment a text***

BOLD OBLIQUE

Eurostile STD Condensed and Extended

Aldo Novarese and A. Butti, Nebiolo

A-Z €

Typography

ABCDEFGHIJKLMNOPQRSTUVW
XYZabcdefghijklmnopqrstuvwxyz&
0123456789$€!?.;:,""{½}

Letterforms have tone, timbre, character,
just as words and sentences do. The mo
ment a text and typeface are chosen, two

CONDENSED

**Letterforms have tone, timbre, character,
just as words and sentences do. The mo
ment a text and typeface are chosen, two**

BOLD CONDENSED

Typography

ABCDEFGHIJKLMN
OPQRSTUVWXYZ
abcdefghijklmnopqrst
uvwxyz&01234567
89$€!?.;:,""{½}

Letterforms have tone,
timbre, character, just as
words and sentences do.

EXTENDED NO. 2

**Letterforms have tone,
timbre, character, just as
words and sentences do.**

BOLD EXTENDED NO. 2

Ex Ponto PRO

Jovica Veljovic, Adobe Systems

A-z € ffi 619 123 e

Typography

ABCDEFGHIJKLMNP
QRSTUVWXYZabcdefghijklm
nopqrstuvwxyz&

ABCDEFGHIJKLMNOPQRST
UVWXYZ
Titling

0123456789 0123456789

0123456789
Proportional and Tabular Figures

A E F H J L Y Z d e g k p s v w z
ct ff ffi ffi ffl fi fl ft st st tf tt tz
Alternates and Ligatures

f i m n r r t u u v w
Beginning

a a d e f h l l m n r s t n
Ending

Ø $¢£¥ƒ€¤#%‰$¢£¥ƒ€$¢£¥ƒ€
#%‰123¼½¾^~·+±<=>-|¦×÷∂μπ
ΔΠΣΩ√∞∫≈≠≤≥∂¬el°ao ___—- ' " (")

„" ‚‹›‹› ,.:; ...·!?¡¿()[]{}/\ *·ſſt
≠¢©®™@
Currency, Punctuation, and Related Forms

ÆŁØŒÞÐÁÂÄÀÅÃÇÉÊÊ
ÈÍÎÏÌÑÓÔÖÒÕŠÚÛÜÙÝŸŽ
ĂĄÇĆČĎĐĚĖĒĘĞĢĪĮĶĹĽĻ
ŃŇŅŐŐŘŘŖŚŞŤŢŬŪŲŮ
ŹŻæłøœßþðáâäàåãçéêëèíîïìñóôöòõ
úûüùýÿžăāąćčďěėēęğğįĳķĺľļńňņőőŕřŗ
śşťţŭūųůžż
Accented Characters

*Letterforms have tone, timbre, character,
just as words and 567 sentences do. The mo*
LIGHT

*Letterforms have tone, timbre, character,
just as words and 567 sentences do. The*
REGULAR

**Letterforms have tone, timbre, charac
ter, just as words and 567 sentences do.**
BOLD

The moment a text and typeface
are chosen, two streams of thought,
two rhythmical systems,
two sets of habits, or if you like,
two personalities, intersect.

To download a complete glyph complement PDF, please visit
www.adobe.com/type.

F

Excelsior STD

Chauncey H. Griffith and Linotype Staff,
Linotype Library GmbH

[A-Z] [€]

Typography

ABCDEFGHIJKLMNOPQRS
TUVWXYZabcdefghijklmnop
qrstuvwxyz&0123456789$€!?
.;:;""{½}

Типографика

АБВГЃҐЂЕЁЄЖЗЅИЙIЇJК
ЌЛЉЬМНЊОПРСТЋУЎФХЦ
ЏЧШЩЪЫЬЭЮЯабвгѓґђеё
єжзѕийіїjкќлљьмнњопрстћуў
фхцџчшщъыьэюя

ABCDEFGHIJKLMNOPQRS
TUVWXYZabcdefghijklmnop
qrstuvwxyz&0123456789$€!?
.;:;""{½}

АБВГЃҐЂЕЁЄЖЗЅИЙIЇJК
ЌЛЉЬМНЊОПРСТЋУЎФХЦ
ЏЧШЩЪЫЬЭЮЯабвгѓґђеё
єжзѕийіїjкќлљьмнњопрстћу
ўфхцџчшщъыьэюя

Letterforms have tone, timbre, char
acter, just as words and sentences do.
The moment a text and typeface are

Точно найденные слова достойны
точности в подборе шрифтов; те, в
свою очередь, заслуживают чутко
ROMAN

Letterforms have tone, timbre, char
acter, just as words and sentences do.
The moment a text and typeface are

Точно найденные слова достойны
точности в подборе шрифтов; те,
в свою очередь, заслуживают чут
ITALIC

Letterforms have tone, timbre, char
acter, just as words and sentences do.
The moment a text and typeface

Точно найденные слова достойны
точности в подборе шрифтов; те, в
свою очередь, заслуживают чутко
BOLD

Fairfield STD

Rudolph Ruzicka and Alex Kaczun, Linotype Library GmbH

[A-Z] [€] [BB] [619] [A]

Typography

ABCDEFGHIJKLMNOPQRST
UVWXYZabcdefghijklmnopqrstu
vwxyz&0123456789$€!?.;:,""{½}

ABCDEFGHIJKLMNOPQRSTUVWXYZ&
0123456789

ABCDEFGHIJKLMNOPQRST
UVWXYZabcdefghijklmnopqrstu
vwxyz&0123456789$€!?.;:,""{½}
0123456789

ABCDEFGHIJKLMNOPQ
RSTUVWXYZ&
Swash

LETTERFORMS HAVE TONE, timbre, charac
ter, just as words and 567 sentences do.
The moment a text and typeface are cho
45 LIGHT

*Letterforms have tone, timbre, character, just
as words and 567 sentences do. The moment
a text and typeface are chosen, two streams*
46 LIGHT ITALIC

LETTERFORMS HAVE TONE, timbre, charac
ter, just as words and 567 sentences do.
The moment a text and typeface are cho
55 MEDIUM

*Letterforms have tone, timbre, character,
just as words and 567 sentences do. The
moment a text and typeface are chosen,*
56 MEDIUM ITALIC

**LETTERFORMS HAVE TONE, timbre, char
acter, just as words and 567 sentences
do. The moment a text and typeface**
75 BOLD

***Letterforms have tone, timbre, charac
ter, just as words and 567 sentences do.
The moment a text and typeface are***
76 BOLD ITALIC

**LETTERFORMS HAVE TONE, timbre,
character, just as words and 567
sentences do. The moment a text**
85 HEAVY

***Letterforms have tone, timbre, char
acter, just as words and 567 senten
ces do. The moment a text and type***
86 HEAVY ITALIC

Fairfield STD Caption

Rudolph Ruzicka and Alex Kaczun, Linotype Library GmbH

`A-Z` `€`

*Letterforms have tone, timbre, character, just as words and sen
tences do. The moment a text and typeface are chosen, two*
45 LIGHT CAPTION

*Letterforms have tone, timbre, character, just as words and
sentences do. The moment a text and type face are chosen,*
55 CAPTION MEDIUM

***Letterforms have tone, timbre, character, just as words
and sentences do. The moment a text and typeface are***
75 BOLD CAPTION

***Letterforms have tone, timbre, character, just as
words and sentences do. The moment a text and type***
85 HEAVY CAPTION

Falstaff STD

Unknown, Monotype Corp.

`A-Z` `€`

Typography

ABCDEFGHIJKLMNO
PQRSTUVWXYZabcde
fghijklmnopqrstuvwxy
z&0123456789$€!?.;:,
""{½}

**Letterforms have tone,
timbre, character, just**
REGULAR

ITC Fenice STD

Aldo Novarese, ITC

A-z **€**

Typography

ABCDEFGHIJKLMNOPQRSTUVW
XYZabcdefghijklmnopqrstuvwxyz
&0123456789$€!?.;:,""{½}

*ABCDEFGHIJKLMNOPQRSTUVW
XYZabcdefghijklmnopqrstuvwxyz
&0123456789$€!?.;:,""{½}*

Letterforms have tone, timbre, character,
just as words and sentences do. The mo
ment a text and typeface are chosen, two
LIGHT

*Letterforms have tone, timbre, character,
just as words and sentences do. The mo
ment a text and typeface are chosen, two*
LIGHT OBLIQUE

Letterforms have tone, timbre, charac
ter, just as words and sentences do. The
moment a text and typeface are chosen,
REGULAR

*Letterforms have tone, timbre, charac
ter, just as words and sentences do. The
moment a text and typeface are chosen,*
REGULAR OBLIQUE

**Letterforms have tone, timbre, char
acter, just as words and sentences
do. The moment a text and typeface**
BOLD

***Letterforms have tone, timbre, char
acter, just as words and sentences
do. The moment a text and typeface***
BOLD OBLIQUE

**Letterforms have tone,
timbre, character, just**
ULTRA

***Letterforms have tone,
timbre, character, just***
ULTRA OBLIQUE

Fette Fraktur STD

Unknown, Linotype Library GmbH

A-z **€** **ffi** **123** **tʒ**

Typography

ABCDEFGHIJKLM
NOPQRSTUVWXYZ
abcdefghijklmnopqrstuv
wxyz&0123456789$€
!?.;:,""{½}

ch ck ff ft ll ſ ſi ſſ ß ſt tʒ
Historic Blackletter

**Letterforms have tone, tim
bre, character, just as word**
REGULAR

Flood STD

Joachim Müller-Lancé, Adobe Systems

A-Z €

TYPOGRAPHY

ABCDEFGHIJKLMNOPQ
RSTUVWXYZ&0123456
789$€!?.,:;,""{½}

LETTERFORMS HAVE TO
NE, TIMBRE, CHARACTER,

REGULAR

ITC Flora STD

Gerard Unger, ITC

A-Z €

Typography

ABCDEFGHIJKLMNOPQRSTUVWXYZ
abcdefghijklmnopqrstuvwxyz&01
23456789$€!?.;:,""{ ½ }

Letterforms have tone, timbre, character,
just as words and sentences do. The mo
ment a text and typeface are chosen, two

MEDIUM

Letterforms have tone, timbre, charac
ter, just as words and sentences do.
The moment a text and typeface are

BOLD

Florens STD

Garrett Boge, LetterPerfect

A-Z € 123 &

Typography

ABCDEFGHIJKLMNOPQRSTUVWX
YZabcdefghijklmnopqrstuvwxyz&01234
56789$€!?.;:,""{½}

Aa Bb Cc Dd Ee Ff Gg Hh
Ii Jj Kk Ll Mm Nn Oo Pp
Qq Rr Ss Tt Uu Vv Ww Xx
Yy Zz 0123456789 &

Letterforms have tone, timbre, charac
ter, just as words and sentences do. The

REGULAR

Flyer STD

Unknown, Linotype Library GmbH

A-Z € 123

Typography

ABCDEFGHIJKLMNOPQRST
UVWXYZabcdefghijklmno
pqrstuvwxyz&0123456789
$€!?.;:,""{½}

Letterforms have tone, tim bre, character, just as words
BLACK CONDENSED

Letterforms have tone, timbre, charac ter, just as words and sentences do.
EXTRA BLACK CONDENSED

Folio STD

Konrad F. Bauer and Walter Baum, Bauer Types, S.A.

Typography

ABCDEFGHIJKLMNOPQRSTU
VWXYZabcdefghijklmnopqrstuv
wxyz&0123456789$€!?.,:;""{½}

Letterforms have tone, timbre, charac ter, just as words and sentences do. The moment a text and typeface are chosen
LIGHT

Letterforms have tone, timbre, charac ter, just as words and sentences do. The moment a text and typeface are
MEDIUM

Letterforms have tone, timbre, character, just as words and sen tences do. The moment a text
BOLD

Letterforms have tone, timbre, character, just as words and sentences do. The moment a
EXTRA BOLD

Letterforms have tone, timbre, character, just as words and sentences do. The moment a text and typeface are chosen, two streams of thought, two
BOLD CONDENSED

Forte STD

Carl Reissberger, Monotype Corp.

Typography

ABCDEFGHIJKLMNOP QRSTUVWXYZabcdefghi jklmnopqrstuvwxyz&012 3456789$€!?.,;:, ""{½}

Letterforms have tone, timbre, character, just as words and
REGULAR

Fournier STD

Pierre Simon Fournier, Monotype Corp.

Typography

ABCDEFGHIJKLMNOPQRSTUV
WXYZabcdefghijklmnopqrstuvwxyz
&0123456789$€!?.;:,"" {½}

ABCDEFGHIJKLMNOPQRSTUVWXYZ&
0123456789 ffi ⅛ 0123456789

ABCDEFGHIJKLMNOPQRSTUV
WXYZ
Tall Capitals

JQwɪQ ɛt fb fh fj fk ſt
Alternates and Ligatures

ABCDEFGHIJKLMNOPQRSTUV WXYZabcdefghijklmnopqrstuvwxyz& 0123456789$€!?.;:, ""{½}

0123456789 ffi ⅛ 0123456789

ABCDEFGHIJKLMNOPQRST UVWXYZ
Tall Capitals

JQw ct fb fh fj fk st
Alternates and Ligatures

LETTERFORMS HAVE TONE, timbre, character, just as words and 567 sentences do. The moment a text and typeface are chosen, two streams of
REGULAR

Letterforms have tone, timbre, character, just as words and 567 sentences do. The moment a text and typeface are chosen, two streams of thought,
ITALIC

Franklin Gothic STD

Morris Fuller Benton

Typography

ABCDEFGHIJKLMNOPQRS TUVWXYZabcdefghijklmno pqrstuvwxyz&012345678 9$€!?.;:, ""{½}

Letterforms have tone, timbre, character, just as words and sen tences do. The moment a text
NO. 2 ROMAN

Letterforms have tone, timbre, character, just as words and sentences do. The mo ment a text and typeface are chosen, two
CONDENSED

Letterforms have tone, timbre, character, just as words and sentences do. The moment a text and typeface are chosen, two streams of thought, two rhythmical systems
EXTRA CONDENSED

ITC Franklin Gothic STD

Vic Caruso, ITC

Typography

ABCDEFGHIJKLMNOPQRSTUVW XYZabcdefghijklmnopqrstuvwxyz &0123456789$€!?.;:, ""{½}

ABCDEFGHIJKLMNOPQRSTUVWX YZabcdefghijklmnopqrsluvwxyz& 0123456789$€!?.;:, ""{½}

Letterforms have tone, timbre, charac ter, just as words and sentences do. The moment a text and typeface are
BOOK

Letterforms have tone, timbre, character, just as words and sentences do. The mo ment a text and typeface are chosen,
BOOK ITALIC

Letterforms have tone, timbre, character, just as words and sentences do. The mo ment a text and typeface are chosen,
MEDIUM

Letterforms have tone, timbre, character, just as words and sentences do. The mo ment a text and typeface are chosen,
MEDIUM ITALIC

Letterforms have tone, timbre, charac ter, just as words and sentences do. The moment a text and typeface are
DEMI

Letterforms have tone, timbre, charac ter, just as words and sentences do. The moment a text and typeface are
DEMI ITALIC

Letterforms have tone, timbre, char acter, just as words and sentences do. The moment a text and typeface
HEAVY

Letterforms have tone, timbre, char acter, just as words and sentences do. The moment a text and typeface
HEAVY ITALIC

ITC Franklin Gothic STD Compressed

Vic Caruso, ITC

A-z €

Typography

ABCDEFGHIJKLMNOPQRSTUVWXYZ
abcdefghijklmnopqrstuvwxyz&0123456789
$€!?.;:,"" {½}

*ABCDEFGHIJKLMNOPQRSTUVWXYZ
abcdefghijklmnopqrstuvwxyz&0123456789
$€!?.;:, ""{½}*

Letterforms have tone, timbre, character, just as words and sentences do. The moment a text and typeface are chosen, two streams of thought, two rhythmical systems
BOOK COMPRESSED

Letterforms have tone, timbre, character, just as words and sentences do. The moment a text and typeface are chosen, two streams of thought, two rhythmical system
BOOK COMPRESSED ITALIC

Letterforms have tone, timbre, character, just as words and sentences do. The moment a text and type face are chosen, two streams of thought, two rhythm
DEMI COMPRESSED

Letterforms have tone, timbre, character, just as words and sentences do. The moment a text and typeface are chosen, two streams of
DEMI COMPRESSED ITALIC

Letterforms have tone, timbre, character, just as words and sentences do. The moment a text and
BOOK EXTRA COMPRESSED

Letterforms have tone, timbre, character, just as words and sentences do. The moment a text and
DEMI EXTRA COMPRESSED

ITC Franklin Gothic STD Condensed

Vic Caruso, ITC

A-z €

Typography

ABCDEFGHIJKLMNOPQRSTUVWXYZ
abcdefghijklmnopqrstuvwxyz&012345
6789$€!?.;:,""{½}

*ABCDEFGHIJKLMNOPQRSTUVWXYZ
abcdefghijklmnopqrstuvwxyz&012345
6789$€!?.;:,""{½}*

Letterforms have tone, timbre, character, just as words and sentences do. The moment a text and typeface are chosen, two streams of thoug
BOOK CONDENSED

Letterforms have tone, timbre, character, just as words and sentences do. The moment a text and typeface are chosen, two streams of thoug
BOOK CONDENSED ITALIC

Letterforms have tone, timbre, character, just as words and sentences do. The moment a text and typeface are chosen, two streams of thoug
MEDIUM CONDENSED

Letterforms have tone, timbre, character, just as words and sentences do. The moment a text and typeface are chosen, two streams of
MEDIUM CONDENSED ITALIC

Letterforms have tone, timbre, character, just as words and sentences do. The moment a text and typeface are chosen, two streams of
DEMI CONDENSED

Letterforms have tone, timbre, character, just as words and sentences do. The moment a text and typeface are chosen, two streams of
DEMI CONDENSED ITALIC

Freestyle Script STD

Martin Wait, Esselte Pendaflex, Letrasct, Esselte Letraset

A-Z €

Typography

ABCDEFGHIJKLMNOPQRSTUVW XYZabcdefghijklmnopqrstuvwxyz& 0123 456789$€!?.,:;""{½}

Letterforms have tone, timbre, character, just as words and sentences do. The moment a text
REGULAR

Friz Quadrata STD

Ernst Friz

A-Z €

Typography

ABCDEFGHIJKLMNOPQ RSTUVWXYZabcdefghijk lmnopqrstuvwxyz&012 3456789$€!?.,:;,""{½}

Letterforms have tone, tim bre, character, just as words
REGULAR

Letterforms have tone, tim bre, character, just as wor
BOLD

Frutiger STD

Adrian Frutiger, Linotype Library GmbH

A-Z €

Typography

ABCDEFGHIJKLMNOPQRSTUV WXYZabcdefghijklmnopqrstuv wxyz&0123456789$€!?.,:;,""{½}

ABCDEFGHIJKLMNOPQRSTUV WXYZabcdefghijklmnopqrstuv wxyz&0123456789$€!?.,:;,""{½}

Letterforms have tone, timbre, character, just as words and sentences do. The mo ment a text and typeface are chosen,
45 LIGHT

Letterforms have tone, timbre, character, just as words and sentences do. The mo ment a text and typeface are chosen,
46 LIGHT ITALIC

Letterforms have tone, timbre, char acter, just as words and sentences do. The moment a text and typeface are
55 ROMAN

Letterforms have tone, timbre, char acter, just as words and sentences do. The moment a text and typeface are
56 ITALIC

Letterforms have tone, timbre, char acter, just as words and sentences do. The moment a text and typeface
65 BOLD

Letterforms have tone, timbre, char acter, just as words and sentences do. The moment a text and typeface
66 BOLD ITALIC

Letterforms have tone, timbre, character, just as words and sen tences do. The moment a text
75 BLACK

Letterforms have tone, timbre, character, just as words and sen tences do. The moment a text
76 BLACK ITALIC

Letterforms have tone, timbre, character, just as words and sentences do. The moment a
95 ULTRA BLACK

Frutiger STD Condensed

Adrian Frutiger, Linotype Library GmbH

A-z €

Typography

ABCDEFGHIJKLMNOPQRSTUVWXYZ
abcdefghijklmnopqrstuvwxyz&01234
56789$€!?.;:,""{½}

Letterforms have tone, timbre, character, just as words and sentences do. The moment a text and typeface are chosen, two streams of thought,
47 LIGHT CONDENSED

Letterforms have tone, timbre, character, just as words and sentences do. The moment a text and typeface are chosen, two streams of
57 CONDENSED

Letterforms have tone, timbre, character, just as words and sentences do. The mo ment a text and typeface are chosen, two
67 BOLD CONDENSED

Letterforms have tone, timbre, charac ter, just as words and sentences do. The moment a text and typeface are
77 BLACK CONDENSED

Letterforms have tone, timbre, charac ter, just as words and sentences do. The moment a text and typeface are
87 EXTRA BLACK CONDENSED

Fusaka STD

Michael Want, Adobe Systems

A-z € e

Alternates

REGULAR

Futura STD

Paul Renner, Bauer Types, S.A.

A-z €

Typography

ABCDEFGHIJKLMNOPQRSTUV
WXYZabcdefghijklmnopqrstuvw
xyz&0123456789$€!?.;:,""{½}

ABCDEFGHIJKLMNOPQRSTUV
WXYZabcdefghijklmnopqrstuvw
xyz&0123456789$€!?.;:,""{½}

Letterforms have tone, timbre, character,
just as words and sentences do. The mo
ment a text and typeface are chosen, two
LIGHT

Letterforms have tone, timbre, character,
just as words and sentences do. The mo
ment a text and typeface are chosen, two
LIGHT OBLIQUE

Letterforms have tone, timbre, character,
just as words and sentences do. The mo
ment a text and typeface are chosen,
BOOK

Letterforms have tone, timbre, character,
just as words and sentences do. The mo
ment a text and typeface are chosen,
BOOK OBLIQUE

Letterforms have tone, timbre, character,
just as words and sentences do. The mo
ment a text and typeface are chosen, two
MEDIUM

Letterforms have tone, timbre, character,
just as words and sentences do. The mo
ment a text and typeface are chosen, two
MEDIUM OBLIQUE

Letterforms have tone, timbre, character,
just as words and sentences do. The mo
ment a text and typeface are chosen,
HEAVY

Letterforms have tone, timbre, character,
just as words and sentences do. The mo
ment a text and typeface are chosen,
HEAVY OBLIQUE

Letterforms have tone, timbre,
character, just as words and sen
tences do. The moment a text an
BOLD

Letterforms have tone, timbre,
character, just as words and sen
tences do. The moment a text an
BOLD OBLIQUE

Letterforms have tone, tim bre, character, just as words and sentences do. The mom

EXTRA BOLD

Letterforms have tone, tim bre, character, just as words and sentences do. The mom

EXTRA BOLD OBLIQUE

Letterforms have tone, timbre, character, just as words and sentences do. The moment a text and typeface are chosen, two streams of thought,

BOLD

Letterforms have tone, timbre, character, just as words and sentences do. The moment a text and typeface are chosen, two streams of thought,

BOLD OBLIQUE

Letterforms have tone, timbre, charac ter, just as words and sentences do. The moment a text and typeface are

EXTRA BOLD

Letterforms have tone, timbre, charac ter, just as words and sentences do. The moment a text and typeface are

EXTRA BOLD OBLIQUE

Futura STD Condensed

Paul Renner, Bauer Types, S.A.

A-z €

Typography

ABCDEFGHIJKLMNOPQRSTUVWXYZabcdefghijkl
mnopqrstuvwxyz&0123456789$€!?.;:,""{½}

ABCDEFGHIJKLMNOPQRSTUVWXYZabcdefghijkl
mnopqrstuvwxyz&0123456789$€!?.;:,""{½}

Letterforms have tone, timbre, character, just as words and sentences do. The moment a text and typeface are chosen, two streams of thought, two rhythmical systems, two sets

LIGHT

Letterforms have tone, timbre, character, just as words and sentences do. The moment a text and typeface are chosen, two streams of thought, two rhythmical systems, two sets

LIGHT OBLIQUE

Letterforms have tone, timbre, character, just as words and sentences do. The moment a text and typeface are chosen, two streams of thought, two rhythmical systems,

MEDIUM

Letterforms have tone, timbre, character, just as words and sentences do. The moment a text and typeface are chosen, two streams of thought, two rhythmical systems,

MEDIUM OBLIQUE

Galahad STD

Alan Blackman, Adobe Systems

A-z € ffi 619 123 ę̃

Typography

ABCDEFGHIJKLMNOPQ
RSTUVWXYZabcdefghijkl
mnopqrstuvwxyz&012345
6789$€!?.;:,""{½}

0123456789 0123456789
Old Style and Proportional Figures

A-AAEE FF GHHH JKK KLMNQQRRRTTWYZZ e g g k l q o r t t x z & &

Alternates

Ll TH ll ff ffi ffi fi fj fl ft gg gg tt

Ligatures

Letterforms have tone, timbre, character, just as words and 567

REGULAR

THE MOMENT A TEXT & A TYPEFACE ARE CHOSEN two streams of thought two rhythmical systems, two sets of habits or if you like, two personalities, intersect.

ITC Galliard STD

Matthew Carter, ITC

A-Z €

Typography

ABCDEFGHIJKLMNOPQRST UVWXYZabcdefghijklmnopqrstu vwxyz&0123456789$€!?.;:,""{½}

ABCDEFGHIJKLMNOPQRSTU VWXYZabcdefghijklmnopqrstuvwx yz&0123456789$€!?.;:,""{½}

Letterforms have tone, timbre, character, just as words and sentences do. The mo ment a text and typeface are chosen, two

ROMAN

Letterforms have tone, timbre, character, just as words and sentences do. The mo ment a text and typeface are chosen, two

ITALIC

Letterforms have tone, timbre, char acter, just as words and sentences do. The moment a text and typeface are

BOLD

Letterforms have tone, timbre, character, just as words and sentences do. The mo ment a text and typeface are chosen, two

BOLD ITALIC

Letterforms have tone, timbre, char acter, just as words and sentences do. The moment a text and typeface are

BLACK

Letterforms have tone, timbre, charac ter, just as words and sentences do. The moment a text and typeface are chosen,

BLACK ITALIC

Letterforms have tone, timbre, character, just as words and senten ces do. The moment a text and type

ULTRA

Letterforms have tone, timbre, charac ter, just as words and sentences do. The moment a text and typeface are

ULTRA ITALIC

Linotype Game Pi STD

Linotype Staff

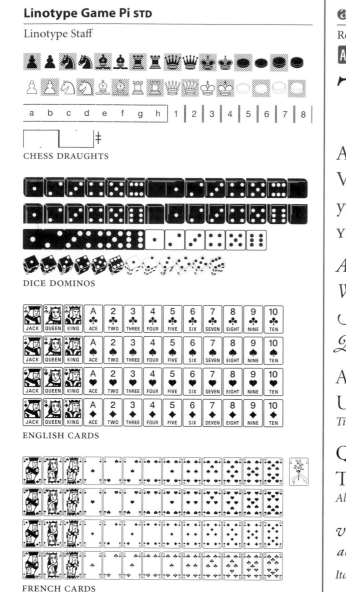

CHESS DRAUGHTS

DICE DOMINOS

ENGLISH CARDS

FRENCH CARDS

Adobe Garamond PRO

Robert Slimbach, Adobe Systems

Typography

ABCDEFGHIJKLMNOPQRSTU
VWXYZabcdefghijklmnopqrstuvwx
yz& ABCDEFGHIJKLMNOPQRSTUVWX
YZ&

ABCDEFGHIJKLMNOPQRSTUV
WXYZabcdefghijklmnopqrstuvwxyz&
ABCDEFGHIJKLMNOP
QRSTUVWXYZ&

ABCDEFGHIJKLMNOPQQRST
UVWXYZ
Titling Capitals

QQ a e n r t z & ff ffi ffi ffl fi fj fl
Th abdehilmnorst
Alternates, Ligatures & Superiors

v & ct ff ffi ffi ffl fi fj fl st Th
abdehilmnorst
Italic Alternates, Ligatures & Superiors

0123456789 0123456789
0123456789 0123456789
0123456789 0123456789
0123456789 0123456789
Proportional and Tabular Figures

Ø$¢£¥ʃ₣£₽€#¤Rp₡%‰$¢£¥ƒ₡€#
$¢€%‰0123456789($¢-.,)0123456789($¢-.,)/
0123456789($¢-.,)0123456789($¢-.,)¼½¾
⅛⅜⅝⅞⅓⅔^~·+±<=>-|¦×÷∂μπΔΠΣ
Ω√∞∫≈≠≤≥◊¬℮ℓ°ªº_——–-—---—' "
"",',«»«»‹›‹›,.:; … … .. ..·!?¡¿⁀()()[][]{}{}
/ \ *•§†‡¶©®™@@

Currency, Punctuation, and Related Forms

Ø$¢£¥ƒF₣£₽€#¤%‰₡Rp$¢£¥ƒ₡€#%
‰$¢%0123456789($¢-.,)0123456789($¢-.,)
/0123456789($¢-.,)0123456789($¢-.,) ¼½¾
⅛⅜⅝⅞⅓⅔^~·+±<=>-|¦×÷∂μπΔΠ
ΣΩ√∞∫≈≠≤≥◊¬℮ℓ°ªº_———
—' " "",',«»«»‹›‹›,.:; … … .. ..·!?¡¿⁀()
*[][]{}{}/ \ *•§†‡¶©®™@@*

Italic Currency, Punctuation, and Related Forms

ÆŁØŒÞÐÁÂÄÀÅÃÇÉÊËÈÍÎÏÌÍŃ
ÓÔÖÒÕŠÚÛÜÙÝŸŽĂĀĄĆČĎ
ĐĚĒĘĢĞĪĮĶĹĽĻŃŇŅŇŐŌŔŘŖ
ŚŞŠŢŤŰŪŲŮŹŻÆıłøœßþðáâäàåãç
éêëíîïìñóôöòõšúûüùýÿžăāąćčďděėēę
ğġīįķĺľļńňņňőōŕřŗśşšţťűūųůźżÆŁØŒÞÐ
ÁÂÄÀÅÃÇÉÊËÈÍÎÏÌÌŃÓÔÖÒÕŠÚÛÜÙÝŸŽ
ĂĀĄĆČĐĎĚĒĘĢĞĪĮĶĹĽĻŃŇŅŇŐŌŔŘŖŚŞŞ
ŤŢŰŪŲŮŹŻ

Accented Characters

ÆŁØŒÞÐÁÂÄÀÅÃÇÉÊËÈÍÎÏÌÍŃ
ÓÔÖÒÕŠÚÛÜÙÝŸŽĂĀĄĆČĎĐĚ
ĒĘĢĞĪĮĶĹĽĻŃŇŅŇŐŌŔŘŖŚŞŞŤ
ŤŰŪŲŮŹŻÆıłøœßþðáâäàåãçéêëíîï
ñóôöòõšúûüùýÿžăāąćčďděėēęğġīįķĺľļńň
ņňőōŕřŗśşšţťűūųůźż

Italic Accented Characters

❧ ☙ ❦

Ornaments

Lᴇᴛᴛᴇʀꜰᴏʀᴍꜱ ʜᴀᴠᴇ ᴛᴏɴᴇ, timbre, character,
just as words and 567 sentences do. The mo
ment a text and typeface are chosen, two
ʀᴇɢᴜʟᴀʀ

Letterforms have tone, timbre, character, just as
words and 567 sentences do. The moment a text
and typeface are chosen, two streams of thought
ɪᴛᴀʟɪᴄ

Lᴇᴛᴛᴇʀꜰᴏʀᴍꜱ ʜᴀᴠᴇ ᴛᴏɴᴇ, timbre, character,
just as words and 567 sentences do. The mo
ment a text and typeface are chosen, two
ꜱᴇᴍɪʙᴏʟᴅ

Letterforms have tone, timbre, character, just
as words and 567 sentences do. The moment a
text and typeface are chosen, two streams of
ꜱᴇᴍɪʙᴏʟᴅ ɪᴛᴀʟɪᴄ

Letterforms have tone, timbre, character,
just as words and 567 sentences do. The
moment a text and typeface are chosen,
ʙᴏʟᴅ

Letterforms have tone, timbre, character,
just as words and 567 sentences do. The mo
ment a text and typeface are chosen, two
ʙᴏʟᴅ ɪᴛᴀʟɪᴄ

To download a complete glyph complement PDF, please visit
www.adobe.com/type.

Garamond 3 STD

Morris Fuller Benton and Thomas M. Cleland,
Linotype Library GmbH

A-z € BB 619

Typography

ABCDEFGHIJKLMNOPQRSTUV
WXYZabcdefghijklmnopqrstuvwxy
z&0123456789$€!?.;:,""{½}

ABCDEFGHIJKLMNOPQRSTUVWXYZ&
0123456789

*ABCDEFGHIJKLMNOPQRSTUV
WXYZabcdefghijklmnopqrstuvwxyz&
0123456789$€!?.;:,""{½}*

0123456789

LETTERFORMS HAVE TONE, timbre, character,
just as words and 567 sentences do. The mo
ment a text and typeface are chosen, two
REGULAR

*Letterforms have tone, timbre, character, just as
words and 567 sentences do. The moment a text
and typeface are chosen, two streams of thought,*
ITALIC

**LETTERFORMS HAVE TONE, timbre, charac
ter, just as words and 567 sentences do.
The moment a text and typeface are cho**
BOLD

***Letterforms have tone, timbre, character,
just as words and 567 sentences do. The mo
ment a text and typeface are chosen, two***
BOLD ITALIC

ITC Garamond STD

Tony Stan, ITC

A-z €

Typography

ABCDEFGHIJKLMNOPQRSTU
VWXYZabcdefghijklmnopqrstu
vwxyz&0123456789$€!?.;:,""{½}

*ABCDEFGHIJKLMNOPQRSTU
WXYZabcdefghijklmnopqrstuv
wxyz&0123456789$€!?.;:,""{½}*

Letterforms have tone, timbre, charac
ter, just as words and sentences do. The
moment a text and typeface are chosen,
LIGHT

*Letterforms have tone, timbre, character,
just as words and sentences do. The mo
ment a text and typeface are chosen,*
LIGHT ITALIC

Letterforms have tone, timbre, charac
ter, just as words and sentences do.
The moment a text and typeface are
BOOK

*Letterforms have tone, timbre, charac
ter, just as words and sentences do.
The moment a text and typeface are*
BOOK ITALIC

**Letterforms have tone, timbre, char
acter, just as words and sentences
do. The moment a text and typeface**
BOLD

***Letterforms have tone, timbre, char
acter, just as words and sentences
do. The moment a text and typeface***
BOLD ITALIC

Letterforms have tone, timbre, character, just as words and sen tences do. The moment a text and
ULTRA

Letterforms have tone, timbre, character, just as words and sen tences do. The moment a text and
ULTRA ITALIC

ITC Garamond STD Condensed

Tony Stan, ITC

A-Z €

Typography

ABCDEFGHIJKLMNOPQRSTUVWXYZ
abcdefghijklmnopqrstuvwxyz&01234567
89$€!?.;:,""{½}

ABCDEFGHIJKLMNOPQRSTUVWXYZ
abcdefghijklmnopqrstuvwxyz&0123456
789$€!?.;:,""{½}

Letterforms have tone, timbre, character, just as words and sentences do. The moment a text and typeface are chosen, two streams of thought, two rhythmical system
LIGHT

Letterforms have tone, timbre, character, just as words and sentences do. The moment a text and typeface are chosen, two streams of thought, two
LIGHT ITALIC

Letterforms have tone, timbre, character, just as words and sentences do. The moment a text and typeface are chosen, two streams of thought, two
BOOK

Letterforms have tone, timbre, character, just as words and sentences do. The moment a text and typeface are chosen, two streams of thought, two
BOOK ITALIC

Letterforms have tone, timbre, character, just as words and sentences do. The moment a text and typeface are chosen, two streams of
BOLD

Letterforms have tone, timbre, character, just as words and sentences do. The mo ment a text and typeface are chosen, two
BOLD ITALIC

Letterforms have tone, timbre, character, just as words and sentences do. The mo ment a text and typeface are chosen, two
ULTRA

Letterforms have tone, timbre, charac ter, just as words and sentences do. The moment a text and typeface are chosen,
ULTRA ITALIC

ITC Garamond STD Narrow

Tony Stan, ITC

A-Z €

Typography

ABCDEFGHIJKLMNOPQRSTUVWXYZ
abcdefghijklmnopqrstuvwxyz&0123456
789$€!?.;:,""{½}

ABCDEFGHIJKLMNOPQRSTUVWXYZ
abcdefghijklmnopqrstuvwxyz&01234
56789$€!?.;:,""{½}

Letterforms have tone, timbre, character, just as words and sentences do. The moment a text and typeface are chosen, two streams of thought, two
LIGHT

Letterforms have tone, timbre, character, just as words and sentences do. The moment a text and typeface are chosen, two streams of thought, two
LIGHT ITALIC

Letterforms have tone, timbre, character, just as words and sentences do. The moment a text and typeface are chosen, two streams of thought, two
BOOK

Letterforms have tone, timbre, character, just as words and sentences do. The moment a text and typeface are chosen, two streams of
BOOK ITALIC

Letterforms have tone, timbre, character, just as words and sentences do. The moment a text and typeface are chosen, two streams
BOLD

Letterforms have tone, timbre, character, just as words and sentences do. The mo ment a text and typeface are chosen, two
BOLD ITALIC

Letterforms have tone, timbre, charac ter, just as words and sentences do. The moment a text and typeface are chosen,
ULTRA

Letterforms have tone, timbre, charac ter, just as words and sentences do. The moment a text and typeface are chosen
ULTRA ITALIC

ITC Garamond Handtooled STD

Ed Benguiat, ITC

A-z €

Typography

ABCDEFGHIJKLMNOPQRS TUVWXYZabcdefghijklmn opqrstuvwxyz&012345678 9$€!?.;:,""{½}

ABCDEFGHIJKLMNOPQRS TUVWXYZabcdefghijklmn opqrstuvwxyz&012345678 9$€!?.;:,""{½}

Letterforms have tone, timbre, character, just as
BOLD

Letterforms have tone, timbre, character, just as
BOLD ITALIC

Simoncini Garamond STD

Francesco Simoncini and W. Bilz, Bauer Types, S.A.

A-z €

Typography

ABCDEFGHIJKLMNOPQRST UVWXYZabcdefghijklmnopqrstu vwxyz&0123456789$€!?.;:,""{½}

ABCDEFGHIJKLMNOPQRSTU
VWXYZabcdefghijklmnopqrstuvw
xyz&0123456789$€!?.;:, ""{½}

Letterforms have tone, timbre, character,
just as words and sentences do. The mo
ment a text and typeface are chosen, two
REGULAR

*Letterforms have tone, timbre, character,
just as words and sentences do. The mo
ment a text and typeface are chosen, two*
ITALIC

**Letterforms have tone, timbre, character,
just as words and sentences do. The mo
ment a text and typeface are chosen, two**
BOLD

Stempel Garamond STD

Stempel Staff, Linotype Library GmbH

A-z € BB 619

Typography

ABCDEFGHIJKLMNOPQRST
UVWXYZabcdefghijklmnopqrstu
vwxyz&0123456789$€!?.;:, ""{½}

ABCDEFGHIJKLMNOPQRSTUVWXYZ
&0123456789

*ABCDEFGHIJKLMNOPQRST
UVWXYZabcdefghijklmnopqrstu
vwxyz&0123456789$€!?.;:, ""{½}
0123456789*

LETTERFORMS HAVE TONE, timbre, charac
ter, just as words and 567 sentences do.
The moment a text and typeface are cho
ROMAN

*Letterforms have tone, timbre, character,
just as words and 567 sentences do. The
moment a text and typeface are chosen,*
ITALIC

**Letterforms have tone, timbre, charac
ter, just as words and 567 sentences do.
The moment a text and typeface are**
BOLD

**Letterforms have tone, timbre, character,
just as words and 567 sentences do. The
moment a text and typeface are chosen,**
BOLD ITALIC

Garth Graphic

Constance Blanchard, Renee Le Winter, and John Matt,
Agfa Division, Bayer Corp.

Typography

ABCDEFGHIJKLMNOPQRSTU
VWXYZabcdefghijklmnopqrstu
vwxyz&0123456789$!?.;:, ""{½}

*ABCDEFGHIJKLMNOPQRSTU
VWXYZabcdefghijklmnopqrstuvw
xyz&0123456789$!?.;:, ""{½}*

Letterforms have tone, timbre, charac
ter, just as words and sentences do.
The moment a text and typeface are
REGULAR

*Letterforms have tone, timbre, character,
just as words and sentences do. The mo
ment a text and typeface are chosen, two*
ITALIC

Letterforms have tone, timbre, char acter, just as words and sentences do. The moment a text and type
BOLD

Letterforms have tone, timbre, char acter, just as words and sentences do. The moment a text and typeface
BOLD ITALIC

Letterforms have tone, timbre, character, just as words and sen tences do. The moment a text
EXTRA BOLD

Letterforms have tone, timbre, character, just as words and sen tences do. The moment a text
BLACK

Letterforms have tone, timbre, character, just as words and sentences do. The moment a text and typeface are chosen, two streams of thought, two
CONDENSED

Letterforms have tone, timbre, character, just as words and sentences do. The mo ment a text and typeface are chosen, two
CONDENSED BOLD

Gazette STD

Unknown, Linotype Library GmbH

Typography

ABCDEFGHIJKLMNOPQRS
TUVWXYZabcdefghijklmno
pqrstuvwxyz&0123456789$€
!?.;:, ""{½}

ABCDEFGHIJKLMNOPQRS TUVWXYZabcdefghijklmno pqrstuvwxyz&0123456789$€ !?.;:, ""{½}

Letterforms have tone, timbre, char acter, just as words and sentences do. The moment a text and typeface
ROMAN

Letterforms have tone, timbre, char acter, just as words and sentences do. The moment a text and typeface
ITALIC

Letterforms have tone, timbre, char acter, just as words and sentences do. The moment a text and typeface
BOLD

Giddyup STD

Laurie Szujewska, Adobe Systems

Aa Bb Cc Dd Ee Ff Gg Hh Ii Jj Kk Ll Mm Nn Oo Pp Qq Rr Ss Tt Uu Vv Ww Xx Yy Zz &0123456789$€!?.;:, ""{½}

Letterforms have tone, timbre, character, just as words and sentences do. The mo
REGULAR

THANGS

Gill Floriated Capitals STD

Eric Gill, Monotype Corp.

TYPOGRA

ABCDEFGHIJKL
MNOPQRSTUV
WXYZ

EFHSTWY

Alternates

LETTERFORMS

REGULAR

Gill Sans STD

Eric Gill, Monotype Corp.

A-z €

Typography

ABCDEFGHIJKLMNOPQRSTUV
WXYZabcdefghijklmnopqrstuvwx
yz&0123456789$€!?.;:,""''{½}

*ABCDEFGHIJKLMNOPQRSTUVWX
YZabcdefghijklmnopqrstuvwxyz&012
3456789$€!?.;:,""''{½}*

Letterforms have tone, timbre, character, just
as words and sentences do. The moment a
text and typeface are chosen, two streams

LIGHT

*Letterforms have tone, timbre, character, just as
words and sentences do. The moment a
text and typeface are chosen, two streams of*

LIGHT ITALIC

Letterforms have tone, timbre, character,
just as words and sentences do. The mo
ment a text and typeface are chosen, two

REGULAR

*Letterforms have tone, timbre, character, just
as words and sentences do. The moment a
text and typeface are chosen, two streams of*

ITALIC

**Letterforms have tone, timbre, char
acter, just as words and sentences do.
The moment a text and typeface are**

BOLD

***Letterforms have tone, timbre, charac
ter, just as words and sentences do. The
moment a text and typeface are chosen***

BOLD ITALIC

**Letterforms have tone timbre,
character, just as words and sen
tences do. The moment a text**

EXTRA BOLD

**Letterforms have to
ne, timbre, charac**

ULTRA BOLD

Gill Sans STD Condensed

Eric Gill, Monotype Corp.

Letterforms have tone, timbre, character, just as words and sentences do. The moment a text and typeface are chosen, two streams of thought, two rhthmical systems, two sets
CONDENSED

Letterforms have tone, timbre, charac ter, just as words and sentences do. The moment a text and typeface are chosen,
BOLD CONDENSED

Letterforms have tone, tim bre, character, just as word
ULTRA BOLD CONDENSED

Gill Sans STD Display

Eric Gill, Monotype Corp.

Letterforms have tone, timbre, character, just
DISPLAY EXTRA BOLD

Letterforms have tone, timbre, character, just as words and sentences to. The moment a text and typeface are
BOLD EXTRA CONDENSED

Letterforms have tone, timbre, character, just as
LIGHT SHADOWED

LETTERFORMS HAVE TO NE, TIMBRE, CHARACTER,
SHADOWED

ITC Giovanni STD

Robert Slimbach, ITC

Typography

ABCDEFGHIJKLMNOPQRSTU VWXYZabcdefghijklmnopqrstuv wxyz&0123456789$€!?.;:,""{½}

ABCDEFGHIJKLMNOPQRSTU VWXYZabcdefghijklmnopqrstuvwx yz&0123456789$€!?.;:,""{½}

Letterforms have tone, timbre, character, just as words and sentences do. The mo ment a text and typeface are chosen, two
BOOK

Letterforms have tone, timbre, character, just as words and sentences do. The mo ment a text and typeface are chosen, two
BOOK ITALIC

Letterforms have tone, timbre, charac ter, just as words and sentences do. The moment a text and typeface are
BOLD

Letterforms have tone, timbre, character, just as words and sentences do. The mo ment a text and typeface are chosen, two
BOLD ITALIC

Letterforms have tone, timbre, charac ter, just as words and sentences do. The moment a text and typeface are
BLACK

Letterforms have tone, timbre, charac ter, just as words and sentences do. The moment a text and typeface are
BLACK ITALIC

Glypha STD

Adrian Frutiger, Linotype Library GmbH

A-Z €

Typography

ABCDEFGHIJKLMNOPQRST
UVWXYZabcdefghijklmnopq
rstuvwxyz&0123456789$€!?.;
:," "{½}

*ABCDEFGHIJKLMNOPQRST
UVWXYZabcdefghijklmnopq
rstuvwxyz&0123456789$€!?.;
:," "{½}*

Letterforms have tone, timbre, character,
just as words and sentences do. The
moment a text and typeface are chosen,
35 THIN

*Letterforms have tone, timbre, character,
just as words and sentences do. The
moment a text and typeface are chosen,*
35 THIN OBLIQUE

Letterforms have tone, timbre, character,
just as words and sentences do. The
moment a text and typeface are chosen,
45 LIGHT

*Letterforms have tone, timbre, character,
just as words and sentences do. The
moment a text and typeface are chosen,*
45 LIGHT OBLIQUE

Letterforms have tone, timbre, char
acter, just as words and sentences
do. The moment a text and typeface
55 ROMAN

*Letterforms have tone, timbre, char
acter, just as words and sentences
do. The moment a text and typeface*
55 OBLIQUE

**Letterforms have tone, timbre, char
acter, just as words and sentences
do. The moment a text and typefac**
65 BOLD

***Letterforms have tone, timbre, char
acter, just as words and sentences
do. The moment a text and typefac***
65 BOLD OBLIQUE

**Letterforms have tone, timbre,
character, just as words and sen
tences do. The moment a text and**
75 BLACK

***Letterforms have tone, timbre,
character, just as words and sen
tences do. The moment a text and***
75 BLACK OBLIQUE

Gothic 13 STD

Unknown

A-Z €

Typography

ABCDEFGHIJKLMNOPQRSTUVWXYZ
abcdefghijklmnopqrstuvwxyz&0123456
789$€!?.;:," "{½}

**Letterforms have tone, timbre, character, just
as words and sentences do. The moment a
text and typeface are chosen, two streams of**
REGULAR

Goudy STD

Frederic W. Goudy

A-z € BB 619

Typography

ABCDEFGHIJKLMNOPQRSTU
VWXYZabcdefghijklmnopqrstuvw
xyz&0123456789$€!?.;:,""{½}

ABCDEFGHIJKLMNOPQRSTUVWXYZ&
0123456789

*ABCDEFGHIJKLMNOPQRSTU
VWXYZabcdefghijklmnopqrstuvwxyz
&0123456789$€!?.;:,""{½}*

0123456789

LETTERFORMS HAVE TONE, timbre, charac
ter, just as words and 567 sentences do.
The moment a text and typeface are cho
OLD STYLE

*Letterforms have tone, timbre, character, just
as words and 567 sentences do. The moment
a text and typeface are chosen, two streams of*
OLD STYLE ITALIC

**Letterforms have tone, timbre, character,
just as words and 567 sentences do. The
moment a text and typeface are chosen,**
BOLD

***Letterforms have tone, timbre, character,
just as words and 567 sentences do. The
moment a text and typeface are chosen,***
BOLD ITALIC

**Letterforms have tone, timbre, charac
ter, just as words and 567 sentences
do. The moment a text and typeface**
EXTRA BOLD

**Letterforms have tone, timbre,
character, just as words and 567
sentences do. The moment a text**
HEAVYFACE

***Letterforms have tone, timbre, character,
just as words and 567 sentences do. The moment a***
HEAVYFACE ITALIC

ITC Goudy Sans STD

Frederic W. Goudy, ITC

A-z €

Typography

ABCDEFGHIJKLMNOPQRSTUVWXY
Zabcdefghijklmnopqrstuvwxyz&0123
456789$€!?.;:,""{½}

*ABCDEFGHIJKLMNOPQRSTUVWXYZ
abcdefghijklmnopqrstuvwxyz&01234
56789$€!?.;:,""{½}*

Letterforms have tone, timbre, character, just
as words and sentences do. The moment a
text and typeface are chosen, two streams of
BOOK

*Letterforms have tone, timbre, character, just
as words and sentences do. The moment a
text and typeface are chosen, two streams of*
BOOK ITALIC

Letterforms have tone, timbre, character, just as words and sentences do. The moment a text and typeface are chosen, two streams of
MEDIUM

Letterforms have tone, timbre, character, just as words and sentences do. The moment a text and typeface are chosen, two streams of
MEDIUM ITALIC

Letterforms have tone, timbre, character, just as words and sentences do. The mo ment a text and typeface are chosen,
BOLD

Letterforms have tone, timbre, character, just as words and sentences do. The mo ment a text and typeface are chosen, two
BOLD ITALIC

Letterforms have tone, timbre, char acter, just as words and sentences do. The moment a text and typeface are
BLACK

Letterforms have tone, timbre, character, just as words and sentences do. The mo ment a text and typeface are chosen, two
BLACK ITALIC

Goudy Text STD

Frederic W. Goudy, Monotype Corp.

Typography

ABCDEFGHIJKLMN
OPQRSTUVWXYZ
abcdefghijklmnopqrstuvwxyz&
0123456789$€!?.;:,""{½}

Alternates and Ligatures

Alternates and Ligatures

Historic Blackletter

Historic Blackletter

Lombardic Capitals

ABCDEFGHIJKLM
NOPQRSTUVWXYZ
Lombardic Capitals

Letterforms have tone, timbre, char acter, just as words and sentences
REGULAR

Monotype Goudy Modern STD

Frederic W. Goudy, Monotype Typography Ltd.

Typography

ABCDEFGHIJKLMNOPQRSTUV
WXYZabcdefghijklmnopqrstuvwxyz
&0123456789$€!?.;:,""{½}

*ABCDEFGHIJKLMNOPQRSTUV
WXYZabcdefghijklmnopqrstuvwxyz
&0123456789$€!?.;:,""{½}*

Letterforms have tone, timbre, character, just as words and sentences do. The moment a text and typeface are chosen, two streams of thought,
REGULAR

Letterforms have tone, timbre, character, just as words and sentences do. The moment a text and typeface are chosen, two streams of thought,
ITALIC

Granjon STD

George W. Jones, Linotype Library GmbH

A-Z € BB 619

Typography

ABCDEFGHIJKLMNOPQRST
UVWXYZabcdefghijklmnopqrstu
vwxyz&0123456789$€!?.,:,""{½}

ABCDEFGHIJKLMNOPQRSTUVWXYZ&
0123456789

*ABCDEFGHIJKLMNOPQRSTUV
WXYZabcdefghijklmnopqrstuvwxyz&
0123456789$€!?.,:,""{½}*

0123456789

LETTERFORMS HAVE TONE, timbre, character,
just as words and 567 sentences do. The
moment a text and typeface are chosen, two
ROMAN

*Letterforms have tone, timbre, character, just as
words and 567 sentences do. The moment a text
and typeface are chosen, two streams of thought,*
ITALIC

**Letterforms have tone, timbre, character, just
as words and 567 sentences do. The moment
a text and typeface are chosen, two streams of**
BOLD

Graphite STD

David Siegel, David Siegel

A-Z € 123

Typography

ABCDEFGHIJKLMNOPQRSTUV
WXYZabcdefghijklmnopqrstuvwxyz$
0123456789$€!?.,:,""{½}

Letterforms have tone, timbre, character, just as words and sen
tences do. The moment a text and typeface are chosen, two
streams of thought, two rhythmical systems, two sets of habits
LIGHT NARROW

Letterforms have tone, timbre, character, just as words and
sentences do. The moment a text and typeface are chosen,
two streams of thought, two rhythmical systems, two sets of
REGULAR NARROW

**Letterforms have tone, timbre, character, just as words
and sentences do. The moment a text and typeface are
chosen, two streams of thought, two rhythmical systems,**
BOLD NARROW

Letterforms have tone, timbre, character, just as
words and sentences do. The moment a text and
typeface are chosen, two streams of thought,
LIGHT

Letterforms have tone, timbre, character, just
as words and sentences do. The moment a
text and typeface are chosen, two streams
REGULAR

**Letterforms have tone, timbre, character,
just as words and sentences do. The mo
ment a text and typeface are chosen, two**
BOLD

Letterforms have tone, timbre, charac
ter, just as words and sentences do.
The moment a text and typeface are
LIGHT WIDE

Letterforms have tone, timbre, char
acter, just as words and sentences
do. The moment a text and typeface
WIDE

Letterforms have tone, timbre,
character, just as words and sen
tences do. The moment a text and
BOLD WIDE

MVB Greymantle STD

Kanna Aoki and Mark van Bronkhorst, MVB Fonts

Typography

ABCDEFGHIJKLMNOPQ
RSTUVWXYZabcdefghijklm
nopqrstuvwxyz&0123456789
9$€!?.;:,""{½}

As A B C D E F G H I J
K L M N O P Q R S T U
V W X Y Z 0123456789

Alternates

Letterforms have tone, timbre, charac
ter, just as words and sentences do.
REGULAR

ORNAMENTS

Monotype Grotesque STD

Unknown, Monotype Typography Ltd.

Typography

ABCDEFGHIJKLMNOPQRST
UVWXYZabcdefghijklmnopqrst
uvwxyz&0123456789$€!?.;:,""{½}

*ABCDEFGHIJKLMNOPQRSTUV
WXYZabcdefghijklmnopqrstuvw
xyz&0123456789$€!?.;:,""{½}*

Letterforms have tone, timbre, charac
ter, just as words and sentences do. The
moment a text and typeface are chosen
LIGHT

*Letterforms have tone, timbre, charac
ter, just as words and sentences do. The
moment a text and typeface are chosen*
LIGHT ITALIC

Letterforms have tone, timbre, charac
ter, just as words and sentences do.
The moment a text and typeface are
REGULAR

*Letterforms have tone, timbre, charac
ter, just as words and sentences do. The
moment a text and typeface are chosen*
ITALIC

**Letterforms have tone, timbre, char
acter, just as words and sentences
do. The moment a text and typefac**
BOLD

**Letterforms have tone, timbre, charac
ter, just as words and sentences do. The
moment a text and typeface are chosen**
BLACK

Monotype Grotesque STD
Condensed and Extended

Unknown, Monotype Typography, Ltd.

Letterforms have tone, timbre, character, just as words and sentences do. The moment a text and typeface are chosen, two streams of thought, two

LIGHT CONDENSED

Letterforms have tone, timbre, character, just as words and sentences do. The moment a text and typeface are chosen, two streams of thought, two

CONDENSED

Letterforms have tone, timbre, character, just as words and sentences do. The moment a text and typeface are chosen, two streams of thought, two rhythmical systems, two sets of habits

EXTRA CONDENSED

Letterforms have tone, timbre, character, just as words and sentences do. The mom

BOLD EXTENDED

Guardi STD

Reinhard Haus, Linotype Library GmbH

Typography

ABCDEFGHIJKLMNOPQRST
UVWXYZabcdefghijklmnopqrst
uvwxyz&0123456789$€!?.;:, {½}

*ABCDEFGHIJKLMNOPQRSTU
VWXYZabcdefghijklmnopqrstuvwxy
z&0123456789$€!?.;:, ""{½}*

Letterforms have tone, timbre, charac ter, just as words and sentences do. The moment a text and typeface are

55 ROMAN

Letterforms have tone, timbre, character, just as words and sentences do. The moment a text and typeface are chosen, two streams of

56 ITALIC

Letterforms have tone, timbre, char acter, just as words and sentences do. The moment a text and typeface

75 BOLD

Letterforms have tone, timbre, charac ter, just as words and sentences do. The moment a text and typeface are chosen,

76 BOLD ITALIC

Letterforms have tone, timbre, character, just as words and sen tences do. The moment a text

95 BLACK

Letterforms have tone, timbre, character, just as words and sen tences do. The moment a text and

96 BLACK ITALIC

Hadriano

Frederic W. Goudy, Agfa Division, Bayer Corp.

Typography

ABCDEFGHIJKLMNOPQRSTU
VWXYZabcdefghijklmnopqrstuv
wxyz&0123456789$!?.;:,""{ ½}

Letterforms have tone, timbre, character, just as words and sentences do. The moment a text and typeface are chosen,

LIGHT

Letterforms have tone, timbre, char
acter, just as words and sentences
do. The moment a text and typeface
BOLD

Letterforms have tone, timbre,
character, just as words and sen
tences do. The moment a text and
EXTRA BOLD

Letterforms have tone, timbre, charac
ter, just as words and sen tences do.
The moment a text and typeface are
EXTRA BOLD CONDENSED

Neue Hammer Unziale STD

Victor Hammer, Linotype Library GmbH

Typograph

ABCDEFGHIJKLMNOPQR
STUVWXYZabcdefghijkl
mnopqrstuvwxyz&012
3456789$€!?.,;:/""{½}

BDEFGI 0123456789
Alternates

Letterforms have tone, tim
bre, character, just as word
and sentences do. The mo
REGULAR

Hardwood STD

Garrett Boge, LetterPerfect

Typography

ABCDEFGHIJKLMNOPQRSTUV
WXYZabcdefghijklmnopqrstuvw
xyz&0123456789$€!?.,;:,""{½}

Letterforms have tone, timbre, char
acter, just as words and sentences
REGULAR

Helvetica STD

Max Miedinger, Linotype Library GmbH

Typography

ABCDEFGHIJKLMNOPQRSTU
VWXYZabcdefghijklmnopqrstuv
wxyz&0123456789$€!?.,;:,""{½}

Типография

АБВГЃҐЂЋЕЁЄЖЗЅИЙІЇЈКЌЛ
ЉМНЊОПРСТЋУЎФХЦЏЧШ
ЩЪЫЬЭЮЯабвгѓґђеёєжзѕи
йіїјкќлљмнњопрстћуўфхцџчш
щъыьэюя

ABCDEFGHIJKLMNOPQRSTU
VWXYZabcdefghijklmnopqrstuv
wxyz&0123456789$€!?.,;:,""''{½}

АБВГЃҐДЂЕЁЄЖЗЅИЙЍЇЈКЌЛ
ЉМНЊОПРСТЋУЎФХЦЏЧШ
ЩЪЫЬЭЮЯабвгѓґдђеёєжзѕи
йѝїјкќлљмнњопрстћуўфхцџчш
щъыьэюя

Letterforms have tone, timbre, charac
ter, just as words and sentences do.
The moment a text and typeface are
LIGHT

Letterforms have tone, timbre, charac
ter, just as words and sentences do.
The moment a text and typeface are
LIGHT OBLIQUE

Letterforms have tone, timbre, charac
ter, just as words and sentences do.
The moment a text and typeface are

Точно найденные слова достойны
точности в подборе шрифтов; те, в
свою очередь, заслуживают чутко
ROMAN

Letterforms have tone, timbre, charac
ter, just as words and sentences do.
The moment a text and typeface are

Точно найденные слова достойны
точ ности в подборе шрифтов; те, в
свою очередь, заслуживают чуткого,
OBLIQUE

Letterforms have tone, timbre, charac
ter, just as words and sentences do.
The moment a text and typeface are

Точно найденные слова достойны
точности в подборе шрифтов; те, в
свою очередь, заслуживают чутко
BOLD

Letterforms have tone, timbre, charac
ter, just as words and sentences do.
The moment a text and typeface are

Точно найденные слова достойны
точности в подборе шрифтов; те, в
свою очередь, заслуживают чутко
BOLD OBLIQUE

Letterforms have tone, timbre,
character, just as words and
sentences do. The moment a
BLACK

Letterforms have tone, timbre,
character, just as words and
sentences do. The moment a
BLACK OBLIQUE

Helvetica STD Compressed

Max Miedinger, Linotype Library GmbH

A-z €

Typography

ABCDEFGHIJKLMNOPQRSTUVWXYZ
abcdefghijklmnopqrstuvwxyz&012
3456789$€!?.,;:,""''{½}

Letterforms have tone, timbre, character,
just as words and sentences do. The mo
ment a text and typeface are chosen, two
REGULAR

Letterforms have tone, timbre, character, just as words and sentences do. The moment a text and typeface are chosen, two streams of thought, two

EXTRA

Letterforms have tone, timbre, character, just as words and sentences do. The moment a text and typeface are chosen, two streams of thought, two rhythmical systems, two sets

ULTRA

Helvetica STD Condensed

Max Miedinger, Linotype Library GmbH

A-z €

Typography

ABCDEFGHIJKLMNOPQRSTUVW
XYZabcdefghijklmnopqrstuvwxyz&
0123456789$€!?.;:,""{½}

*ABCDEFGHIJKLMNOPQRSTUVW
XYZabcdefghijklmnopqrstuvwxyz&
0123456789$€!?.;:,""{½}*

Letterforms have tone, timbre, character, just as words and sentences do. The moment a text and typeface are chosen, two streams of thought, two

LIGHT

Letterforms have tone, timbre, character, just as words and sentences do. The moment a text and typeface are chosen, two streams of thought, two

LIGHT OBLIQUE

Letterforms have tone, timbre, character, just as words and sentences do. The mo ment a text and typeface are chosen, two

REGULAR

Letterforms have tone, timbre, character, just as words and sentences do. The mo ment a text and typeface are chosen, two

OBLIQUE

Letterforms have tone, timbre, character, just as words and sentences do. The mo ment a text and typeface are chosen, two

BOLD

Letterforms have tone, timbre, character, just as words and sentences do. The mo ment a text and typeface are chosen, two

BOLD OBLIQUE

Letterforms have tone, timbre, character, just as words and sentences do. The mo ment a text and typeface are chosen, two

BLACK

Letterforms have tone, timbre, character, just as words and sentences do. The mo ment a text and typeface are chosen, two

BLACK OBLIQUE

Helvetica STD Fractions

Max Miedinger, Linotype Library GmbH

0123456789/0123456789

0123456789 0123456789 0123456789

½ ⁷⁄₁₆ ⁶³⁄₆₄ 1⅓ ²⁄₇₇ ⁴⁴⁄₁₀₀ $\frac{1}{2}$ $\frac{7}{16}$ $\frac{63}{64}$ 1$\frac{1}{3}$ $\frac{22}{7}$ $\frac{44}{100}$

REGULAR

½ ⁷⁄₁₆ ⁶³⁄₆₄ 1⅓ ²⁄₇₇ ⁴⁴⁄₁₀₀ $\frac{1}{2}$ $\frac{7}{16}$ $\frac{63}{64}$ 1$\frac{1}{3}$ $\frac{22}{7}$ $\frac{44}{100}$

BOLD

Helvetica Inserat STD

Max Miedinger, Linotype Library GmbH

A-z **€**

Typography

**ABCDEFGHIJKLMNOPQRS
TUVWXYZabcdefghijklmn
opqrstuvwxyz&01234567
89$€!?.:;,""{½}**

Типография

**АБВГЃҐДЂЕЁЄЖЗЅЅИЙІЇЈКЌЛЉЛЬМН
ЊОПРСТЋУЎФХЦЏЧШЩЪЫЬЭЮЯ
абвгѓґдђеёєжзѕѕийіїјкќлљльмнњо
прстћуўфхцџчшщъыьэюяя**

**Letterforms have tone, timbre,
character, just as words and**

**Точно найденные слова до
стойны точно сти в подборе**

ROMAN

Helvetica Neue STD

Linotype Staff, Linotype Library GmbH

A-z **€**

Typography

ABCDEFGHIJKLMNOPQRSTU
VWXYZabcdefghijklmnopqrstuv
wxyz&0123456789$€.:;,!?{½}

*ABCDEFGHIJKLMNOPQRSTU
VWXYZabcdefghijklmnopqrstuv
wxyz&0123456789$€.:;,!?{½}*

Letterforms have tone, timbre, character,
just as words and sentences do. The mo
ment a text and typeface are chosen, two

25 ULTRA LIGHT

*Letterforms have tone, timbre, character,
just as words and sentences do. The mo
ment a text and typeface are chosen, two*

26 ULTRA LIGHT ITALIC

Letterforms have tone, timbre, character,
just as words and sentences do. The mo
ment a text and typeface are chosen,

35 THIN

*Letterforms have tone, timbre, character,
just as words and sentences do. The mo
ment a text and typeface are chosen,*

36 THIN ITALIC

Letterforms have tone, timbre, character,
just as words and sentences do. The
moment a text and typeface are chosen,

45 LIGHT

*Letterforms have tone, timbre, character,
just as words and sentences do. The
moment a text and typeface are chosen,*

46 LIGHT ITALIC

Letterforms have tone, timbre, charac
ter, just as words and sentences do.
The moment a text and typeface are
55 ROMAN

*Letterforms have tone, timbre, charac
ter, just as words and sentences do.
The moment a text and typeface are*
56 ITALIC

Letterforms have tone, timbre, charac
ter, just as words and sentences do.
The moment a text and typeface are
65 MEDIUM

*Letterforms have tone, timbre, charac
ter, just as words and sentences do.
The moment a text and typeface are*
66 MEDIUM ITALIC

**Letterforms have tone, timbre, char
acter, just as words and sentences
do. The moment a text and typeface**
75 BOLD

***Letterforms have tone, timbre, char
acter, just as words and sentences
do. The moment a text and typeface***
76 BOLD ITALIC

**Letterforms have tone, timbre,
character, just as words and sen
tences do. The moment a text and**
85 HEAVY

***Letterforms have tone, timbre,
character, just as words and sen
tences do. The moment a text***
86 HEAVY ITALIC

**Letterforms have tone, timbre,
character, just as words and sen
tences do. The moment a text**
95 BLACK

***Letterforms have tone, timbre,
character, just as words and sen
tences do. The moment a text***
96 BLACK ITALIC

Helvetica Neue STD Bold Outline

Linotype Staff, Linotype Library GmbH

A-Z €

Typography

ABCDEFGHIJKLMNOPQRSTUV
WXYZabcdefghijklmnopqrstuv
wxyz&0123456789$€!?.;:""{½}

Letterforms have tone, timbre,
character, just as words and
75 BOLD

Helvetica Neue STD Condensed

Linotype Staff, Linotype Library GmbH

A-Z €

Typography

ABCDEFGHIJKLMNOPQRSTUVWXYZ
abcdefghijklmnopqrstuvwxyz&012345
6789$€!?.;:,""{½}

*ABCDEFGHIJKLMNOPQRSTUVWXYZ
abcdefghijklmnopqrstuvwxyz&012345
6789$€!?.;:,""{½}*

Letterforms have tone, timbre, character, just as words
and sentences do. The moment a text and typeface are
chosen, two streams of thought, two rhythmical systems
27 ULTRA LIGHT

*Letterforms have tone, timbre, character, just as words
and sentences do. The moment a text and typeface are
chosen, two streams of thought, two rhythmical systems*
27 ULTRA LIGHT OBLIQUE

Letterforms have tone, timbre, character, just as words and sentences do. The moment a text and typeface are chosen, two streams of thought, two

37 THIN

Letterforms have tone, timbre, character, just as words and sentences do. The moment a text and typeface are chosen, two streams of thought, two

37 THIN OBLIQUE

Letterforms have tone, timbre, character, just as words and sentences do. The moment a text and typeface are chosen, two streams of thought, two

47 LIGHT

Letterforms have tone, timbre, character, just as words and sentences do. The moment a text and typeface are chosen, two streams of thought, two

47 LIGHT OBLIQUE

Letterforms have tone, timbre, character, just as words and sentences do. The moment a text and typeface are chosen, two streams of

57 REGULAR

Letterforms have tone, timbre, character, just as words and sentences do. The moment a text and typeface are chosen, two streams of

57 OBLIQUE

Letterforms have tone, timbre, character, just as words and sentences do. The moment a text and typeface are chosen, two streams of

67 MEDIUM

Letterforms have tone, timbre, character, just as words and sentences do. The moment a text and typeface are chosen, two streams of

67 MEDIUM OBLIQUE

Letterforms have tone, timbre, character, just as words and sentences do. The mo ment a text and typeface are chosen, two

77 BOLD

Letterforms have tone, timbre, character, just as words and sentences do. The mo ment a text and typeface are chosen, two

77 BOLD OBLIQUE

Letterforms have tone, timbre, character, just as words and sentences do. The mo ment a text and typeface are chosen, two

87 HEAVY

Letterforms have tone, timbre, character, just as words and sentences do. The mo ment a text and typeface are chosen, two

87 HEAVY OBLIQUE

Letterforms have tone, timbre, character, just as words and sentences do. The mo ment a text and typeface are chosen, two

97 BLACK

Letterforms have tone, timbre, character, just as words and sentences do. The mo ment a text and typeface are chosen, two

97 BLACK OBLIQUE

Letterforms have tone, timbre, character, just as words and sentences do. The mo ment a text and typeface are chosen, two

107 EXTRA BLACK

Letterforms have tone, timbre, character, just as words and sentences do. The mo ment a text and typeface are chosen, two

107 EXTRA BLACK OBLIQUE

Helvetica Neue STD Extended

Linotype Staff, Linotype Library GmbH

A-Z | €

Typograph

ABCDEFGHIJKLMNOPQR
STUVWXYZabcdefghijklmn
opqrstuvwxyz&012345678
9$€.;:,!?{½}

ABCDEFGHIJKLMNOPQR
STUVWXYZabcdefghijklmn
opqrstuvwxyz&012345678
9$€!?.;:,""{½}

Letterforms have tone, timbre, charac
ter, just as words and sentences do.
The moment a text and typeface are

23 ULTRA LIGHT

*Letterforms have tone, timbre, charac
ter, just as words and sentences do.
The moment a text and typeface are*

23 ULTRA LIGHT OBLIQUE

Letterforms have tone, timbre, char
acter, just as words and sentences
do. The moment a text and typeface

33 THIN

*Letterforms have tone, timbre, char
acter, just as words and sentences
do. The moment a text and typeface*

33 THIN OBLIQUE

Letterforms have tone, timbre,
character, just as words and sen
tences do. The moment a text

43 LIGHT

*Letterforms have tone, timbre,
character, just as words and sen
tences do. The moment a text*

43 LIGHT OBLIQUE

Letterforms have tone, timbre,
character, just as words and sen
tences do. The moment a text

53 REGULAR

*Letterforms have tone, timbre,
character, just as words and sen
tences do. The moment a text*

53 OBLIQUE

Letterforms have tone, timbre,
character, just as words and
sentences do. The moment a

63 MEDIUM

*Letterforms have tone, timbre,
character, just as words and
sentences do. The moment a*

63 MEDIUM OBLIQUE

**Letterforms have tone, tim
re, character, just as words
and sentences do. The mo**

73 BOLD

***Letterforms have tone, tim
re, character, just as words
and sentences do. The mo***

73 BOLD OBLIQUE

**Letterforms have tone,
timbre, character, just as
words and sentences do.**

83 HEAVY

***Letterforms have tone,
timbre, character, just as
words and sentences do.***

83 HEAVY OBLIQUE

**Letterforms have tone,
timbre, character, just as
words and sentences**

93 BLACK

***Letterforms have tone,
timbre, character, just as
words and sentences***

93 BLACK OBLIQUE

158
H

Helvetica Rounded STD
Unknown, Linotype Library GmbH

Typography

ABCDEFGHIJKLMNOPQR STUVWXYZabcdefghijklmn opqrstuvwxyz&0123456789 $€.;:,!?{½}

ABCDEFGHIJKLMNOPQR STUVWXYZabcdefghijklmn opqrstuvwxyz&0123456789 $€!?.;:,""{½}

Letterforms have tone, tim bre, character, just as word
BOLD

Letterforms have tone, tim bre, character, just as wor
BOLD OBLIQUE

Letterforms have tone, timbre, character, just
BLACK

Letterforms have tone, timbre, character, just
BLACK OBLIQUE

Letterforms have tone, timbre, char acter, just as words and sentences
BOLD CONDENSED

Letterforms have tone, timbre, char acter, just as words and sentences
BOLD CONDENSED OBLIQUE

Herculanum STD
Adrian Frutiger, Linotype Library GmbH

TYPOGRAPHY

ABCDEFGHIJKLMNOP QRSTUVWXYZ&0123 456789$€!?.;:,""{½}

AKMNRUVXYZ
Alternates

LETTERFORMS HAVE TONE, TIMBRE, CHARACTER, JUST
REGULAR

ITC Highlander STD
David Farey, ITC

Typography

ABCDEFGHIJKLMNOPQRSTUVW XYZabcdefghijklmnopqrstuvwxyz& 0123456789$€!?.;:,""{½}

ABCDEFGHIJKLMNOPQRSTUVW XYZabcdefghijklmnopqrstuvwxyz& 0123456789$€!?.;:, ""{½}

Letterforms have tone, timbre, character, just as words and sentences do. The moment a text and typeface are chosen, two streams
BOOK

Letterforms have tone, timbre, character, just as words and sentences do. The moment a text and typeface are chosen, two streams
BOOK ITALIC

Letterforms have tone, timbre, character, just as words and sentences do. The mo ment a text and typeface are chosen, two
MEDIUM

Letterforms have tone, timbre, character, just as words and sentences do. The mo ment a text and typeface are chosen, two
MEDIUM ITALIC

Letterforms have tone, timbre, charac ter, just as words and sentences do. The moment a text and typeface are
BOLD

Letterforms have tone, timbre, char acter, just as words and sentences do. The moment a text and typeface are
BOLD ITALIC

Hiroshige STD

Cynthia Hollandsworth, AlphaOmega Typography

Typography

ABCDEFGHIJKLMNOPQRSTU
VWXYZabcdefghijklmnopqrstuv
wxyz&0123456789$€!?.;:,""{½}

*ABCDEFGHIJKLMNOPQRSTU
VWXYZabcdefghijklmnopqrstuv
wxyz&0123456789$€!?.;:,""{½}*

Letterforms have tone, timbre, charac ter, just as words and sentences do. The moment a text and typeface are
BOOK

Letterforms have tone, timbre, character, just as words and sentences do. The mo ment a text and typeface are chosen, two
BOOK ITALIC

Letterforms have tone, timbre, charac ter, just as words and sentences do. The moment a text and typeface are
MEDIUM

Letterforms have tone, timbre, charac ter, just as words and sentences do. The moment a text and typeface are
MEDIUM ITALIC

Letterforms have tone, timbre, char acter, just as words and sentences do. The moment a text and typeface
BOLD

Letterforms have tone, timbre, char acter, just as words and sentences do. The moment a text and typeface
BOLD ITALIC

Letterforms have tone, timbre, character, just as words and sen tences do. The moment a text
BLACK

Letterforms have tone, timbre, character, just as words and sen tences do. The moment a text
BLACK ITALIC

www.adobe.com/type

Hobo STD

Morris Fuller Benton

A-Z **€**

Typography

ABCDEFGHIJKLMNOPQ RSTUVWXYZabcdefghij klmnopqrstuvwxyz&01 23456789$€!?.:;,""{½}

Letterforms have tone, tim bre, character, just as words

REGULAR

Linotype Holiday Pi STD

Linotype Staff

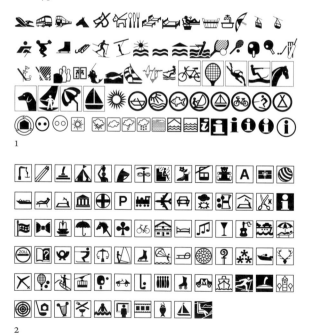

1

2

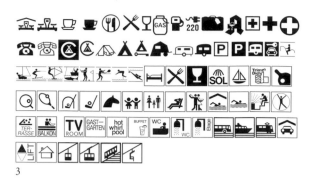

3

Horley Old Style STD

Unknown, Monotype Corp.

A-Z **€**

Typography

ABCDEFGHIJKLMNOPQRST
UVWXYZabcdefghijklmnopqrstu
vwxyz&0123456789$€!?.;:,""{½}

*ABCDEFGHIJKLMNOPQRSTU
VWXYZabcdefghijklmnopqrstuvwx
yz&0123456789$€!?.;:,""{½}*

Letterforms have tone, timbre, character,
just as words and sentences do. The mo
ment a text and typeface are chosen, two
LIGHT

*Letterforms have tone, timbre, character, just
as words and sentences do. The moment a
text and typeface are chosen, two streams of*
LIGHT ITALIC

Letterforms have tone, timbre, character,
just as words and sentences do. The mo
ment a text and typeface are chosen, two
REGULAR

Letterforms have tone, timbre, character, just as words and sentences do. The moment a text and typeface are chosen, two streams
ITALIC

Letterforms have tone, timbre, charac ter, just as words and sentences do. The moment a text and typeface are chosen,
SEMI BOLD

Letterforms have tone, timbre, character, just as words and sentences do. The mo ment a text and typeface are chosen, two
SEMI BOLD ITALIC

Letterforms have tone, timbre, charac ter, just as words and sentences do. The moment a text and typeface are chosen
BOLD

Letterforms have tone, timbre, charac ter, just as words and sentences do. The moment a text and typeface are chosen,
BOLD ITALIC

Immi 505 STD

Tim Donaldson, Adobe Systems

A-z €

Typograph

ABCDEFGHIJKLMNO
PQRSTUVWXYZabcd
efghijklmnopqrstuv
wxyz&0123456789$€!
?.;:,""{½}

Letterforms have tone,
timbre, character, just
REGULAR

Impact STD

Geoffrey Lee, S. Blake

A-z €

Typography

ABCDEFGHIJKLMNOPQRSTUVWX
YZabcdefghijklmnopqrstuvwx
yz&0123456789$€!?.;:,""{½}

Letterforms have tone, timbre,
character, just as words and sen
REGULAR

Impressum STD

Konrad F. Bauer and Walter Baum, Bauer Types, S.A.

A-z €

Typograph

ABCDEFGHIJKLMNOPQR
STUVWXYZabcdefghijklmn
opqrstuvwxyz&0123456789$
€!?.;:,""{½}

*ABCDEFGHIJKLMNOPQRS
TUVWXYZabcdefghijklmno
pqrstuvwxyz&0123456789$€
!?.;:,""{½}*

Letterforms have tone, timbre,
character, just as words and sen
tences do. The moment a text
ROMAN

Letterforms have tone, timbre, character, just as words and sen tences do. The moment a text and
ITALIC

Letterforms have tone, timbre, character, just as words and sen tences do. The moment a text
BOLD

Industria STD

Neville Brody, Linotype Library GmbH

A-z € ę̃

Typography

ABCDEFGHIJKLMNOPQRSTUVWXYZ abcdefghijklmnopqrstuvwxyz&01234 56789$€!?.;:,""'{½}

glt
Alternates

Letterforms have tone, timbre, character, just as words and sentences do. The moment
SOLID

Letterforms have tone, timbre, character, just as words and sentences do. The moment
INLINE

Inflex STD

Unknown, Monotype Corp.

A-z €

Typograph

ABCDEFGHIJKLMNO PQRSTUVWXYZabcdef ghijklmnopqrstuvwxyz &0123456789$€!?.;:,""'{½}

Letterforms have tone, timbre, character just as
BOLD

Insignia STD

Neville Brody, Linotype Library GmbH

A-z € ę̃

Typography

ABCDEFGHIJKLMNOP QRSTUVWXYZabcdefg hijklmnopqrstuvwxyz& 0123456789$€!?.;:,""'{½}

EFJPRSZst
Alternates

Letterforms have tone, tim bre, character, just as word
REGULAR

Ironwood STD

Joy Redick, Adobe Systems

A-Z €

TYPOGRAPHY

ABCDEFGHIJKLMNOPQRSTUVWX
YZ&0123456789$€!?.,:,.""{½}

LETTERFORMS HAVE TONE, TIMBRE,
CHARACTER, JUST AS WORDS AND
MEDIUM

Isabella STD

Herman Ihlenburg, Agfa Division, Bayer Corp.

A-Z €

Typography

ABCDEFGHIJKLMNOPQRST
UVWXYZabcdefghijklmnopqrstuvwx
yz&0123456789$€!?.,:,.""{½}

Letterforms have tone, timbre, char
acter, just as words and sentences
REGULAR

ITC Isadora STD

Kris Holmes, ITC

A-Z €

Typography

ABCDEFGHIJKLMNO
PQRSTUVWXYZabcde
fghijklmnopqrstuvwxyz&
0123456789$€.,:,!?{½}

Letterforms have tone, timbre,
character, just as words and
REGULAR

Letterforms have tone, timbre,
character, just as words and
BOLD

Italia STD

Colin Brignall, Esselte Pendaflex, Letraset, Esselte Letraset

A-Z €

Typography

ABCDEFGHIJKLMNOPQRSTUVW
XYZabcdefghijklmnopqrstuvwxy
z&0123456789$€!?.,:,.""{½}

Letterforms have tone, timbre, charac
ter, just as words and sentences do. The
moment a text and typeface are chosen,
BOOK

Letterforms have tone, timbre, charac
ter, just as words and sentences do. The
moment a text and typeface are chosen,
MEDIUM

**Letterforms have tone, timbre, char
acter, just as words and sentences do.
The moment a text and typeface are**
BOLD

Monotype Italian Old Style STD

Unknown, Monotype Typography Ltd.

A-z €

Typography

ABCDEFGHIJKLMNOPQRST
UVWXYZabcdefghijklmnopqrstu
vwxyz&0123456789$€!?.;:,""{½}

*ABCDEFGHIJKLMNOPQRSTU
VWXYZabcdefghijklmnopqrstuvwx
yz&0123456789$€!?.;:,""{½}*

Letterforms have tone, timbre, character,
just as words and sentences do. The mo
ment a text and typeface are chosen, two
REGULAR

*Letterforms have tone, timbre, character, just
as words and sentences do. The moment a text
and typeface are chosen, two streams of thou*
ITALIC

**Letterforms have tone, timbre, charac
ter, just as words and sentences do. The
moment a text and typeface are chose**
BOLD

***Letterforms have tone, timbre, character,
just as words and sentences do. The moment
a text and typeface are chosen, two streams***
BOLD ITALIC

Janson Text STD

Nicholas Kis, Linotype Library GmbH

A-z € BB 619 123

Typography

ABCDEFGHIJKLMNOPQRS
TUVWXYZabcdefghijklmnopqr
stuvwxyz&0123456789$€!?.;:,""
{½}

ABCDEFGHIJKLMNOPQRSTUVWXYZ&
0123456789 0123456789

*ABCDEFGHIJKLMNOPQRSTU
VWXYZabcdefghijklmnopqrstuvwx
yz&0123456789$€!?.;:,""{½}*

0123456789 0123456789

LETTERFORMS HAVE TONE, timbre, charac
ter, just as words and 567 sentences do.
The moment a text and typeface are cho
55 ROMAN

*Letterforms have tone, timbre, character,
just as words and 567 sentences do. The mo
ment a text and typeface are chosen, two*
56 ITALIC

**Letterforms have tone, timbre, char
acter, just as words and 567 sentences
do. The moment a text and typeface**
75 BOLD

***Letterforms have tone, timbre, character,
just as words and 567 sentences do. The
moment a text and typeface are chosen,***
76 BOLD ITALIC

Adobe Jenson PRO

Robert Slimbach, Adobe Systems

A-z € ffi Bb 619 123 ⅞ H₂ 1st 𝒜 ᵉ꜀ ✎ aA

Typography

ABCDEFGHIJKLMNOPQRSTUV
WXYZabcdefghijklmnopqrstuvwxyz
&ABCDEFGHIJKLMNOPQRSTUVWXYZ&

ABCDEFGHIJKLMNOPQRSTUV
WXYZabcdefghijklmnopqrstuvwxyz&
ABCDEFGHIJKLMNOPQRSTUVWXYZ&

A B C D E F G H I J K L M N O P Q
R S T U V W X Y Z b d f g h j k l p q y
Swash

0123456789 0123456789
0123456789 0123456789
0123456789 0123456789
0123456789 0123456789
Proportional and Tabular Figures

MQZ mqz ſ Th ᵬ ff ffi ffj ffl fi fj fl ſp
ſt fh fi fl ſſ ft abdehilmnorst
Alternates, Ligatures & Superiors

veſ Th Th ᵬ ff ffi ffj ffl fi fj fl ſp ſt ſh ſi ſl
ſſ ſt ff abdehilmnorst
Italic Alternates, Ligatures & Superiors

Ø$¢£¥ƒ€#¤Rp₡%‰$¢£¥ƒ€#$¢₡%‰⁰¹²
3456789($¢-.,)0123456789($¢-.,)/₀₁₂₃₄₅₆₇₈₉($¢-.,)
0123456789($¢-.,)¼½¾⅛⅜⅝⅞⅓⅔^~·+±
<=>-|¦×÷∂µπΔΠΣΩ√∞∫≈≠≤≥◊¬℮
ℓ°ᵃᵒ__——-·--—''"""„",«»‹›,.;: …
.. .·!?¡¿¡¿()()[][]{}{}/ *·§†‡₡©®™ @@
Currency, Punctuation, and Related Forms

Ø$¢£¥ƒ€#¤Rp₡%‰$¢£¥ƒ€#$¢₡%‰⁰¹
23456789($¢-.,)0123456789($¢-.,)/0123456789
($¢-.,)0123456789($¢-.,)¼½¾⅛⅜⅝⅞⅓⅔
^~·+± <=>-|¦×÷∂µπΔΠΣΩ√∞∫≈
≠≤≥◊¬℮ℓ°ᵃᵒ__——-·--—'"""„",'
*«»‹›,.;: … .. .·!?¡¿¡¿()()[][]{}{}/ *
·§†‡₡©®™@@
Italic Currency, Punctuation, and Related Forms

ÆŁØŒÞÐÁÂÄÀÅÃÇÉÊËÈÍÎÏÌ
 İÑÓÔÖÒÕŠÚÛÜÙÝŸŽĂĀĄĆ
ČĎĚĖĒĘĞĠĪĮĶĹĽĻŃŇŅŐŌŔŘ
ŖŚŞŠŤŢŰŪŲŮŹŻÆıłøœßþðáâäà
ãçéêëèíîïìñóôöòõšúûüùýÿžăāąćčďěė
ęğġīįķĺľļńňņőōŕřŗśşşťţűūųůźżÆŁØŒÞ
ÐÁÂÄÀÅÃÇÉÊËÈÍÎÏÌİÑÓÔÖÒÕŠÚÛÜÙ
ÝŸŽĂĀĄĆČĎĚĖĒĘĞĠĪĮĶĹĽĻŃŇŅŐŌŔŘ
ŖŚŞŠŤŢŰŪŲŮŹŻ
Accented Characters

ÆŁØŒÞÐÁÂÄÀÅÃÇÉÊËÈÍÎÏÌÌÑ
ÓÔÖÒÕŠÚÛÜÙÝŸŽĂĀĄĆČĎĚĖ
ĒĘĞĠĪĮĶĹĽĻŃŇŅŐŌŔŘŖŚŞŠŤŢ
ŰŪŲŮŹŻÆıłøœßþðáâäàãçéêëèíîï
ñóôöòõšúûüùýÿžăāąćčďěėęğġīįķĺľļ

*ńňņŏōŕřŗśşŝţťűūųůźż&ŁØŒÞÐÁÂÄÀ
ÅÃÇÉÊËÈÍÎÏÌÑÓÔÖÒÕŠÚÛÜÙÝŸŽĂÃ
ĄĆČĎĖĒĘĞĢĪĮĶĹĽĻŃŇŅŐŌŔŘŖŚŞŠŤ
ŢŰŪŲŮŹŻ*

Italic Accented Characters

~ : ~ ❦ ❧ ❦

Ornaments

Letterforms have tone, timbre, character,
just as words and 567 sentences do. The mo
ment a text and typeface are chosen, two strea
LIGHT

*Letterforms have tone, timbre, character,
just as words and 567 sentences do. The moment
a text and typeface are chosen, two streams of*
LIGHT ITALIC

Letterforms have tone, timbre, character,
just as words and 567 sentences do. The mo
ment a text and typeface are chosen, two strea
REGULAR

*Letterforms have tone, timbre, character,
just as words and 567 sentences do. The moment
a text and typeface are chosen, two streams of*
ITALIC

**Letterforms have tone, timbre, charac
ter, just as words and 567 sentences do. The
moment a text and typeface are chosen, two**
SEMIBOLD

***Letterforms have tone, timbre, character,
just as words and 567 sentences do. The mo
ment a text and typeface are chosen, two stream***
SEMIBOLD ITALIC

**Letterforms have tone, timbre, charac
ter, just as words and 567 sentences do. The
moment a text and typeface are chosen, two**
BOLD

***Letterforms have tone, timbre, charac
ter, just as words and 567 sentences do. The
moment a text and typeface are chosen, two***
BOLD ITALIC

*To download a complete glyph complement PDF, please visit
www.adobe.com/type.*

Adobe Jenson PRO Opticals

Robert Slimbach, Adobe Systems

Letterforms have tone, timbre, character, just as words and 567
sentences do. The moment a text and typeface are chosen, two streams

Letterforms have tone, timbre, character,
just as words and 567 sentences do. The mo

Letterforms have tone, timbre,
character, just as words and 567 sen

Letterforms have tone,
LIGHT: CAPTION, REGULAR, SUBHEAD, DISPLAY

*Letterforms have tone, timbre, character, just as words and
567 sentences do. The moment a text and typeface are chosen, two*

*Letterforms have tone, timbre, character,
just as words and 567 sentences do. The moment*

*Letterforms have tone, timbre,
character, just as words and 567*

Letterforms have tone,
LIGHT ITALIC: CAPTION, REGULAR, SUBHEAD, DISPLAY

LETTERFORMS HAVE TONE, timbre, character, just as words and 567 sentences do. The moment a text and typeface are chosen,

LETTERFORMS HAVE TONE, timbre, character, just as words and 567 sentences do. The mo

LETTERFORMS have tone, timbre, character, just as words and 567

LETTERFORMS have tone,

CAPTION, REGULAR, SUBHEAD, DISPLAY

LETTERFORMS HAVE TONE, timbre, character, just as words and 567 sentences do. The moment a text and typeface are chosen, two

LETTERFORMS HAVE TONE, timbre, character, just as words and 567 sentences do. The moment

LETTERFORMS have tone, timbre, character, just as words and 567 sen

LETTERFORMS have tone,

ITALIC: CAPTION, REGULAR, SUBHEAD, DISPLAY

LETTERFORMS HAVE TONE, timbre, character, just as words and 567 sentences do. The moment a text and typeface are cho

LETTERFORMS HAVE TONE, timbre, charac ter, just as words and 567 sentences do. The

LETTERFORMS have tone, timbre, character, just as words and sen

LETTERFORMS have tone

SEMIBOLD: CAPTION, REGULAR, SUBHEAD, DISPLAY

LETTERFORMS HAVE TONE, timbre, character, just as words and 567 sentences do. The moment a text and typeface are cho

LETTERFORMS HAVE TONE, timbre, charac ter, just as words and 567 sentences do. The

LETTERFORMS have tone, timbre, character, just as words and senten

LETTERFORMS have tone,

SEMIBOLD ITALIC: CAPTION, REGULAR, SUBHEAD, DISPLAY

LETTERFORMS HAVE TONE, timbre, character, just as words and 567 sentences do. The moment a text and typeface are

LETTERFORMS HAVE TONE, timbre, charac ter, just as words and 567 sentences do. The

LETTERFORMS have tone, tim bre, character, just as words and

LETTERFORMS have

BOLD: CAPTION, REGULAR, SUBHEAD, DISPLAY

LETTERFORMS HAVE TONE, timbre, character, just as words and 567 sentences do. The moment a text and typeface are cho

LETTERFORMS HAVE TONE, timbre, charac ter, just as words and 567 sentences do. The

LETTERFORMS have tone, timbre, character, just as words and sen

LETTERFORMS have tone,

BOLD ITALIC: CAPTION, REGULAR, SUBHEAD, DISPLAY

To download a complete glyph complement PDF, please visit www.adobe.com/type.

Jimbo STD

Jim Parkinson, Adobe Systems

A-Z €

Typograph

ABCDEFGHIJKLMNOPQR STUVWXYZabcdefghijkl mnopqrstuvwxyz&01234 56789$€!?.;:,""{½}

Letterforms have tone, timbre, character, just as words and senten

REGULAR CONDENSED

Letterforms have tone, timbre, character, just as words and
BOLD CONDENSED

Letterforms have tone, tim bre, character, just as words
BLACK CONDENSED

Letterforms have tone, timbre, character, just as
REGULAR

Letterforms have tone, timbre, character, just
BOLD

Letterforms have to ne, timbre, character
BLACK

Letterforms have tone, timbre, charac
EXPANDED

Letterforms have tone, timbre, char
BOLD EXPANDED

Letterforms ha ve tone, timbre,
BLACK EXPANDED

Joanna STD

Eric Gill, Monotype Corp.

A-z €

Typography

ABCDEFGHIJKLMNOPQRSTUVW
XYZabcdefghijklmnopqrstuvwxyz&
0123456789$€!?.,:,""{½}

ABCDEFGHIJKLMNOPQRSTUVWXYZ
abcdefghijklmnopqrstuvwxyz&0123456789
$€!?.,:,""{½}

Letterforms have tone, timbre, character, just as words and sentences do. The moment a text and typeface are chosen, two streams of
REGULAR

Letterforms have tone, timbre, character, just as words and sentences do. The moment a text and typeface are chosen, two streams of thought, two rhythmical systems
ITALIC

Letterforms have tone, timbre, character, just as words and sentences do. The mo ment a text and typeface are chosen, two
SEMI BOLD

Letterforms have tone, timbre, character, just as words and sentences do. The moment a text and typeface are chosen, two streams of thought, two rhythmical sys
SEMI BOLD ITALIC

Letterforms have tone, timbre, character, just as words and sentences do. The mo ment a text and typeface are chosen, two
BOLD

Letterforms have tone, timbre, character, just as words and sentences do. The moment a text and type face are chosen, two streams of thought, two rhyth
BOLD ITALIC

Letterforms have tone, timbre, charac ter, just as words and sentences do. The moment a text and typeface are chosen
EXTRA BOLD

Juniper STD

Joy Redick, Adobe Systems

A-z **€**

TYPOGRAPHY

ABCDEFGHIJKLMNOPQRST UVWXYZ&0123456789$€!? .;:,""{½}

LETTERFORMS HAVE TONE, TIMBRE, CHARACTER, JUST AS
MEDIUM

Kabel STD

Rudolf Koch, Linotype Library GmbH

A-z **€**

Typography

ABCDEFGHIJKLMNOPQRSTUVWX
YZabcdefghijklmnopqrstuvwxyz&0123456
789$€!?.;:,""{½}

Letterforms have tone, timbre, character, just as words and sentences do. The moment a text and typeface are chosen, two streams of thought, two rhythmical
LIGHT

Letterforms have tone, timbre, character, just as words and sentences do. The moment a text and typeface are chosen, two streams of thought, two
BOOK

Letterforms have tone, timbre, character, just as words and sentences do. The moment a text and typeface are chosen, two streams of thought, two
HEAVY

Letterforms have tone, timbre, character, just as words and sentences do. The mo ment a text and typeface are chosen,
BLACK

ITC Kabel STD

Rudolf Koch, ITC

A-z **€**

Typography

ABCDEFGHIJKLMNOPQRSTUVWX
YZabcdefghijklmnopqrstuvwxyz&
0123456789$€!?.;:,""{½}

Letterforms have tone, timbre, character, just as words and sentences do. The mo ment a text and typeface are chosen, two
BOOK

Letterforms have tone, timbre, charac ter, just as words and sentences do. The moment a text and typeface are
MEDIUM

Letterforms have tone, timbre, charac ter, just as words and sentences do. The moment a text and typeface are
DEMI

Letterforms have tone, timbre, charac ter, just as words and sentences do. The moment a text and typeface are
BOLD

Letterforms have tone, timbre, charac ter, just as words and sentences do. The moment a text and typeface are
ULTRA

Kaufmann STD

Max R. Kaufmann, Kingsley/ATF

Typography

*ABCDEFGHIJKLMNOP2RSTU
VWXYZabcdefghijklmnopqrstuv
wxyz&0123456789$€!?.,;:, ""{½}*

*Letterforms have tone, timbre, char
acter, just as words and sentences*
REGULAR

**Letterforms have tone, timbre,
character, just as words and**
BOLD

Kepler STD

Robert Slimbach, Adobe Systems

Typography

ABCDEFGHIJKLMNOPQRSTUVW
XYZabcdefghijklmnopqrstuvwxyz
&0123456789$€!?.,;:,""{½}

ABCDEFGHIJKLMNOPQRSTUVWXYZ
&0123456789 ffi ⅛ 0123456789

*ABCDEFGHIJKLMNOPQRSTUVW
XYZabcdefghijklmnopqrstuvwxyz&
0123456789$€!?.,;:,""{½}*

*ABCDEFGHIJKLMNOPQRSTUVWXYZ&
0123456789 ffi ⅛ 0123456789*

*ABCDEFGHIJKLMNOPQRSTU
VWXYZ*
Swash

Ornaments

Letterforms have tone, timbre, character,
just as words and 567 sentences do. The mo
ment a text and typeface are chosen, two
LIGHT

*LETTERFORMS HAVE TONE, timbre, character,
just as words and 567 sentences do. The mo
ment a text and typeface are chosen, two*
LIGHT ITALIC

LETTERFORMS HAVE TONE, timbre, charac
ter, just as words and 567 sentences do.
The moment a text and typeface are cho
ROMAN

LETTERFORMS HAVE TONE, timbre, charac ter, just as words and 567 sentences do. The moment a text and typeface are chosen, two
ITALIC

LETTERFORMS HAVE TONE, timbre, charac ter, just as words and 567 sentences do. The moment a text and typeface are cho
MEDIUM

LETTERFORMS HAVE TONE, timbre, charac ter, just as words and 567 sentences do. The moment a text and typeface are chosen,
MEDIUM ITALIC

LETTERFORMS HAVE TONE, timbre, charac ter, just as words and 567 sentences do. The moment a text and typeface are cho
SEMIBOLD

LETTERFORMS HAVE TONE, timbre, charac ter, just as words and 567 sentences do. The moment a text and typeface are cho
SEMIBOLD ITALIC

LETTERFORMS HAVE TONE, timbre, char acter, just as words and 567 sentences do. The moment a text and typeface are
BOLD

LETTERFORMS HAVE TONE, timbre, charac ter, just as words and 567 sentences do. The moment a text and typeface are cho
BOLD ITALIC

LETTERFORMS HAVE TONE, timbre, char acter, just as words and 567 sentences do. The moment a text and typeface are
BLACK

LETTERFORMS HAVE TONE, timbre, char acter, just as words and 567 sentences do. The moment a text and typeface are
BLACK ITALIC

Robert Slimbach, Adobe Systems

A-z € ffi BB 619 123 ⅞ H₂ 1st 𝒜 ✍ aA

Typography

LETTERFORMS HAVE TONE, timbre, character, just as words and 567 sentences do. The mo ment a text and typeface are chosen, two
LIGHT SEMICONDENSED

LETTERFORMS HAVE TONE, timbre, character, just as words and 567 sentences do. The moment a text and typeface are chosen, two streams of
LIGHT SEMICONDENSED ITALIC

LETTERFORMS HAVE TONE, timbre, character, just as words and 567 sentences do. The mo ment a text and typeface are chosen, two
SEMICONDENSED

LETTERFORMS HAVE TONE, timbre, character, just as words and 567 sentences do. The mo ment a text and typeface are chosen, two
SEMICONDENSED ITALIC

LETTERFORMS HAVE TONE, timbre, character, just as words and 567 sentences do. The mo ment a text and typeface are chosen, two
MEDIUM SEMICONDENSED

LETTERFORMS HAVE TONE, timbre, character, just as words and 567 sentences do. The mo ment a text and typeface are chosen, two
MEDIUM SEMICONDENSED ITALIC

LETTERFORMS HAVE TONE, timbre, charac ter, just as words and 567 sentences do. The moment a text and typeface are chosen, two
SEMIBOLD SEMICONDENSED

LETTERFORMS HAVE TONE, timbre, character, just as words and 567 sentences do. The mo ment a text and typeface are chosen, two
SEMIBOLD SEMICONDENSED ITALIC

LETTERFORMS HAVE TONE, timbre, charac ter, just as words and 567 sentences do. The moment a text and typeface are cho
BOLD SEMICONDENSED

LETTERFORMS HAVE TONE, timbre, charac ter, just as words and 567 sentences do. The moment a text and typeface are chosen, two
BOLD SEMICONDENSED ITALIC

LETTERFORMS HAVE TONE, timbre, charac ter, just as words and 567 sentences do. The moment a text and typeface are cho
BLACK SEMICONDENSED

LETTERFORMS HAVE TONE, timbre, charac ter, just as words and 567 sentences do. The moment a text and typeface are cho
BLACK SEMICONDENSED ITALIC

Kepler STD Extended

Robert Slimbach, Adobe Systems

A-Z € ffi BB 619 123 ⅞ H₂ 1st 𝒜 ✍ aA

Typograph

LETTERFORMS HAVE TONE, timbre, character, just as words and 567 sen tences do. The moment a text and
LIGHT EXTENDED

LETTERFORMS HAVE TONE, timbre, character, just as words and 567 sen tences do. The moment a text and type
LIGHT EXTENDED ITALIC

LETTERFORMS HAVE TONE, timbre, character, just as words and 567 sentences do. The moment a text
EXTENDED

LETTERFORMS HAVE TONE, timbre, character, just as words and 567 sen tences do. The moment a text and
EXTENDED ITALIC

LETTERFORMS HAVE TONE, timbre, character, just as words and 567 sentences do. The moment a text
MEDIUM EXTENDED

LETTERFORMS HAVE TONE, timbre, character, just as words and 567 sen tences do. The moment a text and
MEDIUM EXTENDED ITALIC

LETTERFORMS HAVE TONE, timbre, character, just as words and 567 sentences do. The moment a text
SEMIBOLD EXTENDED

LETTERFORMS HAVE TONE, timbre, character, just as words and 567 sen tences do. The moment a text and
SEMIBOLD EXTENDED ITALIC

LETTERFORMS HAVE TONE, tim bre, character, just as words and 567 sentences do. The moment a
BOLD EXTENDED

LETTERFORMS HAVE TONE, timbre, character, just as words and 567 sentences do. The moment a text
BOLD EXTENDED ITALIC

LETTERFORMS HAVE TONE, tim bre, character, just as words and 576 sentences do. The moment a
BLACK EXTENDED

LETTERFORMS HAVE TONE, timbre, character, just as words and 567 sentences do. The moment a text
BLACK EXTENDED ITALIC

Robert Slimbach, Adobe Systems

A-z € ffi BB 619 123 ⅞ H₂ 1ˢᵗ 𝒜 ✒ aA

LETTERFORMS HAVE TONE, timbre, character, just as words and 567 sentences do. The moment a text and typeface are chosen,

LETTERFORMS HAVE TONE, timbre, character, just as words and 567 sentences do. The

LETTERFORMS have tone, timbre, character, just as words and 567

LETTERFORMS have tone

LIGHT: CAPTION, REGULAR, SUBHEAD, DISPLAY

LETTERFORMS HAVE TONE, timbre, character, just as words and 567 sentences do. The moment a text and typeface are chosen, two

LETTERFORMS HAVE TONE, timbre, character, just as words and 567 sentences do. The mo

LETTERFORMS have tone, timbre, character, just as words and 567

LETTERFORMS have tone,

LIGHT ITALIC: CAPTION, REGULAR, SUBHEAD, DISPLAY

LETTERFORMS HAVE TONE, timbre, character, just as words and 567 sentences do. The moment a text and typeface are chosen,

LETTERFORMS HAVE TONE, timbre, character, just as words and 567 sentences do.

LETTERFORMS have tone, timbre, character, just as words

LETTERFORMS have to

CAPTION, REGULAR, SUBHEAD, DISPLAY

LETTERFORMS HAVE TONE, timbre, character, just as words and 567 sentences do. The moment a text and typeface are chosen,

LETTERFORMS have tone, timbre, character, just as words and 567

LETTERFORMS have tone

ITALIC: CAPTION, REGULAR, SUBHEAD, DISPLAY

LETTERFORMS HAVE TONE, timbre, character, just as words and 567 sentences do. The moment a text and typeface are

LETTERFORMS HAVE TONE, timbre, character, just as words and 567 sentences do.

LETTERFORMS have tone, timbre, character, just as words

LETTERFORMS have to

MEDIUM: CAPTION, REGULAR, SUBHEAD, DISPLAY

LETTERFORMS HAVE TONE, timbre, character, just as words and 567 sentences do. The moment a text and typeface are chosen,

LETTERFORMS HAVE TONE, timbre, charac ter, just as words and 567 sentences do. The

LETTERFORMS have tone, timbre, character, just as words and 567

LETTERFORMS have to

MEDIUM ITALIC: CAPTION, REGULAR, SUBHEAD, DISPLAY

LETTERFORMS HAVE TONE, timbre, character, just as words and 567 sentences do. The moment a text and typeface are

LETTERFORMS HAVE TONE, timbre, charac ter, just as words and 567 sentences do.

LETTERFORMS have tone, tim bre, character, just as words

LETTERFORMS have to

SEMIBOLD: CAPTION, REGULAR, SUBHEAD, DISPLAY

www.adobe.com/type

K

LETTERFORMS HAVE TONE, timbre, character, just as words and 567 sentences do. The moment a text and typeface are chosen,

LETTERFORMS HAVE TONE, timbre, character, just as words and 567 sentences do. The mo

LETTERFORMS have tone, tim bre, character, just as words an

LETTERFORMS have to

SEMIBOLD ITALIC: CAPTION, REGULAR, SUBHEAD, DISPLAY

LETTERFORMS HAVE TONE, timbre, character, just as words and 567 sentences do. The moment a text and typeface are

LETTERFORMS HAVE TONE, timbre, char acter, just as words and 567 sentences

LETTERFORMS have tone, tim bre, character, just as words

LETTERFORMS have

BOLD: CAPTION, REGULAR, SUBHEAD, DISPLAY

LETTERFORMS HAVE TONE, timbre, character, just as words and 567 sentences do. The moment a text and typeface are

LETTERFORMS HAVE TONE, timbre, charac ter, just as words and 567 sentences do.

LETTERFORMS have tone, tim bre, character, just as words

LETTERFORMS have to

BOLD ITALIC: CAPTION, REGULAR, SUBHEAD, DISPLAY

LETTERFORMS HAVE TONE, timbre, character, just as words and 567 sentences do. The moment a text and type

LETTERFORMS HAVE TONE, timbre, char acter, just as words and 567 sentences

LETTERFORMS have tone, timbre, character, just as

LETTERFORMS have

BLACK: CAPTION, REGULAR, SUBHEAD, DISPLAY

LETTERFORMS HAVE TONE, timbre, character, just as words and 567 sentences do. The moment a text and typeface are

LETTERFORMS HAVE TONE, timbre, char acter, just as words and 567 sentences

LETTERFORMS have tone, tim bre, character, just as words

LETTERFORMS have

BLACK ITALIC: CAPTION, REGULAR, SUBHEAD, DISPLAY

Kepler STD Condensed Opticals

Robert Slimbach, Adobe Systems

LETTERFORMS have tone, timbre, charac ter, just as words and 567 sentences do.

LETTERFORMS have tone, timbre,

LIGHT: SUBHEAD, DISPLAY

LETTERFORMS have tone, timbre, charac ter, just as words and 567 sentences do.

LETTERFORMS have tone, timbre,

LIGHT ITALIC: SUBHEAD, DISPLAY

LETTERFORMS have tone, timbre, char acter, just as words and 567 sentences

LETTERFORMS have tone, tim

SUBHEAD, DISPLAY

LETTERFORMS have tone, timbre, charac ter, just as words and 567 sentences do.

LETTERFORMS have tone, timbre

ITALIC: SUBHEAD, DISPLAY

LETTERFORMS have tone, timbre, char
acter, just as words and 567 sentences

LETTERFORMS have tone,

MEDIUM: SUBHEAD, DISPLAY

*LETTERFORMS have tone, timbre, charac
ter, just as words and 567 sentences do.*

LETTERFORMS have tone, tim

MEDIUM ITALIC: SUBHEAD, DISPLAY

LETTERFORMS have tone, timbre, char
acter, just as words and 567 sentences

LETTERFORMS have tone,

SEMIBOLD: SUBHEAD, DISPLAY

*LETTERFORMS have tone, timbre, char
acter, just as words and 567 sentences*

LETTERFORMS have tone, tim

SEMIBOLD ITALIC: SUBHEAD, DISPLAY

**LETTERFORMS have tone, timbre,
character, just as words and 567 sen**

LETTERFORMS have tone,

BOLD: SUBHEAD, DISPLAY

***LETTERFORMS have tone, timbre,
character, just as words and 567 sen***

LETTERFORMS have tone,

BOLD ITALIC: SUBHEAD, DISPLAY

Robert Slimbach, Adobe Systems

LETTERFORMS HAVE TONE, timbre, character, just as words and 567
sentences do. The moment a text and typeface are chosen, two

LETTERFORMS HAVE TONE, timbre, character,
just as words and 567 sentences do. The mo

LETTERFORMS have tone, timbre,
character, just as words and 567 sen

LETTERFORMS have tone,

LIGHT: CAPTION, REGULAR, SUBHEAD, DISPLAY

*LETTERFORMS HAVE TONE, timbre, character, just as words and 567
sentences do. The moment a text and typeface are chosen, two streams*

*LETTERFORMS HAVE TONE, timbre, character, just
as words and 567 sentences do. The moment a*

*LETTERFORMS have tone, timbre, char
acter, just as words and 567 sentences*

LETTERFORMS have tone, tim

LIGHT ITALIC: CAPTION, REGULAR, SUBHEAD, DISPLAY

LETTERFORMS HAVE TONE, timbre, character, just as words and
567 sentences do. The moment a text and typeface are chosen, two

LETTERFORMS HAVE TONE, timbre, character,
just as words and 567 sentences do. The mo

LETTERFORMS have tone, timbre,
character, just as words and 567

LETTERFORMS have tone,

CAPTION, REGULAR, SUBHEAD, DISPLAY

LETTERFORMS HAVE TONE, timbre, character, just as words and 567 sentences do. The moment a text and typeface are chosen, two

LETTERFORMS HAVE TONE, timbre, character, just as words and 567 sentences do. The mo

LETTERFORMS have tone, timbre, character, just as words and 567 sen

LETTERFORMS have tone,

ITALIC: CAPTION, REGULAR, SUBHEAD, DISPLAY

LETTERFORMS HAVE TONE, timbre, character, just as words and 567 sentences do. The moment a text and typeface are chosen,

LETTERFORMS HAVE TONE, timbre, character, just as words and 567 sentences do. The mo

LETTERFORMS have tone, timbre, character, just as words and 567

LETTERFORMS have tone,

MEDIUM: CAPTION, REGULAR, SUBHEAD, DISPLAY

LETTERFORMS HAVE TONE, timbre, character, just as words and 567 sentences do. The moment a text and typeface are chosen, two

LETTERFORMS HAVE TONE, timbre, character, just as words and 567 sentences do. The mo

LETTERFORMS have tone, timbre, character, just as words and 567

LETTERFORMS have tone,

MEDIUM ITALIC: CAPTION, REGULAR, SUBHEAD, DISPLAY

LETTERFORMS HAVE TONE, timbre, character, just as words and 567 sentences do. The moment a text and typeface are chosen,

LETTERFORMS HAVE TONE, timbre, charac ter, just as words and 567 sentences do. The

LETTERFORMS have tone, timbre, character, just as words and 567

LETTERFORMS have tone,

SEMIBOLD: CAPTION, REGULAR, SUBHEAD, DISPLAY

LETTERFORMS HAVE TONE, timbre, character, just as words and 567 sentences do. The moment a text and typeface are chosen, two

LETTERFORMS HAVE TONE, timbre, character, just as words and 567 sentences do. The mo

LETTERFORMS have tone, timbre, character, just as words and 567

LETTERFORMS have tone,

SEMIBOLD ITALIC: CAPTION, REGULAR, SUBHEAD, DISPLAY

LETTERFORMS HAVE TONE, timbre, character, just as words and 567 sentences do. The moment a text and typeface are cho

LETTERFORMS HAVE TONE, timbre, charac ter, just as words and 567 sentences do.

LETTERFORMS have tone, tim bre, character, just as words and

LETTERFORMS have tone

BOLD: CAPTION, REGULAR, SUBHEAD, DISPLAY

LETTERFORMS HAVE TONE, timbre, character, just as words and 567 sentences do. The moment a text and typeface are chosen,

LETTERFORMS HAVE TONE, timbre, character, just as words and 567 sentences do. The mo

LETTERFORMS have tone, timbre, character, just as words and 567

LETTERFORMS have tone,

BOLD ITALIC: CAPTION, REGULAR, SUBHEAD, DISPLAY

LETTERFORMS HAVE TONE, timbre, character, just as words and 567 sentences do. The moment a text and typeface are

LETTERFORMS HAVE TONE, timbre, charac ter, just as words and 567 sentences do.

LETTERFORMS have tone, tim bre, character, just as words

LETTERFORMS have ton

BLACK: CAPTION, REGULAR, SUBHEAD, DISPLAY

Letterforms have tone, timbre, character, just as words and 567 sentences do. The moment a text and typeface are chosen,

Letterforms have tone, timbre, charac ter, just as words and 567 sentences do.

Letterforms have tone, tim bre, character, just as words

Letterforms have tone

BLACK ITALIC: CAPTION, REGULAR, SUBHEAD, DISPLAY

Kepler std Extended Opticals

Robert Slimbach, Adobe Systems

Letterforms have tone, timbre, character, just as words and 567 sentences do. The moment a text and

Letterforms have tone, timbre, character, just as words and 567 sen

Letterforms have tone, timbre, character, just as

Letterforms have

LIGHT: CAPTION, REGULAR, SUBHEAD, DISPLAY

Letterforms have tone, timbre, character, just as words and 567 sentences do. The moment a text and

Letterforms have tone, timbre, character, just as words and 567 senten

Letterforms have tone, tim bre, character, just as words

Letterforms have

LIGHT ITALIC: CAPTION, REGULAR, SUBHEAD, DISPLAY

Letterforms have tone, timbre, character, just as words and 567 sentences do. The moment a text and

Letterforms have tone, timbre, character, just as words and 567 sen

Letterforms have tone, timbre, character, just as

Letterforms have

CAPTION, REGULAR, SUBHEAD, DISPLAY

Letterforms have tone, timbre, character, just as words and 567 sentences do. The moment a text and

Letterforms have tone, timbre, character, just as words and 567 sen

Letterforms have tone, timbre, character, just as

Letterforms have

ITALIC: CAPTION, REGULAR, SUBHEAD, DISPLAY

Letterforms have tone, timbre, character, just as words and 567 sentences do. The moment a text

Letterforms have tone, timbre, character, just as words and 567

Letterforms have tone, timbre, character, just as

Letterforms have

MEDIUM: CAPTION, REGULAR, SUBHEAD, DISPLAY

Letterforms have tone, timbre, character, just as words and 567 sentences do. The moment a text and

Letterforms have tone, timbre, character, just as words and 567 sen

Letterforms have tone, timbre, character, just as

Letterforms have

MEDIUM ITALIC: CAPTION, REGULAR, SUBHEAD, DISPLAY

LETTERFORMS HAVE TONE, timbre, character, just as words and 567 sentences do. The moment a text

LETTERFORMS HAVE TONE, timbre, charac ter, just as words and sen

LETTERFORMS have tone, timbre, character, just as

LETTERFORMS hav

SEMIBOLD: CAPTION, REGULAR, SUBHEAD, DISPLAY

LETTERFORMS HAVE TONE, timbre, character, just as words and 567 sentences do. The moment a text and

LETTERFORMS HAVE TONE, timbre, character, just as words and 567 sen

LETTERFORMS have tone, timbre, character, just as

LETTERFORMS have

SEMIBOLD ITALIC: CAPTION, REGULAR, SUBHEAD, DISPLAY

LETTERFORMS HAVE TONE, timbre, character, just as words and 567 sentences do. The moment

LETTERFORMS HAVE TONE, tim bre, character, just as words and

LETTERFORMS have tone, timbre, character,

LETTERFORMS hav

BOLD: CAPTION, REGULAR, SUBHEAD, DISPLAY

LETTERFORMS HAVE TONE, timbre, character, just as words and 567 sentences do. The moment a text

LETTERFORMS HAVE TONE, timbre, character, just as words and 567

LETTERFORMS have tone, timbre, character, just as

LETTERFORMS hav

BOLD ITALIC: CAPTION, REGULAR, SUBHEAD, DISPLAY

LETTERFORMS HAVE TONE, timbre, character, just as words and 567 sentences do. The mo

LETTERFORMS HAVE TONE, tim bre, character, just as words and

LETTERFORMS have tone, timbre, character,

LETTERFORMS ha

BLACK: CAPTION, REGULAR, SUBHEAD, DISPLAY

LETTERFORMS HAVE TONE, timbre, character, just as words and 567 sentences do. The moment a text

LETTERFORMS HAVE TONE, timbre, character, just as words and 567

LETTERFORMS have tone, timbre, character, just as

LETTERFORMS hav

BLACK ITALIC: CAPTION, REGULAR, SUBHEAD, DISPLAY

Khaki STD

Steve Miggas, Aerotype

A-Z € 123

Typography

ABCDEFGHIJKLMNOPQRSTUV WXYZabcdefghijklmnopqrstuvw xyz&0123456789$€!?.;:,""{½}

Letterforms have tone, timbre, character, just as words and sen
ONE

Letterforms have tone, timbre, character, just as words and sen
TWO

Arthur Baker, Arthur Baker Design

A-z € 123 é

Typography

ABCDEFGHIJKLMNOPQRS
TUVWXYZabcdefghijklmnop
qrstuvwxyz&0123456789
$€!?.;:,""{½}

ABCDEFGHIJKLMNOPQRS
TUVWXYZ&0123456789

b d f g h j k l p q y b d f k k l
Alternates

ABCDEFGHIJKLMNOPQRS
TUVWXYZabcdefghijklmnn
pqrstuvwxyz&0123456789
$€!?.;:,""{½}

ABCDEFGHIJKLMNOPQRS
TUVWXYZ&0123456789

b d f g h j k l p e y b d f k k l
Alternates

Letterforms have tone, timbre,
character, just as words and
ROMAN

Letterforms have tone, timbre,
character, just as words and
ITALIC

ABCDEFGHIJKLMNOPQRS
TUVWXYZabcdefghijklmnop
qrstuvwxyz&0123456789
$€!?.;:,""{½}

ABCDEFGHIJKLM
NOPQRSTUVWXYZ
ABCDEFGHIJKLM
NOPQRSTUVWXYZ
Alternates

Letterforms have tone, timbre,
character, just as words and
ZIGZAG

Kinesis STD

Mark Jamra, Adobe Systems

A-z € ffi BB 619 123 ⅞ H₂ 1st

Typography

ABCDEFGHIJKLMNOPQRSTUV
WXYZabcdefghijklmnopqrstuvwxyz&
0123456789$€!?.;:,""{½}

ABCDEFGHIJKLMNOPQRSTUVWXYZ&
0123456789 ffi ⅛ 0123456789

ABCDEFGHIJKLMNOPQRSTUVWXYZ
abcdefghijklmnopqrstuvwxyz&0123456789
$€!?.,:;""{½}

ABCDEFGHIJKLMNOPQRSTUVWXYZ&
0123456789 ffi ⅛ 0123456789

LETTERFORMS HAVE TONE, timbre, character,
just as words and 567 sentences do. The moment
a text and typeface are chosen, two streams of
LIGHT

LETTERFORMS HAVE TONE, timbre, character, just as
words and 567 sentences do. The moment a text and
typeface are chosen, two streams of thought, two rhyth
LIGHT ITALIC

LETTERFORMS HAVE TONE, timbre, character,
just as words and 567 sentences do. The moment
a text and typeface are chosen, two streams of
REGULAR

LETTERFORMS HAVE TONE, timbre, character, just as
words and 567 sentences do. The moment a text and
type face are chosen, two streams of thought, two
ITALIC

LETTERFORMS HAVE TONE, timbre, character,
just as words and 567 sentences do. The mo
ment a text and typeface are chosen, two
SEMIBOLD

LETTERFORMS HAVE TONE, timbre, character, just as
words and 567 sentences do. The moment a text and
typeface are chosen, two streams of thought, two
SEMIBOLD ITALIC

LETTERFORMS HAVE TONE, timbre, character,
just as words and 567 sentences do. The mo
ment a text and typeface are chosen, two
BOLD

LETTERFORMS HAVE TONE, timbre, character, just
as words and 567 sentences do. The moment a text
and typeface are chosen, two streams of thought,
BOLD ITALIC

LETTERFORMS HAVE TONE, timbre, character,
just as words and 567 sentences do. The mo
ment a text and typeface are chosen, two
BLACK

LETTERFORMS HAVE TONE, timbre, character, just
as words and 567 sentences do. The moment a text
and typeface are chosen, two streams of thought,
BLACK ITALIC

Kino STD

Martin Dovey, Monotype Corp.

Typography

ABCDEFGHIJKLMNOPQRSTUV
WXYZabcdefghijklmnopqrstuvwx
yz&0123456789$€!?.,:;""{½}

Letterforms have tone, timbre, charac
ter, just as words and sentences do.
REGULAR

Klang STD

Will Carter, Monotype Corp.

Typography

ABCDEFGHIJKLMNOPQR
STUVWXYZabcdefghijklm

nopqrstuvwxyz&0123456
789$€!?.,:;""{½}

Letterforms have tone, timbre,
character, just as words and
REGULAR

Koch Antiqua STD

Rudolf Koch, Linotype Library GmbH

Typography

ABCDEFGHIJKLMNOPQR
STUVWXYZabcdefghijklmnopqrst
uvwxyz&0123456789 $€!?.,;:,""{½}

Letterforms have tone, timbre, character,
just as words and sentences do. The mo
REGULAR

Kolo STD

Paul Shaw, LetterPerfect

TYPOGRAPHY

ABCDEFGHIJKLMNOPQ
RSTUVWXYZ&0123456
789$€!?.,;:, ``"{½}

AABCDEFGHHIJKLM
NOPQRSTUVWXYz
AEIOUŒ
Alternates

Ornaments

LETTERFORMS HAVE TONE, TIM
BRE, CHARACTER, JUST AS WORDS
NARROW

LETTERFORMS HAVE TONE,
TIMBRE, CHARACTER, JUST
REGULAR

LETTERFORMS HA
VE TONE, TIMBRE,
WIDE

Kompakt STD

Hermann Zapf, Linotype Library GmbH

Typography

ABCDEFGHIJKLMNOPQ
RSTUVWXYZabcdefghijkl
mnopqrstuvwxyz&012345
6789$€!?.,;:,""{½}

Letterforms have tone,
timbre, character, just as
REGULAR

ITC Korinna STD

Ed Benguiat and Vic Caruso, ITC

`A-z` `€`

Typography

ABCDEFGHIJKLMNOPQRSTUV
WXYZabcdefghijklmnopqrstuvwx
yz&0123456789$€!?.,;:,""{½}

ABCDEFGHIJKLMNOPQRSTUVW
XYZabcdefghijklmnopqrstuvwxyz
&0123456789$€!?.,;:,""{½}

Letterforms have tone, timbre,
character, just as words and sen
REGULAR

Letterforms have tone, timbre,
character, just as words and sen
KURSIV REGULAR

Letterforms have tone, timbre,
character, just as words and
BOLD

Letterforms have tone, tim
bre, character, just as words
KURSIV BOLD

Künstler Script STD

Hans Bohn, Linotype Library GmbH

`A-z` `€`

Typography

Aa Bb Cc Dd Ee Ff Gg Hh Ii
Jj Kk Ll Mm Nn Oo Pp Qq
Rr Ss Tt Uu Vv Ww Xx Yy Zz
&0123456789$€!?.,;: ""{½}

Letterforms have tone, timbre, char
acter, just as words and sentences
MEDIUM

Letterforms have tone, timbre,
character, just as words and
BLACK

Letterforms have tone, timbre, character just as
words and sentences do. The moment a text and
NO. 2 BOLD

Latin STD

Unknown, Monotype Corp.

`A-z` `€`

Typography

ABCDEFGHIJKLMNOPQRSTUVW
XYZabcdefghijklmnopqrstuvwxyz&
0123456789$€!?.,;:,""{½}

Letterforms have tone, timbre, character, just as words and sentences do. The mo
CONDENSED

ITC Leawood STD

Leslie Usherwood, ITC

[A-z] [€]

Typography

ABCDEFGHIJKLMNOPQRSTUV
WXYZabcdefghijklmnopqrstuv
wxyz&0123456789$€!?.;:,""{½}

*ABCDEFGHIJKLMNOPQRSTUV
WXYZabcdefghijklmnopqrstuv
wxyz&0123456789$€!?.;:,""{½}*

Letterforms have tone, timbre, char
acter, just as words and sentences
do. The moment a text and a type
BOOK

*Letterforms have tone, timbre, char
acter, just as words and sentences
do. The moment a text and a type*
BOOK ITALIC

**Letterforms have tone, timbre,
character, just as words and sen
tences do. The moment a text**
MEDIUM

*Letterforms have tone, timbre,
character, just as words and sen
tences do. The moment a text and*
MEDIUM ITALIC

**Letterforms have tone, timbre,
character, just as words and
sentences do. The moment a**
BOLD

*Letterforms have tone, timbre,
character, just as words and sen
tences do. The moment a text*
BOLD ITALIC

**Letterforms have tone, timbre,
character, just as words and
sentences do. The moment a**
BLACK

***Letterforms have tone, timbre,
character, just as words and
sentences do. The moment a***
BLACK ITALIC

ITC Legacy Sans STD

Ronald Arnholm, ITC

[A-z] [€]

Typography

ABCDEFGHIJKLMNOPQRSTUV
WXYZabcdefghijklmnopqrstuvwxy
z&0123456789$€!?.;:,""{½}

*ABCDEFGHIJKLMNOPQRSTUVWX
YZabcdefghijklmnopqrstuvwxyz&0123
456789$€!?.;:,""{½}*

Letterforms have tone, timbre, character,
just as words and sentences do. The mo
ment a text and typeface are chosen, two
BOOK

*Letterforms have tone, timbre, character, just as
words and sentences do. The moment a text and
typeface are chosen, two streams of thought, two*
BOOK ITALIC

Letterforms have tone, timbre, character, just as words and sentences do. The mo ment a text and typeface are chosen, two
MEDIUM

Letterforms have tone, timbre, character, just as words and sentences do. The moment a text and typeface are chosen, two streams of thou
MEDIUM ITALIC

Letterforms have tone, timbre, character, just as words and sentences do. The mo ment a text and typeface are chosen, two
BOLD

Letterforms have tone, timbre, character, just as words and sentences do. The moment a text and typeface are chosen, two streams
BOLD ITALIC

Letterforms have tone, timbre, char acter, just as words and sentences do. The moment a text and typeface
ULTRA

ITC Legacy Serif STD

Ronald Arnholm, ITC

A-Z €

Typography

ABCDEFGHIJKLMNOPQRSTU
VWXYZabcdefghijklmnopqrstuv
wxyz&0123456789$€!?.;:,{½}

*ABCDEFGHIJKLMNOPQRSTUV
WXYZabcdefghijklmnopqrstuvwxyz
&0123456789$€!?.;:, ""{½}*

Letterforms have tone, timbre, character, just as words and sentences do. The mo ment a text and typeface are chosen, two
BOOK

Letterforms have tone, timbre, character, just as words and sentences do. The moment a text and typeface are chosen, two streams of thought, two
BOOK ITALIC

Letterforms have tone, timbre, character, just as words and sentences do. The mo ment a text and typeface are chosen, two
MEDIUM

Letterforms have tone, timbre, character, just as words and sentences do. The moment a text and typeface are chosen, two streams of though
MEDIUM ITALIC

Letterforms have tone, timbre, charac ter, just as words and sentences do. The moment a text and typeface are chosen,
BOLD

Letterforms have tone, timbre, character, just as words and sentences do. The moment a text and typeface are chosen, two streams
BOLD ITALIC

Letterforms have tone, timbre, char acter, just as words and sentences do. The moment a text and typeface
ULTRA

Legault STD

Diana Craft, Communicative Arts Group

A-Z €

Typography

ABCDEFGHIJKLMNOPQRSTUVW
XYZabcdefghijklmnopqrstuvwxyz&
0123456789$€!?.:;, ""{½}

a E J S T a c e f g h i l m n o o r s t t u x & ff ff ft tt Th TT

Alternates and Ligatures

Letterforms have tone, timbre, charac ter, just as words and sentences do. The
REGULAR

Letterforms have tone, timbre, charac ter, just as words and sentences do. The
BOLD

Letter Gothic STD

Roger Roberson

A-z €

Typography

ABCDEFGHIJKLMNOPQRSTUVW
XYZabcdefghijklmnopqrst
uvwxyz&0123456789$€!?.;
:,""{½}

ABCDEFGHIJKLMNOPQRSTUVW
XYZabcdefghijklmnopqrst
uvwxyz&0123456789$€!?.;
:,""{½}

Letterforms have tone, tim
bre, character, just as words
and sentences do. The moment
MEDIUM

Letterforms have tone, tim
bre, character, just as words
and sentences do. The moment
SLANTED

Letterforms have tone, tim
bre, character, just as words
and sentences do. The moment
BOLD

Letterforms have tone, timbre
character, just as words and
sentences do. The moment a
BOLD SLANTED

Life STD

W. Bilz, Simoncini S.A.

A-z €

Typography

ABCDEFGHIJKLMNOPQRSTU
VWXYZabcdefghijklmnopqrstuv
wxyz&0123456789$€!?.;:,""{½}

ABCDEFGHIJKLMNOPQRSTU
VWXYZabcdefghijklmnopqrstuv
wxyz&0123456789$€!?.;:,""{½}

Letterforms have tone, timbre, charac
ter, just as words and sentences do. The
moment a text and typeface are chosen,
ROMAN

Letterforms have tone, timbre, character,
just as words and sentences do. The
moment a text and typeface are chosen,
ITALIC

Letterforms have tone, timbre, charac
ter, just as words and sentences do. The
moment a text and typeface are chosen
BOLD

L

LinoLetter STD

Andre Gürtler and Reinhard Haus,
Linotype Library GmbH

A-Z € BB 619

Typography

ABCDEFGHIJKLMNOPQRS
TUVWXYZabcdefghijklmno
pqrstuvwxyz&0123456789$€
!?.;:,""{½}

ABCDEFGHIJKLMNOPQRSTUVWX
YZ&0123456789

*ABCDEFGHIJKLMNOPQRS
TUVWXYZabcdefghijklmnop
qrstuvwxyz&0123456789$€!?
.;:,""{½}*

0123456789

LETTERFORMS HAVE TONE, timbre,
character, just as words and 567 sen
tences do. The moment a text and
ROMAN

*Letterforms have tone, timbre, charac
ter, just as words and 567 sentences
do. The moment a text and typeface*
ITALIC

LETTERFORMS HAVE TONE, timbre,
character, just as words and 567
sentences do. The moment a text
MEDIUM

*Letterforms have tone, timbre, char
acter, just as words and 567 senten
ces do. The moment a text and type*
MEDIUM ITALIC

**LETTERFORMS HAVE TONE, timbre,
character, just as words and 567
sentences do. The moment a text**
BOLD

***Letterforms have tone, timbre, char
acter, just as words and 567 senten
ces do. The moment a text and type***
BOLD ITALIC

**LETTERFORMS HAVE TONE, timbre,
character, just as words and 567
sentences do. The moment a**
BLACK

***Letterforms have tone, timbre,
character, just as words and 567
sentences do. The moment a text***
BLACK ITALIC

Linoscript STD

Morris Fuller Benton, Linotype Library GmbH

A-Z €

Typography

ABCDEFGHIJKLMNOPQR
STUVWXYZabcdefghijklmnopqrs
tuvwxyz&0123456789$€!?.;:,""{½}

Letterforms have tone, timbre, charac
ter, just as words and sentences do. The
MEDIUM

Linotext STD

Morris Fuller Benton, Linotype Library GmbH

Typography

ABCDEFGHIJKLMN
OPQRSTUVWXYZabc
defghijklmnopqrstuvwxyz&
0123456789$€!?.,;.,"''{½}

ch ck ff ft ll ſ ſi ſſ ſt ħ ẗ

Historic Blackletter

Letterforms have tone, timbre,
character, just as words and

REGULAR

Lithos PRO

Carol Twombly, Adobe Systems

TYPOGRAPHY

ABCDEFGHIJKLMNOP
QRSTUVWXYZABCDEF
GHIJKLMNOPQRSTUVW
XYZ&

YY

Alternates

0123456789
0123456789
0123456789
0123456789

Proportional and Tabular Figures

Ø $ ¢ £ ¥ ƒ €¤$¢£¥ƒ€%‰
#$ ¢£¥ƒ€$¢£¥ƒ€%‰¹²³⁴
¼½¾/^~·+±<=>−|¦×÷∂µ
ΠΔΣΩ√∞∫ \≈≠≤≥◊¬℮ℓ
ºªº ——–-'"˝˘ˇ˛„ „‚«»‹›,.:; … !?
¡¿¡¿!?()[]{}/*·§†‡¶©®™Ⓐ

Currency, Punctuation, and Related Forms

ÆŁØŒÞÐÁÂÄÀÅÃÇÉ
ÊËÈÍÎÏÌİÑÓÔÖÒÕŠÚÛ
ÜÙÝŸŽĂĀĄĆČĎĚĖĒĘ
ĞĢĪĮĶĹĽĻŃŇŅŇŐŌŔŘŖ
ŚŞŠŢŤŰŪŲŮŹŻÆŁØŒ
ÞÐÁÂÄÀÅÃÇÉÊËÈÍÎÏÌÑ
ÓÔÖÒÕŠÚÛÜÙÝŸŽĂĀĄ
ĆČĎĚĖĒĘĞĢĪĮĶĹĽĻŃŇŅ
ŐŌŔŘŖŚŞŠŢŤŰŪŲŮŹŻ

Accented Characters

LETTERFORMS HAVE TO
NE, TIMBRE, CHARACTER,

EXTRA LIGHT

LETTERFORMS HAVE TO
NE, TIMBRE, CHARACTER,
LIGHT

LETTERFORMS HAVE TO
NE, TIMBRE, CHARACTER,
REGULAR

**LETTERFORMS HAVE TO
NE, TIMBRE, CHARACTER**
BOLD

**LETTERFORMS HAVE TO
NE, TIMBRE, CHARAC**
BLACK

ΑΒΓΔΕΖΗΘΙΚΛΜΝΞΟ
ΠΡΣΤΥΦΧΨΩΆΈΉΊΪΪΟ
ΎΫΫΩΑΒΓΔΕΖΗΘΙΚΛΜΝ
ΞΟΠΡΣΤΥΦΧΨΩΆΈΉΊΪ
ΪΟΎΫΫΩ
Greek

ΚΎΨΣΚΎΨΣ
Greek Alternates

ΣΤΙΣ ΠΎΛΕΣ ΤΟΥ ΔΆΣΟΥΣ
Ο ΈΚΠΛΗΚΤΟΣ ΆΝΘΡΩ
EXTRA LIGHT

ΣΤΙΣ ΠΎΛΕΣ ΤΟΥ ΔΆΣΟΥΣ
Ο ΈΚΠΛΗΚΤΟΣ ΆΝΘΡΩ
LIGHT

ΣΤΙΣ ΠΎΛΕΣ ΤΟΥ ΔΆΣΟΥΣ
Ο ΈΚΠΛΗΚΤΟΣ ΆΝΘΡΩ
REGULAR

**ΣΤΙΣ ΠΎΛΕΣ ΤΟΥ ΔΆ
ΣΟΥΣ Ο ΈΚΠΛΗΚΤΟΣ**
BOLD

**ΣΤΙΣ ΠΎΛΕΣ ΤΟΥ ΔΆ
ΣΟΥΣ Ο ΈΚΠΛΗΚΤΟΣ**
BLACK

*To download a complete glyph complement PDF, please visit
www.adobe.com/type.*

ITC Lubalin Graph STD

Herb Lubalin, ITC

Typography

ABCDEFGHIJKLMNOPQRSTUV
WXYZabcdefghijklmnopqrstuv
wxyz&0123456789$€!?.;:, ""{½}

*ABCDEFGHIJKLMNOPQRSTUV
WXYZabcdefghijklmnopqrstuv
wxyz&0123456789$€!?.;:, ""{½}*

Letterforms have tone, timbre, char
acter, just as words and sentences
do. The moment a text and typefa
BOOK

*Letterforms have tone, timbre, char
acter, just as words and sentences
do. The moment a text and typefa*
BOOK OBLIQUE

**Letterforms have tone, timbre, char
acter, just as words and sentences
do. The moment a text and typefa**
DEMI

Letterforms have tone, timbre, char acter, just as words and sentences do. The moment a text and typefa
DEMI OBLIQUE

Lucida STD

Charles Bigelow and Kris Holmes, Bigelow & Holmes

A-z € ffi

Typography

ABCDEFGHIJKLMNOPQRSTU VWXYZabcdefghijklmnopqr stuvwxyz&0123456789$€!? .;:, ""{½} ffi

ABCDEFGHIJKLMNOPQRSTU VWXYZabcdefghijklmnopqr stuvwxyz&0123456789$€!? .;:, ""{½} ffi

Letterforms have tone, timbre, character, just as words and sen tences do. The moment a text and
ROMAN

Letterforms have tone, timbre, character, just as words and sen tences do. The moment a text and
ITALIC

Letterforms have tone, timbre, character, just as words and sentences do. The moment a
BOLD

Letterforms have tone, timbre, character, just as words and sentences do. The moment a
BOLD ITALIC

Lucida Sans STD

Charles Bigelow and Kris Holmes, Bigelow & Holmes

A-z € ffi

Typography

ABCDEFGHIJKLMNOPQRSTUV WXYZabcdefghijklmnopqrstu vwxyz&0123456789$€!?.;:, ""{½} ffi

ABCDEFGHIJKLMNOPQRSTUV WXYZabcdefghijklmnopqrstu vwxyz&0123456789$€!?.;:, ""{½} ffi

Letterforms have tone, timbre, char acter, just as words and sentences do. The moment a text and type
ROMAN

Letterforms have tone, timbre, char acter, just as words and sentences do. The moment a text and typeface
ITALIC

Letterforms have tone, timbre, character, just as words and sentences do. The moment a
BOLD

Letterforms have tone, timbre, character, just as words and sentences do. The moment a
BOLD ITALIC

L

Lucida Typewriter STD

Charles Bigelow and Kris Holmes, Bigelow & Holmes

A-z €

Typograph

ABCDEFGHIJKLMNOPQRS
TUVWXYZabcdefghijkl
mnopqrstuvwxyz&0123
456789$€!?.;:,""{½}

ABCDEFGHIJKLMNOPQRS
TUVWXYZabcdefghijkl
mnopqrstuvwxyz&0123
456789$€!?.;:,""{½}

Letterforms have tone,
timbre, character, just
as words and sentences
REGULAR

Letterforms have tone,
timbre, character, just
as words and sentences
OBLIQUE

Letterforms have tone,
timbre, character, just
as words and sentences
BOLD

Letterforms have tone,
timbre, character, just
as words and sentences
BOLD OBLIQUE

Lucida Sans Typewriter STD

Charles Bigelow and Kris Holmes, Bigelow & Holmes

A-z €

Typography

ABCDEFGHIJKLMNOPQRSTUVW
XYZabcdefghijklmnopqrst
uvwxyz&0123456789$€!?.;
:,""{½}

ABCDEFGHIJKLMNOPQRSTUVW
XYZabcdefghijklmnopqrst
uvwxyz&0123456789$€!?.;
:,""{½}

Letterforms have tone, tim
bre, character, just as words
and sentences do. The moment
REGULAR

Letterforms have tone, tim
bre, character, just as words
and sentences do. The moment
OBLIQUE

Letterforms have tone, tim
bre, character, just as words
and sentences do. The moment
BOLD

Letterforms have tone, tim
bre, character, just as words
and sentences do. The moment
BOLD OBLIQUE

Lucida Math STD

Charles Bigelow and Kris Holmes, Bigelow & Holmes

Extension

ABCDEFGHIJKLMNOPQRSTUVWX
YZ.abcdefghijklmnopqrstuvwxyz
0123456789ΓΔΘΛΞΠΣΥΦΨΩαβγδ
εζηθικλμνξπρστυφχψωεϑϖϱ
φ⟶ ⟶ ⟶°◁▷ ♭♮♯≈∼℘ℓ∂ </>★

Italic

ABCDEFGHIJKLMNOPQRST
UVWXYZ {}()\/↕↔⇕⇔↑⇑↞⟵⟸
⇒↘↙↗‖⊢⊤⊥⊣∏∐∈∀∃⊐
ℵℶ−×÷±∓≡∞∝∼≃≈≦≪≫≺≻⋨⋩
⊓⊑⊒⊏⊐⊇∪∩⊎△▽▽∧∨♠♡◇♣¶§†
‡∗⊕⊖⊗⊙∅·•◇∘≍○   √

Symbol

Bonder & Carnase, Inc., ITC

`A-z` `€`

TYPOGRAPHY

ABCDEFGHIJKLMNOPQRSTUVWXY
Z&0123456789$€!?.,:.,""''{½}

**LETTERFORMS HAVE TONE, TIMBRE,
CHARACTER, JUST AS WORDS AND**

MEDIUM

**LETTERFORMS HAVE TONE, TIMBRE,
CHARACTER, JUST AS WORDS AND**

BOLD

Madrone STD

Barbara Lind, Adobe Systems

`A-z` `€`

Typogra

ABCDEFGHIJ
KLMNOPQRST
UVWXYZabcde
fghijklmnopqr
stuvwxyz&012
3456789$€!?.,:;,
""''{½}

Letterforms
have tone, tim

REGULAR

M

192

MVB Magnesium STD
Mark van Bronkhorst, MVB Fonts

TYPOGRAPH
ABCDEFGHIJKLMN
OPQRSTUVWXYZ&
0123456789$€!?.;:,
""{½}

LETTERFORMS HAVE TONE, TIMBRE, CHARACTER, JUST
REGULAR

LETTERFORMS HAVE TONE, TIMBRE, CHAR
GRIME

MVB Magnolia STD
Mark van Bronkhorst, MVB Fonts

TYPOGRAPHY
ABCDEFGHIJKLMNOPQRSTUVWXYZ
&0123456789$€!?.;:,""{½}

CT ST TT
Ligatures

LETTERFORMS HAVE TONE, TIMBRE, CHARACTER, JUST AS WORDS AND SENTENCES
REGULAR

Manito STD
Garrett Boge, LetterPerfect

TYPOGRAPH
ABCDEFGHIJKLMNOP
QRSTUVWXYZABCDE
FGHIJKLMNOPQRSTU
VWXYZ&012345678
9$!?.;:,""{½}

LETTERFORMS HAVE TONE, TIMBRE, CHARAC
REGULAR

Marigold
Arthur Baker, AlphaOmega Typography

Typography
ABCDEFGHIJKLMNOPQRSTUVWX
YZabcdefghijklmnopqrstuvwxyz&012345
6789$!?.;:,""{½}

Letterforms have tone, timbre, character, just as words and sentences do. The moment a text and
REGULAR

Mathematical Pi STD

Linotype Staff

ABCDEFGHIJKLMNOPQRSTUVW XYZghlzghlzABCDEFGHIJKLMN OPQRSTUVWXYZ abcdefghijflmnno pqrstuvwxyz ABCDEFGHIJKLMNOP QRSTUVWXYZ **ABΓΔEZHΘIKΛMN ΞΟΠΡΘΣΤΥΦΧΨΩ∇αβδγδεζηθικλ μνξοπρστυφχψωдеϑκφϖ** ABΓΔEZH ΘIKΛMNΞΟΠΡΘΣΤΥΦΧΨΩ∇αβγδεζ ηθικλμνξοπρστυφχψωдеϑκφϖ()<>[]{}

REGULAR

Matura STD

Imre Reiner, Monotype Corp.

Typography

ABCDEFGHIJKLMNOPQR STUVWXYZabcdefghijklm nopqrstuvwxyz&01234567 89$€!?.;:,{½}

ABCDEFGHIJ KLMNOPQRS TUVWXYZ&

Scriptorial Capitals

Letterforms have tone, timbre, character, just as words and

REGULAR

Maximus STD

Unknown, Linotype Library GmbH

Typography

ABCDEFGHIJKLMN OPQRSTUVWXYZ abcdefghijklmnopqrst uvwxyz&0123456789 $€!?.;:,"" {½}

Letterforms have tone, timbre, character, just

MEDIUM

Medici Script STD

Hermann Zapf, Linotype Library GmbH

A-z €

Typography

ABCDEFGHIJKLMNO
PQRSTUVWXYZabcdefgh
ijklmnopqrstuvwxyz&01234
56789$€!?.;:,""{½}

Letterforms have tone, timbre, char
acter, just as words and sentences
MEDIUM

Melior STD

Hermann Zapf, Linotype Library GmbH

A-z €

Typography

ABCDEFGHIJKLMNOPQRSTUV
WXYZabcdefghijklmnopqrstuvw
xyz&0123456789$€!?.;:, ""{½}

*ABCDEFGHIJKLMNOPQRSTUV
WXYZabcdefghijklmnopqrstuvw
xyz&0123456789$€!?.;:, ""{½}*

Letterforms have tone, timbre, charac
ter, just as words and sentences do.
The moment a text and typeface are
REGULAR

*Letterforms have tone, timbre, charac
ter, just as words and sentences do.
The moment a text and typeface are*
ITALIC

**Letterforms have tone, timbre, charac
ter, just as words and sentences do.
The moment a text and typeface are**
BOLD

***Letterforms have tone, timbre, char
acter, just as words and sentences
do. The moment a text and typeface***
BOLD ITALIC

Memphis STD

Dr. Rudolf Wolf, Linotype Library GmbH

A-z €

Typography

ABCDEFGHIJKLMNOPQRSTU
VWXYZabcdefghijklmnopqrstu
vwxyz&0123456789$€!?.;:,""{½}

*ABCDEFGHIJKLMNOPQRSTU
VWXYZabcdefghijklmnopqrstu
vwxyz&0123456789$€!?.;:,""{½}*

Letterforms have tone, timbre, char
acter, just as words and sentences do.
The moment a text and typeface are
LIGHT

*Letterforms have tone, timbre, char
acter, just as words and sentences do.
The moment a text and typeface are*
LIGHT ITALIC

**Letterforms have tone, timbre, char
acter, just as words and sentences
do. The moment a text and typeface**
MEDIUM

Letterforms have tone, timbre, char acter, just as words and sentences do. The moment a text and typeface are
MEDIUM ITALIC

Letterforms have tone, timbre, char acter, just as words and sentences do. The moment a text and typeface
BOLD

Letterforms have tone, timbre, char acter, just as words and sentences do. The moment a text and typeface are
BOLD ITALIC

Letterforms have tone, timbre, character, just as words and sentences do. The moment a
EXTRA BOLD

ITC Mendoza Roman STD

José Mendoza y Almeida, ITC

A-z €

Typography

ABCDEFGHIJKLMNOPQRSTUV
WXYZabcdefghijklmnopqrstuvw
xyz&0123456789$€!?.;:,""{½}

*ABCDEFGHIJKLMNOPQRSTUV
WXYZabcdefghijklmnopqrstuvwxy
z&0123456789$€!?.;:,""{½}*

Letterforms have tone, timbre, char acter, just as words and sentences do. The moment a text and typeface are
BOOK

Letterforms have tone, timbre, character, just as words and sentences do. The mo ment a text and typeface are chosen, two
BOOK ITALIC

Letterforms have tone, timbre, char acter, just as words and sentences do. The moment a text and typeface are
MEDIUM

Letterforms have tone, timbre, charac ter, just as words and sentences do. The moment a text and typeface are chosen
MEDIUM ITALIC

Letterforms have tone, timbre, char acter, just as words and sentences do. The moment a text and typeface
BOLD

Letterforms have tone, timbre, char acter, just as words and sentences do. The moment a text and typeface are
BOLD ITALIC

Mercurius STD

Imre Reiner, Monotype Corp.

A-z €

Typography

*ABCDEFGHIJKLM
NOPQRSTUVWXYZ
abcdefghijklmnopqrst
uvwxyz&0123456789
$€!?.;:,""{½}*

Letterforms have tone, tim bre, character, just as words
BOLD SCRIPT

Club Type Mercurius STD

Adrian Williams, Adrian Williams Design Ltd.

A-z €

Typography

ABCDEFGHIJKLMNOPQRSTUVWX
YZabcdefghijklmnopqrstuvwxyz&
0123456789$€!?.,;:,""{½}

*ABCDEFGHIJKLMNOPQRSTUVWX
YZabcdefghijklmnopqrstuvwxyz&01
23456789$€!?.,;:,""{½}*

Letterforms have tone, timbre, character, just as
words and sentences do. The moment a text and
typeface are chosen, two streams of thought, two
LIGHT

*Letterforms have tone, timbre, character, just as words
and sentences do. The moment a text and typeface are
chosen, two streams of thought, two rhythmical sys*
LIGHT ITALIC

**Letterforms have tone, timbre, character,
just as words and sentences do. The mo
ment a text and typeface are chosen, two**
MEDIUM

***Letterforms have tone, timbre, character,
just as words and sentences do. The moment
a text and typeface are chosen, two streams***
MEDIUM ITALIC

**Letterforms have tone, timbre, char
acter, just as words and sentences do.
The moment a text and typeface are**
BLACK

***Letterforms have tone, timbre, char
acter, just as words and sentences do.
The moment a text and typeface are***
BLACK ITALIC

Meridien STD

Adrian Frutiger, Linotype Library GmbH

A-z €

Typography

ABCDEFGHIJKLMNOPQRSTUV
WXYZabcdefghijklmnopqrstuvw
xyz&0123456789$€!?.,;:,""{½}

*ABCDEFGHIJKLMNOPQRSTUVW
XYZabcdefghijklmnopqrstuvwxyz&
0123456789$€!?.,;:,""{½}*

Letterforms have tone, timbre, char
acter, just as words and sentences do.
The moment a text and typeface are
ROMAN

*Letterforms have tone, timbre, character,
just as words and sentences do. The moment
a text and typeface are chosen, two streams*
ITALIC

Letterforms have tone, timbre, char
acter, just as words and sentences do.
The moment a text and typeface are
MEDIUM

*Letterforms have tone, timbre, character,
just as words and sentences do. The moment
a text and typeface are chosen, two streams*
MEDIUM ITALIC

**Letterforms have tone, timbre,
character, just as words and sen
tences do. The moment a text and**
BOLD

***Letterforms have tone, timbre, charac
ter, just as words and sentences do. The
moment a text and typeface are chosen***
BOLD ITALIC

Mesquite STD

Joy Redick, Adobe Systems

A-z €

TYPOGRAPHY

ABCDEFGHIJKLMNOPQRSTUVW
XYZ&0123456789$€!?.,:;, ""{½}

LETTERFORMS HAVE TONE, TIMBRE,
CHARACTER, JUST AS WORDS AND

MEDIUM

Mezz STD

Michael Harvey, Adobe Systems

A-z €

Typography

ABCDEFGHIJKLMNOPQRSTUVWXYZ
abcdefghijklmnopqrstuvwxyz&012
3456789$€!?.,:;, ""{½}

Letterforms have tone, timbre, character, just as
words and sentences do. The moment a text and

LIGHT

Letterforms have tone, timbre, character,
just as words and sentences do. The momen

REGULAR

Letterforms have tone, timbre, charac
ter, just as words and sentences do. The

SEMIBOLD

Letterforms have tone, timbre, cha
racter, just as words and sentences

BOLD

Letterforms have tone, timbre,
character, just as words and

BLACK

MICR STD

Unknown

⑆⑆⑈⑉⑈⑇0123456789

MEDIUM

Minion PRO

Robert Slimbach, Adobe Systems

A-z € ffi BB 619 123 ⅞ H₂ 1st 𝒜 ê ✧ aA

Typography

ABCDEFGHIJKLMNOPQRSTUV
WXYZabcdefghijklmnopqrstuvwx
yz&ABCDEFGHIJKLMNOPQRSTUVW
XYZ&

*ABCDEFGHIJKLMNOPQRSTUV
WXYZabcdefghijklmnopqrstuvwxyz
&ABCDEFGHIJKLMNOPQRSTUVWX
YZ&*

*ABCDEFGHIJKLMNOPQR
STUVWXYZ*

Swash

0123456789 0123456789

0123456789 0123456789

0123456789 0123456789

0123456789 0123456789

Proportional and Tabular Figures

KRkſ ae mn r Th ch ck ct fb ff fh
fi fj fk fl ft ffb ffh ffi ffj ffk ffl fft sp
st fb fh fi fk fl ff ft ffi ffl ^{abdehilmnorst}

Alternates, Ligatures, and Superiors

*KRkſ ch ck ct fb ff fh fi fj fk fl ft ffb
ffh ffi ffj ffk ffl fft sp st fb fh fi fk fl ff
ft ffi ffl Th* ^{abdehilmnorst}

Italic Alternates, Ligatures, and Superiors

Ø$¢£¥ƒ₡F£P€#¤$¢£¥ƒ₡F£€#RpPs%
‰$¢£¥ƒ₡F£€#$¢£¥ƒ₡F£€#%‰℮
0123456789($¢-.,)0123456789($¢-.,)/0123456789
($¢-.,)0123456789($¢-.,) ¼½¾⅛⅜⅝⅞⅓⅔
∧~·+±<=>−|¦×÷∂μπΔΠΣΩ√∞∫≈≠
≤≥◊¬№℮ℓºao_——-----—'''"«»„'‹›«»
«»‹›‹› ,.:; … .. .·!?¡¿!?¡¿()()[][]{}{}
/\\⁎•§†‡¶©®™@@

Currency, Punctuation, and Related Forms

*Ø$¢£¥ƒ₡F£P€#¤$¢£¥ƒ₡F£€#RpPs%
‰$¢£¥ƒ₡F£€#$¢£¥ƒ₡F£€#%‰℮
0123456789($¢-.,)0123456789($¢-.,)/0123456789
($¢-.,)0123456789($¢-.,) ¼½¾⅛⅜⅝⅞⅓⅔
∧~+±<=>-|¦×÷∂μπΔΠΣΩ√∞∫≈≠
≤≥◊¬№℮ℓºao_——-----—""«»„'‹›«»*

«»‹›‹›,.:; … .. .·!?¡¿!?¡¿()()[][]{}{}
/\\⁎•§†‡¶©®™@@

Italic Currency, Punctuation, and Related Forms

ÆŁØŒÞÐÁÂÄÀÅÃÇÉÊËÈÍÎÏÌIÑ
ÓÔÖÒÕŠÚÛÜÙÝŸŽĂÀĄĆČĎÐ
ĚÈĒĘĞĠĨĮĶĹĽĻŃŇŅŐŌŔŘŖŚŞŞ
ŤŢŰŪŲŮŽŻÆĈĊČĚŊĜĠĦĤĨ IJ Ĩ
ĴĻŎØŚŤŬŨŴŴŴŴŶŸŸæıłøœßþ
ðáâäàåãçéêëèíîïì ñóôöòõšúûüùýÿžăā
ąćčďðěèēęğġĩįķĺľļńňņőōŕřŗśşşťťűūų
ůžżæĉċčěŋĝġħĥĩ ij ĩĵļŀnŏøśťŭũẃŵẅẁŵŷ
ỳķÆŁØŒÞÐÁÂÄÀÅÃÇÉÊËÍÎÏÌÑÓÔ
ÖÒÕŠÚÛÜÙÝŸŽĂÀĄĆČĎÐĚÈĒĘĞĨĮ
ĶĹĽĻŃŇŅŐŌŔŘŖŚŞŞŤŢŰŪŲŮŽŻÆĈ
ĚŊĜĠĦĤĨ IJ ĨĴĻŎØŚŤŬŨŴŴŴŴŶŸ

Latin Alphabetic

*ÆŁØŒÞÐÁÂÄÀÅÃÇÉÊËÍÎÏÌIÑ
ÓÔÖÒÕŠÚÛÜÙÝŸŽĂÀĄĆČĎÐĚ
ÈĒĘĞĠĨĮĶĹĽĻŃŇŅŐŌŔŘŖŚŞŞŤŢ
ŰŪŲŮŽŻÆĈĊČĚŊĜĠĦĤĨ IJ ĨĴĻŎ
ØŚŤŬŨŴŴŴŴŶŸŸæıłøœßþðáâäà
åãçéêëèíîïì ñóôöòõšúûüùýÿžăāąćčďðě
éēęğġĩįķĺľļńňņőōŕřŗśşşťťűūųůžżæĉċčěŋ
ĝġħĥĩ ij ĩĵļŀnŏøśťŭũẃŵẅẁŷỳķÆŁØŒÞ
ÐÁÂÄÀÅÃÇÉÊËÍÎÏÌIÑÓÔÖÒÕŠÚÛÜÙ
ÝŸŽĂÀĄĆČĎÐĚÈĒĘĞĠĨĮĶĹĽĻŃŇŅŐŌ
ŔŘŖŚŞŞŤŢŰŪŲŮŽŻÆĈĊČĚŊĜĠĦĤĨ IJ
ĨĴĻŎØŚŤŬŨŴŴŴŴŶŸ*

Italic Accented Characters

Ornaments

LETTERFORMS HAVE TONE, timbre, charac
ter, just as words and 567 sentences do. The
moment a text and typeface are chosen, two
REGULAR

*LETTERFORMS HAVE TONE, timbre, character,
just as words and 567 sentences do. The mo
ment a text and typeface are chosen, two*
ITALIC

LETTERFORMS HAVE TONE, timbre, charac
ter, just as words and 567 sentences do. The
moment a text and typeface are chosen, two
MEDIUM

*LETTERFORMS HAVE TONE, timbre, charac
ter, just as words and 567 sentences do. The
moment a text and typeface are chosen, two*
MEDIUM ITALIC

LETTERFORMS HAVE TONE, timbre, charac
ter, just as words and 567 sentences do. The
moment a text and typeface are chosen,
SEMIBOLD

*LETTERFORMS HAVE TONE, timbre, charac
ter, just as words and 567 sentences do. The
moment a text and typeface are chosen, two*
SEMIBOLD ITALIC

**LETTERFORMS HAVE TONE, timbre, char
acter, just as words and 567 sentences do.
The moment a text and typeface are cho**
BOLD

***LETTERFORMS HAVE TONE, timbre, charac
ter, just as words and 567 sentences do. The
moment a text and typeface are chosen,***
BOLD ITALIC

АБВГЃҐДЂЕЁЄЖЗЅИЙІЇЈКЌЛЉ
МНЊОПРСТЋУЎФХЦЏЧШЩ
ЪЫЬЭЮЯабвгѓґдђеёєжзѕийіїјк
ќлљмнњопрстћуўфхцџчшщъыьэ
юя
Cyrillic

*АБВГЃҐДЂЕЁЄЖЗЅИЙІЇЈКЌЛЉ
МНЊОПРСТЋУЎФХЦЏЧШЩЪ
ЫЬЭЮЯабвгѓґдђеёєжзѕийіїјкќлљ
мнњопрстћуўфхцџчшщъыьэюя*
Italic Cyrillic

ѲѴѢѳѵѣ
Cyrillic Alternates

дбшлі ѲѴѢѳѵљ
Italic Cyrillic Alternates

Точно найденные слова достойны точно
сти в подборе шрифтов; те, в свою оче
REGULAR, ITALIC

Точно найденные слова достойны точно
сти в подборе шрифтов; те, в свою оче
MEDIUM, MEDIUM ITALIC

Точно найденные слова достойны точ
ности в подборе шрифтов; те, в свою
SEMIBOLD, SEMIBOLD ITALIC

Точно найденные слова достойны точ
ности в подборе шрифтов; те, в свою
BOLD, BOLD ITALIC

ΑΒΓΔΕΖΗΘΙΚΛΜΝΞΟΠΡΣΤΥΦΧ
ΨΩΆΈΉΊΪΌΎ ΫΩαβγδεζηθικλμνξ
οπρστυφχψωάέήί ϊόύϋώΐΰς
Greek

ΑΒΓΔΕΖΗΘΙΚΛΜΝΞΟΠΡΣΤΥΦΧ
ΨΩΆΈΉΊΪΌΎ ΫΩαβγδεζηθικλμνξ
οπρστυφχψωάέήί ϊόύϋώΐΰς
Italic Greek

ἈΆἌἎἊἌἊΑΑΙἉΙἍΙἋΙἍΙἋΙἍΙἋΙἍΙ
ἈΆἌἊἈΑΈΈἜἛ ἜἛἜἛ ἨἩἭ
Ἣ ἩΉ Ἡ Ηι Ἡι Ἥι Ἣι Ἥι Ἣι Ἥι Ἣι Ηι
Ἡι Ἥι Ἣι ΗΙΙΊΪΊΊ Ἲ ΊΊΊΊΊ ΊΪΩΏΏΏ
ῺὨῺὨ Ωι Ὠι Ὥι Ὣι Ὥι Ὣι Ὥι Ὣι Ωι
Ὥι Ὣι Ωι ΟΌΌΌΟΌΌΌΌΟΡΎΎ
ΎΎΎ Ϋ Ύ Ϋ ἀάᾶᾴᾂᾃᾅᾆᾇέὲἕἒἔἓήῆῆ
ῄἠἡἦἢ ἴ ἲ ϊ ῒ ῑ ῗ ῖ ΐ ῖ ὸόὂὃὄὅ ὺύὒὓ ὔὕ ὖ ὠ ὡ ῶ
ῶ ῴ ᾧ ᾦ ῶ ὠ ὡ ᾳ ᾴ ᾂ ᾃ ᾅ ᾆ ᾇ
ᾇ ἠ ἡ ἦ ἢ ῄ ῆ ἦ ᾧ ᾧ ὢ ὣ ᾦ ῳ ᾷ ᾳ ᾳ ᾳ ᾷ ῂ ῃ
ῃ ῇ ῂ ϊ ῒ ῑ ῗ ῖ ῦ ῢ ῧ ῧ ῥ ῤ ῦ ᾧ ῳ ῴ ῶ ᾷ ᾷ
Greek Polytonic (Classical)

ἈΆἌἊἈΑΈΈἜἛ ἜἛἜἛ ἨΉἭἫ
... (Italic Greek Polytonic Classical)
Italic Greek Polytonic (Classical)

Στις πύλες του δάσους ο έκπληκτος άνθρω
πος του κόσμου είναι αναγκασμένος να εγκα
REGULAR, ITALIC

Στις πύλες του δάσους ο έκπληκτος άνθρω
πος του κόσμου είναι αναγκασμένος να εγκα
MEDIUM, MEDIUM ITALIC

Στις πύλες του δάσους ο έκπληκτος άνθρω
πος του κόσμου είναι αναγκασμένος να
SEMIBOLD, SEMIBOLD ITALIC

Στις πύλες του δάσους ο έκπληκτος άνθρω
πος του κόσμου είναι αναγκασμένος να
BOLD, BOLD ITALIC

*To download a complete glyph complement PDF, please visit
www.adobe.com/type.*

Robert Slimbach, Adobe Systems

A-z € ffi Bb 619 123 ⅞ H₂ 1ˢᵗ 𝒜 ℰ ✍ aA

Typography

LETTERFORMS HAVE TONE, timbre, character,
just as words and 567 sentences do. The mo
ment a text and typeface are chosen, two stream
CONDENSED

*LETTERFORMS HAVE TONE, timbre, character,
just as words and 567 sentences do. The moment
a text and typeface are chosen, two streams of*
CONDENSED ITALIC

LETTERFORMS HAVE TONE, timbre, character,
just as words and 567 sentences do. The mo
ment a text and typeface are chosen, two
MEDIUM CONDENSED

*LETTERFORMS HAVE TONE, timbre, character,
just as words and 567 sentences do. The moment
a text and typeface are chosen, two streams of*
MEDIUM CONDENSED ITALIC

**LETTERFORMS HAVE TONE, timbre, character,
just as words and 567 sentences do. The mo
ment a text and typeface are chosen, two**
SEMIBOLD CONDENSED

***LETTERFORMS HAVE TONE, timbre, character,
just as words and 567 sentences do. The mo
ment a text and typeface are chosen, two***
SEMIBOLD CONDENSED ITALIC

**LETTERFORMS HAVE TONE, timbre, character,
just as words and 567 sentences do. The mo
ment a text and typeface are chosen, two**
BOLD CONDENSED

***LETTERFORMS HAVE TONE, timbre, character,
just as words and 567 sentences do. The mo
ment a text and typeface are chosen, two***
BOLD CONDENSED ITALIC

Точно найденные слова достойны точности
в подборе шрифтов; те, в свою очередь, за
CONDENSED, CONDENSED ITALIC

Точно найденные слова достойны точности
в подборе шрифтов; те, в свою очередь, за
MEDIUM CONDENSED, MEDIUM CONDENSED ITALIC

Точно найденные слова достойны точности
в подборе шрифтов; те, в свою очередь, за
SEMIBOLD CONDENSED, SEMIBOLD CONDENSED ITALIC

**Точно найденные слова достойны точно
*сти в подборе шрифтов; те, в свою оче***
BOLD CONDENSED, BOLD CONDENSED ITALIC

Στις πύλες του δάσους ο έκπληκτος άνθρωπος
του κόσμου είναι αναγκασμένος να εγκαταλεί
CONDENSED, CONDENSED ITALIC

Στις πύλες του δάσους ο έκπληκτος άνθρωπος
του κόσμου είναι αναγκασμένος να εγκαταλεί
MEDIUM CONDENSED, MEDIUM CONDENSED ITALIC

Στις πύλες του δάσους ο έκπληκτος άνθρωπος
του κόσμου είναι αναγκασμένος να εγκαταλεί
SEMIBOLD CONDENSED, SEMIBOLD CONDENSED ITALIC

**Στις πύλες του δάσους ο έκπληκτος άνθρω
*πος του κόσμου είναι αναγκασμένος να εγκα***
BOLD CONDENSED, BOLD CONDENSED ITALIC

*To download a complete glyph complement PDF, please visit
www.adobe.com/type.*

ⓔ **Minion PRO Opticals**

Robert Slimbach, Adobe Systems

A-Z € ffi BB 619 123 ⅞ H₂ 1st 𝒜 è ✎ aA

LETTERFORMS HAVE TONE, timbre, character, just as words and 567 sentences do. The moment a text and typeface are chosen,

LETTERFORMS HAVE TONE, timbre, charac ter, just as words and 567 sentences do.

LETTERFORMS have tone, tim bre, character, just as words and

LETTERFORMS have tone, timbre, character,

CAPTION, REGULAR, SUBHEAD, DISPLAY

LETTERFORMS HAVE TONE, timbre, character, just as words and 567 sentences do. The moment a text and typeface are chosen,

LETTERFORMS HAVE TONE, timbre, character, just as words and 567 sentences do. The mo

LETTERFORMS have tone, timbre, character, just as words and sen

LETTERFORMS have tone, timbre character,

ITALIC: CAPTION, REGULAR, SUBHEAD, DISPLAY

LETTERFORMS HAVE TONE, timbre, character, just as words and 567 sentences do. The moment a text and typeface are chosen,

LETTERFORMS HAVE TONE, timbre, charac ter, just as words and 567 sentences do.

LETTERFORMS have tone, tim bre, character, just as words and

LETTERFORMS have tone, timbre, character,

MEDIUM: CAPTION, REGULAR, SUBHEAD, DISPLAY

LETTERFORMS HAVE TONE, timbre, character, just as words and 567 sentences do. The moment a text and typeface are chosen,

LETTERFORMS HAVE TONE, timbre, charac ter, just as words and 567 sentences do. The

LETTERFORMS have tone, timbre, character, just as words and sen

LETTERFORMS have tone, timbre character,

MEDIUM ITALIC: CAPTION, REGULAR, SUBHEAD, DISPLAY

LETTERFORMS HAVE TONE, timbre, character, just as words and 567 sentences do. The moment a text and typeface are

LETTERFORMS HAVE TONE, timbre, charac ter, just as words and 567 sentences do.

LETTERFORMS have tone, tim bre, character, just as words

LETTERFORMS have tone, timbre, character,

SEMIBOLD: CAPTION, REGULAR, SUBHEAD, DISPLAY

LETTERFORMS HAVE TONE, timbre, character, just as words and 567 sentences do. The moment a text and typeface are chosen,

LETTERFORMS HAVE TONE, timbre, charac ter, just as words and 567 sentences do.

LETTERFORMS have tone, tim bre, character, just as words and

LETTERFORMS have tone, timbre, character,

SEMIBOLD ITALIC: CAPTION, REGULAR, SUBHEAD, DISPLAY

LETTERFORMS HAVE TONE, timbre, character, just as words and 567 sentences do. The moment a text and typeface are

LETTERFORMS HAVE TONE, timbre, char acter, just as words and 567 sentences do.

LETTERFORMS have tone, tim bre, character, just as words

LETTERFORMS have tone, timbre, character

BOLD: CAPTION, REGULAR, SUBHEAD, DISPLAY

LETTERFORMS HAVE TONE, timbre, character, just as words and 567 sentences do. The moment a text and typeface are

LETTERFORMS HAVE TONE, timbre, charac ter, just as words and 567 sentences do.

LETTERFORMS have tone, tim bre, character, just as words

LETTERFORMS have tone, timbre, character,

BOLD ITALIC: CAPTION, REGULAR, SUBHEAD, DISPLAY

Точно найденные слова достойны точности в подборе *шрифтов; те, в свою очередь, заслуживают чуткого, осмы*

Точно найденные слова достойны точно *сти в подборе шрифтов; те, в свою оче*

Точно найденные слова до *стойны точности в подборе*

Точно найденные сло *ва достойны точно*

CAPTION, ITALIC CAPTION, REGULAR, ITALIC, SUBHEAD, ITALIC SUBHEAD, DISPLAY, ITALIC DISPLAY

Точно найденные слова достойны точности в подборе *шрифтов; те, в свою очередь, заслуживают чуткого, осмы*

Точно найденные слова достойны точно *сти в подборе шрифтов; те, в свою оче*

Точно найденные слова до *стойны точности в подборе*

Точно найденные сло *ва достойны точно*

MEDIUM: CAPTION, ITALIC CAPTION, REGULAR, ITALIC, SUBHEAD, ITALIC SUBHEAD, DISPLAY, ITALIC DISPLAY

Точно найденные слова достойны точности в подборе *шрифтов; те, в свою очередь, заслуживают чуткого, осмы*

Точно найденные слова достойны точ *ности в подборе шрифтов; те, в свою*

Точно найденные слова до *стойны точности в подборе*

Точно найденные сло *ва достойны точно*

SEMIBOLD: CAPTION, ITALIC CAPTION, REGULAR, ITALIC, SUBHEAD, ITALIC SUBHEAD, DISPLAY, ITALIC DISPLAY

Точно найденные слова достойны точности в подборе *шрифтов; те, в свою очередь, заслуживают чуткого,*

Точно найденные слова достойны точ *ности в подборе шрифтов; те, в свою*

Точно найденные слова до *стойны точности в подборе*

Точно найденные слова достойны точ

BOLD: CAPTION, ITALIC CAPTION, REGULAR, ITALIC, SUBHEAD, ITALIC SUBHEAD, DISPLAY, ITALIC DISPLAY

Στις πύλες του δάσους ο έκπληκτος άνθρωπος του κόσμου είναι αναγκασμένος να εγκαταλείψει τις αστικές του εκτιμήσεις της

Στις πύλες του δάσους ο έκπληκτος άνθρω πος του κόσμου είναι αναγκασμένος να εγκα

Στις πύλες του δάσους ο έκπλη κτος άνθρωπος του κόσμου είναι

Στις πύλες του δάσους ο έκπληκτος άνθρωπος

CAPTION, ITALIC CAPTION, REGULAR, ITALIC, SUBHEAD, ITALIC SUBHEAD, DISPLAY, ITALIC DISPLAY

Στις πύλες του δάσους ο έκπληκτος άνθρωπος του κόσμου είναι αναγκασμένος να εγκαταλείψει τις αστικές του εκτιμήσεις της

Στις πύλες του δάσους ο έκπληκτος άνθρω πος του κόσμου είναι αναγκασμένος να εγκα

Στις πύλες του δάσους ο έκπλη κτος άνθρωπος του κόσμου είναι

Στις πύλες του δάσους ο έκπληκτος άνθρωπος

MEDIUM: CAPTION, ITALIC CAPTION, REGULAR, ITALIC, SUBHEAD, ITALIC SUBHEAD, DISPLAY, ITALIC DISPLAY

Στις πύλες του δάσους ο έκπληκτος άνθρωπος του κόσμου είναι αναγκασμένος να εγκαταλείψει τις αστικές του εκτιμή

Στις πύλες του δάσους ο έκπληκτος άνθρω πος του κόσμου είναι αναγκασμένος να

Στις πύλες του δάσους ο έκπλη κτος άνθρωπος του κόσμου εί

Στις πύλες του δάσους ο έκπληκτος άνθρωπος

SEMIBOLD: CAPTION, ITALIC CAPTION, REGULAR, ITALIC, SUBHEAD, ITALIC SUBHEAD, DISPLAY, ITALIC DISPLAY

Στις πύλες του δάσους ο έκπληκτος άνθρωπος του κόσμου είναι αναγκασμένος να εγκαταλείψει τις αστικές του εκτιμή

Στις πύλες του δάσους ο έκπληκτος άνθρω πος του κόσμου είναι αναγκασμένος να

Στις πύλες του δάσους ο έκπλη κτος άνθρωπος του κόσμου εί

Στις πύλες του δάσους ο έκπληκτος άνθρωπος

BOLD: CAPTION, ITALIC CAPTION, REGULAR, ITALIC, SUBHEAD, ITALIC SUBHEAD, DISPLAY, ITALIC DISPLAY

To download a complete glyph complement PDF, please visit www.adobe.com/type.

Minion PRO Condensed Opticals

Robert Slimbach, Adobe Systems

A-Z € ffi BB 619 123 ⅞ H₂ 1st 𝒜 é̀ ✒ aA

LETTERFORMS HAVE TONE, timbre, character, just as words and 567 sentences do. The moment a text and typeface are chosen, two

LETTERFORMS HAVE TONE, timbre, character, just as words and 567 sentences do. The mo

LETTERFORMS have tone, timbre, character, just as words and 567 sen

LETTERFORMS have tone, timbre, character, just as

CONDENSED: CAPTION, REGULAR, SUBHEAD, DISPLAY

Letterforms have tone, timbre, character, just as words and 567 sentences do. The moment a text and typeface are chosen, two streams

Letterforms have tone, timbre, character, just as words and 567 sentences do. The moment

Letterforms have tone, timbre, character, just as words and 567 sen

Letterforms have tone, timbre, character, just as

CONDENSED ITALIC: CAPTION, REGULAR, SUBHEAD, DISPLAY

Letterforms have tone, timbre, character, just as words and 567 sentences do. The moment a text and typeface are chosen, two

Letterforms have tone, timbre, character, just as words and 567 sentences do. The mo

Letterforms have tone, timbre, character, just as words and 567

Letterforms have tone, timbre, character, just as

MEDIUM CONDENSED: CAPTION, REGULAR, SUBHEAD, DISPLAY

Letterforms have tone, timbre, character, just as words and 567 sentences do. The moment a text and typeface are chosen, two streams

Letterforms have tone, timbre, character, just as words and 567 sentences do. The moment

Letterforms have tone, timbre, character, just as words and 567 sen

Letterforms have tone, timbre, character, just as

MEDIUM CONDENSED ITALIC: CAPTION, REGULAR, SUBHEAD, DISPLAY

Letterforms have tone, timbre, character, just as words and 567 sentences do. The moment a text and typeface are chosen, two

Letterforms have tone, timbre, character, just as words and 567 sentences do. The mo

Letterforms have tone, timbre, character, just as words and 567

Letterforms have tone, timbre, character, just as

SEMIBOLD CONDENSED: CAPTION, REGULAR, SUBHEAD, DISPLAY

Letterforms have tone, timbre, character, just as words and 567 sentences do. The moment a text and typeface are chosen,

Letterforms have tone, timbre, character, just as words and 567 sentences do. The mo

Letterforms have tone, timbre, character, just as words and 567 sen

Letterforms have tone, timbre, character, just as

SEMIBOLD CONDENSED ITALIC: CAPTION, REGULAR, SUBHEAD, DISPLAY

Letterforms have tone, timbre, character, just as words and 567 sentences do. The moment a text and typeface are chosen, two

Letterforms have tone, timbre, character, just as words and 567 sentences do. The mo

Letterforms have tone, timbre, character, just as words and 567

Letterforms have tone, timbre, character, just as

BOLD CONDENSED: CAPTION, REGULAR, SUBHEAD, DISPLAY

www.adobe.com/type

LETTERFORMS HAVE TONE, timbre, character, just as words and 567 sentences do. The moment a text and typeface are chosen, two

LETTERFORMS HAVE TONE, timbre, character, just as words and 567 sentences do. The mo

LETTERFORMS have tone, timbre, character, just as words and 567

LETTERFORMS have tone, timbre, character, just as

BOLD CONDENSED ITALIC: CAPTION, REGULAR, SUBHEAD, DISPLAY

Точно найденные слова достойны точности в подборе шрифтов; те, в свою очередь, заслуживают чуткого, осмысленного, грамот

Точно найденные слова достойны точности в подборе шрифтов; те, в свою очередь, за

Точно найденные слова достойны точности в подборе шрифтов;

Точно найденные слова достойны точности в

CONDENSED: CAPTION, ITALIC CAPTION, REGULAR, ITALIC, SUBHEAD, ITALIC SUBHEAD, DISPLAY, ITALIC DISPLAY

Точно найденные слова достойны точности в подборе шрифтов; те, в свою очередь, заслуживают чуткого, осмысленного, гра

Точно найденные слова достойны точности в подборе шрифтов; те, в свою очередь, за

Точно найденные слова до стой ны точности в подборе шриф

Точно найденные слова достойны точности в

MEDIUM CONDENSED: CAPTION, ITALIC CAPTION, REGULAR, ITALIC, SUBHEAD, ITALIC SUBHEAD, DISPLAY, ITALIC DISPLAY

Точно найденные слова достойны точности в подборе шриф тов; те, в свою очередь, заслуживают чуткого, осмысленного,

Точно найденные слова достойны точности в подборе шрифтов; те, в свою очередь, за

Точно найденные слова достой ны точности в подборе шриф

Точно найденные слова достойны точности в

SEMIBOLD CONDENSED: CAPTION, ITALIC CAPTION, REGULAR, ITALIC, SUBHEAD, ITALIC SUBHEAD, DISPLAY, ITALIC DISPLAY

Точно найденные слова достойны точности в подборе шриф тов; те, в свою очередь, заслуживают чуткого, осмысленного,

Точно найденные слова достойны точно сти в подборе шрифтов; те, в свою оче

Точно найденные слова достой ны точности в подборе шриф

Точно найденные слова достойны точности в

BOLD CONDENSED: CAPTION, ITALIC CAPTION, REGULAR, ITALIC, SUBHEAD, ITALIC SUBHEAD, DISPLAY, ITALIC DISPLAY

Στις πύλες του δάσους ο έκπληκτος άνθρωπος του κόσμου είναι ανα γκασμένος να εγκαταλείψει τις αστικές του εκτιμήσεις της μικρότη

Στις πύλες του δάσους ο έκπληκτος άνθρωπος του κόσμου είναι αναγκασμένος να εγκαταλεί

Στις πύλες του δάσους ο έκπληκτος άνθρωπος του κόσμου είναι αναγκα

Στις πύλες του δάσους ο έκπληκτος άνθρωπος του

CONDENSED: CAPTION, ITALIC CAPTION, REGULAR, ITALIC, SUBHEAD, ITALIC SUBHEAD, DISPLAY, ITALIC DISPLAY

Στις πύλες του δάσους ο έκπληκτος άνθρωπος του κόσμου είναι ανα
γκασμένος να εγκαταλείψει τις αστικές του εκτιμήσεις της μικρότη

Στις πύλες του δάσους ο έκπληκτος άνθρωπος
του κόσμου είναι αναγκασμένος να εγκαταλεί

Στις πύλες του δάσους ο έκπλη
κτος άνθρωπος του κόσμου είναι

Στις πύλες του δάσους ο
έκπληκτος άνθρωπος του

MEDIUM CONDENSED: CAPTION, ITALIC CAPTION,
REGULAR, ITALIC, SUBHEAD, ITALIC SUBHEAD, DISPLAY,
ITALIC DISPLAY

Στις πύλες του δάσους ο έκπληκτος άνθρωπος του κόσμου είναι ανα
γκασμένος να εγκαταλείψει τις αστικές του εκτιμήσεις της μικρότη

Στις πύλες του δάσους ο έκπληκτος άνθρωπος
του κόσμου είναι αναγκασμένος να εγκαταλεί

Στις πύλες του δάσους ο έκπλη
κτος άνθρωπος του κόσμου είναι

Στις πύλες του δάσους ο
έκπληκτος άνθρωπος του

SEMIBOLD CONDENSED: CAPTION, ITALIC CAPTION,
REGULAR, ITALIC, SUBHEAD, ITALIC SUBHEAD, DISPLAY,
ITALIC DISPLAY

Στις πύλες του δάσους ο έκπληκτος άνθρωπος του κόσμου είναι
αναγκασμένος να εγκαταλείψει τις αστικές του εκτιμήσεις της μι

Στις πύλες του δάσους ο έκπληκτος άνθρω
πος του κόσμου είναι αναγκασμένος να εγκα

Στις πύλες του δάσους ο έκπλη
κτος άνθρωπος του κόσμου είναι

Στις πύλες του δάσους ο
έκπληκτος άνθρωπος του

BOLD CONDENSED: CAPTION, ITALIC CAPTION,
REGULAR, ITALIC, SUBHEAD, ITALIC SUBHEAD, DISPLAY,
ITALIC DISPLAY

*To download a complete glyph complement PDF, please visit
www.adobe.com/type.*

Minion STD

Robert Slimbach, Adobe Systems

A-z € ffi 619 123 ⅞ H₂ 1ˢᵗ

Typography

ABCDEFGHIJKLMNO
PQRSTUVWXYZabcdef
ghijklmnopqrstuvwxyz
&0123456789$€!?.,:;{½}

0123456789 ffi ⅛
0123456789

Letterforms have tone, tim
bre, character, just as words

BLACK

Minister STD

M. Fahrenwaldt

A-z €

Typography

ABCDEFGHIJKLMNOPQR
STUVWXYZabcdefghijklmno
pqrstuvwxyz&0123456789$€
!?.;:,""{½}

ABCDEFGHIJKLMNOPQRS
TUVWXYZabcdefghijklmnopqrs
tuvwxyz&0123456789$€!?.,:,
""{½}

Letterforms have tone, timbre, charac
ter, just as words and sentences do. The
moment a text and typeface are chosen
LIGHT

Letterforms have tone, timbre, character,
just as words and sentences do. The mo
ment a text and typeface are chosen, two
LIGHT ITALIC

Letterforms have tone, timbre, char
acter, just as words and sentences do.
The moment a text and typeface are
BOOK

Letterforms have tone, timbre, charac
ter, just as words and sentences do. The
moment a text and typeface are chosen,
BOOK ITALIC

Letterforms have tone, timbre,
character, just as words and senten
ces do. The moment a text and
BOLD

Letterforms have tone, timbre, char
acter, just as words and sentences
do. The moment a text and typeface
BOLD ITALIC

Letterforms have tone, timbre,
character, just as words and sen
tences do. The moment a text
BLACK

Letterforms have tone, timbre,
character, just as words and sen
tences do. The moment a text
BLACK ITALIC

Mistral STD

Roger Excoffon, M. Olive

A-z € 123

Typography

ABCDEFGHIJKLMNOPQRSTUV
WXYZabcdefghijklmnopqrstuv
wxyz&0123456789$€!?.,:;{½}

Letterforms have tone, timbre, char
acter, just as words and sentences
ROMAN

Monotype Modern STD

Unknown, Monotype Typography Ltd.

A-z €

Typography

ABCDEFGHIJKLMNOPQRSTUV
WXYZabcdefghijklmnopqrstuvwxyz
&0123456789$€!?.,:,""{½}

ABCDEFGHIJKLMNOPQRSTUV
WXYZabcdefghijklmnopqrstuvwxyz&
0123456789$€!?.,:,""{½}

Letterforms have tone, timbre, character, just as
words and sentences do. The moment a text and
typeface are chosen, two streams of thought, two
CONDENSED

Letterforms have tone, timbre, character, just as words and sentences do. The moment a text and typeface are chosen, two streams of thought, two
CONDENSED ITALIC

Letterforms have tone, timbre, character, just as words and sentences do.The mo ment a text and typeface are chosen, two
BOLD

Letterforms have tone, timbre, character, just as words and sentences do. The mo ment a text and typeface are chosen, two
BOLD ITALIC

Letterforms have tone, timbre, character, just as words and sentences do.The mo ment a text and typeface are chosen, two
EXTENDED

Letterforms have tone, timbre, character, just as words and sentences do. The mo ment a text and typeface are chosen, two
EXTENDED ITALIC

Letterforms have tone, timbre, character, just as words and senten ces do. The moment a text and
WIDE

Letterforms have tone, timbre, char acter, just as words and sentences do. The moment a text and typeface
WIDE ITALIC

Mojo STD

Jim Parkinson, Adobe Systems

A-z €

TYPOGRAPHY

ABCDEFGHIJKLMNOPQRSTUVWXYZ
&0123456789$£!?.,;;""{½}

LETTERFORMS HAVE TONE, TIMBRE, CHARACTER, JUST AS WORDS AND

REGULAR

ITC Mona Lisa STD

Pat Hickson, ITC

A-z €

Typography

ABCDEFGHIJKLMNOPQRS
TUVWXYZabcdefghijklmnop
qrstuvwxyz&0123456789$£!?
.;:," "{½}

Letterforms have tone, timbre, charac ter, just as words and sentences do.
SOLID

Letterforms have tone, timbre, charac ter, just as words and sentences do.
RECUT

Monoline Script STD

Unknown, Monotype Corp.

Typography

ABCDEFGHIJKLMNOPQ
RSTUVWXYZabcdefghijkl
mnopqrstuvwxyz&012345
6789$€!?.;:,""{½}

Letterforms have tone, timbre,
character, just as words and

REGULAR

Montara STD

Jim Parkinson, Adobe Systems

Typography

ABCDEFGHIJKLMNOPQRSTUVWXYZ
abcdefghijklmnopqrstuvwxyz&0123
456789$€!?.;:,""{½}

ABCDEFGHIJKLMNOPQRSTUVWXYZ
abcdefghijklmnopqrstuvwxyz&01234
56789$€!?.;:,""{½}

Letterforms have tone, timbre, character, just
as words and sentences do. The moment a
text and typeface are chosen, two streams of

GOTHIC

Letterforms have tone, timbre, character, just
as words and sentences do. The moment a
text and typeface are chosen, two streams of

ITALIC

**Letterforms have tone, timbre, character,
just as words and sentences do. The mo
ment a text and typeface are chosen, two**

BOLD GOTHIC

***Letterforms have tone, timbre, character,
just as words and sentences do. The mo
ment a text and typeface are chosen, two***

BOLD ITALIC

LETTERFORMS HAVE TONE, TIMBRE, CHARAC

BOLD INITIALS

Moonglow STD

Michael Harvey, Adobe Systems

TYPOGRAPH

ABCDEFGHIJKLMNOPQR
STUVWXYZ&0123456789
$€!?.·. ""{½}

ÆEGJKPRU

Alternates

LETTERFORMS HAVE TONE,
TIMBRE, CHARACTER, JUST AS

LIGHT

LETTERFORMS HAVE TONE, TIMBRE, CHARACTER, JUST

REGULAR

LETTERFORMS HAVE TONE, TIMBRE, CHARACTER, JUST

SEMIBOLD

LETTERFORMS HAVE TONE, TIMBRE, CHARAC

BOLD

Moonglow STD Condensed and Extended

Michael Harvey, Adobe Systems

A-Z € 123 e ¢

TYPOGRAPHY

ABCDEFGHIJKLMNOPQRSTUVWXY
Z&0123456789$€!?.·„"""{½}

ÆEGJKPRU

Alternates

LETTERFORMS HAVE TONE, TIMBRE, CHARAC TER, JUST AS WORDS AND SENTENCES DO.

LIGHT CONDENSED

LETTERFORMS HAVE TONE, TIMBRE, CHARACTER, JUST AS WORDS AND SEN

CONDENSED

LETTERFORMS HAVE TONE, TIMBRE, CHARACTER, JUST AS WORDS AND

SEMIBOLD CONDENSED

LETTERFORMS HAVE TONE, TIMBRE, CHARACTER, JUST AS

BOLD CONDENSED

TYPOGRA

ABCDEFGHIJKLMNOP
QRSTUVWXYZ&01234
56789$€!?.·„"""{½}

ÆEGJKPRU

Alternates

LETTERFORMS HAVE TONE, TIMBRE, CHARACTER, JUST

LIGHT EXTENDED

LETTERFORMS HAVE TONE, TIMBRE, CHARAC

EXTENDED

LETTERFORMS HAVE TONE, TIMBRE, CHARAC

SEMIBOLD EXTENDED

LETTERFORMS HAVE TONE, TIMBRE, CHAR

BOLD EXTENDED

www.adobe.com/type

M

ITC Motter Corpus STD

Othmar Motter, ITC

`A-z` `€`

Typography

ABCDEFGHIJKLMNOPQRS
TUVWXYZabcdefghijklm
nopqrstuvwxyz&001234
56789$€!?.,;:,""{½}

**Letterforms have tone, tim
bre, character, just as words**
CONDENSED

**Letterforms have tone,
timbre, character, just**
SEMI CONDENSED

**Letterforms have
tone, timbre, charac**
REGULAR

Myriad PRO

Carol Twombly, Robert Slimbach, Fred Brady, and
Christopher Slye, Adobe Systems

`A-z` `€` `ffi` `619` `123` `⅞` `H₂` `1ˢᵗ` `aA`

Typography

ABCDEFGHIJKLMNOPQRSTUVWX
YZabcdefghijklmnopqrstuvwxyz&

*ABCDEFGHIJKLMNOPQRSTUVWXY
Zabcdefghijklmnopqrstuvwxyz&*

---

ff fi fj fl ffi ffj ffl *ff fi fj fl ffi ffj ffl*
Ligatures

0123456789 0123456789
0123456789 0123456789
0123456789 0123456789
0123456789 0123456789
Proportional and Tabular Figures

Ø$¢£¥ƒ€¤#%‰$¢£¥ƒ€#%⁰¹²³⁴⁵⁶⁷⁸⁹(($¢-.,)0123456789($¢-.,)/0123456789($¢-.,)01234567
89($¢-.,)¼½¾∧~·+±<=>-|¦×÷∂μπΔΠΣ
Ω√∞∫≈≠≤≥◊¬℮ℓ°ªº_ —·-·-—''""„
"‚«»‹›⟨⟩,.:; ….·!?¡¿¿()()[][]{}{} / *•§
†‡¶©®™@@
Currency, Punctuation, and Related Forms

*Ø$¢£¥ƒ€¤#%‰$¢£¥ƒ€#%⁰¹²³⁴⁵⁶⁷⁸⁹
($¢-.,)0123456789($¢-.,)/0123456789($¢-.,)0123456789
($¢-.,)¼½¾∧~·+±<=>-|¦×÷∂μπΔΠΣΩ
√∞∫≈≠≤≥◊¬℮ℓ°ªº_ —·-·-—''""„‚
«»‹›⟨⟩,.:; ….·!?¡¿¿()()[][]{}{} / *•§†‡¶
©®™@@*
Italic Currency, Punctuation, and Related Forms

ÆŁØŒÞÐÁÂÄÀÅÃÇÉÊËÈÍÎÏÌÑÓ
ÔÖÒÕŠÚÛÜÙÝŸŽĂĀĄĆĈĎĚĖĒĘĜ
ĢĪĮĶĹĽĻŃŇŅŐŌŔŘŖŚŞŠŢŤŰŪŲŮŹ
ŻÆĈĊĚŊĜĠĦĤĨ IJ ĨĴĿŎØŜŦŬŨŴ
ŴŴŴŶŶÝæıłøœßþðáâäàåãçéêëèíîï
ìñóôöòõšúûüùýÿžăāąćčďděėēęğǵ
īįķĺľļńňņőōôřŗśşşţţűūųůźżæĉċěŋ
ġħĥĩ ij ĩĵŀňŏøŝŧŭũẃŵẅẁŷỳк
Accented Characters

ÆŁØŒÞÐÁÂÄÀÅÃÇÉÊËÈÍÎÏÌÑÓÔ
ÖÒÕŠÚÛÜÙÝŸŽÅĀĄĆĈĎĚĒĘĞĜĮ
ĶĹĽĿŃŇŅŐŌŘŔŖŚŞŠŢŤŲÚÛŲŮŹŽÆ
ĈČĚŊĜĠĦĤİ IJ ĨĴĿĿĥŎŐŚŦŬŨŴŴŴ
ẀŶŸĸæıłœßþðáâäàåãçéêëèíîïìñó
ôöòõšúûüùýÿžåāąćĉďđěėēęǧĝįĩĵķĺľļ
ńňņőōřŕŗśşšţťŲúûŲůźžæĉčěŋĝĝħĥ ij
ĩĵŀħŏőśŧŭũŵŵẁẃŵŷ ẁ ĸ

Italic Accented Characters

Letterforms have tone, timbre, character,
just as words and 567 sentences do. The mo
ment a text and typeface are chosen, two
LIGHT

Letterforms have tone, timbre, character, just
as words and 567 sentences do. The moment a
text and typeface are chosen, two streams of
LIGHT ITALIC

Letterforms have tone, timbre, character,
just as words and 567 sentences do. The
moment a text and typeface are chosen,
REGULAR

Letterforms have tone, timbre, character,
just as words and 567 sentences do. The mo
ment a text and typeface are chosen, two
ITALIC

Letterforms have tone, timbre, character,
just as words and 567 sentences do. The
moment a text and typeface are chosen,
SEMIBOLD

Letterforms have tone, timbre, character,
just as words and 567 sentences do. The
moment a text and typeface are chosen,
SEMIBOLD ITALIC

Letterforms have tone, timbre, charac
ter, just as words and 567 sentences do.
The moment a text and typeface are
BOLD

Letterforms have tone, timbre, character,
just as words and 567 sentences do. The
moment a text and typeface are chosen,
BOLD ITALIC

Letterforms have tone, timbre, char
acter, just as words and 567 sentences
do. The moment a text and typeface
BLACK

Letterforms have tone, timbre, charac
ter, just as words and 567 sentences do.
The moment a text and typeface are
BLACK ITALIC

АБВГЃЌДЂЕЁЄЖЗЅИЙІЇЈКЌЛЉМН
ЊОПРСТЋЎУЎФХЦЏЧШЩЪЫЬЭЮ
Яабвгѓѓдђеёєжзѕийіїјкќллљмнњо
прстћўуўфхцџчшщъыьэюя
Cyrillic

АБВГЃЃДЂЕЁЄЖЗЅИЙІЇЈКЌЛЉМНЊ
ОПРСТЋЎУЎФХЦЏЧШЩЪЫЬЭЮЯ
абвгѓѓдђеёєжзѕийіїјкќллљмнњопр
стћўуўфхцџчшщъыьэюя
Italic Cyrillic

ә әīдūш
Cyrillic Alternates

Точно найденные слова достойны точно
сти в подборе шрифтов; те, в свою оче
LIGHT, LIGHT ITALIC

Точно найденные слова достойны точно
сти в подборе шрифтов; те, в свою оче
REGULAR, ITALIC

Точно найденные слова достойны точ
ности в подборе шрифтов; те, в свою
SEMIBOLD, SEMIBOLD ITALIC

Точно найденные слова достойны
точности в подборе шрифтов; те, в
BOLD, BOLD ITALIC

Точно найденные слова достойны
точности в подборе шрифтов; те,
BLACK, BLACK ITALIC

ΑΒΓΔΕΖΗΘΙΚΛΜΝΞΟΠΡΣΤΥΦΧΨΩ
ΆΈΉΊΪΌΎΫ Ὠαβγδεζηθικλμνξοπρ
στυφχψωάέήί ϊόύϋώϊϋς
Greek

ΑΒΓΔΕΖΗΘΙΚΛΜΝΞΟΠΡΣΤΥΦΧΨΩΆ
ΈΉΊΪ ΌΎ ΫΩαβγδεζηθικλμνξοπρστ
υφχψωάέή ίϊόύϋώϊϋς
Italic Greek

Στις πύλες του δάσους ο έκπληκτος άνθρω
πος του κόσμου είναι αναγκασμένος να εγκατα
LIGHT, LIGHT ITALIC

Στις πύλες του δάσους ο έκπληκτος άν
θρω πος του κόσμου είναι αναγκασμένος να
REGULAR, ITALIC

Στις πύλες του δάσους ο έκπληκτος άν
θρω πος του κόσμου είναι αναγκασμένος
SEMIBOLD, SEMIBOLD ITALIC

Στις πύλες του δάσους ο έκπληκτος άν
θρωπος του κόσμου είναι αναγκασμένος
BOLD, BOLD ITALIC

Στις πύλες του δάσους ο έκπληκτος άν
θρωπος του κόσμου είναι αναγκασμέ
BLACK, BLACK ITALIC

To download a complete glyph complement PDF, *please visit*
www.adobe.com/type.

 Myriad PRO Condensed

Carol Twombly, Robert Slimbach, Fred Brady, and
Christopher Slye, Adobe Systems

A-z € ffi 619 123 ⅞ H₂ 1ˢᵗ aA

Typography

Letterforms have tone, timbre, character, just as words and 567
sentences do. The moment a text and typeface are chosen, two
streams of thought, two rhythmical systems, two sets of habits
LIGHT CONDENSED

Letterforms have tone, timbre, character, just as words and 567
sentences do. The moment a text and typeface are chosen, two
streams of thought, two rhythmical systems, two sets of habits
LIGHT CONDENSED ITALIC

Letterforms have tone, timbre, character, just as words
and 567 sentences do. The moment a text and typeface
are chosen, two streams of thought, two rhythmical sys
CONDENSED

Letterforms have tone, timbre, character, just as words and
567 sentences do. The moment a text and typeface are cho
sen, two streams of thought, two rhythmical systems, two
CONDENSED ITALIC

Letterforms have tone, timbre, character, just as
words and 567 sentences do. The moment a text and
typeface are chosen, two streams of thought, two
SEMIBOLD CONDENSED

Letterforms have tone, timbre, character, just as words
and 567 sentences do. The moment a text and typeface
are chosen, two streams of thought, two streams of
SEMIBOLD CONDENSED ITALIC

Letterforms have tone, timbre, character, just as
words and 567 sentences do. The moment a text
and typeface are chosen, two streams of thought,
BOLD CONDENSED

Letterforms have tone, timbre, character, just as
words and 567 sentences do. The moment a text and
typeface are chosen, two streams of thought, two
BOLD CONDENSED ITALIC

Letterforms have tone, timbre, character, just as words and 567 sentences do. The moment a text and typeface are chosen, two streams of
BLACK CONDENSED

Letterforms have tone, timbre, character, just as words and 567 sentences do. The moment a text and typeface are chosen, two streams of thought,
BLACK CONDENSED ITALIC

Точно найденные слова достойны точности в подборе шрифтов; те, в свою очередь, заслуживают чуткого,
LIGHT CONDENSED, LIGHT CONDENSED ITALIC

Точно найденные слова достойны точности в подборе шрифтов; те, в свою очередь, заслуживают чуткого,
CONDENSED, CONDENSED ITALIC

Точно найденные слова достойны точности в под боре шрифтов; те, в свою очередь, заслуживают
SEMIBOLD CONDENSED, SEMIBOLD CONDENSED ITALIC

Точно найденные слова достойны точности в подборе шрифтов; те, в свою очередь, заслужи
BOLD CONDENSED, BOLD CONDENSED ITALIC

Точно найденные слова достойны точности в подборе шрифтов; те, в свою очередь, заслу
BLACK CONDENSED, BLACK CONDENSED ITALIC

Στις πύλες του δάσους ο έκπληκτος άνθρωπος του κόσμου είναι αναγκασμένος να εγκαταλείψει τις αστικές του εκτιμήσεις της
LIGHT CONDENSED, LIGHT CONDENSED ITALIC

Στις πύλες του δάσους ο έκπληκτος άνθρωπος του κόσμου είναι αναγκασμένος να εγκαταλείψει τις αστικές του εκτιμή
CONDENSED, CONDENSED ITALIC

Στις πύλες του δάσους ο έκπληκτος άνθρωπος του κό σμου είναι αναγκασμένος να εγκαταλείψει τις αστικές
SEMIBOLD CONDENSED, SEMIBOLD CONDENSED ITALIC

Στις πύλες του δάσους ο έκπληκτος άνθρωπος του κόσμου είναι αναγκασμένος να εγκαταλείψει τις αστι
BOLD CONDENSED, BOLD CONDENSED ITALIC

Στις πύλες του δάσους ο έκπληκτος άνθρωπος του κόσμου είναι αναγκασμένος να εγκαταλείψει
BLACK CONDENSED, BLACK CONDENSED ITALIC

To download a complete glyph complement PDF, please visit www.adobe.com/type.

Myriad PRO SemiCondensed

Carol Twombly, Robert Slimbach, Fred Brady, and Christopher Slye, Adobe Systems

`A-z` `€` `ffi` `619` `123` `⅞` `H₂` `1ˢᵗ` `aA`

Typography

Letterforms have tone, timbre, character, just as words and 567 sentences do. The moment a text and typeface are chosen, two streams of
LIGHT SEMICONDENSED

l etterforms have tone, timbre, character, just as words and 567 sentences do. The moment a text and typeface are chosen, two streams of thought,
LIGHT SEMICONDENSED ITALIC

Letterforms have tone, timbre, character, just as words and 567 sentences do. The moment a text and typeface are chosen, two streams
SEMICONDENSED

Letterforms have tone, timbre, character, just as words and 567 sentences do. The moment a text and typeface are chosen, two streams of
SEMICONDENSED ITALIC

Letterforms have tone, timbre, character, just as words and 567 sentences do. The mo ment a text and typeface are chosen, two
SEMIBOLD SEMICONDENSED

Letterforms have tone, timbre, character, just as words and 567 sentences do. The moment a text and typeface are chosen, two streams
SEMIBOLD SEMICONDENSED ITALIC

Letterforms have tone, timbre, character, just as words and 567 sentences do. The moment a text and typeface are chosen,
BOLD SEMICONDENSED

Letterforms have tone, timbre, character, just as words and 567 sentences do. The mo ment a text and typeface are chosen, two
BOLD SEMICONDENSED ITALIC

Letterforms have tone, timbre, character, just as words and 567 sentences do. The moment a text and typeface are chosen,
BLACK SEMICONDENSED

Letterforms have tone, timbre, character, just as words and 567 sentences do. The moment a text and typeface are chosen,
BLACK SEMICONDENSED ITALIC

Точно найденные слова достойны точности в *подборе шрифтов; те, в свою очередь, заслу*
LIGHT SEMICONDENSED, LIGHT SEMICONDENSED ITALIC

Точно найденные слова достойны точности *в подборе шрифтов; те, в свою очередь, за*
SEMICONDENSED, SEMICONDENSED ITALIC

Точно найденные слова достойны точно сти в под боре шрифтов; те, в свою оче
SEMIBOLD SEMICONDENSED,
SEMIBOLD SEMICONDENSED ITALIC

Точно найденные слова достойны точно сти в подборе шрифтов; те, в свою оче
BOLD SEMICONDENSED, BOLD SEMICONDENSED ITALIC

Точно найденные слова достойны точ ности в подборе шрифтов; те, в свою
BLACK SEMICONDENSED, BLACK SEMICONDENSED ITALIC

Στις πύλες του δάσους ο έκπληκτος άνθρωπος *του κόσμου είναι αναγκασμένος να εγκαταλείψει τις*
LIGHT SEMICONDENSED, LIGHT SEMICONDENSED ITALIC

Στις πύλες του δάσους ο έκπληκτος άνθρω *πος του κόσμου είναι αναγκασμένος να εγκατα*
SEMICONDENSED, SEMICONDENSED ITALIC

Στις πύλες του δάσους ο έκπληκτος άνθρω *πος του κόσμου είναι αναγκασμένος να εγκα*
SEMIBOLD SEMICONDENSED,
SEMIBOLD SEMICONDENSED ITALIC

Στις πύλες του δάσους ο έκπληκτος άνθρω *πος του κόσμου είναι αναγκασμένος να εγκα*
BOLD SEMICONDENSED, BOLD SEMICONDENSED ITALIC

Στις πύλες του δάσους ο έκπληκτος άν *ρωπος του κόσμου είναι αναγκασμένος να*
BLACK SEMICONDENSED, BLACK SEMICONDENSED ITALIC

To download a complete glyph complement PDF, please visit www.adobe.com/type.

Myriad PRO SemiExtended

Carol Twombly, Robert Slimbach, Fred Brady, and Christopher Slye, Adobe Systems

A-Z € ffi 619 123 ⅞ H₂ 1st aA

Typograph

Letterforms have tone, timbre, charac ter, just as words and 567 sentences do. The moment a text and typeface are
LIGHT SEMIEXTENDED

Letterforms have tone, timbre, character, just as words and 567 sentences do. The moment a text and typeface are chosen,
LIGHT SEMIEXTENDED ITALIC

Letterforms have tone, timbre, char acter, just as words and 567 sentences do. The moment a text and typeface
SEMIEXTENDED

Letterforms have tone, timbre, character, just as words and 567 sentences do. The moment a text and typeface are chosen,
SEMIEXTENDED ITALIC

Letterforms have tone, timbre, charac ter, just as words and 567 sentences do. The moment a text and typeface
SEMIBOLD SEMIEXTENDED

Letterforms have tone, timbre, charac ter, just as words and 567 sentences do. The moment a text and typeface are
SEMIBOLD SEMIEXTENDED ITALIC

Letterforms have tone, timbre, char acter, just as words and 567 senten ces do. The moment a text and type
BOLD SEMIEXTENDED

Letterforms have tone, timbre, charac ter, just as words and 567 sentences do. The moment a text and typeface
BOLD SEMIEXTENDED ITALIC

Letterforms have tone, timbre, char acter, just as words and 567 senten ces do. The moment a text and type
BLACK SEMIEXTENDED

Letterforms have tone, timbre, char acter, just as words and 567 sentenc es do. The moment a text and type
BLACK SEMIEXTENDED ITALIC

Точно найденные слова достойны точ *ности в подборе шрифтов; те, в свою*
LIGHT SEMIEXTENDED, LIGHT SEMIEXTENDED ITALIC

Точно найденные слова достойны *точности в подборе шрифтов; те, в*
SEMIEXTENDED, SEMIEXTENDED ITALIC

Точно найденные слова достойны *точности в подборе шрифтов; те,*
SEMIBOLD SEMIEXTENDED,
SEMIBOLD SEMIEXTENDED ITALIC

Точно найденные слова достойны *точности в подборе шрифтов;*
BOLD SEMIEXTENDED, BOLD SEMIEXTENDED ITALIC

Точно найденные слова достойны *точности в подборе шрифтов;*
BLACK SEMIEXTENDED, BLACK SEMIEXTENDED ITALIC

Στις πύλες του δάσους ο έκπληκτος άν θρωπος του κόσμου είναι αναγκασμένος
LIGHT SEMIEXTENDED, LIGHT SEMIEXTENDED ITALIC

Στις πύλες του δάσους ο έκπληκτος άν θρωπος του κόσμου είναι αναγκασμένος
SEMIEXTENDED, SEMIEXTENDED ITALIC

Στις πύλες του δάσους ο έκπληκτος άνθρωπος του κόσμου είναι αναγκασμέ
SEMIBOLD SEMIEXTENDED,
SEMIBOLD SEMIEXTENDED ITALIC

Στις πύλες του δάσους ο έκπληκτος *άνθρωπος του κόσμου είναι αναγκα*
BOLD SEMIEXTENDED, BOLD SEMIEXTENDED ITALIC

Στις πύλες του δάσους ο έκπληκτος *άνθρωπος του κόσμου είναι αναγκα*
BLACK SEMIEXTENDED ITALIC

To download a complete glyph complement PDF, *please visit* www.adobe.com/type.

Myriad STD Wild

Carol Twombly and Robert Slimbach, Adobe Systems

A-z €

Typography

ABCDEFGHIJKLMNOPQRSTUV WXYZabcdefghijklmnopqrst uvwxyz&0123456789$€!?.:; ""{½}

Letterforms have tone, timbre, charac ter, just as words and sentences do.
SKETCH

Typography

ABCDEFGHIJKLMNOPQRSTUVWX
YZabcdefghijklmnopqrstuvwxyz
&0123456789$€!?.;:, ""{½}

Letterforms have tone, timbre, charac
ter, just as words and sentences do.
TILT

Mythos STD

Min Wang & Jim Wasco, Adobe Systems

A-z €

ABCDEFGHIJKL
MNOPQRSTUVW
XYZ&0123456789$€!?.;:, ""{½}

LETTERFORMS HA
VE TONE, TIMBRE,
REGULAR

National Codes Pi STD

Unknown

Ⓐ Ⓑ Ⓒ Ⓓ Ⓔ Ⓕ Ⓖ Ⓗ Ⓘ Ⓙ Ⓚ Ⓛ
Ⓜ Ⓝ Ⓞ Ⓟ Ⓠ Ⓡ Ⓢ Ⓣ Ⓤ Ⓥ Ⓦ Ⓧ
Ⓨ Ⓩ ⬭ ABCDEFGHIJLMNOPQRSTUVWXYZ (AFG) (AG) (AK) (AL)
(AND) (AR) (ARM) (ASE) (AUS) (AZ) (BG) (BD) (BDS) (BF) (BG) (BIH)
(BLR) (BOL) (BR) (BRN) (BRU) (BS) (BZ) (CA) (CAN) (CDN) (CH) (CI)
(CL) (CHL) (CN) (CO) (CR) (CT) (CV) (CY) (CZ) (DC) (DE) (DK)
(DOM) (DZ) (EAK) (EAT) (EAU) (EC) (EHT) (ES) (EST) (ET) (EU) (EUR)
(FIN) (FJI) (FL) (FR) (FSM) (FX) (GA) (GBG) (GBJ) (GBM) (GBZ) (GCA)
(GEO) (GH) (GR) (GT) (GTM) (GU) (GUY) (HCA) (HI) (HK) (HN) (HND)
(HR) (HU) (IA) (ID) (IL) (IN) (IND) (IR) (IRL) (IRQ) (IS) (JA)
(JOR) (KAS) (KGZ) (KS) (KWT) (KY) (LA) (LAO) (LAR) (LI) (LR) (LS)
(LT) (LV) (MA) (MAL) (MB) (MC) (MD) (ME) (MEX) (MI) (MM) (MN)
(MO) (MOC) (MOL) (MS) (MT) (MW) (NA) (NB) (NC) (ND) (NE) (NEP)
(NF) (NH) (NIC) (NJ) (NL) (NM) (NS) (NT) (NV) (NY) (NZ) (OH)
(OK) (OM) (ON) (OR) (PA) (PE) (PEI) (PK) (PL) (PNG) (PQ) (PR)
(PRT) (PY) (QC) (RA) (RB) (RC) (RCA) (RCB) (RCH) (RH) (RI) (RIM)
(RL) (RM) (RMM) (RN) (RO) (ROK) (ROU) (RP) (RSM) (RU) (RUS) (RWA)
(SA) (SC) (SD) (SGP) (SK) (SLO) (SME) (SN) (SO) (STP) (SUD) (SVN)
(SY) (SYR) (TAD) (TCH) (TG) (TN) (TR) (TT) (TUR) (TW) (TX) (UKR)
(URY) (USA) (USB) (UT) (VA) (VEN) (VI) (VN) (VT) (WA) (WAG) (WD)
(WG) (WI) (WL) (WS) (WV) (WY) (YU) (YV) (ZA) (ZRE) (ZW)
UNIVERSAL

Neuland STD

Rudolf Koch, Linotype Library GmbH

A-z €

ABCDEFGHIJKLMNO
PQRSTUVWXYZ&012
3456789$€!?.;:, ""{½}

LETTERFORMS HAVE
TONE, TIMBRE, CHARAC
BLACK

Neuzeit S STD

C. Wilhelm Pischiner, Linotype Library GmbH

A-z **€**

Typography

ABCDEFGHIJKLMNOPQRSTU
VWXYZabcdefghijklmnopqrstuv
wxyz&0123456789$€!?.;:,""''{½}

Letterforms have tone, timbre, charac
ter, just as words and sentences do.
The moment a text and typeface are
BOOK

**Letterforms have tone, timbre, char
acter, just as words and sentences
do. The moment a text and typefac**
BOOK HEAVY

News Gothic STD

Morris Fuller Benton

A-z **€**

Typography

ABCDEFGHIJKLMNOPQRSTUVWX
YZabcdefghijklmnopqrstuvwxyz&
0123456789$€!?.;:,""''{½}

*ABCDEFGHIJKLMNOPQRSTUVWX
YZabcdefghijklmnopqrstuvwxyz&
0123456789$€!?.;:,""''{½}*

Letterforms have tone, timbre, character,
just as words and sentences do. The mo
ment a text and typeface are chosen, two
MEDIUM

*Letterforms have tone, timbre, character,
just as words and sentences do. The mo
ment a text and typeface are chosen, two*
OBLIQUE

**Letterforms have tone, timbre, char
acter, just as words and sentences
do. The moment a text and typeface**
BOLD

***Letterforms have tone, timbre, char
acter, just as words and sentences
do. The moment a text and typeface***
BOLD OBLIQUE

Notre Dame STD

Karlgeorg Hoefer, Linotype Library GmbH

A-z **€** **ß**

𝕿𝖞𝖕𝖔𝖌𝖗𝖆𝖕𝖍𝖞

𝕬𝕭𝕮𝕯𝕰𝕱𝕲𝕳𝕴𝕵𝕶𝕷𝕸𝕹𝕺
𝕻𝕼𝕽𝕾𝕿𝖀𝖁𝖂𝖃𝖄𝖅𝖆𝖇𝖈𝖉𝖊𝖋𝖌𝖍
𝖎𝖏𝖐𝖑𝖒𝖓𝖔𝖕𝖖𝖗𝖘𝖙𝖚𝖛𝖜𝖝𝖞𝖟&0123456
789$€!?.;:,""''{½}

ch ck ff ft ll ſ ſi ſſ ſt ſz tz
Historic Blackletter

Letterforms have tone, timbre, charac
ter, just as words and sentences do.
ROMAN

ORNAMENTS

www.adobe.com/type

ITC Novarese STD

Aldo Novarese, ITC

A-z €

Typography

ABCDEFGHIJKLMNOPQRSTUVW
XYZabcdefghijklmnopqrstuvwxyz
&0123456789$€!?.;:,""''{½}

ABCDEFGHIJKLMNOPQRSTUVW
XYZabcdefghijklmnopqrstuvwxyz&01
23456789$€!?.;:,""''{½}

Letterforms have tone, timbre, character,
just as words and sentences do. The mo
ment a text and typeface are chosen, two
BOOK

Letterforms have tone, timbre, character, just as
words and sentences do. The moment a text and
typeface are chosen, two streams of thought, two
BOOK ITALIC

Letterforms have tone, timbre, charac
ter, just as words and sentences do. The
moment a text and typeface are chosen
MEDIUM

Letterforms have tone, timbre, character, just
as words and sentences do. The moment a text
and typeface are chosen, two streams of though
MEDIUM ITALIC

Letterforms have tone, timbre, charac
ter, just as words and sentences do.
The moment a text and typeface are
BOLD

Letterforms have tone, timbre, character,
just as words and sentences do. The mo
ment a text and typeface are chosen, two
BOLD ITALIC

Letterforms have tone, timbre,
character, just as words and sen
tences do. The moment a text
ULTRA

€ Nueva STD

Carol Twombly, Adobe Systems

A-z €

Typography

ABCDEFGHIJKLMNOPQRST
UVWXYZabcdefghijklmno
pqrstuvwxyz&0123456789$
€!?.;:,""''{½}

ABCDEFGHIJKLMNOPQRSTUV
WXYZabcdefghijklmnopqrst
uvwxyz&0123456789$€!?.;:,""''{½}

Letterforms have tone, timbre,
character, just as words and sen
LIGHT

Letterforms have tone, timbre, char
acter, just as words and sentences
LIGHT ITALIC

Letterforms have tone, tim
bre, character, just as words
REGULAR

Letterforms have tone, timbre, character, just as words and sent

ITALIC

Letterforms have tone, tim bre, character, just as words

BOLD

Letterforms have tone, timbre, character, just as words and

BOLD ITALIC

Nueva STD Condensed

Carol Twombly, Adobe Systems

A-z €

Typography

Letterforms have tone, timbre, character, just as words and sentences do. The moment a text

LIGHT CONDENSED

Letterforms have tone, timbre, character, just as words and sentences do. The moment a text and

LIGHT CONDENSED ITALIC

Letterforms have tone, timbre, character, just as words and sentences do. The mo

CONDENSED

Letterforms have tone, timbre, character, just as words and sentences do. The moment a type

CONDENSED ITALIC

Letterforms have tone, timbre, char acter, just as words and sentences

BOLD CONDENSED

Letterforms have tone, timbre, charac ter, just as words and sentences do. The

BOLD CONDENSED ITALIC

Nueva STD Extended

Carol Twombly, Adobe Systems

A-z €

Typograph

Letterforms have tone, timbre, character, just as

LIGHT EXTENDED

Letterforms have tone, tim bre, character, just as words

LIGHT EXTENDED ITALIC

Letterforms have tone, timbre, character, just

EXTENDED

Letterforms have tone, tim bre, character, just as word

EXTENDED ITALIC

Letterforms have to ne, timbre, character,

BOLD EXTENDED

Letterforms have tone, timbre, character, just as

BOLD EXTENDED ITALIC

Nuptial Script STD

Edwin Shaar, Intertype

A-z €

Typography

Aa Bb Cc Dd Ee Ff Gg Hh Ii Jj Kk Ll Mm Nn Oo Pp Qq Rr Ss Tt Uu Vv Ww Xx Yy Zz &012 3456789$€!?.;:, ""{½}

Letterforms have tone, timbre, charac ter, just as words and sentences do. The
MEDIUM

Nyx STD

Rick Cusick, Adobe Systems

A-z €

TYPOGRAPHY

ABCDEFGHIJKLMNOPQ
RSTUVWXYZ&0123456
789$€!?.;:, ""{½}

LETTERFORMS HAVE TONE,
TIMBRE, CHARACTER, JUST
REGULAR

Ocean Sans STD

Chong Wah, Monotype Corp.

A-z €

Typography

ABCDEFGHIJKLMNOPQRSTUVWXYZ
abcdefghijklmnopqrstuvwxyz&012
3456789$€!?.;:, ""{½}

*ABCDEFGHIJKLMNOPQRSTUVWXYZ
abcdefghijklmnopqrstuvwxyz&0123
456789$€!?.;:, ""{½}*

Letterforms have tone, timbre, character,
just as words and sentences do. The mo
ment a text and typeface are chosen, two
LIGHT

*Letterforms have tone, timbre, character, just
as words and sentences do. The moment a
text and typeface are chosen, two streams of*
LIGHT ITALIC

Letterforms have tone, timbre, character,
just as words and sentences do. The mo
ment a text and typeface are chosen, two
BOOK

*Letterforms have tone, timbre, character,
just as words and sentences do. The moment
a text and typeface are chosen, two streams*
BOOK ITALIC

**Letterforms have tone, timbre, character,
just as words and sentences do. The mo
ment a text and typeface are chosen, two**
SEMIBOLD

***Letterforms have tone, timbre, character,
just as words and sentences do. The mo
ment a text and typeface are chosen, two***
SEMIBOLD ITALIC

Letterforms have tone, timbre, character, just as words and sentences do. The mo ment a text and typeface are chosen, two
BOLD

Letterforms have tone, timbre, character, just as words and sentences do. The mo ment a text and typeface are chosen, two
BOLD ITALIC

Letterforms have tone, timbre, charac ter, just as words and sentences do. The moment a text and typeface are chosen
EXTRA BOLD

Letterforms have tone, timbre, character, just as words and sentences do. The mo ment a text and typeface are chosen, two
EXTRA BOLD ITALIC

Ocean Sans STD SemiExtended

Chong Wah, Monotype Corp.

A-z €

Typography

ABCDEFGHIJKLMNOPQRSTUVWXY
Zabcdcfghijklmnopqrstuvwxyz&
0123456789$€!?.;:,""{½}

*ABCDEFGHIJKLMNOPQRSTUVWX
YZabcdefghijklmnopqrstuvwxyz&
0123456789$€!?.;:,""{½}*

Letterforms have tone, timbre, character, just as words and sentences do. The mo ment a text and typeface are chosen,
BOOK SEMIEXTENDED

Letterforms have tone, timbre, character, just as words and sentences do. The mo ment a text and typeface are chosen, two
BOOK SEMIEXTENDED ITALIC

Letterforms have tone, timbre, char acter, just as words and sentences do. The moment a text and typeface are
BOLD SEMIEXTENDED

Letterforms have tone, timbre, charac ter, just as words and sentences do. The moment a text and typeface are chosen
BOLD SEMIEXTENDED ITALIC

Ocean Sans STD Extended

Chong Wah, Monotype Corp.

A-z €

Typograph

ABCDEFGHIJKLMNOPQRSTU
VWXYZabcdefghijklmnopqrs
tuvwxyz&0123456789$€!?.;:,
""{½}

*ABCDEFGHIJKLMNOPQRSTU
VWXYZabcdefghijklmnopqrst
uvwxyz&0123456789$€!?.;:,
""{½}*

Letterforms have tone, timbre, char acter, just as words and sentences do. The moment a text and typeface
LIGHT EXTENDED

Letterforms have tone, timbre, char acter, just as words and sentences do. The moment a text and typeface are
LIGHT EXTENDED ITALIC

Letterforms have tone, timbre, char
acter, just as words and sentences
do. The moment a text and type

BOOK EXTENDED

*Letterforms have tone, timbre, char
acter, just as words and sentences
do. The moment a text and typeface*

BOOK EXTENDED ITALIC

**Letterforms have tone, timbre,
character, just as words and sent
ences do. The moment a text and**

SEMIBOLD EXTENDED

***Letterforms have tone, timbre, char
acter, just as words and sentences
do. The moment a text and type***

SEMIBOLD EXTENDED ITALIC

**Letterforms have tone, timbre,
character, just as words and sen
tences do. The moment a text**

BOLD EXTENDED

***Letterforms have tone, timbre,
character, just as words and sen
tences do. The moment a text and***

BOLD EXTENDED ITALIC

**Letterforms have tone, timbre,
character, just as words and sen
tences do. The moment a text**

EXTRA BOLD EXTENDED

***Letterforms have tone, timbre,
character, just as words and sen
tences do. The moment a text***

EXTRA BOLD EXTENDED ITALIC

OCR-A STD

American Type Founders Staff

A-z €

Typography

ABCDEFGHIJKLMNOPQRS
TUVWXYZabcdefghijkl
mnopqrstuvwxyz&0123
456789$€!?.;:,""{½}

Letterforms have tone,
timbre, character, just
as words and sentences

MEDIUM

OCR-B STD

Adrian Frutiger

A-z €

Typography

ABCDEFGHIJKLMNOPQRS
TUVWXYZabcdefghijkl
mnopqrstuvwxyz&0123
456789$€!?.;:,""{½}

Letterforms have tone,
timbre, character, just
as words and sentences

MEDIUM

Octavian STD

Will Carter and David Kindersley, Monotype Corp.

A-Z € ffi BB 619 123 ⅞ H₂ 1ˢᵗ

Typography

ABCDEFGHIJKLMNOPQRSTUV
WXYZabcdefghijklmnopqrstuvwxyz&
0123456789$€!?.;:,""{½}

ABCDEFGHIJKLMNOPQRSTUVWXYZ&
0123456789$¢ ffi ⅛

ABCDEFGHIJKLMNOPQRSTUV
WXYZabcdefghijklmnopqrstuvwxyz&
0123456789$€!?.;:,""{½}

0123456789$¢ ffi ⅛

LETTERFORMS HAVE TONE, timbre, character,
just as words and 567 sentences do. The moment
a text and typeface are chosen, two streams of
REGULAR

*Letterforms have tone, timbre, character, just as
words and 567 sentences do. The moment a text
and typeface are chosen, two streams of thought,*
ITALIC

ITC Officina Sans STD

Erik Spiekermann, ITC

A-Z €

Typography

ABCDEFGHIJKLMNOPQRSTUVWXYZ
abcdefghijklmnopqrstuvwxyz&0123
456789$€!?.;:,""{½}

ABCDEFGHIJKLMNOPQRSTUVWXYZ
abcdefghijklmnopqrstuvwxyz&0123
456789$€!?.;:,""{½}

Letterforms have tone, timbre, character,
just as words and sentences do. The mo
ment a text and typeface are chosen, two
BOOK

Letterforms have tone, timbre, character,
just as words and sentences do. The mo
ment a text and typeface are chosen, two
BOOK ITALIC

Letterforms have tone, timbre, character,
just as words and sentences do. The mo
ment a text and typeface are chosen,
BOLD

Letterforms have tone, timbre, character,
just as words and sentences do. The mo
ment a text and typeface are chosen, two
BOLD ITALIC

ITC Officina Serif STD

Erik Spiekermann, ITC

A-z €

Typography

ABCDEFGHIJKLMNOPQRSTUVWXYZ
abcdefghijklmnopqrstuvwxyz&01
23456789$€!?.;:,""{½}

ABCDEFGHIJKLMNOPQRSTUVWXYZ
abcdefghijklmnopqrstuvwxyz&0123
456789$€!?.;:,""{½}

Letterforms have tone, timbre, character,
just as words and sentences do. The mo
ment a text and typeface are chosen, two
BOOK

Letterforms have tone, timbre, character,
just as words and sentences do. The mo
ment a text and typeface are chosen, two
BOOK ITALIC

Letterforms have tone, timbre, char
acter, just as words and sentences do.
The moment a text and typeface are
BOLD

Letterforms have tone, timbre, charac
ter, just as words and sentences do. The
moment a text and typeface are chosen
BOLD ITALIC

Old Claude STD

Paul Shaw, LetterPerfect

A-z € Bb 619

Typography

ABCDEFGHIJKLMNO
PQRSTUVWXYZabcdef
ghijklmnopqrstuvwxyz&
0123456789$€!?.;:,""{½}
abcdefghijklmnopqrstuv
wxyz&0123456789

LETTERFORMS HAVE TONE, tim
bre, character, just as words
REGULAR

Monotype Old Style STD

Unknown, Monotype Typography Ltd.

A-z €

Typography

ABCDEFGHIJKLM
NOPQRSTUVWXY
Zabcdefghijklmnopqr
stuvwxyz&012345678
9$€!?.;:,""{½}

Letterforms have tone, timbre, character, just as
BOLD OUTLINE

Old Style 7 STD

Unknown

A-z € BB 619

Typography

ABCDEFGHIJKLMNOPQRST
UVWXYZabcdefghijklmnopqrs
tuvwxyz&0123456789$€!?.;:,""{½}

ABCDEFGHIJKLMNOPQRSTUVWX
YZ&0123456789

ABCDEFGHIJKLMNOPQRST
UVWXYZabcdefghijklmnopqrstu
vwxyz&0123456789$€!?.;:,""{½}
0123456789

LETTERFORMS HAVE TONE, timbre, char
acter, just as words and 567 sentences do.
The moment a text and typeface are cho
ROMAN

Letterforms have tone, timbre, character,
just as words and 576 sentences do. The
moment a text and typeface are chosen,
ITALIC

Olympian STD

Matthew Carter, Linotype Library GmbH

A-z €

Typography

ABCDEFGHIJKLMNOPQR
STUVWXYZabcdefghijklm
nopqrstuvwxyz&0123456789
$€!?.;:,""{½}

ABCDEFGHIJKLMNOPQRS
TUVWXYZabcdefghijklmno
pqrstuvwxyz&0123456789$€
!?.;:,""{½}

Letterforms have tone, timbre, char
acter, just as words and sentences
do. The moment a text and typeface
ROMAN

Letterforms have tone, timbre, char
acter, just as words and sentences
do. The moment a text and typeface
ITALIC

Letterforms have tone, timbre, char
acter, just as words and sentences
do. The moment a text and typeface
BOLD

Letterforms have tone, timbre, char
acter, just as words and sentences
do. The moment a text and typeface
BOLD ITALIC

www.adobe.com/type

228

O

Omnia STD

Karlgeorg Hoefer, Linotype Library GmbH

A-z €

TYPOGRAPH

ABCDEFGHIJKLMNOP
QRSTUVWXYZ&0123456
789$€!?.,;:,""{½}

LETTERFORMS HAVE TO
NE, TIMBRE, CHARACTER,
ROMAN

Ondine STD

Adrian Frutiger, Linotype Library GmbH

A-z €

Typography

ABCDEFGHIJKLMNOPQR
STUVWXYZabcdefghijkl
mnopqrstuvwxyz&012345
6789$€!?.;:,""{½}

Letterforms have tone, timbre,
character, just as words and
REGULAR

Onyx STD

Gerry Powell, Monotype Corp.

A-z €

Typography

ABCDEFGHIJKLMNOPQRSTUVWXYZ
abcdefghijklmnopqrstuvwxyz&0123
456789$€!?.:.,;,"" {½}

Letterforms have tone, timbre, character,
just as words and sentences do. The moment
REGULAR

Optima STD

Hermann Zapf, Linotype Library GmbH

A-z €

Typography

ABCDEFGHIJKLMNOPQRSTUV
WXYZabcdefghijklmnopqrstuvw
xyz&0123456789$€!?.;:,""{½}

*ABCDEFGHIJKLMNOPQRSTUV
WXYZabcdefghijklmnopqrstuvw
xyz&0123456789$€!?.;:,""{½}*

Letterforms have tone, timbre, character,
just as words and sentences do. The
moment a text and typeface are chosen,
ROMAN

Letterforms have tone, timbre, character, just as words and sentences do. The moment a text and typeface are chosen,
ITALIC

Letterforms have tone, timbre, character, just as words and sentences do. The moment a text and typeface are
MEDIUM

Letterforms have tone, timbre, character, just as words and sentences do. The moment a text and typeface are
MEDIUM ITALIC

Letterforms have tone, timbre, character, just as words and sentences do. The moment a text and typeface are chosen
DEMI

Letterforms have tone, timbre, character, just as words and sentences do. The moment a text and typeface are
DEMI ITALIC

Letterforms have tone, timbre, character, just as words and sentences do. The moment a text and typeface are chosen
BOLD

Letterforms have tone, timbre, character, just as words and sentences do. The moment a text and typeface are chosen
BOLD ITALIC

Letterforms have tone, timbre, character, just as words and sentences do. The moment a text and typeface are
BLACK

Letterforms have tone, timbre, character, just as words and sentences do. The moment a text and typeface are
BLACK ITALIC

Letterforms have tone, timbre, character, just as words and sentences do. The moment a text and type
EXTRA BLACK

Letterforms have tone, timbre, character, just as words and sentences do. The moment a text and type
EXTRA BLACK ITALIC

Orator STD

John Scheppler

A-z €

TYPOGRAPHY

ABCDEFGHIJKLMNOPQRSTUVWXYZ
ABCDEFGHIJKLMNOPQRSTUVWXYZ
&0123456789$€!?.;:,""{½}

ABCDEFGHIJKLMNOPQRSTUVWXYZ
ABCDEFGHIJKLMNOPQRSTUVWXYZ
&0123456789$€!?.;:,""{½}

LETTERFORMS HAVE TONE, TIMBRE, CHARACTER, JUST AS WORDS AND SENTENCES DO. THE MOMENT
MEDIUM

LETTERFORMS HAVE TONE, TIMBRE, CHARACTER, JUST AS WORDS AND SENTENCES DO. THE MOMENT
SLANTED

O

Orgánica STD

Gabriel Martínez Meave, Gabriel Martínez Meave

A-z € 123

Typography

ABCDEFGHIJKLMNOP
QRSTUVWXYZabcdefgh
ijklmnopqrstuvwxyz&O
123456789$€!?.;:,""{½}

Letterforms have tone,
timbre, character, just as

SEMISERIF ROMAN

Origami STD

Carl Crossgrove, Carl Crossgrove

A-z €

Typography

ABCDEFGHIJKLMNOPQRSTUVWXY
Zabcdefghijklmnopqrstuvwxyz&01234
56789$€!?.;:,""{½}

ABCDEFGHIJKLMNOPQRSTUVWXY
Zabcdefghijklmnopqrstuvwxyz&01234567
89$€!?.;:,""{½}

Letterforms have tone, timbre, character, just as
words and sentences do. The moment a text
and typeface are chosen, two streams of thought,

REGULAR

*Letterforms have tone, timbre, character, just as
words and sentences do. The moment a text and
typeface are chosen, two streams of thought, two*

ITALIC

Letterforms have tone, timbre, character, just
as words and sentences do. The moment a
text and typeface are chosen, two streams of

MEDIUM

*Letterforms have tone, timbre, character, just as
words and sentences do. The moment a text and
typeface are chosen, two streams of thought, two*

MEDIUM ITALIC

**Letterforms have tone, timbre, character,
just as words and sentences do. The moment
a text and typeface are chosen, two streams**

SEMIBOLD

***Letterforms have tone, timbre, character, just
as words and sentences do. The moment a text
and typeface are chosen, two streams of thought,***

SEMIBOLD ITALIC

**Letterforms have tone, timbre, character,
just as words and sentences do. The mo
ment a text and typeface are chosen, two**

BOLD

***Letterforms have tone, timbre, character, just
as words and sentences do. The moment a
text and typeface are chosen, two streams of***

BOLD ITALIC

Ouch! STD

Joachim Müller-Lancé, Adobe Systems

A-z €

TYPOGRAPH

ABCDEFGHIJKLMN
OPQRSTUVWXYZ&012
3456789$€!?.,;;""{½}

LETTERFORMS HAVE
TONE, TIMBRE, CHAR

REGULAR

Oxford

Arthur Baker, AlphaOmega Typography

Typography

ABCDEFGHIJKLMNOPQRSTUV
WXYZabcdefghijklmnopqrstuvw
xyz&0123456789$!?.;:, ""{ ½ }

Letterforms have tone, timbre, char
acter, just as words and sentences

REGULAR

ITC Ozwald STD

David Farey, ITC

A-z €

Typograph

ABCDEFGHIJKL
MNOPQRSTUVW
XYZabcdefghijkl
mnopqrstuvwxyz
&0123456789$€
!?.;:,""{½}

Letterforms have
tone, timbre, cha

REGULAR

Palace Script STD

Unknown, Monotype Corp.

A-z €

Typography

Aa Bb Cc Dd Ee Ff Gg Hh
Ii Jj Kk Ll Mm Nn Oo Pp
Qq Rr Ss Tt Uu Vv Ww Xx Yy
Zz &0123456789$€!?.;:. ""{½}

Letterforms have tone, timbre, character,
just as words and sentences do. The mo

REGULAR

Letterforms have tone, timbre, character,
just as words and sentences do. The mo

SEMIBOLD

Palatino STD

Hermann Zapf, Linotype Library GmbH

A-z € BB 619

Typography

ABCDEFGHIJKLMNOPQRST
UVWXYZabcdefghijklmnopqrs
tuvwxyz&0123456789$€!?.;:,""
{½}

ABCDEFGHIJKLMNOPQRSTUVWXY
z&0123456789

*ABCDEFGHIJKLMNOPQRSTU
VWXYZabcdefghijklmnopqrstuvw
xyz&0123456789$€!?.;:,""{½}*

0123456789

Letterforms have tone, timbre, character,
just as words and sentences do. The mo
ment a text and typeface are chosen, two
LIGHT

*Letterforms have tone, timbre, character, just
as words and sentences do. The moment a
text and typeface are chosen, two streams of*
LIGHT ITALIC

LETTERFORMS HAVE TONE, timbre, char
acter, just as words and 567 sentences
do. The moment a text and typeface are
ROMAN

*Letterforms have tone, timbre, character,
just as words and 567 sentences do. The
moment a text and typeface are chosen, two*
ITALIC

Letterforms have tone, timbre, charac
ter, just as words and sentences do.
The moment a text and typeface are
MEDIUM

*Letterforms have tone, timbre, character,
just as words and sentences do. The mo
ment a text and typeface are chosen, two*
MEDIUM ITALIC

**Letterforms have tone, timbre, charac
ter, just as words and 567 sentences
do. The moment a text and typeface**
BOLD

***Letterforms have tone, timbre, charac
ter, just as words and 567 sentences do.
The moment a text and typeface are***
BOLD ITALIC

**Letterforms have tone, timbre, char
acter, just as words and sentences
do. The moment a text and typeface**
BLACK

***Letterforms have tone, timbre, char
acter, just as words and sentences
do. The moment a text and typeface***
BLACK ITALIC

Parisian STD

Morris Fuller Benton

A-z € 123

Typography

ABCDEFGHIJKLMNOPQ
RSTUVWXYZabcdefghijklmno
pqrstuvwxyz&0123456789$€
!?.;:,""{½}

Letterforms have tone, timbre, character, just as words and sentences do. The mo
MEDIUM

Park Avenue STD

Robert E. Smith, Kingsley/ATF

A-z € 619

Typography

Aa Bb Cc Dd Ee Ff Gg Hh Ii
Jj Kk Ll Mm Nn Oo Pp Qq
Rr Ss Tt Uu Vv Ww Xx Yy
Zz & 0123456789$€!?.;:,"" {½}

Letterforms have tone, timbre, character, just as words and sentences do. The mo
MEDIUM

Peignot STD

A.M. Cassandre, Linotype Library GmbH

A-z €

Typography

ABCDEFGHIJKLMNOPQR
STUVWXYZabcdefghijklmno
pqrstuvwxyz&012345678
9$€!?.;:,""'{½}

Letterforms have tone, timbre, character, just as words and sent
LIGHT

Letterforms have tone, timbre, character, just as words and sent
DEMI

Letterforms have tone, timbre, character, just as words
BOLD

Pelican

Arthur Baker, AlphaOmega Typography

Typography

ABCDEFGHIJKLMNOPQRS
TUVWXYZabcdefghijklmnopqrst
uvwxyz&0123456789$!?.;:,""
{½}

Letterforms have tone, timbre, character, just as words and sentences do. The mo
REGULAR

ⓔ **Penumbra Sans** STD

Lance Hidy, Adobe Systems

A-z €

TYPOGRAPHY

ABCDEFGHIJKLMNOP QRSTUVWXYZ&012345 6789$€!?.;:,""'{½}

LETTERFORMS HAVE TONE,
TIMBRE, CHARACTER, JUST AS
LIGHT SANS

LETTERFORMS HAVE TONE,
TIMBRE, CHARACTER, JUST
REGULAR SANS

**LETTERFORMS HAVE TONE,
TIMBRE, CHARACTER, JUST**
SEMIBOLD SANS

**LETTERFORMS HAVE TO
NE, TIMBRE, CHARACTER,**
BOLD SANS

ⓔ **Penumbra Flare** STD

Lance Hidy, Adobe Systems

A-z €

TYPOGRAPHY

LETTERFORMS HAVE TONE,
TIMBRE, CHARACTER, JUST AS
LIGHT FLARE SERIF

LETTERFORMS HAVE TONE,
TIMBRE, CHARACTER, JUST
REGULAR FLARE SERIF

**LETTERFORMS HAVE TONE,
TIMBRE, CHARACTER, JUST**
SEMIBOLD FLARE SERIF

**LETTERFORMS HAVE TO
NE, TIMBRE, CHARACTER**
BOLD FLARE SERIF

ⓔ **Penumbra HalfSerif** STD

Lance Hidy, Adobe Systems

A-z €

TYPOGRAPHY

LETTERFORMS HAVE TONE,
TIMBRE, CHARACTER, JUST
LIGHT HALF SERIF

LETTERFORMS HAVE TONE,
TIMBRE, CHARACTER, JUST
REGULAR HALF SERIF

**LETTERFORMS HAVE TO
NE, TIMBRE, CHARACTER**
SEMIBOLD HALF SERIF

**LETTERFORMS HAVE TO
NE, TIMBRE, CHARACTER**
BOLD HALF SERIF

Penumbra Serif STD

Lance Hidy, Adobe Systems

TYPOGRAPHY

LETTERFORMS HAVE TONE, TIMBRE, CHARACTER, JUST

LIGHT SERIF

LETTERFORMS HAVE TO NE, TIMBRE, CHARACTER

REGULAR SERIF

LETTERFORMS HAVE TO NE, TIMBRE, CHARAC

SEMIBOLD SERIF

LETTERFORMS HAVE TONE, TIMBRE, CHAR

BOLD SERIF

Pepita STD

Imre Reiner, Monotype Corp.

Typography

*Aa Bb Cc Dd Ee Ff Gg
Hh Ii Jj Kk Ll Mm Nn
Oo Pp Qq Rr Ss Tt Uu
Vv Ww Xx Yy Zz &0123
456789$€!?.;:,""{½}*

*Letterforms have tone, timbre, char
acter, just as words and sentences*

REGULAR

Pepperwood STD

Kim Buker Chansler, Adobe Systems

TYPOGRAPHY

ABCDEFGHIJKLMNOPQRSTUV

WXYZ&0123456789$€!?.;:,""{½}

LETTERFORMS HAVE TONE, TIMBRE,

REGULAR

LETTERFORMS HAVE TONE, TIMBRE,

FILL

LETTERFORMS HAVE TONE, TIMBRE,

OUTLINE

LETTERFORMS HAVE TONE, TIMBRE

USE EACH STYLE AS IS OR OVERLAP AND COLOR THEM.

Perpetua STD

Eric Gill, Monotype Corp.

A-z € ffi Bb 619 123 ⅞ H₂ 1ˢᵗ

Typography

ABCDEFGHIJKLMNOPQRSTUVW
XYZabcdefghijklmnopqrstuvwxyz&01
23456789$€!?.;:,""{½}

ABCDEFGHIJKLMNOPQRSTUVWXYZ&
0123456789$¢ ffi ⅛

ABCDEFGHIJKLMNOPQRSTUVWXYZ
abcdefghijklmnopqrstuvwxyz&012345678
9$€!?.;:,""{½}

0123456789$¢ ffi ⅛

LETTERFORMS HAVE TONE, timbre, character,
just as words and 567 sentences do. The moment
a text and typeface are chosen, two streams of
REGULAR

*Letterforms have tone, timbre, character, just as words
and 567 sentences do. The moment a text and typeface
are chosen, two streams of thought, two rhythmical sys*
ITALIC

**Letterforms have tone, timbre, character,
just as words and 567 sentences do. The
moment a text and typeface are chosen,**
BOLD

***Letterforms have tone, timbre, character, just
as words and 567 sentences do. The moment a
text and typeface are chosen, two streams of***
BOLD ITALIC

Photina STD

José Mendoza y Almeida, Monotype Corp.

A-z €

Typography

ABCDEFGHIJKLMNOPQRSTUVW
XYZabcdefghijklmnopqrstuvwxyz
&0123456789$€!?.;:,""{½}

*ABCDEFGHIJKLMNOPQRSTUV
WXYZabcdefghijklmnopqrstuvwxyz
&0123456789$€!?.;:,""{½}*

Letterforms have tone, timbre, character,
just as words and sentences do. The mo
ment a text and typeface are chosen, two
REGULAR

*Letterforms have tone, timbre, character, just
as words and sentences do. The moment a
text and typeface are chosen, two streams of*
ITALIC

**Letterforms have tone, timbre, character,
just as words and sentences do. The mo
ment a text and typeface are chosen, two**
SEMIBOLD

***Letterforms have tone, timbre, character,
just as words and sentences do. The mo
ment a text and typeface are chosen, two***
SEMIBOLD ITALIC

**Letterforms have tone, timbre, char
acter, just as words and sentences do.
The moment a text and typeface are**
BOLD

***Letterforms have tone, timbre, charac
ter, just as words and sentences do. The
moment a text and typeface are chosen***
BOLD ITALIC

Letterforms have tone, timbre, character, just as words and sen tences do. The moment a text
ULTRA BOLD

Letterforms have tone, timbre, char acter, just as words and sentences do. The moment a text and typeface
ULTRA BOLD ITALIC

Plantin STD

F.H. Pierpont, Monotype Corp.

A-Z €

Typography

ABCDEFGHIJKLMNOPQRS
TUVWXYZabcdefghijklmnopq
rstuvwxyz&0123456789$€!?.;:,
"" {½}

*ABCDEFGHIJKLMNOPQRST
UVWXYZabcdefghijklmnopqrstuv
wxyz&0123456789$€!?.;:, "" {½}*

Letterforms have tone, timbre, character,
just as words and sentences do. The mo
ment a text and typeface are chosen, two
LIGHT

*Letterforms have tone, timbre, character, just
as words and sentences do. The moment a
text and typeface are chosen, two streams of*
LIGHT ITALIC

Letterforms have tone, timbre, charac
ter, just as words and sentences do. The
moment a text and typeface are chosen,
REGULAR

*Letterforms have tone, timbre, character,
just as words and sentences do. The moment
a text and typeface are chosen, two streams*
ITALIC

Letterforms have tone, timbre, char
acter, just as words and sentences do.
The moment a text and typeface are
SEMIBOLD

*Letterforms have tone, timbre, charac
ter, just as words and sentences do.
The moment a text and typeface are*
SEMIBOLD ITALIC

**Letterforms have tone, timbre, char
acter, just as words and sentences
do. The moment a text and typeface**
BOLD

***Letterforms have tone, timbre, char
acter, just as words and sentences
do. The moment a text and typeface***
BOLD ITALIC

**Letterforms have tone, timbre, character,
just as words and sentences do. The moment
a text and typeface are chosen, two streams**
BOLD CONDENSED

Poetica STD

Robert Slimbach, Adobe Systems

A-Z € ffi BB 619 123 ⅞ H₂ 1st 𝒜 ᵉᵉ 🖉

Typography

ABCDEFGHIJKLMNOPQRSTU
VWXYZabcdefghijklmnopqrstuvwx
yz&0123456789$€!?.;:, ""{½}

ABCDEFGHIJKLMNOPQRSTUV
WXYZABCDEFGHIJKLMNOP
QRSTUVWXYZ&0123456789

AAAAAAAAAABBBB
BBBBBBBCCCCCCC
DDDDDDDDDDEEE
EEEEEEEFFFFFF
FFGGGGGGGGGGHH
HHHHHHHHIIIIIII
IJJJJJJJJJKKKKK
KKKKKLLLLLLLLL
MMMMMMMMMMMMNN
NNNNNNNXOOOO
OOOOOOOPPPPPPP
PQQQQQQQQQQRRR

R R R R R R R S S S S S S S S
S T T T T T T T T T T U U U
U U U U U U UV V V V V
V V V V V W W W W W W W
W W W W W W X X X X X X X
X X X Y Y Y Y Y Y Y Y Y Y Y
Z Z Z Z Z Z Z Z Z
Swash Capitals

Initial Swash Capitals

b b b c d d d d f f g g g g g h
h j j k k k k k l l l p p p p
q g g s ſ t v v v v w w w x
x x y y y y y 3 z z z
Lowercase Alternates

K K M N N Q R R V X X Z
Small Capitals Alternates

Lowercase Beginnings

Lowercase Endings

Ligatures

Ampersands

Ornaments

LETTERFORMS HAVE TONE, *timbre, character, just as words and sentences do. The*
REGULAR

The moment a text and typeface are chosen,
two streams of thought,
two rhythmical systems, two sets of habits,
or if you like, two personalities,
intersect.

Pompeia STD

Victor de Castro, Unitype

A-Z € 123

Typography

ABCDEFGHIJKLMNOPQRST
UVWXYZabcdefghijklmnop
qrstuvwxyz&0123456789$€
!?.,;:,""''{1/2}

ABCDEFGHIJKLMNOPQRST
UVWXYZabcdefghijklmnop
qrstuvwxyz&0123456789$€
!?.,;:,""''{1/2}

Letterforms have tone,
timbre, character, just as
INLINE

*Letterforms have tone,
timbre, character, just*
INLINE ITALIC

Pompeijana STD

Adrian Frutiger, Linotype Library GmbH

`A-z` `€` `123`

TYPOGRAPHY

ABCDEFGHIJKLMNOPQRST
UVWXYZ&0123456789$€
!?.;:,""{½}

LETTERFORMS HAVE TONE,
TIMBRE, CHARACTER, JUST AS

ROMAN

BORDERS

Ponderosa STD

Kim Buker Chansler, Adobe Systems

`A-z` `€`

789$€!?.·:,""{½}

LETTERFORMS HAVE TONE, TIMBRE, CHAR

REGULAR

Poplar STD

Barbara Lind, Adobe Systems

`A-z` `€`

Typography

ABCDEFGHIJKLMNOPQRSTUV
WXYZabcdefghijklmnopqrstuvwxy
z&0123456789$€!?.;:,""{½}

Letterforms have tone, timbre, char
acter, just as words and sentences

BLACK

Postino STD

Tim Donaldson, Adobe Systems

`A-z` `€`

Typograph

ABCDEFGHIJKLM
NOPQRSTUVWXYZ
abcdefghijklmnopqr
stuvwxyz&01234567
89$€ !?.;:,""{½}

ABCDEFGHIJKLMN
OPQRSTUVWXYZab
cdefghijklmnopqrstu
vwxyz&0123456789$€
!?.;:,""{½}

Letterforms have tone, timbre, charac
REGULAR

Letterforms have tone, timbre, charac
ITALIC

Present STD

Friedrich Karl Sallwey, Linotype Library GmbH

A-Z €

Typography

ABCDEFGHIJKLMN
OPQRSTUVWXYZabc
defghijklmnopqrstuvwxyz&
0123456789$€!? .,:,""{½}

Letterforms have tone, tim
bre, character, just as words
ROMAN

**Letterforms have tone,
timbre, character, just as**
BOLD

**Letterforms have tone,
timbre, character, just**
BLACK

Letterforms have tone, timbre, character,
just as words and sentences do. The moment
CONDENSED

Letterforms have tone, timbre, char
acter, just as words and sentences do.
BOLD CONDENSED

**Letterforms have tone, timbre,
character, just as words and sen**
BLACK CONDENSED

Prestige Elite STD

Howard Kettler

A-Z €

Typography

ABCDEFGHIJKLMNOPQRSTUVWXYZ
abcdefghijklmnopqrstuvwxyz
&0123456789$€!?.;:,""{½}

ABCDEFGHIJKLMNOPQRSTUVWXYZ
abcdefghijklmnopqrstuvwxyz
&0123456789$€!?.;:,""{½}

Letterforms have tone, tim
bre, character, just as words
and sentences do. The moment
REGULAR

Letterforms have tone, tim
bre, character, just as words
and sentences do. The moment
SLANTED

Letterforms have tone, tim
bre, character, just as words
and sentences do. The moment
BOLD

Letterforms have tone, tim
bre, character, just as words
and sentences do. The moment
BOLD SLANTED

Quake STD

Fryda Berd, Adobe Systems

A-z €

Typography

ABCDEFGHIJKLMNOP
QRSTUVWXYZabcdefghi
jklmnopqrstuvwxyz&012
3456789$€!?.;:,""{½}

Letterforms have tone, timbre,
character, just as words and
REGULAR

ITC Quorum STD

Ray Baker, ITC

A-z €

Typography

ABCDEFGHIJKLMNOPQR
STUVWXYZabcdefghijklm
nopqrstuvwxyz&012345
6789$€!?.;:,""{½}

Letterforms have tone, timbre,
character, just as words and sen
LIGHT

Letterforms have tone, timbre,
character, just as words and sen
BOOK

Letterforms have tone, tim
bre, character, just as words
MEDIUM

**Letterforms have tone, tim
bre, character, just as words**
BOLD

**Letterforms have tone, tim
bre, character, just as words**
BLACK

Rad STD

John Ritter, Adobe Systems

A-z €

REGULAR

Raleigh STD

Robert Norton, Linotype Library GmbH

A-Z €

Typography

ABCDEFGHIJKLMNOPQRSTUVW
XYZabcdefghijklmnopqrstuvwxyz
&0123456789$€!?.;:,""[½]

Letterforms have tone, timbre, character,
just as words and sentences do. The mo
ment a text and typeface are chosen, two
ROMAN

Letterforms have tone, timbre, character,
just as words and sentences do. The mo
ment a text and typeface are chosen, two
MEDIUM

Letterforms have tone, timbre, character,
just as words and sentences do. The mo
ment a text and typeface are chosen,
DEMI BOLD

Letterforms have tone, timbre, charac
ter, just as words and sentences do.
The moment a text and typeface are
BOLD

Raphael STD

Unknown

A-Z €

Typography

ABCDEFGHIJKLMNOPQ
RSTUVWXYZabcdefghijkl
mnopqrstuvwxyz&012345
6789$€!?.;:,""{½}

Letterforms have tone, timbre,
character, just as words and sen
REGULAR

Reliq STD Calm

Carl Crossgrove, Adobe Systems

A-Z € 619 123

Typography

ABCDEFGHIJKLMNOPQRSTUV
WXYZabcdefghijklmnopqrstuvw
xyz&0123456789$€!?.;:,""{½}

Letterforms have tone, timbre, character,
just as words and 567 sentences do. The
LIGHT CALM

Letterforms have tone, timbre, charac
ter, just as words and 567 sentences do
CALM

Letterforms have tone, timbre, char
acter, just as words and 567 senten
SEMIBOLD CALM

Letterforms have tone, timbre,
character, just as words and 567
BOLD CALM

Reliq STD Active

Carl Crossgrove, Adobe Systems

A-z € 619 123

Typography

Letterforms have tone, timbre, character,
just as words and 567 sentences do. The
LIGHT ACTIVE

Letterforms have tone, timbre, charac
ter, just as words and 567 sentences do
ACTIVE

Letterforms have tone, timbre, char
acter, just as words and 567 senten
SEMIBOLD ACTIVE

Letterforms have tone, timbre,
character, just as words and 567
BOLD ACTIVE

Reliq STD Extra Active

Carl Crossgrove, Adobe Systems

A-z € 619 123

Typography

Letterforms have tone, timbre, character,
just as words and 567 sentences do. The
LIGHT EXTRA ACTIVE

Letterforms have tone, timbre, charac
ter, just as words and sentences do.
EXTRA ACTIVE

Letterforms have tone, timbre,
character, just as words and 567
SEMIBOLD EXTRA ACTIVE

Letterforms have tone, timbre,
character, just as words and 567
BOLD EXTRA ACTIVE

Reporter STD

C. Winkow, J. Wagner

A-z €

Typography

ABCDEFGHIJKLMNOPQR
STUVWXYZabcdefghijklmnop
qrstuvwxyz&0123456789$€!?
.;:,""''{½}

Letterforms have tone, timbre, charac
ter, just as words and sentences do.

2

Revue STD

Colin Brignall, Esselte Pendaflex, Letraset, Esselte Letraset

[A-Z] [€]

Typography

ABCDEFGHIJKLMNOPQ
RSTUVWXYZabcdefghij
klmnopqrstuvwxyz&012
3456789$€!?.;:,""{½}

Letterforms have tone,
timbre, character, just as

BOLD

Rockwell STD

Unknown, Monotype Corp.

[A-Z] [€]

Typography

ABCDEFGHIJKLMNOPQRSTUV
WXYZabcdefghijklmnopqrstuv
wxyz&0123456789$€!?.;:,"" {½}

ABCDEFGHIJKLMNOPQRSTUVW
XYZabcdefghijklmnopqrstuvwxy
z&0123456789$€!?.;:,""{½}

Letterforms have tone, timbre, character,
just as words and sentences do. The mo
ment a text and typeface are chosen

LIGHT

Letterforms have tone, timbre, character,
just as words and sentences do. The mo
ment a text and typeface are chosen, two

LIGHT ITALIC

Letterforms have tone, timbre, charac
ter, just as words and sentences do.
The moment a text and typeface are

REGULAR

Letterforms have tone, timbre, charac
ter, just as words and sentences do. The
moment a text and typeface are chosen

ITALIC

Letterforms have tone, timbre, char
acter, just as words and sentences
do. The moment a text and typeface

BOLD

Letterforms have tone, timbre, char
acter, just as words and sentences
do. The moment a text and typeface

BOLD ITALIC

Letterforms have tone, tim
bre, character, just as words
and sentences do. The mom

EXTRA BOLD

Rockwell STD Condensed

Unknown, Monotype Corp.

[A-Z] [€]

Typography

ABCDEFGHIJKLMNOPQRSTUVWX
YZabcdefghijklmnopqrstuvwxyz&
0123456789$€!?.;:,""{½}

Letterforms have tone, timbre, charac ter, just as words and sentences do.
CONDENSED

Letterforms have tone, timbre, character, just as words and
BOLD CONDENSED

Romic STD

Colin Brignall, Esselte Pendaflex, Letraset, Esselte Letraset

Typography

ABCDEFGHIJKLMNOPQR
STUVWXYZabcdefghijklm
nopqrstuvwxyz&012345
6789$€!?.;:,""{½}

ABCDEFGHIJKLMNOPQR
STUVWXYZabcdefghijkl
mnopqrstuvwxyz&0123
456789$€!?.;:,""{½}

Letterforms have tone, tim bre, character, just as words
LIGHT

Letterforms have tone, timbre, character, just as
LIGHT ITALIC

Letterforms have tone, timbre, character, just as
MEDIUM

Letterforms have tone, timbre, character, just as
BOLD

Letterforms have tone, timbre, character, just as
EXTRA BOLD

Rosewood STD

Kim Buker Chansler, Adobe Systems

TYPOGRAPH

ABCDEFGHIJKLMNOPQ
RSTUVWXYZ&01234567
89$€!?.;:,""{½}

LETTERFORMS HAVE TONE, TIMBRE, CHARACTER, JUST
REGULAR

LETTERFORMS HAVE TONE, TIMBRE, CHARACTER, JUST
FILL

LETTERFORMS HAVE TONE,
USE EACH STYLE AS IS OR OVERLAP AND COLOR THEM.

Arthur Ritzel, Linotype Library GmbH

A-z €

Typography

ABCDEFGHIJKLMNOPQRSTU
VWXYZabcdefghijklmnopqrstuv
wxyz&0123456789$€!?.;:,""{½}

*ABCDEFGHIJKLMNOPQRSTU
VWXYZabcdefghijklmnopqrstuv
wxyz&0123456789$€!?.;:,""{½}*

Letterforms have tone, timbre, charac
ter, just as words and sentences do. The
moment a text and typeface are chosen
ROMAN

*Letterforms have tone, timbre, charac
ter, just as words and sentences do. The
moment a text and typeface are chosen*
ITALIC

**Letterforms have tone, timbre, charac
ter, just as words and sentences do. The
moment a text and typeface are chosen**
BOLD

Otl Aicher, Agfa Division, Bayer Corp.

Typography

ABCDEFGHIJKLMNOPQRSTUVWXYZ
abcdefghijklmnopqrstuvwxyz&01234
56789$!?.;:,""{½}

*ABCDEFGHIJKLMNOPQRSTUVWXYZ
abcdefghijklmnopqrstuvwxyz&01234
56789$!?.;:,""{½}*

Letterforms have tone, timbre, character, just
as words and sentences do. The moment a
text and typeface are chosen, two streams
45 LIGHT

*Letterforms have tone, timbre, character, just
as words and sentences do. The moment a
text and typeface are chosen, two streams of*
46 LIGHT ITALIC

Letterforms have tone, timbre, character, just
as words and sentences do. The moment a
text and typeface are chosen, two streams
55 REGULAR

*Letterforms have tone, timbre, character, just
as words and sentences do. The moment a
text and typeface are chosen, two streams of*
56 ITALIC

**Letterforms have tone, timbre, character,
just as words and sentences do. The mo
ment a text and typeface are chosen, two**
65 BOLD

**Letterforms have tone, timbre, character,
just as words and sentences do. The mo
ment a text and typeface are chosen, two**
75 EXTRA BOLD

Rotis Semi Sans

Otl Aicher, Agfa Division, Bayer Corp.

Typography

ABCDEFGHIJKLMNOPQRSTUVWXYZ
abcdefghijklmnopqrstuvwxyz&0123
456789$!?.;:,""{½}

*ABCDEFGHIJKLMNOPQRSTUVWXYZ
abcdefghijklmnopqrstuvwxyz&0123
456789$!?.;:,""{½}*

Letterforms have tone, timbre, character, just
as words and sentences do. The moment a
text and typeface are chosen, two streams
45 LIGHT

*Letterforms have tone, timbre, character, just
as words and sentences do. The moment a
text and typeface are chosen, two streams of*
46 LIGHT ITALIC

Letterforms have tone, timbre, character,
just as words and sentences do. The mo
ment a text and typeface are chosen, two
55 REGULAR

*Letterforms have tone, timbre, character,
just as words and sentences do. The mo
ment a text and typeface are chosen, two*
56 ITALIC

Letterforms have tone, timbre, character,
just as words and sentences do. The mo
ment a text and typeface are chosen, two
65 BOLD

**Letterforms have tone, timbre, character,
just as words and sentences do. The mo
ment a text and typeface are chosen,**
75 EXTRA BOLD

Rotis Semi Serif

Otl Aicher, Agfa Division, Bayer Corp.

Typography

ABCDEFGHIJKLMNOPQRSTUVWXY
Zabcdefghijklmnopqrstuvwxyz&012
3456789$!?.;:,""{½}

Letterforms have tone, timbre, character,
just as words and sentences do. The mo
ment a text and typeface are chosen, two
55 REGULAR

**Letterforms have tone, timbre, character,
just as words and sentences do. The mo
ment a text and typeface are chosen,**
65 BOLD

Rotis Serif

Otl Aicher, Agfa Division, Bayer Corp.

Typography

ABCDEFGHIJKLMNOPQRSTUVW
XYZabcdefghijklmnopqrstuvwxyz
&0123456789$!?.;:,""{½}

*ABCDEFGHIJKLMNOPQRSTUVW
XYZabcdefghijklmnopqrstuvwxyz&
0123456789$!?.;:,""{½}*

Letterforms have tone, timbre, character,
just as words and sentences do. The mo
ment a text and typeface are chosen, two
55 REGULAR

Letterforms have tone, timbre, character, just as words and sentences do. The mo ment a text and typeface are chosen, two

56 ITALIC

Letterforms have tone, timbre, charac ter, just as words and sentences do. The moment a text and typeface are chosen

65 BOLD

Ruling Script STD

Gottfried Pott, Linotype Library GmbH

Typography

ABCDEFGHIJKLMNO
PQRSTUVWXYZabcdef
ghijklmnopqrstuvwxyz
&0123456789$€!?.;:,""{½}

Letterforms have tone, timbre, character, just as

2

Unknown, Monotype Corp.

Typography

ABCDEFGHIJKLMNOPQRSTUVWXYZ
abcdefghijklmnopqrstuvwxyz&012
3456789$€!?.;:,""{½}

Letterforms have tone, timbre, charac ter, just as words and sentences do.

CONDENSED

Russell Oblique STD

Karen Ackoff, Karen Ackoff

Typography

ABCDEFGHIJKLMNOPQRSTUV
WXYZabcdefghijklmnopqrstuv
WXYZ&0123456789$€!?.;:,""{½}

Letterforms have tone, timbre, char acter, just as words and sentences

REGULAR

Typography

ABCDEFGHIJKLMNOPQRSTU
WXYZabcdefghijklmnopqrstuv
wxyz&0123456789$€!?.;:,""{½}

Alternates

Letterforms have tone, timbre,
character, just as words and sen
INFORMAL

Russell Square

John Russell, Visual Graphics Corp.

Typography

ABCDEFGHIJKLMNOPQRSTU
VWXYZabcdefghijklmnopqrs
tuvwxyz&0123456789$!?.;:,
""{½}

*ABCDEFGHIJKLMNOPQRSTU
VWXYZabcdefghijklmnopqrs
tuvwxyz&0123456789$!?.;:,
""{½}*

Letterforms have tone, timbre,
character, just as words and
REGULAR

*Letterforms have tone, timbre,
character, just as words and*
OBLIQUE

Rusticana STD

Adrian Frutiger, Linotype Library GmbH

A-Z € 123

TYPOGRAPH

ABCDEFGHIJKLMNO
PQRSTUVWXYZ&01
23456789$€!?.;:,""{½}

LETTERFORMS HAVE
TONE, TIMBRE, CHAR
ROMAN

BORDERS

Ruzicka Freehand STD

Ann Chaisson, Mark Altman, and Rudolph Ruzicka
Linotype Library GmbH

A-Z € BB 619 123

Typography

ABCDEFGHIJKLMNOPQRST
UVWXYZabcdefghijklmnopqrstuv
wxyz&0123456789$€!?.;:,""{½}

ABCDEFGHIJKLMNOPQRSTUVWXYZ&

0123456789

LETTERFORMS HAVE TONE, timbre, char
acter, just as words and 567 sentenc
ROMAN

LETTERFORMS HAVE TONE, timbre,
character, just as words and 567
BOLD

Sabon STD

Jan Tschichold, Linotype Library GmbH

A-Z € BB 619

Typography

ABCDEFGHIJKLMNOPQRSTU
VWXYZabcdefghijklmnopqrstuv
wxyz&0123456789$€!?.;:,""{½}

ABCDEFGHIJKLMNOPQRSTUVWXYZ
&0123456789

ABCDEFGHIJKLMNOPQRSTU
VWXYZabcdefghijklmnopqrstuv
wxyz&0123456789$€!?.;:,""{½}

0123456789

LETTERFORMS HAVE TONE, timbre, char
acter, just as words and 567 sentences
do. The moment a text and typeface are
ROMAN

Letterforms have tone, timbre, character,
just as words and 567 sentences do. The
moment a text and typeface are chosen,
ITALIC

Letterforms have tone, timbre, character,
just as words and 567 sentences do. The
moment a text and typeface are chosen,
BOLD

Letterforms have tone, timbre, character,
just as words and 567 sentences do. The
moment a text and typeface are chosen,
BOLD ITALIC

San Marco STD

Karlgeorg Hoefer, Linotype Library GmbH

A-Z € ffi 123 ʦ

Typography

ABCDEFGHIJKLMNO
PQRSTUVWXYZabcdefg
hijklmnopqrstuvwxyz&012
3456789$€!?.;:,""{½}

ch ck ff ft ll ſ ſi ſſ ß ſt ʦ

Historic Blackletter

Letterforms have tone, timbre,
character, just as words and
ROMAN

Sanvito PRO

Robert Slimbach, Adobe Systems

A-Z € 619 123 ⅞ H₂ 1ˢᵗ

Typography

ABCDEFGHIJKLMNOPQRSTU
VWXYZabcdefghijklmnopqrst
uvwxyz&

0123456789 0123456789
0123456789 0123456789
Proportional and Tabular Figures

Ø$¢£¥ƒ€#¤%‰$¢£¥ƒ€#$¢£¥ƒ
€#%‰0123456789($¢-.,)0123456789
($¢-.,)0123456789($¢-.,)0123456789($¢-
.,)¼½¾⅛⅜⅝⅞⅓⅔^~.+±<=>
−|¦×÷∂μπΔΠΣΩ√∞∫≈≠≤≥◊¬℮
ℓ°ªº_—-–'"“”„'‚«»‹›,.:; … ·!?¡¿
()[]{}/*•§†‡ƍ©®™@
Currency, Punctuation, and Related Forms

ÆŁØŒÞÐÁÂÄÀÅÃÇÉÊËÈÍÎÏÌ
ÑÓÔÖÒÕŠÚÛÜÙÝŸŽĂĀĄĆ
ČĎĐĖÈĘĢĞĪĮĶĹĽĻŃŇŅŎŌŔ
ŘŖŚŞŠŢŤŲŰÛŪŲŮŹŻÆɪłøœßþð
áâäàåãçéêëèíîïìñóôöòõšúûüùý
ÿžăāąćčďđėèęğġīįķĺľļńňņŏōŕř
ŗśşšťțŭűūųůźż
Accented Characters

Letterforms have tone, timbre, char
acter, just as words and sentences do.
LIGHT

Letterforms have tone, timbre, char
acter, just as words and sentences
REGULAR

**Letterforms have tone, timbre,
character, just as words and sen**
SEMIBOLD

**Letterforms have tone, timbre,
character, just as words and sen**
BOLD

*To download a complete glyph complement PDF, please visit
www.adobe.com/type.*

Sanvito PRO Opticals

Robert Slimbach, Adobe Systems

A-Z € 619 123 ⅞ H₂ 1ˢᵗ

Letterforms have tone, timbre, character, just as words and 567 sentences
do. The moment a text and typeface are chosen, two streams of thought,

Letterforms have tone, timbre, character, just as
words and 567 sentences do. The moment a text

Letterforms have tone, timbre, charac
ter, just as words and 567 sentences do

Letterforms have tone, tim
bre character, just as words
LIGHT: CAPTION, REGULAR, SUBHEAD, DISPLAY

Letterforms have tone, timbre, character, just as words and 567 sentenc es do. The moment a text and typeface are chosen, two streams of

Letterforms have tone, timbre, character, just as words and 567 sentences do. The moment a text

Letterforms have tone, timbre, char acter, just as words and 567 sentenc

Letterforms have tone, tim bre character, just as words

CAPTION, REGULAR, SUBHEAD, DISPLAY

Letterforms have tone, timbre, character, just as words and 567 sen tences do. The moment a text and typeface are chosen, two streams of

Letterforms have tone, timbre, character, just as words and 567 sentences do. The moment a text

Letterforms have tone, timbre, character, just as words and 567

Letterforms have tone, timbre character, just as

SEMIBOLD: CAPTION, REGULAR, SUBHEAD, DISPLAY

Letterforms have tone, timbre, character, just as words and 567 sentences do. The moment a text and typeface are chosen, two

Letterforms have tone, timbre, character, just as words and 567 sentences do. The moment a

Letterforms have tone, timbre, character, just as words and 567

Letterforms have tone, timbre character, just as

BOLD: CAPTION, REGULAR, SUBHEAD, DISPLAY

To download a complete glyph complement PDF, please visit www.adobe.com/type.

Arthur Baker, Arthur Baker Design

A-Z € 123 €

Typography

ABCDEFGHIJKLMNOPQRSTU VWXYZabcdefghijklmnopqrstuvwxyz &0123456789$€!?.,;:,""{½}

b d f g h j k l p q y b d f h k l
Alternates

ABCDEFGHIJKLMNOPQRSTU VWXYZabcdefghijklmnopqrstuvwxyz &0123456789$€!?.,;:,""{½}

b d f g h j k l p q y b d f h k l
Alternates

Letterforms have tone, timbre, character, just as words and sentences do. The moment a
ROMAN

Letterforms have tone, timbre, character, just as words and sentences do. The moment a text
ITALIC

Stempel Schneidler STD

F.H. Ernst Schneidler, Bauer Types, S.A.

A-Z €

Typography

ABCDEFGHIJKLMNOPQRSTU
VWXYZabcdefghijklmnopqrstu
vwxyz&0123456789$€!¿.;:,""{½}

*ABCDEFGHIJKLMNOPQRSTU
VWXYZabcdefghijklmnopqrstuvwx
yz&0123456789$€!¿.;:,""{½}*

Letterforms have tone, timbre, character,
just as words and sentences do. The mo
ment a text and typeface are chosen, two
LIGHT

*Letterforms have tone, timbre, character, just
as words and sentences do. The moment a
text and typeface are chosen, two streams of*
LIGHT ITALIC

Letterforms have tone, timbre, charac
ter, just as words and sentences do. The
moment a text and typeface are chosen,
ROMAN

*Letterforms have tone, timbre, character, just
as words and sentences do. The moment a
text and typeface are chosen, two streams of*
ITALIC

Letterforms have tone, timbre, charac
ter, just as words and sentences do.
The moment a text and typeface are
MEDIUM

*Letterforms have tone, timbre, character,
just as words and sentences do. The mo
ment a text and typeface are chosen, two*
MEDIUM ITALIC

**Letterforms have tone, timbre, char
acter, just as words and sentences
do. The moment a text and typeface**
BOLD

***Letterforms have tone, timbre, charac
ter, just as words and sentences do.
The moment a text and typeface are***
BOLD ITALIC

**Letterforms have tone, timbre,
character, just as words and sen
tences do. The moment a text and**
BLACK

***Letterforms have tone, timbre, char
acter, just as words and sentences
do. The moment a text and typeface***
BLACK ITALIC

Monotype Scotch Roman STD

Unknown, Monotype Typography Ltd.

A-Z €

Typography

ABCDEFGHIJKLMNOPQRST
UVWXYZabcdefghijklmnopqrstu
vwxyz&0123456789$€!?.;:,""{½}

*ABCDEFGHIJKLMNOPQRSTU
VWXYZabcdefghijklmnopqrstuvwx
yz&0123456789$€!?.;:,""{½}*

Letterforms have tone, timbre, charac
ter, just as words and sentences do. The
moment a text and typeface are chosen
REGULAR

Letterforms have tone, timbre, character, just as words and sentences do. The mo ment a text and typeface are chosen, two
ITALIC

Monotype Script STD

Unknown, Monotype Typography Ltd.

Typography

ABCDEFGHIJKLMNO PQRSTUVWXYZabcdef ghijklmnopqrstuvwxyz& 0123456789$€!?.;:,""{½}

Letterforms have tone, timbre, character, just as words and
BOLD

ITC Serif Gothic STD

Herb Lubalin and Tony DeSpigna, ITC

Typography

ABCDEFGHIJKLMNOPQ RSTUVWXYZabcdefghijk lmnopqrstuvwxyz&012 3456789$€!?.;:,""{½}

Letterforms have tone, tim bre, character, just as words
LIGHT

Letterforms have tone, tim bre, character, just as words
REGULAR

Letterforms have tone, tim bre, character, just as word
BOLD

Letterforms have tone, tim bre, character, just as word
EXTRA BOLD

Letterforms have tone, timbre, character, just as
HEAVY

Letterforms have tone, tim bre, character, just as word
BLACK

Serifa STD

Adrian Frutiger, Bauer Types, S.A.

Typography

ABCDEFGHIJKLMNOPQRSTUV WXYZabcdefghijklmnopqrstuv wxyz&0123456789$€!?.;:," "{½}

ABCDEFGHIJKLMNOPQRSTUV WXYZabcdefghijklmnopqrstuv wxyz&0123456789$€!?.;:," "{½}

Letterforms have tone, timbre, charac ter, just as words and sentences do. The moment a text and typeface are chosen

45 LIGHT

Letterforms have tone, timbre, character, just as words and sentences do. The mo ment a text and typeface are chosen,

46 LIGHT ITALIC

Letterforms have tone, timbre, char acter, just as words and sentences do. The moment a text and typeface

55 ROMAN

Letterforms have tone, timbre, char acter, just as words and sentences do. The moment a text and typeface are

56 ITALIC

Letterforms have tone, timbre, char acter, just as words and sentences do. The moment a text and typeface

65 BOLD

Letterforms have tone, timbre, character, just as words and sen tences do. The moment a text

75 BLACK

Serlio STD

Unknown

TYPOGRAPHY

ABCDEFGHIJKLMNOPQRS TUVWXYZABCDEFGHIJKLM NOPQRSTUVWXYZ&O123456 789$€!?.:;,""{½}

LETTERFORMS HAVE TONE, TIMBRE, CHARACTER, JUST AS WORDS AND

REGULAR

Serpentine

Dick Jensen, Visual Graphics Corp.

ABCDEFGHIJKLMNOPQR STUVWXYZabcdefghijklm nopqrstuvwxyz&012345 6789$!?.:;,""{½}

ABCDEFGHIJKLMNOPQR STUVWXYZabcdefghijklm nopqrstuvwxyz&012345 6789$!?.:;,""{½}

Letterforms have tone, tim bre, character, just as words

LIGHT

Letterforms have tone, tim bre, character, just as words

LIGHT OBLIQUE

Letterforms have tone, timbre, character, just

MEDIUM

Letterforms have tone, timbre, character, just

MEDIUM OBLIQUE

Letterforms have tone, timbre, character, just

BOLD

Letterforms have tone, timbre, character, just

BOLD OBLIQUE

Shannon

Kris Holmes and Janice Prescott, Agfa Division, Bayer Corp.

Typography

ABCDEFGHIJKLMNOPQRSTUVWX
YZabcdefghijklmnopqrstuvwxyz&
0123456789$!?.;:,""{ ½ }

*ABCDEFGHIJKLMNOPQRSTUVWXYZ
abcdefghijklmnopqrstuvwxyz&01234
56789$!?.;:,""{ ½ }*

Letterforms have tone, timbre, charac
ter, just as words and sentences do. The
moment a text and typeface are chosen

BOOK

*Letterforms have tone, timbre, character,
just as words and sentences do. The mo
ment a text and typeface are chosen, two*

OBLIQUE

**Letterforms have tone, timbre, char
acter, just as words and sentences
do. The moment a text and typeface**

BOLD

**Letterforms have tone, timbre, char
acter, just as words and sentences
do. The moment a text and type**

EXTRA BOLD

Matthew Carter, Linotype Library GmbH

A-z € A

Typography

*abcdefghijklmnopqrstuvwxyz
0123456789$€!?.;:,""{½}*

*A B C D E F G H I J K
L M N O P Q R S T U V
W X Y Z*

Andante

*A B C D E F G H I
J K L M N O P Q R
S T U V W X Y Z*

Allegro

*A B C D E F G H I
J K L M N O P Q R
S T U V W X Y Z bhklz*

Volante

*Letterforms have tone, timbre, charac
ter, just as words and sentences do. The*

REGULAR

Sho STD

Karlgeorg Hoefer, Linotype Library GmbH

A-z €

Typography

ABCDEFGHIJKLMNOPQR
STUVWXYZabcdefghijklm
nopqrstuvwxyz&012345678
9$€!?.;:,""{½}

Letterforms have tone,
timbre, character, just as

ROMAN

Shuriken Boy STD

Joachim Müller-Lancé, Adobe Systems

A-z €

Typography

ABCDEFGHIJKLMN
OPQRSTUVWXYZ
abcdefghijklmnop
qrstuvwxyz&0123
456789$€!?.;:,""{½}

Letterforms have tone,
timbre, character, just

REGULAR

Silentium PRO

Jovica Veljović, Adobe Systems

A-z € ffi 619 123 e A aA

Typography

ABCDEFGHIJKLMNOPQR
STUVWXYZabcdefghijklmn
opqrstuvwxyz&0123456789
$€!?.;:,""{½}
Roman I

ABCDEFGHIJKLMNOPQR
STUVWXYZ0123456789
Roman I Titling

ABCDEFGHIJKLMNOPQR
STUVWXYZabcdefghijklmn
opqrstuvwxyz&0123456789
$€!?.;:,""{½}
Roman II

0123456789 0123456789
0123456789 0123456789
Roman I Proportional and Tabular Figures

0123456789 0123456789
0123456789 0123456789
Roman II Proportional and Tabular Figures

ABCDEFGGHIJKLM
MNOPQRRSTTUVW
XYZ ÆEGMMPQRTaaegiior
ftvwx ert
Roman I Alternates

A̋ Ⓐ Ⓒ Ⓒ Ⓒ Ⓒ Ⓐ Ⓓ Ⓔ Ⓗ Ⓡ Ⓛ
M̋ NK Ⓐ Ⓔ Ⓘ Ⓞ Te Ti To TT VE
Ct ex fa fb ff ffi ffi ffl fh fi fj fk
fl fr ft ft fð gg æ ra rt sh sp st
ta tt ty tz zz
Roman I Ligatures

CNRaaegiiorftvwx ert Th
Tl AV CT ME NE NN ST TT TV
TW TY VR WR ct ex fa fb ff
ffi ffi ffl fh fi fj fk fl fr ft ft fð
gg ra rt sh sp st ta tt ty tz zz
Roman II Alternates and Ligatures

0$¢£¥ƒ€#¤$¢£¥€¤%‰$¢£¥ƒ
€#0$¢£¥€%‰^+±<=>−×÷≈≠≤≥¬
₀1234₁₂₃₄¼½¾ / ^~.+±<=>−|¦×
÷∂µπΔΠΣΩ√∞∫≈≠≤≥◊¬⊖ℓ°
ao __ –--- —'"“”„‚,‹›«»‹›⟨⟩,.:;
… ··!?¡¿¡¿()()[][]{}{}/ \★•§†‡¶
©®™@@
Roman I Currency, Punctuation, and Related Forms

ÆLØŒÞÐÁÂÄÀÅÃÇÉÊËÈÍ
ÎÏÌÑÓÔÖÒÕŠÚÛÜÙÝŸŽ
ĂĀĄĆČĎĐĚÈĒĘĞĢĪĮĶĹĽĻ
ŃŇŅŐŌŔŘŖŚŞŠŢŤŰŪŲŮ
ŹŻæıłøœßþðáâäàåãçéêëèíîïìñ
óôöòõšúûüùýÿžăāąćčďđěèēę
ğġīįķĺľļńňņőōŕřŗśşşťţűūuůźż
Roman I Accented Characters

0$¢£¥ƒ€#¤$¢£¥€¤%‰$¢£¥ƒ
€#0$¢£¥€%‰^+±<=>−×÷≈≠≤≥¬
₀1234₁₂₃₄¼½¾ / ^~.+±<=>−|¦×
÷∂µπΔΠΣΩ√∞∫≈≠≤≥◊¬⊖ℓ°
ao __ –--- —'"“”„‚,‹›«»‹›⟨⟩,.:;
… ··!?¡¿¡¿()()[][]{}{}/ \★•§†‡¶
©®™@@
Roman II Currency, Punctuation, and Related Forms

ÆLØŒÞÐÁÂÄÀÅÃÇÉÊËÈÍ
ÎÏÌÑÓÔÖÒÕŠÚÛÜÙÝŸŽ
ĂĀĄĆČĎĐĚÈĒĘĞĢĪĮĶĹĽĻ
ŃŇŅŐŌŔŘŖŚŞŠŢŤŰŪŲŮ
ŹŻæıłøœßþðáâäàåãçéêëèíîïìñ
óôöòõšúûüùýÿžăāąćčďđěèēęğ
ġīįķĺľļńňņőōŕřŗśşşťţűūuůźż
Roman II Accented Characters

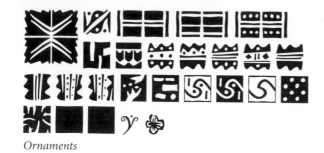

Ornaments

Letterforms have tone, timbre,
character, just as words and 567

LETTERFORMS HAVE TONE,
TIMBRE, CHARACTER, JUST AS

LETTERFORMS HAVE TONE
TIMBRE, CHARACTER, JUST AS

LETTERFORMS HAVE
ROMAN I

Letterforms have tone, timbre,
character, just as words and sen
ROMAN II

*To download a complete glyph complement PDF, please visit
www.adobe.com/type.*

ITC Slimbach STD

Robert Slimbach, ITC

A-z €

Typography

ABCDEFGHIJKLMNOPQRSTUV
WXYZabcdefghijklmnopqrstuvw
xyz&0123456789$€!?.;:, ""{ ½ }

ABCDEFGHIJKLMNOPQRSTUVW
XYZabcdefghijklmnopqrstuvwxyz
&0123456789$€!?.;:, ""{ ½ }

Letterforms have tone, timbre, charac
ter, just as words and sentences do. The
moment a text and typeface are chosen,
BOOK

*Letterforms have tone, timbre, character,
just as words and sentences do. The
moment a text and typeface are chosen,*
BOOK ITALIC

Letterforms have tone, timbre, charac
ter, just as words and sentences do.
The moment a text and typeface are
MEDIUM

*Letterforms have tone, timbre, charac
ter, just as words and sentences do. The
moment a text and typeface are chosen,*
MEDIUM ITALIC

**Letterforms have tone, timbre, charac
ter, just as words and sentences do.
The moment a text and typeface are**
BOLD

***Letterforms have tone, timbre, charac
ter, just as words and sentences do.
The moment a text and typeface are***
BOLD ITALIC

**Letterforms have tone, timbre, char
acter, just as words and sentences
do. The moment a text and typeface**
BLACK

***Letterforms have tone, timbre, char
acter, just as words and sentences
do. The moment a text and typeface***
BLACK ITALIC

Smaragd STD

Gudrun Zapf von Hesse, Linotype Library GmbH

A-z €

TYPOGRAPH

ABCDEFGHIJKLMN
OPQRSTUVWXYZ&O
123456789$€!?.;:,""[½]

LETTERFORMS HAVE
TONE, TIMBRE, CHAR

REGULAR

Snell Roundhand STD

Matthew Carter, Linotype Library GmbH

A-z €

Typography

Aa Bb Cc Dd Ee Ff Gg
Hh Ii Jj Kk Ll Mm Nn
Oo Pp Qq Rr Ss Tt Uu
Vv Ww Xx Yy Zz &
0123456789$€!?..;, ""{ ½}

*Letterforms have tone, timbre, char
acter, just as words and sentences*

SCRIPT

*Letterforms have tone, timbre,
character, just as words and*

BOLD SCRIPT

*Letterforms have tone, tim
bre, character, just as word*

BLACK SCRIPT

♫ Sonata STD

Cleo Huggins, Adobe Systems

f ff fff fz m mf mp mf mp p pp

ppp r s sf tr tr z

7890123456789**——**

MEDIUM

S

ITC Souvenir STD

Ed Benguiat, ITC

A-z €

Typography

ABCDEFGHIJKLMNOPQRSTU
VWXYZabcdefghijklmnopqrstuvw
xyz&0123456789$€!?.;:,""{½}

*ABCDEFGHIJKLMNOPQRSTU
VWXYZabcdefghijklmnopqrstuv
wxyz&0123456789$€!?.;:,""{½}*

Letterforms have tone, timbre, charac
ter, just as words and sentences do. The
moment a text and typeface are chosen
LIGHT

*Letterforms have tone, timbre, charac
ter, just as words and sentences do.
The moment a text and typeface are*
LIGHT ITALIC

**Letterforms have tone, timbre, char
acter, just as words and sentences
do. The moment a text and typeface**
MEDIUM

***Letterforms have tone, timbre, char
acter, just as words and sentences
do. The moment a text and type***
MEDIUM ITALIC

**Letterforms have tone, timbre,
character, just as words and sen
tences do. The moment a text and**
DEMI

***Letterforms have tone, timbre,
character, just as words and sen
tences do. The moment a text***
DEMI ITALIC

**Letterforms have tone, timbre,
character, just as words and sen
tences do. The moment a text**
BOLD

***Letterforms have tone, timbre,
character, just as words and
sentences do. The moment a***
BOLD ITALIC

Spartan STD

Unknown, Linotype Library GmbH

A-z €

Typography

ABCDEFGHIJKLMNOPQ
RSTUVWXYZabcdefghijk
lmnopqrstuvwxyz&01234567
89$€!?.;:,""''{½}

Letterforms have tone, timbre,
character, just as words and sen
tences do. The moment a text and
CLASSIFIED

**Letterforms have tone, timbre,
character, just as words and sen
tences do. The moment a text and**
HEAVY CLASSIFIED

Spectrum STD

Jan van Krimpen, Monotype Corp.

A-Z € ffi BB 619 123 ⅞ H₂ 1st

Typography

ABCDEFGHIJKLMNOPQRSTUVWX
YZabcdefghijklmnopqrstuvwxyz&01
23456789$€!?.,:,"" {½}

ABCDEFGHIJKLMNOPQRSTUVWXYZ&
0123456789$¢ ffi ⅛

*ABCDEFGHIJKLMNOPQRSTUVWXY
Zabcdefghijklmnopqrstuvwxyz&0123456789
$€!?"" {½}*

0123456789$¢ ffi ⅛

LETTERFORMS HAVE TONE, timbre, character, just
as words and 567 sentences do. The moment a
text and typeface are chosen, two streams of
REGULAR

*Letterforms have tone, timbre, character, just as words and
567 sentences do. The moment a text and typeface are cho
sen, two streams of thought, two rhythmical systems, two
ITALIC*

**Letterforms have tone, timbre, character,
just as words and sentences do. The mo
ment a text and typeface are chosen, two**
SEMIBOLD

Spring STD

Garrett Boge, LetterPerfect

A-Z € 123

Typography

ABCDEFGHIJKLM
NOPQRSTUVWXYZ
abcdefghijklmnopqrstuvwxyz
&0123456789$€!?.,:, ""{½}

*Letterforms have tone, timbre, charac
ter, just as words and sentences do. The*
LIGHT

*Letterforms have tone, timbre, char
acter, just as words and sentences do.*
REGULAR

Spumoni STD

Garrett Boge, LetterPerfect

A-Z € 123

Typography

ABCDEFGHIJKLMNOPQRST
UVWXYZabcdefghijklmnopqr
stuvwxyz&0123456789$€!?.,:,
""{½}

**Letterforms have tone, timbre,
character, just as words and sen**
REGULAR

Stencil STD

Gerry Powell

A-z €

TYPOGRAPHY

ABCDEFGHIJKLMNO PQRSTUVWXYZ&012 3456789$€!?.;:,""{½}

LETTERFORMS HAVE TONE, TIMBRE, CHAR

BOLD

ITC Stone Sans STD

Sumner Stone, ITC

A-z €

Typography

ABCDEFGHIJKLMNOPQRSTUVW XYZabcdefghijklmnopqrstuvwxy z&0123456789$€!?.;:,""{½}

ABCDEFGHIJKLMNOPQRSTUVWX YZabcdefghijklmnopqrstuvwxyz& 0123456789$€!?.;:,""{½}

Letterforms have tone, timbre, charac ter, just as words and sentences do. The moment a text and typeface are

MEDIUM

Letterforms have tone, timbre, character, just as words and sentences do. The mo ment a text and typeface are chosen, two

MEDIUM ITALIC

Letterforms have tone, timbre, char acter, just as words and sentences do. The moment a text and typeface

SEMIBOLD

Letterforms have tone, timbre, charac ter, just as words and sentences do. The moment a text and typeface are chosen

SEMIBOLD ITALIC

Letterforms have tone, timbre, character, just as words and sen tences do. The moment a text

BOLD

Letterforms have tone, timbre, char acter, just as words and sentences do. The moment a text and typeface

BOLD ITALIC

ITC Stone Serif STD

Sumner Stone, ITC

A-z €

Typography

ABCDEFGHIJKLMNOPQRSTUV WXYZabcdefghijklmnopqrstuv wxyz&0123456789$€!?.;:,""{½}

ABCDEFGHIJKLMNOPQRSTUV WXYZabcdefghijklmnopqrstuvwx yz&0123456789$€!?.;:,""{½}

Letterforms have tone, timbre, charac
ter, just as words and sentences do.
The moment a text and typeface are
MEDIUM

*Letterforms have tone, timbre, character,
just as words and sentences do. The mo
ment a text and typeface are chosen, two*
MEDIUM ITALIC

Letterforms have tone, timbre, char
acter, just as words and sentences
do. The moment a text and type
SEMIBOLD

*Letterforms have tone, timbre, char
acter, just as words and sentences
do. The moment a text and typeface*
SEMIBOLD ITALIC

**Letterforms have tone, timbre,
character, just as words and sen
tences do. The moment a text**
BOLD

***Letterforms have tone, timbre,
character, just as words and sen
tences do. The moment a text***
BOLD ITALIC

ITC Stone Informal STD

Sumner Stone, ITC

A-z €

Typography

ABCDEFGHIJKLMNOPQRSTUV
WXYZabcdefghijklmnopqrstuv
wxyz&0123456789$€!?.;:,""{½}

*ABCDEFGHIJKLMNOPQRSTUVW
XYZabcdefghijklmnopqrstuvwxyz
&0123456789$€!?.;:,""{½}*

Letterforms have tone, timbre, char
acter, just as words and sentences do.
The moment a text and typeface are
MEDIUM

*Letterforms have tone, timbre, character,
just as words and sentences do. The mo
ment a text and typeface are chosen,*
MEDIUM ITALIC

Letterforms have tone, timbre,
character, just as words and senten
ces do. The moment a text and
SEMIBOLD

*Letterforms have tone, timbre, char
acter, just as words and sentences
do. The moment a text and typeface*
SEMIBOLD ITALIC

**Letterforms have tone, timbre,
character, just as words and sen
tences do. The moment a text**
BOLD

***Letterforms have tone, timbre,
character, just as words and sen
tences do. The moment a text and***
BOLD ITALIC

ITC Stone STD Phonetic

Sumner Stone and John Renner, ITC

aɐɒbʙβccɕdðдɖdeɛʒfɸʏɣgɢ
ɡʰhɦħiɨɪjjɟʄkɪkjlʟɫlmɱɯɰmnɳɲ
oɔəɵøppɸqɟɖɽrɾʀʁsʃşĥtθtʈuʊʉʋʊʌʋw
ɥxx̆yɣʎyzžƶ!oʟ‖ǂ⁝‖ǃ|əɡ̊ǀʔɴ?ʕ?ʃↃ↑
↓ʌ˥˦˧˨˩ʃʃ[]/,,ʰⁿʷˡʰjˠˠ˞

Sans IPA

Sans Alternate

Serif IPA

Serif Alternate

Strayhorn STD

Michael Harvey, Monotype Corp.

A-Z € BB 619

Typography

ABCDEFGHIJKLMNOPQRSTUVW
XYZabcdefghijklmnopqrstuvwxyz&
0123456789$€!?.;:,""{½}

ABCDEFGHIJKLMNOPQRSTUVWXYZ&
0123456789

ABCDEFGHIJKLMNOPQRSTUVW
XYZabcdefghijklmnopqrstuvwxyz&
0123456789$€!?.;:,""{½}

0123456789

LETTERFORMS HAVE TONE, timbre, character, just
as words and 567 sentences do. The moment
a text and typeface are chosen, two streams of
LIGHT

Letterforms have tone, timbre, character, just
as words and 567 sentences do. The moment a
text and typeface are chosen, two streams of
LIGHT ITALIC

LETTERFORMS HAVE TONE, timbre, character,
just as words and 567 sentences do. The mo
ment a text and typeface are chosen, two
REGULAR

Letterforms have tone, timbre, character, just
as words and 567 sentences do. The moment
a text and typeface are chosen, two streams
ITALIC

Letterforms have tone, timbre, character,
just as words and 567 sentences do. The
mo ment a text and typeface are chosen,
BOLD

Letterforms have tone, timbre, character,
just as words and 567 sentences do. The
moment a text and typeface are chosen,
BOLD ITALIC

Letterforms have tone, tim
bre, character, just as words
EXTRA BOLD

Letterforms have tone, tim
bre, character, just as words
EXTRA BOLD ITALIC

Strumpf STD

Mário Feliciano, Adobe Systems

A-z €

Typography

ABCDEFGHIJKLMNOPQR
STUVWXYZabcdefghijkl
mnopqrstuvwxyz&0123
456789$€!?.;:,""{½}

Letterforms have tone,
timbre, character, just as
OPEN

Letterforms have tone,
timbre, character, just as
CONTOUR

Studz STD

Michael Harvey, Adobe Systems

A-z €

TYPOGRAPHY

ABCDEFGHIJKLMNO
PQRSTUVWXYZ&01
23456789$€!?.;:,""{½}

LETTERFORMS HAVE
TONE, TIMBRE, CHAR
REGULAR

Symbol STD

€

ΑΒΧΔΕΓΗΙϑΚΛΜΝΟΠΘΡΣΤΥςΩ
ΞΨΖαβχδεφγηιφκλμνοπθρστυϖω
ξψζ&0123456789€#%!?.;:, … ()[]
{}//*°•_ ¯′″.+±<=>−|×÷√∠¬∧∨
◊~≈≡≅≠≤≥⊗⊕∅ϒ∂϶Σ∇∏ℵℑℜ
℘∃∀∝∞∈∉∴∩∪⊃⊇⊄⊂⊆↔←↑
→↓↵⇔⇐⇑⇒⇓‖—⊥⟨⏐⟩⌈⌉⌊⌋
⏐⌈⌉⌊⌋⎧⎩⎨⎬©®™©®™♣◆♥♠
MEDIUM

ITC Symbol STD

Aldo Novarese, ITC

A-z €

Typography

ABCDEFGHIJKLMNOPQRSTUVW
XYZabcdefghijklmnopqrstuvwxyz
&0123456789$€!?.;:,""{ ½ }

ABCDEFGHIJKLMNOPQRSTUVW
XYZabcdefghijklmnopqrstuvwxyz
&0123456789$€!?.;:,""{ ½ }

Letterforms have tone, timbre, charac
ter, just as words and sentences do.
The moment a text and typeface are
BOOK

Letterforms have tone, timbre, charac
ter, just as words and sentences do.
The moment a text and typeface are
BOOK ITALIC

Letterforms have tone, timbre, charac ter, just as words and sentences do. The moment a text and typeface are
MEDIUM

Letterforms have tone, timbre, charac ter, just as words and sentences do. The moment a text and typeface are
MEDIUM ITALIC

Letterforms have tone, timbre, char acter, just as words and sentences do. The moment a text and type
BOLD

Letterforms have tone, timbre, char acter, just as words and sentences do. The moment a text and typeface
BOLD ITALIC

Letterforms have tone, timbre, character, just as words and sen tences do. The moment a text
BLACK

Letterforms have tone, timbre, character, just as words and sen tences do. The moment a text
BLACK ITALIC

Syntax STD

Hans Eduard Meyer, Linotype Library GmbH

A-z €

Typography

ABCDEFGHIJKLMNOPQRSTUV WXYZabcdefghijklmnopqrstuvw xyz&0123456789$€!?.;:,""{½}

ABCDEFGHIJKLMNOPQRSTUV WXYZabcdefghijklmnopqrstuvw xyz&0123456789$€!?.;:,""{½}

Letterforms have tone, timbre, character, just as words and sentences do. The mo ment a text and typeface are chosen,
ROMAN

Letterforms have tone, timbre, character, just as words and sentences do. The mo ment a text and typeface are chosen,
ITALIC

Letterforms have tone, timbre, charac ter, just as words and sentences do. The moment a text and typeface are chosen,
BOLD

Letterforms have tone, timbre, character, just as words and sen tences do. The moment a text and
BLACK

Letterforms have tone, timbre, character, just as words and sen tences do. The moment a text
ULTRA BLACK

Tekton PRO

David Siegel, Jim Wasco, and Francis Ching,
Adobe Systems

`A-z` `€` `ffi` `BB` `619` `123` `⅞` `H₂` `1ˢᵗ` `aA`

Typography

ABCDEFGHIJKLMNOPQRSTU
VWXYZabcdefghijklmnopqrst
uvwxyz&ABCDEFGHIJKLMNOPQ
RSTUVWXYZ&

ABCDEFGHIJKLMNOPQRSTUV
WXYZabcdefghijklmnopqrstuvw
xyz&ABCDEFGHIJKLMNOPQRSTUV
WXYZ&

0123456789 0123456789
0123456789 0123456789
0123456789 0123456789
0123456789 0123456789
Proportional and Tabular Figures

ff ffi ffj ffl fi fj fl tt ff ffi ffj ffl fi fj fl tt
Ligatures

Ø$ ¢ £¥ƒ €¤#%‰$¢£¥ƒ€#⁰¹²
3456789($¢-.,)0123456789($¢-.,)/01234
56789($¢-.,)0123456789($¢-.,)¼½¾
^~·+±<=>−|¦×÷∂μπΔ∏∑Ω
√∞∫≈≠≤≥◊¬℮ℓ°ᵃᵒ_ —————–-–

I II "" ',,'' «»«»‹›‹›,.:; . . . ··!?¡¿!¿!?¡¿()()
[][]{}{}/*•§†‡¶©®™@@
Figures, Punctuation, and Related Forms

Ø$¢£¥ƒ€¤#%‰$¢£¥ƒ€#⁰¹²³
456789($¢-.,)0123456789($¢-.,)/01234567
89($¢-.,)0123456789($¢-.,)¼½¾ ^~·+
±<=>−|¦×÷∂μπΔ∏∑Ω√∞∫≈≠≤≥
◊¬℮ℓ°ᵃᵒ_ —————–-– I II "" ',,'' «»«›
‹›‹›,.:; . . . ··!?¡¿!¿!?¡¿()()[][]{}{}/\
*•§†‡¶©®™@@
Italic Figures, Punctuation, and Related Forms

ÆŁØŒÞÐÁÂÄÀÅÃÇÈÉÍÎÏÌÑÓ
ÔÖÒÕŠÚÛÜÙÝŸŽĂĀĄĆČĎÐĚ
ÉĒĘĞĢĪĮĶĹĽĻŃŇŅŐŌŔŘŖŚŞ
ŞŤŢŰŪŲŮŹŽÆæıłøœßþðáâäàå
çèéíîïìñóôöòõšúûüùýÿžăāąćčďð
ěéēę ğ ģ ī į ķ ĺ ľ ļ ń ň ņ ő ō ŕ ř ŗ ś ş ş ť ţ ű ū ų ů
ŹŽÆŁØŒÞÐÁÂÄÀÅÃÇÈÉÍÎÏÌÑÓÔÖ
ÒÕŠÚÛÜÙÝŸŽĂĀĄĆČĎÐĚÉĒĘĞĢĪ
ĮĶĹĽĻŃŇŅŐŌŔŘŖŚŞŞŤŢŰŪŲŮŹŽĶ
Accented Characters

ÆŁØŒÞÐÁÂÄÄÀÅÃÇÈÉÍÎÏÌÑÓÔÖ
ÒÕŠÚÛÜÙÝŸŽĂĀĄĆČĎÐĚÉĒĘ
ĞĢĪĮĶĹĽĻŃŇŅŐŌŔŘŖŚŞŞŤŢŰŪ
ŲŮŽŹÆæıłøœßþðâäàåãçèéíîïìñóô
öòõšúûüùýÿžăāąćčďðěéēęğ ğ ĵ ĩ ĵ ĵ ĺ ľ ĺ

ńňņŏōŕřŗśşŝşťţŭūůýÿžŽ ÆŁØŒÞÐÁ ÂÄÀÅÃÇÈÍÎÏÌÍÑÓÔÖÒÕŠÚÛÜÙÝŸŽ ĀĄĆČĎĐĖĖĒĘĞĢĪĮĶĹĽĻŃŇŅŐŌŔŘŖŚ ŞŚŤŢŰŪŮŹŻ
Italic Accented Characters

LETTERFORMS HAVE TONE, timbre, character, just as words and 567
LIGHT

LETTERFORMS HAVE TONE, timbre, character, just as words and 567
LIGHT OBLIQUE

LETTERFORMS HAVE TONE, tim bre, character, just as words
REGULAR

LETTERFORMS HAVE TONE, timbre, character, just as words and 567
OBLIQUE

LETTERFORMS HAVE TONE, tim bre, character, just as words
BOLD

LETTERFORMS HAVE TONE, timbre, character, just as words and 567
BOLD OBLIQUE

To download a complete glyph complement PDF, please visit www.adobe.com/type.

Tekton PRO Condensed and Extended

David Siegel, Jim Wasco, and Francis Ching, Adobe Systems

A-z € ffi BB 619 123 ⅞ H₂ 1st aA

Typography

ABCDEFGHIJKLMNOPQRSTUVWXYZ
abcdefghijklmnopqrstuvwxyz&ABCDEFGHI
JKLMNOPQRSTUVWXYZ&

ABCDEFGHIJKLMNOPQRSTUVWXYZ
abcdefghijklmnopqrstuvw xyz&ABCDEFGHIJK
LMNOPQRSTUVWXYZ&

LETTERFORMS HAVE TONE, timbre, character, just as words and 567 sentences do. The mo
LIGHT CONDENSED

LETTERFORMS HAVE TONE, timbre, character, just as words and 567 sentences do. The moment a
LIGHT CONDENSED OBLIQUE

LETTERFORMS HAVE TONE, timbre, charac ter, just as words and 567 sentences do.
CONDENSED

LETTERFORMS HAVE TONE, timbre, character, just as words and 567 sentences do. The mo
CONDENSED OBLIQUE

LETTERFORMS HAVE TONE, timbre, char acter, just as words and 567 sentenc
BOLD CONDENSED

LETTERFORMS HAVE TONE, timbre, character, just as words and 567
BOLD CONDENSED OBLIQUE

Typograph

LETTERFORMS HAVE TONE,
timbre, character, just as
LIGHT EXTENDED

LETTERFORMS HAVE TONE, tim
bre, character, just as words
LIGHT EXTENDED OBLIQUE

LETTERFORMS HAVE TONE,
timbre, character, just as
EXTENDED

LETTERFORMS HAVE TONE,
timbre, character, just as
EXTENDED OBLIQUE

LETTERFORMS HAVE
TONE, timbre, character
BOLD EXTENDED

LETTERFORMS HAVE TONE,
timbre, character, just as
BOLD EXTENDED OBLIQUE

To download a complete glyph complement PDF, please visit www.adobe.com/type.

Tempo STD

R. Hunter Middleton, Ludlow Type Foundry

A-z €

Typography

ABCDEFGHIJKLMNOPQRSTUVW
XYZabcdefghijklmnopqrstuvwxyz&
0123456789$€!?.;:,'"'{½}

ABCDEFGHIJKLMNOPQRSTUVW
XYZabcdefghijklmnopqrstuvwxyz
&0123456789$€!?.;:,'"'{½}

Letterforms have tone, timbre, char
acter, just as words and sentences
HEAVY CONDENSED

Letterforms have tone, timbre,
character, just as words and senten
HEAVY CONDENSED ITALIC

ITC Tiepolo STD

AlphaOmega Typography, ITC

A-z €

Typography

ABCDEFGHIJKLMNOPQRSTUV
WXYZabcdefghijklmnopqrstuvw
xyz&0123456789$€!?.;:,""{ ½ }

ABCDEFGHIJKLMNOPQRSTUVW XYZabcdefghijklmnopqrstuvwxyz& 0123456789$€!?.;:,"" { ½ }

Letterforms have tone, timbre, character, just as words and sentences do. The mo ment a text and typeface are chosen,
BOOK

Letterforms have tone, timbre, character, just as words and sentences do. The moment a text and typeface are chosen, two streams of
BOOK ITALIC

Letterforms have tone, timbre, charac ter, just as words and sentences do. The moment a text and typeface are
BOLD

Letterforms have tone, timbre, character, just as words and sentences do. The mo ment a text and typeface are chosen, two
BOLD ITALIC

Letterforms have tone, timbre, charac ter, just as words and sentences do. The moment a text and typeface are
BLACK

Letterforms have tone, timbre, charac ter, just as words and sentences do. The moment a text and typeface are chosen
BLACK ITALIC

ITC Tiffany STD

Ed Benguiat, ITC

A-Z €

Typography

ABCDEFGHIJKLMNOPQRS TUVWXYZabcdefghijklmnop qrstuvwxyz&0123456789$€! ?.;:,""{½}

ABCDEFGHIJKLMNOPQR STUVWXYZabcdefghijklmno pqrstuvwxyz&0123456789$€ !?.;:,""{½}

Letterforms have tone, timbre, char acter, just as words and sentences do. The moment a text and typeface
MEDIUM

Letterforms have tone, timbre, char acter, just as words and sentences do. The moment a text and typeface
ITALIC

Letterforms have tone, timbre, char acter, just as words and sentences do. The moment a text and typeface
DEMI

Letterforms have tone, timbre, char acter, just as words and sentences do. The moment a text and typeface
DEMI ITALIC

Letterforms have to ne, timbre, character,
HEAVY

Letterforms have to ne, timbre, characte
HEAVY ITALIC

Times STD

Linotype Staff, Linotype Library GmbH

A-Z € BB 619

Typography

ABCDEFGHIJKLMNOPQRSTU
VWXYZabcdefghijklmnopqrstuv
wxyz&0123456789$€!?.;:,""{½}

ABCDEFGHIJKLMNOPQRSTUVWXYZ
&0123456789

*ABCDEFGHIJKLMNOPQRSTUV
WXYZabcdefghijklmnopqrstuvwxyz
&0123456789$€!?.;:,""{½}*

0123456789

LETTERFORMS HAVE TONE, timbre, charac
ter, just as words and 567 sentences do. The
moment a text and typeface are chosen,
ROMAN

*Letterforms have tone, timbre, character,
just as words and 567 sentences do. The mo
ment a text and typeface are chosen, two*
ITALIC

**Letterforms have tone, timbre, character,
just as words and sentences do. The mo
ment a text and typeface are chosen, two**
SEMIBOLD

*Letterforms have tone, timbre, character,
just as words and sentences do. The mo
ment a text and typeface are chosen, two*
SEMIBOLD ITALIC

**LETTERFORMS HAVE TONE, timbre, char
acter, just as words and 567 sentences do.
The moment a text and typeface are cho**
BOLD

***Letterforms have tone, timbre, character,
just as words and 567 sentences do. The
moment a text and typeface are chosen,***
BOLD ITALIC

**Letterforms have tone, timbre, charac
ter, just as words and sentences do.
The moment a text and typeface are**
EXTRA BOLD

Times STD Phonetic

Linotype Staff, Linotype Library GmbH

aɑɐbʙɓßccɕdðɖʤɛɜʒfɸɣɤgɠ
ɡ́hɦʜɧḥiɨɪɟɟ̑ʄkɪkʲlʟʎ↕mɱɯmɲŋ
oɔɵøɶpɓqɾrʀʁʁʂʃʂɧtΘʈuɥʊʉʌʋʌ
wɪxχ̑yɣʎɥʒʒ̆ʑ!ʘ‖‖/,'nwlhjʏ',

IPA

aɑbʔčçɕɔdʤ̑ɗ̑ɸðɖəɜʒfɣʏhḥiɪɟkɪkʲkʲʎ
ʌ̑ɲŋɔlʂpɾ̑rɾ̑ɿ̑šʂʃʧʦtʊωɷ̆ω̆ω̆*žʒʒ

ɔɔɒɓfiɟmʀʁʁ̑ɿsyɥə0123456789

Alternate

Times Europa STD

Walter Tracy, Linotype Library GmbH

A-z €

Typography

ABCDEFGHIJKLMNOPQRSTUVW
XYZabcdefghijklmnopqrstuvwxyz&
0123456789$€!?.;:,""{½}

ABCDEFGHIJKLMNOPQRSTUVWXY
Zabcdefghijklmnopqrstuvwxyz&01234
56789$€!?.;:,""{½}

Letterforms have tone, timbre, char
acter, just as words and sentences
do. The moment a text and typeface
ROMAN

Letterforms have tone, timbre, charac
ter, just as words and sentences do. The
moment a text and typeface are chose
ITALIC

Letterforms have tone, timbre, char
acter, just as words and sentences
do. The moment a text and typeface
BOLD

Letterforms have tone, timbre, charac
ter, just as words and sentences do.
The moment a text and typeface are
BOLD ITALIC

Times New Roman STD

Stanley Morrison and Victor Lardent, Monotype Corp.

A-z €

Typography

ABCDEFGHIJKLMNOPQRST
UVWXYZabcdefghijklmnopqrstu
vwxyz&0123456789$€!?.;:,""{½}

ABCDEFGHIJKLMNOPQRSTU
VWXYZabcdefghijklmnopqrstuvw
xyz&0123456789$€!?.;:,""{½}

Letterforms have tone, timbre, character,
just as words and sentences do. The mo
ment a text and typeface are chosen, two
REGULAR

Letterforms have tone, timbre, character,
just as words and sentences do. The mo
ment a text and typeface are chosen, two
ITALIC

Letterforms have tone, timbre, character,
just as words and sentences do. The mo
ment a text and typeface are chosen, two
BOLD

Letterforms have tone, timbre, character,
just as words and sentences do. The mo
ment a text and typeface are chosen, two
BOLD ITALIC

Times New Roman STD Condensed

Stanley Morrison and Victor Lardent, Monotype Corp.

A-z €

Typography

ABCDEFGHIJKLMNOPQRSTUVWX
YZabcdefghijklmnopqrstuvwxyz&01234
56789$€!?.;:,""{½}

*ABCDEFGHIJKLMNOPQRSTUVWXY
Zabcdefghijklmnopqrstuvwxyz&0123456
789$€!?.;:,""{½}*

Letterforms have tone, timbre, character, just as
words and sentences do. The moment a text and
typeface are chosen, two streams of thought, two
REGULAR

*Letterforms have tone, timbre, character, just as
words and sentences do. The moment a text and type
face are chosen, two streams of thought, two streams*
ITALIC

**Letterforms have tone, timbre, character, just as
words and sentences do. The moment a text and
typeface are chosen, two streams of thought,**
BOLD

Times Ten STD

Linotype Staff, Linotype Library GmbH

A-z € BB 619

Typography

ABCDEFGHIJKLMNOPQRST
UVWXYZabcdefghijklmnopqrst
uvwxyz&0123456789$€!?.;:;""{½}

ABCDEFGHIJKLMNOPQRSTUVWXYZ&
0123456789

Типографика

АБВГЃГДЂЕЁЁЄЖЗSИЙIЇЈK
ЌЛЉМНЊОПРСТЋУЎФХЦ
ЏЧШЩЪЫЬЭЮЯабвгѓгдђеё
єжзsийіїјкќлљмнњопрстћуўфх
цџчшщъыьэюя

*ABCDEFGHIJKLMNOPQRST
UVWXYZabcdefghijklmnopqrstu
vwxyz&0123456789$€!?.;:,""{½}*

0123456789

*АБВГЃГДЂЕЁЁЄЖЗSИЙIЇЈK
ЌЛЉМНЊОПРСТЋУЎФХЦ
ЏЧШЩЪЫЬЭЮЯабвгѓгдђеё
жзsийіїјкќлљмнњопрстћуўфх
цџчшщъыьэюя*

LETTERFORMS HAVE TONE, timbre, charac
ter, just as words and 567 sentences do.
The moment a text and typeface are cho

Точно найденные слова достойны точ
ности в подборе шрифтов; те, в свою
очередь, заслуживают чуткого, осмы
ROMAN

*Letterforms have tone, timbre, character,
just as words and 567 sentences do. The
moment a text and typeface are chosen,*

*Точно найденные слова достойны
точности в подборе шрифтов; те, в
свою очередь, заслуживают чуткого,*
ITALIC

Letterforms have tone, timbre, charac ter, just as words and 567 sentences do. The moment a text and typeface are cho

Точно найденные слова достойны точности в подборе шрифтов; те, в свою очередь, заслуживают чуткого,
BOLD

Letterforms have tone, timbre, charac ter, just as words and 567 sentences do. The moment a text and typeface are cho

Точно найденные слова достойны точности в подборе шрифтов; те, в свою очередь, заслуживают чут
BOLD ITALIC

Toolbox STD

Brian Strysko, Adobe Systems

A-z €

TYPOGRAPH

ABCDEFGHIJKLM
NOPQRSTUVWXYZ
&0123456789 $€!?
.;:, "" {½}

LETTERFORMS HAVE
TONE, TIMBRE, CHARA
REGULAR

Trade Gothic STD

Jackson Burke, Linotype Library GmbH

A-z €

Typography

ABCDEFGHIJKLMNOPQRSTUV
WXYZabcdefghijklmnopqrstuvwx
yz&0123456789$€!?.;:,""{½}

*ABCDEFGHIJKLMNOPQRSTUV
WXYZabcdefghijklmnopqrstuvwx
yz&0123456789$€!?.;:,""{½}*

Letterforms have tone, timbre, character, just as words and sentences do. The mo ment a text and typeface are chosen, two
LIGHT

Letterforms have tone, timbre, character, just as words and sentences do. The mo ment a text and typeface are chosen, two
LIGHT OBLIQUE

Letterforms have tone, timbre, charac ter, just as words and sentences do. The moment a text and typeface are chosen
REGULAR

Letterforms have tone, timbre, charac ter, just as words and sentences do. The moment a text and typeface are chosen
OBLIQUE

Letterforms have tone, timbre, character, just as words and sentences do. The mo ment a text and typeface are chosen, two
BOLD

Letterforms have tone, timbre, character, just as words and sentences do. The mo ment a text and typeface are chosen, two
BOLD OBLIQUE

Letterforms have tone, timbre, charac
ter, just as words and sentences do. The
moment a text and typeface are chosen,
BOLD 2

Letterforms have tone, timbre, charac
ter, just as words and sentences do. The
moment a text and typeface are chosen
BOLD 2 OBLIQUE

Trade Gothic STD Condensed

Jackson Burke, Linotype Library GmbH

A-z €

Typography

ABCDEFGHIJKLMNOPQRSTUVWXYZ
abcd efghijklmnopqrstuvwxyz&0123456
789$€!?.;:,""{½}

ABCDEFGHIJKLMNOPQRSTUVWXYZ
abcd efghijklmnopqrstuvwxyz&0123456
789$€!?.;:,""{½}

Letterforms have tone, timbre, character, just as
words and sentences do. The moment a text and
typeface are chosen, two streams of thought, two
NO. 18

Letterforms have tone, timbre, character, just as
words and sentences do. The moment a text and
typeface are chosen, two streams of thought, two
NO. 18 OBLIQUE

Letterforms have tone, timbre, character, just
as words and sentences do. The moment a text
and typeface are chosen, two streams of though
BOLD NO. 20

Letterforms have tone, timbre, character, just
as words and sentences do. The moment a text
and typeface are chosen, two streams of though
BOLD NO. 20 OBLIQUE

Trade Gothic STD Extended

Jackson Burke, Linotype Library GmbH

A-z €

Typography

ABCDEFGHIJKLMNOPQ
RSTUVWXYZabcdefghij
klmnopqrstuvwxyz&0123
456789$€!?.;:,""{½}

Letterforms have tone, timbre,
character, just as words and
sentences do. The moment a
REGULAR

Letterforms have tone, timbre,
character, just as words and
sentences do. The moment a
BOLD

Trajan PRO

Carol Twombly, Adobe Systems

A-Z € BB 123

TYPOGRAPHY

ABCDEFGHIJKLMN
OPQRSTUVWXYZ
ABCDEFGHIJKLMNOP
QRSTUVWXYZ&

0123456789
0123456789
0123456789
0123456789

Proportional and Tabular Figures

Ø$¢£¥ƒ€#¤$¢£¥ƒ€%
‰£¹²³⁴/¼½¾^~.+±<=>
–|¦×÷∂μπΔ∏∑Ω√∞∫≈≠≤
≥◊¬℮ℓ°ᴬᴼ_——-‐——'"" ''
« » « » ‹ › ‹ ›,.:;…·!?¡¿¡¿()()
[][]{}⁄∧*'§†‡¶©®™@@

Currency, Punctuation, and Related Forms

ÆŁØŒÞÐÁÂÄÀÅÃÇ
ÉÊËÈÍÎÏÌİÑÓÔÖÒŎ
ŠÚÛÜÙÝŸŽĀĀĄĆČĎ

ĐĚĖĒĘĞĠĪĮĶĹĿĽŅŃŇ
ŊŐŌŔŘŖŚŞŠŢŤŲŰŪŲ
ŮŹŻÆIŁØŒSSÞÐÁÂÄ
ÀÅÃÇÉÊËÈÍÎÏÌÑÓÔÖÖ
ÕŠÚÚÛÜÙÝŸŽĂĀĄĆČĎ
ĐĚĖĒĘĞĠĪĮĶĹĽĽĻŃŇŅ
ŐŌŔŘŖŚŞŠŢŤŰŪŲŮŹŻ

Accented Characters

LETTERFORMS HAVE
TONE, TIMBRE, CHARAC
REGULAR

**LETTERFORMS HAVE
TONE, TIMBRE, CHARAC**
BOLD

*To download a complete glyph complement PDF, please visit
www.adobe.com/type.*

Trump Mediäval STD

Georg Trump, Linotype Library GmbH

A-Z € BB 619

Typography

ABCDEFGHIJKLMNOPQRS
TUVWXYZabcdefghijklmnop
qrstuvwxyz&0123456789$€!?
.;:,""''{½}

ABCDEFGHIJKLMNOPQRSTUVWX
YZ&0123456789

ABCDEFGHIJKLMNOPQRS TUVWXYZabcdefghijklmnop qrstuvwxyz&0123456789$€!? .;:,""{½}

0123456789

LETTERFORMS HAVE TONE, timbre, char acter, just as words and 567 sentenc es do. The moment a text and type
ROMAN

Letterforms have tone, timbre, char acter, just as words and 567 sentenc es do. The moment a text and type
ITALIC

Letterforms have tone, timbre, charac ter, just as words and 567 sentences do. The moment a text and typeface
BOLD

Letterforms have tone, timbre, char acter, just as words and 567 sentenc es do. The moment a text and type
BOLD ITALIC

Umbra STD

R. Hunter Middleton, Ludlow Type Foundry

[A-z] [€]

TYPOGRAPHY

ABCDEFGHIJKLMNOPQ RSTUVWXYZ&012345678 9$€!?.;:,""{½}

LETTERFORMS HAVE TONE, TIMBRE, CHARACTER, JUST

REGULAR

Univers STD

Adrian Frutiger, Linotype Library GmbH

[A-z] [€]

Typography

ABCDEFGHIJKLMNOPQRSTU VWXYZabcdefghijklmnopqrstu vwxyz&0123456789$€!?.;:,""{½}

ABCDEFGHIJKLMNOPQRSTU VWXYZabcdefghijklmnopqrstu vwxyz&0123456789$€!?.;:,""{½}

Letterforms have tone, timbre, charac ter, just as words and sentences do. The moment a text and typeface are
45 LIGHT

Letterforms have tone, timbre, charac ter, just as words and sentences do. The moment a text and typeface are
45 LIGHT OBLIQUE

Letterforms have tone, timbre, char acter, just as words and sentences do. The moment a text and typeface
55 REGULAR

Letterforms have tone, timbre, char acter, just as words and sentences do. The moment a text and typeface
55 OBLIQUE

Letterforms have tone, timbre, char acter, just as words and sentences do. The moment a text and typeface
65 BOLD

Letterforms have tone, timbre, char acter, just as words and sentences do. The moment a text and typeface
65 BOLD OBLIQUE

Letterforms have tone, timbre, character, just as words and sen tences do. The moment a text

75 BLACK

Letterforms have tone, timbre, character, just as words and sen tences do. The moment a text

75 BLACK OBLIQUE

Letterforms have tone, timbre, character, just as words and sen tences do. The moment a text

85 EXTRA BLACK

Letterforms have tone, timbre, character, just as words and sen tences do. The moment a text

85 EXTRA BLACK OBLIQUE

Univers STD Condensed

Adrian Frutiger, Linotype Library GmbH

Typography

ABCDEFGHIJKLMNOPQRSTUVWX YZabcdefghijklmnopqrstuvwxyz&01 23456789$€!?.;:,""{½}

ABCDEFGHIJKLMNOPQRSTUVWX YZabcdefghijklmnopqrstuvwxyz&01 23456789$€!?""{½}

Letterforms have tone, timbre, character, just as words and sentences do. The moment a text and typeface are chosen, two streams of thought

47 LIGHT

Letterforms have tone, timbre, character, just as words and sentences do. The moment a text and typeface are chosen, two streams of though

47 LIGHT OBLIQUE

Letterforms have tone, timbre, character, just as words and sentences do. The mo ment a text and typeface are chosen, two

57 REGULAR

Letterforms have tone, timbre, character, just as words and sentences do. The mo ment a text and typeface are chosen, two

57 OBLIQUE

Letterforms have tone, timbre, character, just as words and sentences do. The mo ment a text and typeface are chosen, two

67 BOLD

Letterforms have tone, timbre, character, just as words and sentences do. The mo ment a text and typeface are chosen, two

67 BOLD OBLIQUE

Univers STD Ultra Condensed

Adrian Frutiger, Linotype Library GmbH

Typography

ABCDEFGHIJKLMNOPQRSTUVWXYZabcdefghijkl mnopqrstuvwxyz&0123456789$€!?.;:,""{½}

Letterforms have tone, timbre, character, just as words and sentences do. The moment a text and typeface

39 THIN

Letterforms have tone, timbre, charac
ter, just as words and sentences do.

49 LIGHT

Letterforms have tone, timbre,
character, just as words and

59 REGULAR

Univers STD Extended

Linotype Library GmbH

A-z €

Typography

ABCDEFGHIJKLMNOPQ
RSTUVWXYZabcdefghij
klmnopqrstuvwxyz&012
3456789$€!?.;:,""'{½}

ABCDEFGHIJKLMNOPQ
RSTUVWXYZabcdefghij
klmnopqrstuvwxyz&012
3456789$€!?.;:,""'{½}

Letterforms have tone, timbre,
character, just as words and
sentences do. The moment a

53 REGULAR

Letterforms have tone, timbre,
character, just as words and
sentences do. The moment a

53 OBLIQUE

Letterforms have tone, tim
bre, character, just as words
and sentences do. The mo

63 BOLD

Letterforms have tone, tim
bre, character, just as words
and sentences do. The mo

63 BOLD OBLIQUE

Letterforms have tone, tim
bre, character, just as word
and sentences do. The mo

73 BLACK

Letterforms have tone, tim
bre, character, just as word
and sentences do. The mo

73 BLACK OBLIQUE

Letterforms have tone,
timbre, character, just
as words and sentence

93 EXTRA BLACK

Letterforms have tone,
timbre, character, just
as words and sentence

93 EXTRA BLACK OBLIQUE

Universal STD

Linotype Staff

ΑΒΨΔΕΦΓΗΙΞΚΛΜΝΟΠΘΡΣ
ΤΘΩ6ΧΥΖαβψδεφγηιξκλμνοπ
ϑρστθωφχυζεχ∇ςϖℏλ∂∝∞∫ΣΠ+
−×÷=±∓+≠≡∓≢<>≥≤≮≯
≰≱≤≥≰≱≰≱∼≈+↗√[]{}⟨⟩()/
⌐°′″‴

GREEK WITH MATH PI

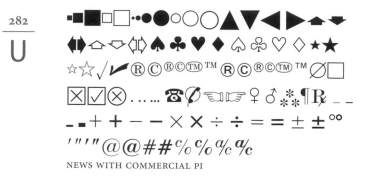

NEWS WITH COMMERCIAL PI

University STD

Mike Daines and Phillip Kelly, Esselte Pendaflex, Letraset, Esselte Letraset

A-z €

Typography

ABCDEFGHIJKLMNOPQRST UVWXYZabcdefghijklmnopqrs tuvwxyz&0123456789$€!?.;:,""
{½}

Letterforms have tone, timbre, character, just as words and sen
ROMAN

ITC Usherwood STD

Leslie Usherwood, ITC

A-z €

Typography

ABCDEFGHIJKLMNOPQRSTUVW XYZabcdefghijklmnopqrstuvwxy z&0123456789$€!?.;:,""{½}

ABCDEFGHIJKLMNOPQRSTUVW XYZabcdefghijklmnopqrstuvwxyz &0123456789$€!?.;:,""{½}

Letterforms have tone, timbre, character, just as words and sentences do. The moment a text and typeface are chosen,
BOOK

Letterforms have tone, timbre, character, just as words and sentences do. The moment a text and typeface are chosen, two
BOOK ITALIC

Letterforms have tone, timbre, character, just as words and sentences do. The moment a text and typeface are chosen,
MEDIUM

Letterforms have tone, timbre, character, just as words and sentences do. The moment a text and typeface are chosen, two
MEDIUM ITALIC

Letterforms have tone, timbre, character, just as words and sentences do. The moment a text and typeface are
BOLD

Letterforms have tone, timbre, character, just as words and sentences do. The moment a text and typeface are
BOLD ITALIC

Letterforms have tone, timbre, char acter, just as words and sentences do. The moment a text and typefac

BLACK

Letterforms have tone, timbre, character, just as words and sen tences do. The moment a text and

BLACK ITALIC

Utopia STD

Robert Slimbach, Adobe Systems

A-Z | € | ffi | Bʙ | 619 | 123 | ⅞ | H₂ | 1ˢᵗ | ✍ | aA

Typography

ΛBCDEFGHIJKLMNOPQRSTUV
WXYZabcdefghijklmnopqrstuvw
xyz&0123456789$€!?.,:;,""{½}

ABCDEFGHIJKLMNOPQRSTUVWXYZ
&0123456789$¢ ffi ⅛

ABCDEFGHIJKLMNOPQRSTUV
WXYZabcdefghijklmnopqrstuvwx
yz&0123456789$€!?.,:;,""{½}

0123456789$¢ ffi ⅛

✍ ◦ ❧ ◇ ▷ ← → ← → ← → ← ✦ ▶ ← →
◁ ▷ ☙ - ❦ □ ✳ ✽ ✱ ⊙ ◆ ■ √ □ ☑

LETTERFORMS HAVE TONE, timbre, charac ter, just as words and 567 sentences do. The moment a text and typeface are cho

REGULAR

Letterforms have tone, timbre, character, just as words and 567 sentences do. The moment a text and typeface are chosen

ITALIC

LETTERFORMS HAVE TONE, timbre, char acter, just as words and 567 sentences do. The moment a text and typeface are

SEMIBOLD

Letterforms have tone, timbre, charac ter, just as words and 567 sentences do. The moment a text and typeface are cho

SEMIBOLD ITALIC

LETTERFORMS HAVE TONE, timbre, char acter, just as words and 567 sentences do. The moment a text and typeface are

BOLD

Letterforms have tone, timbre, charac ter, just as words and 567 sentences do. The moment a text and typeface are cho

BOLD ITALIC

Utopia STD Opticals

Robert Slimbach, Adobe Systems

A-Z | € | ffi | Bʙ | 619 | 123 | ⅞ | H₂ | 1ˢᵗ | ✍ | aA

LETTERFORMS HAVE TONE, timbre, character, just as words and 567 sentences do. The moment a text and typeface are

LETTERFORMS HAVE TONE, timbre, charac ter, just as words and 567 sentences do.

LETTERFORMS have tone, tim bre, character, just as words

LETTERFORMS have tone, timbre, charac

CAPTION, REGULAR, SUBHEAD, DISPLAY

Letterforms have tone, timbre, character, just as words and 567 sentences do. The moment a text and typeface are chosen,

Letterforms have tone, timbre, character, just as words and 567 sentences do. The

Letterforms have tone, timbre, character, just as words

Letterforms have tone, timbre, character, just

ITALIC: CAPTION, REGULAR, SUBHEAD, DISPLAY

Letterforms have tone, timbre, character, just as words and 567 sentences do. The moment a text and typeface are

Letterforms have tone, timbre, character, just as words and 567 sentences

Letterforms have tone, timbre, character, just as words

Letterforms have tone, timbre, charac

SEMIBOLD: CAPTION, REGULAR, SUBHEAD, DISPLAY

Letterforms have tone, timbre, character, just as words and 567 sentences do. The moment a text and typeface are cho

Letterforms have tone, timbre, character, just as words and 567 sentences do.

Letterforms have tone, timbre, character, just as words

Letterforms have to ne, timbre, character,

SEMIBOLD ITALIC: CAPTION, REGULAR, SUBHEAD, DISPLAY

Letterforms have tone, timbre, character, just as words and 567 sentences do. The moment a text and typeface are

Letterforms have tone, char acter, just as words and 567 sentences

Letterforms have tone, tim bre, character, just as words

Letterforms have tone, timbre, charac

BOLD: CAPTION, REGULAR, SUBHEAD, DISPLAY

Letterforms have tone, timbre, character, just as words and 567 sentences do. The moment a text and typeface are

Letterforms have tone, timbre, charac ter, just as words and 567 sentences do.

Letterforms have tone, tim bre, character, just as words

Letterforms have to ne, timbre, character

BOLD ITALIC: CAPTION, REGULAR, SUBHEAD, DISPLAY

Letterforms

BLACK HEADLINE

VAG Rounded STD

Gerry Barney, Terence Griffin, David Bristow, and
Kit Cooper, Sedley Place

A-z €

Typography

ABCDEFGHIJKLMNOPQRSTUVWXY
Zabcdefghijklmnopqrstuvwxyz&01
23456789$€!?.;:,""{½}

Letterforms have tone, timbre, character,
just as words and sentences do. The mo
ment a text and typeface are chosen, two
THIN

Letterforms have tone, timbre, character,
just as words and sentences do. The mo
ment a text and typeface are chosen, two
LIGHT

**Letterforms have tone, timbre, charac
ter, just as words and sentences do. The
moment a text and typeface are chosen**
BOLD

**Letterforms have tone, timbre, charac
ter, just as words and sentences do.
The moment a text and typeface are**
BLACK

Vectora STD

Adrian Frutiger, Linotype Library GmbH

A-z €

Typography

ABCDEFGHIJKLMNOPQRSTUVW
XYZabcdefghijklmnopqrstuvwx
yz&0123456789$€!?.;:,""{½}

*ABCDEFGHIJKLMNOPQRSTUVW
XYZabcdefghijklmnopqrstuvwx
yz&0123456789$€!?.;:,""{½}*

Letterforms have tone, timbre, character,
just as words and sentences do. The mo
ment a text and typeface are chosen,
45 LIGHT

*Letterforms have tone, timbre, charac
ter, just as words and sentences do. The
moment a text and typeface are chosen,*
46 LIGHT ITALIC

Letterforms have tone, timbre, charac
ter, just as words and sentences do.
The moment a text and typeface are
55 ROMAN

*Letterforms have tone, timbre, charac
ter, just as words and sentences do.
The moment a text and typeface are*
56 ITALIC

**Letterforms have tone, timbre, char
acter, just as words and sentences
do. The moment a text and type**
75 BOLD

***Letterforms have tone, timbre, char
acter, just as words and sentences
do. The moment a text and type***
76 BOLD ITALIC

**Letterforms have tone, timbre,
character, just as words and sen
tences do. The moment a text**
95 BLACK

***Letterforms have tone, timbre,
character, just as words and sen
tences do. The moment a text***
96 BLACK ITALIC

ITC Veljovic STD

Jovica Veljovic, ITC

A-z €

Typography

ABCDEFGHIJKLMNOPQRSTU
VWXYZabcdefghijklmnopqrstuv
wxyz&0123456789$€!?.;:,""{½}

*ABCDEFGHIJKLMNOPQRSTUV
WXYZabcdefghijklmnopqrstuvwxy
z&0123456789$€!?.;:,""{½}*

Letterforms have tone, timbre, charac
ter, just as words and sentences do.
The moment a text and typeface are
BOOK

*Letterforms have tone, timbre, character,
just as words and sentences do. The mo
ment a text and typeface are chosen, two*
BOOK ITALIC

Letterforms have tone, timbre, charac
ter, just as words and sentences do.
The moment a text and typeface are
MEDIUM

*Letterforms have tone, timbre, charac
ter, just as words and sentences do.
The moment a text and typeface are*
MEDIUM ITALIC

**Letterforms have tone, timbre, char
acter, just as words and sentences
do. The moment a text and type**
BOLD

***Letterforms have tone, timbre, charac
ter, just as words and sentences do.
The moment a text and typeface are***
BOLD ITALIC

**Letterforms have tone, timbre,
character, just as words and sen
tences do. The moment a text**
BLACK

***Letterforms have tone, timbre, char
acter, just as words and sentences
do. The moment a text and type***
BLACK ITALIC

Versailles STD

Adrian Frutiger, Linotype Library GmbH

A-z €

Typography

ABCDEFGHIJKLMNOPQRS
TUVWXYZabcdefghijklmnop
qrstuvwxyz&0123456789$€!?
.;:,""{½}

*ABCDEFGHIJKLMNOPQRS
TUVWXYZabcdefghijklmnop
qrstuvwxyz&0123456789$€!?
.;:,""{½}*

Letterforms have tone, timbre, charac
ter, just as words and sentences do.
The moment a text and typeface are
45 LIGHT

*Letterforms have tone, timbre, charac
ter, just as words and sentences do.
The moment a text and typeface are*
46 LIGHT ITALIC

Letterforms have tone, timbre, char
acter, just as words and sentences
do. The moment a text and typeface
55 ROMAN

Letterforms have tone, timbre, char acter, just as words and sentences do. The moment a text and typeface
56 ITALIC

Letterforms have tone, timbre, character, just as words and sen tences do. The moment a text
75 BOLD

Letterforms have tone, timbre, character, just as words and sen tences do. The moment a text and
76 BOLD ITALIC

Letterforms have tone, timbre, character, just as words and sentences do. The moment a
95 BLACK

Letterforms have tone, timbre, character, just as words and sentences do. The moment a
96 BLACK ITALIC

Verve STD

Brian Sooy, Brian Sooy

A-z | € | 123

Typography

ABCDEFGHIJKLMNOPQRSTUUWXYZ
abcdefghijklmnopqrstuuwxyz&
0123456789$€!?.;:,""(½)

FSTYfhj kmnr
Alternates

Letterforms have tone, timbre, charac ter, just as words and sentences do.
REGULAR

Letterforms have tone, timbre, character, just as words and sen
BOLD

Letterforms have tone, timbre, character, just as words
BLACK

Visigoth

Arthur Baker, AlphaOmega Typography

Typography

ABCDEFGHIJKLMNOPQ
RSTUVWXYZabcdefghijk
lmnopqrstuvwxyz&O123
456789$!?.;:,""{½}

Letterforms have tone, tim bre, character, just as words
REGULAR

Viva STD

Carol Twombly, Adobe Systems

A-z €

Typography

ABCDEFGHIJKLMNOP
QRSTUVWXYZabcdef
ghijklmnopqrstuvwx
yz&0123456789$€!?.,;
,""{½}

Letterforms have tone, timbre,
character, just as words and sen
LIGHT CONDENSED

Letterforms have tone, timbre
character, just as words and
CONDENSED

**Letterforms have tone, tim
bre, character, just as word**
BOLD CONDENSED

Letterforms have tone,
timbre, character, just as
LIGHT

Letterforms have tone,
timbre, character, just as
REGULAR

**Letterforms have tone
timbre, character, just**
BOLD

Letterforms
have tone, tim
LIGHT EXTRA-EXTENDED

Letterforms
have tone,
EXTRA-EXTENDED

**Letterforms
have tone,**
BOLD EXTRA-EXTENDED

Voluta Script PRO

Viktor Solt, Adobe Systems

€ ffi 619 ę

Typography

Aa Bb Cc Dd Ee ff Gg Ch Ii Jj Kk
Ll Mm Nn Oo Pp Qq Rr Ss Tt
Uu Vv Ww Xx Yy Zz & 0123456789

Ee Ct J ad fg ij op py s t x yz ll ffi ffl
fi fl ß tt
Alternates and Ligatures

°$¢£¥ƒ€¤#%‰0123456789 ¼ ½ ¾ ^~.+ ±
<=>-|/:÷·μπ ΔΠΣΩ√∞∫≈≠≤≥◊· e°
ª°__ __- ' " " " „ '' ,«»‹› ,.:; ... ...!¡?¿
()[]{}/\ *·§ ‡† J© ®™ @@
Currency, Punctuation, and Related Forms

Æ Œ Œ Þ Đ Á Â Ä À Å Ã

Ç É Ê Ë È Í Î Ï Ì Ñ Ó Ô Ö Ò

Õ Ú Û Ü Ù Ý Ÿ Ž á â ä à å

Đ Đ Ě Ê É É Ğ Ğ Ĭ Į Ķ Ĺ Ľ Ł

Ń Ň Ņ Ŏ Ő Ŕ Ř Ŗ Ś Ŝ Ţ Ţ

Ŭ Ũ Ų Ż Ž ą ε ł œ ø β þ ð á â ä à å ā ç é ê ë è í í í

ñ ó ô ö ò õ ș ú û ü ù ý ÿ ž ā ā ą ç đ ě ê é ě ğ ġ ĭ į ķ ĺ ľ ł ș ń ň ņ ŏ ő ŕ ř ŗ ș

ţ ţ ŭ ũ ų ż ž

Accented Characters

Letterforms have tone, timbre, character, just as words and sentences do. The moment

REGULAR

To download a complete glyph complement PDF, *please visit www.adobe.com/type.*

Warning Pi STD

Unknown

REGULAR

Robert Slimbach, Adobe Systems

A-Z € ffi BB 619 123 7/8 H₂ 1st 𝓐 ᵉ 🍃 aA

Typography

ABCDEFGHIJKLMNOPQRSTU
VWXYZabcdefghijklmnopqrstu
vwxyz&ABCDEFGHIJKLMNOPQRS
TUVWXYZ&

ABCDEFGHIJKLMNOPQRSTUV
WXYZabcdefghijklmnopqrstuvw
xyz&ABCDEFGHIJKLMNOPQRSTUV
WXYZ&

ABCDEFGHIJKLMNOPQ
RSTUVWXYZ

Swash Capitals

0123456789 0123456789
0123456789 0123456789
0123456789 *0123456789*
0123456789 *0123456789*

Proportional and Tabular Figures

KQR ᴋǫʀ kſvwy a d e g h l m n
σ r t u Th ᴄt ff ffi ffj ffl fi fj fl ſþ st

abdehilmnorst

Alternates, Ligatures, and Superiors

KQR ᴋǫʀ *kſtvwyz & a d e g h l*
m n σ r t u Th ᴄt ff ffi ffi ffl fi fj fl
ſþ st abdehilmnorst

Italic Alternates, Ligatures, and Superiors

Ø$¢£¥ƒ₡₣£₽€#¤€₨p%‰$¢£¥ƒ₡₣£
₽€#¤%‰ 0123456789($¢-.,)0123456789($¢-.,)%
123456789($¢-.,)0123456789($¢-
.,)¼½¾⅛⅜⅝⅞ ⅓⅔^~˙+±<=>−−|¦×÷
∂µπΔΠΣΩ√∞∫≈≠≤≥◊¬№℮ℓ°ᵃᵒ_____
——-·-——' " "" „‚',«» «»‹›‹› ,.:; … ..
. ·˙!?¡¿!?¡¿()() []{}§§/\
*•§†‡¶©®™@@

Currency, Punctuation, and Related Forms

Ø$¢£¥ƒ₡₣£₽€#¤€₨p%‰$¢£¥ƒ₡₣
£€#¤%‰ 0123456789($¢-.,)0123456789($¢-.,)/
0123456789($¢-.,)0123456789($¢-.,) ¼½¾⅛⅜⅝
⅞⅓⅔^~˙+±<=>−−|¦×÷∂µπΔΠΣΩ√
∞∫≈≠≤≥◊¬№℮ℓ°ᵃᵒ_____——' "
"" „‚',«» «»‹›‹› ,.:; … .. . ·˙!?¡¿!?¡¿()()
*[][]{}§§/\ *•§†‡¶©®™@@*

Italic Currency, Punctuation, and Related Forms

ÆŁØŒÞÐÁÂÄÀÅÃÇÉÊËÈÍÎÏÌ
ÑÓÔÖÒÕŠÚÛÜÙÝŸŽĂĀĄĆČ
ĎĐĚĖĒĘĞĠĪĮĶĹĽĻŃŇŅŐŌŔŘ
ŖŚŞŠŢŤŰŪŲŮŹŻÆĈĊĚŊĜĠĦ
ĤĬ Ĳ ĨĴĿŎØŜŦŬŨŴŴŴŴŶŶÆ
ıłøœßþðáâäàåãçéêëèíîïìñóôöòõšú
ûüùýÿžăāąćčďđěėēęğġīįķĺľļńňņőō
ŕřŗśşšţťűūųůźżæĉċěŋĝġħĥĩ ĳ ĩĵŀňŏø
ŝŧŭũŵŵŵŵŷỳќÆŁØŒÞÐÁÂÄÀÅ
ÇÉÊËÈÍÎÏÌÑÓÔÖÒÕŠÚÛÜÙÝŸŽĂĀ
ĄĆČĎĐĚĖĒĘĞĠĪĮĶĹĽĻŃŇŅŐŌŔŘ

ŚŞŠŢŤŰŪŲŮŹŻÆĈĊĚŊĜĠĦĤĨ Ĳ ĨĴĿŎØŜŦŬŨŴŴŴŴŶŶ

Accented Characters

ÆŁØŒÞÐÁÂÄÀÅÃÇÉÊËÈÍÎÏÌ
ÑÓÔÖÒÕŠÚÛÜÙÝŸŽĂĀĄĆČ
ĎĐĚĖĒĘĞĠĪĮĶĹĽĻŃŇŅŐŌŔŘ
ŚŞŠŢŤŰŪŲŮŹŻÆĈĊĚŊĜĠĦ
ĤĬ Ĳ ĨĴĿŎØŜŦŬŨŴŴŴŴŶŶæıłøœ
ßþðáâäàåãçéêëèíîïìñóôöòõšúûüùý
ÿžăāąćčďđěėēęğġīįķĺľļńňņőōŕřŗśşş
ťţűūųůźżæĉċěŋĝġħĥĩ ĳ ĩĵŀňŏøŝŧŭũŵ
ŵŵŵŷỳќÆŁØŒÞÐÁÂÄÀÅÃÇÉÊËÈÍ
ÎÏÌÑÓÔÖÒÕŠÚÛÜÙÝŸŽĂĀĄĆČĎĐĚ
ĖĒĘĞĠĪĮĶĹĽĻŃŇŅŐŌŔŘŖŚŞŠŢŤŰŪ
ŲŮŹŻÆĈĊĚŊĜĠĦĤĨ Ĳ ĨĴĿŎØŜŦŬŨ
ŴŴŴŴŶŶ

Italic Accented Characters

Ornaments

Italic Ornaments

LETTERFORMS HAVE TONE, timbre, charac
ter, just as words and 567 sentences do. The
moment a text and typeface are chosen, two
REGULAR

LETTERFORMS HAVE TONE, timbre, character,
just as words and 567 sentences do. The mo
ment a text and typeface are chosen, two
ITALIC

LETTERFORMS HAVE TONE, timbre, charac ter, just as words and 567 sentences do. The moment a text and typeface are chosen, two
MEDIUM

LETTERFORMS HAVE TONE, timbre, charac ter, just as words and 567 sentences do. The moment a text and typeface are chosen, two
MEDIUM ITALIC

LETTERFORMS HAVE TONE, timbre, charac ter, just as words and 567 sentences do. The moment a text and typeface are chosen,
SEMIBOLD

LETTERFORMS HAVE TONE, timbre, charac ter, just as words and 567 sentences do. The moment a text and typeface are chosen, two
SEMIBOLD ITALIC

LETTERFORMS HAVE TONE, timbre, char acter, just as words and 567 sentences do. The moment a text and typeface are cho
BOLD

LETTERFORMS HAVE TONE, timbre, charac ter, just as words and 567 sentences do. The moment a text and typeface are chosen,
BOLD ITALIC

АБВГЃДЂЕЁЄЖЗЅИЙЍЇЈКЌЛЉ МНЊОПРСТЋУЎФХЦЏЧШЩ ЪЫЬЭЮЯабвгѓдђеёєжзѕийіїјк ќлљмнњопрстћуўфхцџчшщъыь эюя
Cyrillic

АБВГЃДЂЕЁЄЖЗЅИЙЍЇЈКЌЛЉ МНЊОПРСТЋУЎФХЦЏЧШЩ ЪЫЬЭЮЯабвгѓдђеёєжзѕийіїјкќ лљмнњопрстћуўфхцџчшщъыэ юя
Italic Cyrillic

ДЛЉЬэдллљ ѲѴѢѳѵѢ
Cyrillic Alternates

ДЛЉЬэбдıдйīвлљю̄ ѲѴѢѳѵњ
Italic Cyrillic Alternates

Точно найденные слова достойны точно *сти в подборе шрифтов; те, в свою оче*
LIGHT, LIGHT ITALIC

Точно найденные слова достойны точ *ности в подборе шрифтов; те, в свою*
REGULAR, ITALIC

Точно найденные слова достойны точ *ности в подборе шрифтов; те, в свою*
SEMIBOLD, SEMIBOLD ITALIC

Точно найденные слова достойны ***точности в подборе шрифтов; те, в***
BOLD, BOLD ITALIC

ΑΒΓΔΕΖΗΘΙΚΛΜΝΞΟΠΡΣΤΥ ΦΧΨΩΆΈΉΊΪΌΎ ῨῺαβγδεζηθι κλμνξοπρστυφχψωάέήίϊόύϋώΐΰς
Greek

ΑΒΓΔΕΖΗΘΙΚΛΜΝΞΟΠΡΣΤΥ ΦΧΨΩΆΈΉΊΪΌΎ ῨῺαβγδεζηθικ λμνξοπρστυφχψωάέήίϊόύϋώΐΰς
Italic Greek

ѲѴΦѳνβϰϑ
Greek Alternates

ΘΝΦθνβϰϑ

Italic Greek Alternates

Στις πύλες του δάσους ο έκπληκτος άν
θρωπος του κόσμου είναι αναγκασμένος
LIGHT, LIGHT ITALIC

Στις πύλες του δάσους ο έκπληκτος άν
θρωπος του κόσμου είναι αναγκασμένος
MEDIUM, MEDIUM ITALIC

**Στις πύλες του δάσους ο έκπληκτος άν
θρωπος του κόσμου είναι αναγκασμένος**
SEMIBOLD, SEMIBOLD ITALIC

**Στις πύλες του δάσους ο έκπληκτος άν
θρωπος του κόσμου είναι αναγκασμένος**
BOLD, BOLD ITALIC

To download a complete glyph complement PDF, *please visit*
www.adobe.com/type.

⚫ Warnock PRO Opticals

Robert Slimbach, Adobe Systems

| A-z | € | ffi | Bb | 619 | 123 | ⅞ | H₂ | 1ˢᵗ | 𝒜 | ê̦ | 🖎 | aA |

LETTERFORMS HAVE TONE, timbre, character, just as words
and 567 sentences do. The moment a text and typeface are cho

LETTERFORMS HAVE TONE, timbre, char
acter, just as words and 567 sentences do.

LETTERFORMS have tone, tim
bre, character, just as words and

LETTERFORMS have
tone, timbre, character,
LIGHT: CAPTION, REGULAR, SUBHEAD, DISPLAY

LETTERFORMS HAVE TONE, timbre, character, just as words
and 567 sentences do. The moment a text and typeface are cho

*LETTERFORMS HAVE TONE, timbre, charac
ter, just as words and 567 sentences do. The*

*LETTERFORMS have tone, tim
bre, character, just as words and*

*LETTERFORMS have
tone, timbre character,*
LIGHT ITALIC: CAPTION, REGULAR, SUBHEAD, DISPLAY

LETTERFORMS HAVE TONE, timbre, character, just as words
and 567 sentences do. The moment a text and typeface are

LETTERFORMS HAVE TONE, timbre, char
acter, just as words and 567 sentences do.

LETTERFORMS have tone, tim
bre, character, just as words

LETTERFORMS have
tone, timbre, character
CAPTION, REGULAR, SUBHEAD, DISPLAY

*LETTERFORMS HAVE TONE, timbre, character, just as words
and 567 sentences do. The moment a text and typeface are cho*

*LETTERFORMS HAVE TONE, timbre, charac
ter, just as words and 567 sentences do. The*

*LETTERFORMS have tone, tim
bre, character, just as words*

*LETTERFORMS have
tone, timbre character,*
ITALIC: CAPTION, REGULAR, SUBHEAD, DISPLAY

Letterforms have tone, timbre, character, just as words and 567 sentences do. The moment a text and type

Letterforms have tone, timbre, char acter, just as words and 567 sentences do

Letterforms have tone, tim bre, character, just as words

Letterforms have tone, timbre, charac

SEMIBOLD: CAPTION, REGULAR, SUBHEAD, DISPLAY

Letterforms have tone, timbre, character, just as words and 567 sentences do. The moment a text and type

Letterforms have tone, timbre, char ac ter, just as words and 567 sentences do

Letterforms have tone, tim bre, character, just as words

Letterforms have tone, timbre, charac

SEMIBOLD ITALIC: CAPTION, REGULAR, SUBHEAD, DISPLAY

Letterforms have tone, timbre, character, just as words and 567 sentences do. The moment a text and type

Letterforms have tone, timbre, character, just as words and 567 sentenc

Letterforms have tone, tim bre, character, just as words

Letterforms have tone, timbre, charac

BOLD: CAPTION, REGULAR, SUBHEAD, DISPLAY

Letterforms have tone, timbre, character, just as words and 567 sentences do. The moment a text and type

Letterforms have tone, timbre, character, just as words and 567 sentenc

Letterforms have tone, tim bre, character, just as words

Letterforms have tone, timbre, charact

BOLD ITALIC: CAPTION, REGULAR, SUBHEAD, DISPLAY

Точно найденные слова достойны точности в подборе шрифтов; те, в свою очередь, заслуживают чуткого,

Точно найденные слова достойно сти в подборе шрифтов; те, в свою оче

Точно найденные слова до стойны точности в подборе

Точно найденные сло ва достойны точно

LIGHT: CAPTION, ITALIC CAPTION, REGULAR, ITALIC, SUBHEAD, ITALIC SUBHEAD, DISPLAY, ITALIC DISPLAY

Точно найденные слова достойны точности в подборе шрифтов; те, в свою очередь, заслуживают чуткого,

Точно найденные слова достойны точ ности в подборе шрифтов; те, в свою

Точно найденные слова до стойны точности в подборе

Точно найденные слова достойны точ

CAPTION, ITALIC CAPTION, REGULAR, ITALIC, SUBHEAD, ITALIC SUBHEAD, DISPLAY, ITALIC DISPLAY

Точно найденные слова достойны точности в подборе шрифтов; те, в свою очередь, заслуживают чуткого,

Точно найденные слова достойны точ ности в подборе шрифтов; те, в свою

Точно найденные слова до стойны точности в подбо

Точно найденные слова достойны

SEMIBOLD: CAPTION, ITALIC CAPTION, REGULAR, ITALIC, SUBHEAD, ITALIC SUBHEAD, DISPLAY, ITALIC DISPLAY

Точно найденные слова достойны точности в подборе шрифтов; те, в свою очередь, заслуживают чуткого,

Точно найденные слова достойны точности в подборе шрифтов; те, в

Точно найденные слова до стойны точности в подбо

Точно найденные слова достойны

BOLD: CAPTION, ITALIC CAPTION, REGULAR, ITALIC, SUBHEAD, ITALIC SUBHEAD, DISPLAY, ITALIC DISPLAY

Στις πύλες του δάσους ο έκπληκτος άνθρωπος του κόσμου εί ναι αναγκασμένος να εγκαταλείψει τις αστικές του εκτιμήσεις

Στις πύλες του δάσους ο έκπληκτος άνθρω πος του κόσμου είναι αναγκασμένος να

Στις πύλες του δάσους ο έκπλη κτος άνθρωπος του κόσμου είναι

Στις πύλες του δάσους ο έκπληκτος άνθρωπος

LIGHT: CAPTION, ITALIC CAPTION, REGULAR, ITALIC, SUBHEAD, ITALIC SUBHEAD, DISPLAY, ITALIC DISPLAY

Στις πύλες του δάσους ο έκπληκτος άνθρωπος του κόσμου είναι αναγκασμένος να εγκαταλείψει τις αστικές του εκτιμή

Στις πύλες του δάσους ο έκπληκτος άν θρωπος του κόσμου είναι αναγκασμένος

Στις πύλες του δάσους ο έκπλη κτος άνθρωπος του κόσμου εί

Στις πύλες του δάσους ο έκπληκτος άνθρωπος

CAPTION, ITALIC CAPTION, REGULAR, ITALIC, SUBHEAD, ITALIC SUBHEAD, DISPLAY, ITALIC DISPLAY

Στις πύλες του δάσους ο έκπληκτος άνθρωπος του κόσμου είναι αναγκασμένος να εγκαταλείψει τις αστικές του εκτι

Στις πύλες του δάσους ο έκπληκτος άν θρωπος του κόσμου είναι αναγκασμένος

Στις πύλες του δάσους ο έκ πληκτος άνθρωπος του κό

Στις πύλες του δά σους ο έκπληκτος άν

SEMIBOLD: CAPTION, ITALIC CAPTION, REGULAR, ITALIC, SUBHEAD, ITALIC SUBHEAD, DISPLAY, ITALIC DISPLAY

Στις πύλες του δάσους ο έκπληκτος άνθρωπος του κό σμου είναι αναγκασμένος να εγκαταλείψει τις αστικές του

Στις πύλες του δάσους ο έκπληκτος άν θρωπος του κόσμου είναι αναγκασμένος

Στις πύλες του δάσους ο έκ πληκτος άνθρωπος του κό

Στις πύλες του δά σους ο έκπληκτος άν

BOLD: CAPTION, ITALIC CAPTION, REGULAR, ITALIC, SUBHEAD, ITALIC SUBHEAD, DISPLAY, ITALIC DISPLAY

To download a complete glyph complement PDF, please visit www.adobe.com/type.

Julian Waters, Adobe Systems

A-z € ffi 123 é A

TYPOGRAPHY

ABCDEFGHIJKLMNOP
QRSTUVWXYZ&012345
6789

€ EJKQRTVWYY &aeio

Alternates

ÆA ÆS CA CÆ CC CE CO
CŒ CT DC DG DO DŒ EA
EÆ EE EO ES EY KS LA
LÆ NN ŒA ŒS OC OG OO
RS ST TH TT TY ZA ZÆ *an*
and at for from in of the to

Ligatures

Ø$¢£¥ƒ€#¤%‰¹²³⁴¼½¾^~.
+±<=>−|¦×÷∂μπΔΠΣΩ√∞∫≈
≠≤≥◊¬€ℓ°ᵃᵒ_ ——–-' " "" ",' ,«»‹›
,.:; … ·!?¡¿()[]{} /*·§†‡¶©®™@

Currency, Punctuation, and Related Forms

ÆŁØŒÞÐÁÂÄÀÅÃÇÉÊ
ËÈÍÎÏÌÑÓÔÖÒÕŠÚÛÜÙ
ÝŸŽĂĀĄĆČĎÐĖĖĒĘĞĢ
ĮĶĹĽĻŃŇŅŐŌŔŘŖŚŞŠŢ
ŤŰŪŲŮŹŻ

Accented Characters

LETTERFORMS HAVE TONE, TIMBRE,
CHARACTER, JUST AS WORDS AND SEN
LIGHT CONDENSED

LETTERFORMS HAVE TONE, TIM
BRE, CHARACTER, JUST AS WOR
CONDENSED

**LETTERFORMS HAVE TONE, TIM
BRE, CHARACTER, JUST AS WOR**
SEMIBOLD CONDENSED

**LETTERFORMS HAVE TONE,
TIMBRE, CHARACTER, JUST AS**
BOLD CONDENSED

LETTERFORMS HAVE TONE,
TIMBRE, CHARACTER, JUST AS
LIGHT SEMICONDENSED

LETTERFORMS HAVE TONE,
TIM BRE, CHARACTER, JUST
REGULAR SEMICONDENSED

**LETTERFORMS HAVE TONE,
TIMBRE, CHARACTER, JUST**
SEMIBOLD SEMICONDENSED

LETTERFORMS HAVE TO NE, TIMBRE, CHARACTER,
BOLD SEMICONDENSED

LETTERFORMS HAVE TO NE, TIMBRE, CHARACTER,
LIGHT

LETTERFORMS HAVE TO NE, TIMBRE, CHARACTE
REGULAR

LETTERFORMS HAVE TONE, TIMBRE, CHARA
SEMIBOLD

LETTERFORMS HAVE TONE, TIMBRE, CHAR
BOLD

To download a complete glyph complement PDF, please visit www.adobe.com/type.

ITC Weidemann STD

Kurt Weidemann, ITC

Typography

ABCDEFGHIJKLMNOPQRSTUVW XYZabcdefghijklmnopqrstuvwxyz& 0123456789$€!?.;:,""{½}

ABCDEFGHIJKLMNOPQRSTUVW XYZabcdefghijklmnopqrstuvwxyz& 0123456789$€!?.;:,""{½}

Letterforms have tone, timbre, character, just as words and sentences do. The mo ment a text and typeface are chosen, two
BOOK

Letterforms have tone, timbre, character, just as words and sentences do. The mo ment a text and typeface are chosen, two
BOOK ITALIC

Letterforms have tone, timbre, character, just as words and sentences do. The mo ment a text and typeface are chosen, two
MEDIUM

Letterforms have tone, timbre, character, just as words and sentences do. The mo ment a text and typeface are chosen, two
MEDIUM ITALIC

Letterforms have tone, timbre, charac ter, just as words and sentences do. The moment a text and typeface are chosen
BOLD

Letterforms have tone, timbre, charac ter, just as words and sentences do. The moment a text and typeface are
BOLD ITALIC

Letterforms have tone, timbre, charac ter, just as words and sentences do. The moment a text and typeface are

BLACK

Letterforms have tone, timbre, charac ter, just as words and sentences do. The moment a text and typeface are

BLACK ITALIC

Weiss STD

Rudolf Weiss, Bauer Types, S.A.

Typography

ABCDEFGHIJKLMNOPQRSTUV
WXYZabcdefghijklmnopqrstuvwx
yz&0123456789$€!?.;:,""{½}

*ABCDEFGHIJKLMNOPQRSTUVW
XYZabcdefghijklmnopqrstuvwxyz&01234
56789$€!?.;:,""{½}*

Letterforms have tone, timbre, character, just as words and sentences do. The mo ment a text and typeface are chosen, two

REGULAR

Letterforms have tone, timbre, character, just as words and sentences do. The moment a text and type face are chosen, two streams of thought, two rhythms

ITALIC

Letterforms have tone, timbre, character, just as words and sentences do. The mo ment a text and typeface are chosen, two

BOLD

Letterforms have tone, timbre, charac ter, just as words and sentences do. The moment a text and typeface are chosen

EXTRA BOLD

297

www.adobe.com/type

Wendy STD

Garrett Boge, LetterPerfect

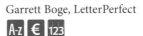

Typography

Aa Bb Cc Dd Ee Ff Gg Hh Ii Jj Kk Ll Mm Nn Oo Pp Qq Rr Ss Tt Uu Vv Ww Xx Yy Zz & 0123456789$€!?.;:,""{½}

Letterforms have tone, timbre, character, just as words and sentences do. The mo

LIGHT

Letterforms have tone, timbre, character, just as words and sentences do. The mo

MEDIUM

Letterforms have tone, timbre, character, just as words and sentences do. The mo

BOLD

Wiesbaden Swing STD

Rosemarie Kloos-Rau, Linotype Library GmbH

A-Z €

Typography

ABCDEFGHIJKLMNOPQRST
UVWXYZabcdefghijklmnopqrstuvwxyz
&0123456789$€!?.;:,"" { ½ }

Letterforms have tone, timbre, character,
just as words and sentences do. The mo
REGULAR

Wiesbaden Swing STD Dingbats

Rosemarie Kloos-Rau, Linotype Library GmbH

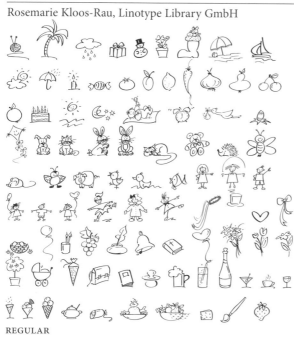

REGULAR

Wilhelm Klingspor Gotisch STD

Rudolf Koch, Linotype Library GmbH

A-Z € ffi 123 ß

Typography

ABCDEFGHIJKLMNOP
QRSTUVWXYZabcdefghijklm
nopqrstuvwxyz&0123456789$€
!?.;:,""{½}

ch ck ff ft ll ſi ſi ſſ ſt ß k
Historic Blackletter

Letterforms have tone, timbre, character,
just as words and sentences do. The
REGULAR

Wilke STD

Martin Wilke, Linotype Library GmbH

A-Z €

Typography

ABCDEFGHIJKLMNOPQRSTU
VWXYZabcdefghijklmnopqrstuv
wxyz&0123456789$€!?.;:,""{½}

ABCDEFGHIJKLMNOPQRSTUV
WXYZabcdefghijklmnopqrstuvwxy
z&0123456789$€!?.;:,""{½}

Letterforms have tone, timbre, character, just as words and sentences do. The moment a text and typeface are chosen,
55 ROMAN

Letterforms have tone, timbre, character, just as words and sentences do. The mo ment a text and typeface are chosen, two
56 ITALIC

Letterforms have tone, timbre, char acter, just as words and sentences do. The moment a text and typeface
75 BOLD

Letterforms have tone, timbre, char acter, just as words and sentences do. The moment a text and typeface
76 BOLD ITALIC

Letterforms have tone, timbre, character, just as words and sen tences do. The moment a text
95 BLACK

Letterforms have tone, timbre, character, just as words and sentences do. The moment a text
96 BLACK ITALIC

Willow STD

Joy Redick, Adobe Systems

A-z €

Typography

ABCDEFGHIJKLMNOPQRSTUVWXYZ
abcdefghijklmnopqrstuvwxyz&0123456789
$¢!?..;., ""(½)

Letterforms have tone, timbre, character, just as words and sentences do. The moment a text
REGULAR

Wittenberger Fraktur STD

Unknown, Monotype Corp.

A-z € ffi 123 tz

Typography

ABCDEFGHIJKLMN
OPQRSTUVWXYZabc
defghijklmnopqrstuvwxyz
&0123456789$€!?.;:, ""{½}

ch ck ff ft ll ſ ſi ſſ ß ſt tz
Historic Blackletter

Letterforms have tone, timbre, character, just as words and
REGULAR

Letterforms have tone, tim bre, character, just as words
BOLD

Adobe Wood Type Ornaments STD

Barbara Lind, Adobe Systems

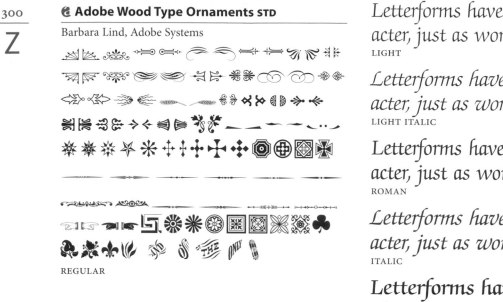

REGULAR

ITC Zapf Chancery STD

Hermann Zapf, ITC

A-Z €

Typography

ABCDEFGHIJKLMNOPQR
STUVWXYZabcdefghijklmno
pqrstuvwxyz&0123456789
$€!?.;:,""{½}

ABCDEFGHIJKLMNOPQ
RSTUVWXYZabcdefghijklm
nopqrstuvwxyz&012345678
9$€!?.;:,""{½}

Letterforms have tone, timbre, char acter, just as words and sentences
LIGHT

Letterforms have tone, timbre, char acter, just as words and sentences
LIGHT ITALIC

Letterforms have tone, timbre, char acter, just as words and sentences
ROMAN

Letterforms have tone, timbre, char acter, just as words and sentences
ITALIC

Letterforms have tone, timbre, character, just as words and sen
DEMI

Letterforms have tone, timbre character, just as words and
BOLD

ITC Zapf Dingbats STD

Hermann Zapf, ITC

REGULAR

❦ Zebrawood STD

Kim Buker Chansler, Adobe Systems

A-z €

TYPOGRAPH

ABCDEFGHIJKLMNOP
QRSTUVWXYZ&0123
56789$€!?.;;,""{½}

LETTERFORMS HAVE
TONE, TIMBRE, CHAR

REGULAR

LETTERFORMS HAVE
TONE, TIMBRE, CHAR

FILL

LETTERFORMS HAVE

USE EACH STYLE AS IS OR OVERLAP AND COLOR THEM.

Zipty Do STD

Robert Alonso, Robert Alonso

A-z € 123

Typography

ABCDEFGHIJKLMNOPQR
STUVWXYZabcdefghijklmnop
qrstuvwxyz&0123456789$
€!?.;;,""{½}

Letterforms have tone, timbre, char
acter, just as words and sentences

REGULAR

Heisei Kaku Gothic STD 平成角ゴ STD

Font Development and Promotion Center

美しい日本語

タイポグラフィをクリスタルの杯にたとえたの
はビアトリス・ウォードでした。原作者の言葉
を正確に印刷された文字の配列に移し変えて、
読みやすい書籍を作ることがタイポグラフィの
役割だとウォードは考えていました。

w3

タイポグラフィをクリスタルの杯にたとえたの
はビアトリス・ウォードでした。原作者の言葉
を正確に印刷された文字の配列に移し変えて、
読みやすい書籍を作ることがタイポグラフィの
役割だとウォードは考えていました。

w5

**タイポグラフィをクリスタルの杯にたとえたの
はビアトリス・ウォードでした。原作者の言葉
を正確に印刷された文字の配列に移し変えて、
読みやすい書籍を作ることがタイポグラフィの
役割だとウォードは考えていました。**

w7

**タイポグラフィをクリスタルの杯にたとえたの
はビアトリス・ウォードでした。原作者の言葉
を正確に印刷された文字の配列に移し変えて、
読みやすい書籍を作ることがタイポグラフィの
役割だとウォードは考えていました。**

w9

Heisei Maru Gothic STD 平成丸ゴ STD

Font Development and Promotion Center

美しい日本語

タイポグラフィをクリスタルの杯にたとえたの
はビアトリス・ウォードでした。原作者の言葉
を正確に印刷された文字の配列に移し変えて、
読みやすい書籍を作ることがタイポグラフィの
役割だとウォードは考えていました。

w4

**タイポグラフィをクリスタルの杯にたとえたの
はビアトリス・ウォードでした。原作者の言葉
を正確に印刷された文字の配列に移し変えて、
読みやすい書籍を作ることがタイポグラフィの
役割だとウォードは考えていました。**

w8

Heisei Mincho STD 平成明朝 STD

Font Development and Promotion Center

美しい日本語

タイポグラフィをクリスタルの杯にたとえたの
はビアトリス・ウォードでした。原作者の言葉
を正確に印刷された文字の配列に移し変えて、
読みやすい書籍を作ることがタイポグラフィの
役割だとウォードは考えていました。

w3

タイポグラフィをクリスタルの杯にたとえたの
はビアトリス・ウォードでした。原作者の言葉
を正確に印刷された文字の配列に移し変えて、
読みやすい書籍を作ることがタイポグラフィの
役割だとウォードは考えていました。

W5

タイポグラフィをクリスタルの杯にたとえたの
はビアトリス・ウォードでした。原作者の言葉
を正確に印刷された文字の配列に移し変えて、
読みやすい書籍を作ることがタイポグラフィの
役割だとウォードは考えていました。

W7

タイポグラフィをクリスタルの杯にたとえたの
はビアトリス・ウォードでした。原作者の言葉
を正確に印刷された文字の配列に移し変えて、
読みやすい書籍を作ることがタイポグラフィの
役割だとウォードは考えていました。

W9

Kozuka Mincho PRO 小塚明朝 PRO

Masahiko Kozuka, Adobe Systems

美しい日本語

タイポグラフィをクリスタルの杯にたとえたの
はビアトリス・ウォードでした。原作者の言葉
を正確に印刷された文字の配列に移し変えて、
読みやすい書籍を作ることがタイポグラフィの
役割だとウォードは考えていました。

EXTRA LIGHT

タイポグラフィをクリスタルの杯にたとえたの
はビアトリス・ウォードでした。原作者の言葉
を正確に印刷された文字の配列に移し変えて、
読みやすい書籍を作ることがタイポグラフィの
役割だとウォードは考えていました。

LIGHT

タイポグラフィをクリスタルの杯にたとえたの
はビアトリス・ウォードでした。原作者の言葉
を正確に印刷された文字の配列に移し変えて、
読みやすい書籍を作ることがタイポグラフィの
役割だとウォードは考えていました。

REGULAR

タイポグラフィをクリスタルの杯にたとえたの
はビアトリス・ウォードでした。原作者の言葉
を正確に印刷された文字の配列に移し変えて、
読みやすい書籍を作ることがタイポグラフィの
役割だとウォードは考えていました。

MEDIUM

タイポグラフィをクリスタルの杯にたとえたの
はビアトリス・ウォードでした。原作者の言葉
を正確に印刷された文字の配列に移し変えて、
読みやすい書籍を作ることがタイポグラフィの
役割だとウォードは考えていました。

BOLD

タイポグラフィをクリスタルの杯にたとえたの
はビアトリス・ウォードでした。原作者の言葉
を正確に印刷された文字の配列に移し変えて、
読みやすい書籍を作ることがタイポグラフィの
役割だとウォードは考えていました。

HEAVY

Kozuka Gothic PRO 小塚ゴシック**PRO**

Masahiko Kozuka, Adobe Systems

美しい日本語

タイポグラフィをクリスタルの杯にたとえたの
はビアトリス・ウォードでした。原作者の言葉
を正確に印刷された文字の配列に移し変えて、
読みやすい書籍を作ることがタイポグラフィの
役割だとウォードは考えていました。

EXTRA LIGHT

タイポグラフィをクリスタルの杯にたとえたの
はビアトリス・ウォードでした。原作者の言葉
を正確に印刷された文字の配列に移し変えて、
読みやすい書籍を作ることがタイポグラフィの
役割だとウォードは考えていました。

LIGHT

タイポグラフィをクリスタルの杯にたとえたの
はビアトリス・ウォードでした。原作者の言葉
を正確に印刷された文字の配列に移し変えて、
読みやすい書籍を作ることがタイポグラフィの
役割だとウォードは考えていました。

REGULAR

タイポグラフィをクリスタルの杯にたとえたの
はビアトリス・ウォードでした。原作者の言葉
を正確に印刷された文字の配列に移し変えて、
読みやすい書籍を作ることがタイポグラフィの
役割だとウォードは考えていました。

MEDIUM

タイポグラフィをクリスタルの杯にたとえたの
はビアトリス・ウォードでした。原作者の言葉
を正確に印刷された文字の配列に移し変えて、
読みやすい書籍を作ることがタイポグラフィの
役割だとウォードは考えていました。

BOLD

**タイポグラフィをクリスタルの杯にたとえたの
はビアトリス・ウォードでした。原作者の言葉
を正確に印刷された文字の配列に移し変えて、
読みやすい書籍を作ることがタイポグラフィの
役割だとウォードは考えていました。**

HEAVY

Ryo Display STD りょう**Display STD**

Ryoko Nishizuka, Adobe Systems

いろはにほへと

タイポグラフィをクリスタルのさかづきにたと
えたのはビアトリスウォードでした。げんさく
しゃのことばをせいかくにいんさつされたもじ
のはいれつにうつしかえて、よみみやすいし

MEDIUM

タイポグラフィをクリスタルのさかづきにたと
えたのはビアトリスウォードでした。げんさく
しゃのことばをせいかくにいんさつされたもじ
のはいれつにうつしかえて、よみみやすいし

SEMI BOLD

タイポグラフィをクリスタルのさかづきにたと
えたのはビアトリスウォードでした。げんさく
しゃのことばをせいかくにいんさつされたもじ
のはいれつにうつしかえて、よみみやすいし

BOLD

タイポグラフィをクリスタルのさかづきにたと
えたのはビアトリスウォードでした。げんさく
しゃのことばをせいかくにいんさつされたもじ
のはいれつにうつしかえて、よみみやすいし

EXTRA BOLD

タイポグラフィをクリスタルのさかづきにたと
えたのはビアトリスウォードでした。げんさく
しゃのことばをせいかくにいんさつされたもじ
のはいれつにうつしかえて、よみみやすいし

HEAVY

Ryoko Nishizuka, Adobe Systems

いろはにほへと

タイポグラフィをクリスタルのさかづきにたと
えたのはビアトリスウォードでした。げんさく
しゃのことばをせいかくにいんさつされたもじ
のはいれつにうつしかえて、よみみやすいし

EXTRA LIGHT

タイポグラフィをクリスタルのさかづきにたと
えたのはビアトリスウォードでした。げんさく
しゃのことばをせいかくにいんさつされたもじ
のはいれつにうつしかえて、よみみやすいし

LIGHT

タイポグラフィをクリスタルのさかづきにたと
えたのはビアトリスウォードでした。げんさく
しゃのことばをせいかくにいんさつされたもじ
のはいれつにうつしかえて、よみみやすいし

REGULAR

タイポグラフィをクリスタルのさかづきにたと
えたのはビアトリスウォードでした。げんさく
しゃのことばをせいかくにいんさつされたもじ
のはいれつにうつしかえて、よみみやすいし

MEDIUM

The following books can be helpful in understanding more about the history, development, and use of typography.

Anatomy of a Typeface by Alexander Lawson (David R. Godine, 2002)

Collier's Rules for Desktop Design and Typography by David Collier (Reading: Riverside Printing Co. Ltd., 1992)

The Complete Manual of Typography by James Felici (San Jose: Adobe Press, 2002)

The Elements of Typographic Style, second edition by Robert Bringhurst (Vancouver: Hartley & Marks Publishers, 1996)

Encyclopaedia of Typefaces by W. Pincus Jaspert, W. Turner Berry, and A. F. Johnson (Seven Dials, 2001)

Graphic Design for the Electronic Age by Jan V. White (New York: Watson-Guptill, 1988)

Language Culture Type: International Type Design in the Age of Unicode by John D. Berry (Graphis Press, 2002)

Letter Forms: Typographic and Scriptorial by Stanley Morison (Hartley & Marks, 1997)

Looking Good in Print: fifth edition by Roger C. Parker (The Coriolis Group, 2000)

The New Typography: A Handbook for Modern Designers by Jan Tschichold, Ruari McLean, and Robin Kinross (University of California Press, 1998)

The Origin of the Serif: Brush Writing & Roman Letters, second edition by Edward M. Catich (Davenport, Iowa: Catich Gallery, St. Ambrose University, 1991)

Stop Stealing Sheep & Find Out How Type Works, second edition by Erik Spiekermann and E.M. Ginger (San Jose: Adobe Press, 2003)

The Thames and Hudson Manual of Typography by Ruari McLean (London: Thames and Hudson, 1988)

Type Rules! by Ilene Strizver (North Light Books, 2001)

TypeStyle: How to Choose and Use Type on a Personal Computer by Daniel Will-Harris (Berkeley: Peachpit Press, Inc., 1990)

Typographica by Rick Poyner (Princeton Architectural Press, 2001)

Typology: Type Design from the Victorian Era to the Digital Age by Steven Heller and Louise Fili (Chronicle Books, 1999)

Using Type Right: One Hundred Twenty-One No-Nonsense Rules for Working with Type by Phillip Brady (NTC/Contemporary Publishing Company, 1994)

Writing: The Story of Alphabets and Scripts by George Jean (New York: Harry N. Abrams, Inc., 1992)

Index de la liste alphabétique

Type designer names on pages 52–301 were originally researched by typographer E.M. Ginger with assistance from Robert Bringhurst. Current sources of information include:

Carter, Sebastian. *Twentieth Century Type Designers.* New York: W.W. Norton & Company, Inc., 1995.

Cleary, Ed, Jurgen Siebert, and Erik Spiekermann. *The FontBook.* Berlin: Fontshop International, 1993.

—*The FontBook,* vol 2. Berlin: Fontshop International, 1995.

Jaspert, Berry and Johnson. *Encyclopedia of Type Faces.* Poole, UK: Blandford Press, 1986.

Level, Jeff, Bruce Newman, and Brenda Newman. *Precision Type Font Reference Guide: The Complete Font Software Resource for Electronic Publishing,* sixth edition, Hartley & Marks, Inc., 2000.

McGrew, Mac. *American Metal Typefaces of the Twentieth Century.* Newcastle: Oak Knoll Books, 1993.

Adobe Western 2 Character Set

Character Name and Glyph Sample		Unicode	Windows U.S. Keyboard	Macintosh U.S. Keyboard	Character Name and Glyph Sample		Unicode	Windows U.S. Keyboard	Macintosh U.S. Keyboard
.notdef	⊠	N/A	N/A	N/A	F	F	0046	Shift+f	Shift+f
space		0020	space bar	space bar	G	G	0047	Shift+g	Shift+g
exclam	!	0021	Shift+1	Shift+1	H	H	0048	Shift+h	Shift+h
quotedbl	"	0022	Shift+'	Shift+'	I	I	0049	Shift+i	Shift+i
numbersign	#	0023	Shift+3	Shift+3	J	J	004A	Shift+j	Shift+j
dollar	$	0024	Shift+4	Shift+4	K	K	004B	Shift+k	Shift+k
percent	%	0025	Shift+5	Shift+5	L	L	004C	Shift+l	Shift+l
ampersand	&	0026	Shift+7	Shift+7	M	M	004D	Shift+m	Shift+m
quoteright	'	2019	Alt+0146	Shift+Option+]	N	N	004E	Shift+n	Shift+n
parenleft	(	0028	Shift+9	Shift+9	O	O	004F	Shift+o	Shift+o
parenright	)	0029	Shift+0	Shift+0	P	P	0050	Shift+p	Shift+p
asterisk	*	002A	Shift+8	Shift+8	Q	Q	0051	Shift+q	Shift+q
plus	+	002B	Shift+=	Shift+=	R	R	0052	Shift+r	Shift+r
comma	,	002C	,	,	S	S	0053	Shift+s	Shift+s
hyphen	-	002D	-	-	T	T	0054	Shift+t	Shift+t
period	.	002E	.	.	U	U	0055	Shift+u	Shift+u
slash	/	002F	/	/	V	V	0056	Shift+v	Shift+v
zero	0	0030	0	0	W	W	0057	Shift+w	Shift+w
one	1	0031	1	1	X	X	0058	Shift+x	Shift+x
two	2	0032	2	2	Y	Y	0059	Shift+y	Shift+y
three	3	0033	3	3	Z	Z	005A	Shift+z	Shift+z
four	4	0034	4	4	bracketleft	[	005B	[	[
five	5	0035	5	5	backslash	\	005C	\	\
six	6	0036	6	6	bracketright	]	005D	]	]
seven	7	0037	7	7	asciicircum	^	005E	Shift+6	Shift+6
eight	8	0038	8	8	underscore	_	005F	Shift+-	Shift+-
nine	9	0039	9	9	quoteleft	'	2018	Alt+0145	Option+]
colon	:	003A	Shift+;	Shift+;	a	a	0061	a	a
semicolon	;	003B	;	;	b	b	0062	b	b
less	<	003C	Shift+,	Shift+,	c	c	0063	c	c
equal	=	003D	=	=	d	d	0064	d	d
greater	>	003E	Shift+.	Shift+.	e	e	0065	e	e
question	?	003F	?	?	f	f	0066	f	f
at	@	0040	Shift+2	Shift+2	g	g	0067	g	g
A	A	0041	Shift+a	Shift+a	h	h	0068	h	h
B	B	0042	Shift+b	Shift+b	i	i	0069	i	i
C	C	0043	Shift+c	Shift+c	j	j	006A	j	j
D	D	0044	Shift+d	Shift+d	k	k	006B	k	k
E	E	0045	Shift+e	Shift+e	l	l	006C	l	l

Character Name and Glyph Sample		Unicode	Windows U.S. Keyboard	Macintosh U.S. Keyboard
m	m	006D	m	m
n	n	006E	n	n
o	o	006F	o	o
p	p	0070	p	p
q	q	0071	q	q
r	r	0072	r	r
s	s	0073	s	s
t	t	0074	t	t
u	u	0075	u	u
v	v	0076	v	v
w	w	0077	w	w
x	x	0078	x	x
y	y	0079	y	y
z	z	007A	z	z
braceleft	{	007B	Shift+[	Shift+[
bar	|	007C	Shift+\	Shift+\
braceright	}	007D	Shift+]	Shift+]
asciitilde	~	007E	Shift+`	Shift+`
exclamdown	¡	00A1	Alt+0161	Option+1
cent	¢	00A2	Alt+0162	Option+4
sterling	£	00A3	Alt+0163	Option+3
fraction	⁄	2044	Char. Map, General Punct.	Shift+Option+1
yen	¥	00A5	Alt+0165	Option+y
florin	ƒ	0192	Alt+0131	Option+f
section	§	00A7	Alt+0167	Option+6
currency	¤	00A4	Alt+0164	Char. Palette
quotesingle	'	0027	'	'
quotedblleft	"	201C	Alt+0147	Option+[
guillemotleft	«	00AB	Alt+0171	Option+\
guilsinglleft	‹	2039	Alt+0139	Shift+Option+3
guilsinglright	›	203A	Alt+0155	Shift+Option+4
endash	–	2013	Alt+0150	Option+-
dagger	†	2020	Alt+0133	Option+t
daggerdbl	‡	2021	Alt+0135	Shift+Option+7
periodcentered	·	00B7	Alt+0183	Shift+Option+9
paragraph	¶	00B6	Alt+0182	Option+7
bullet	•	2022	Alt+0149	Option+8
quotesinglbase	‚	201A	Alt+0130	Shift+Option+0

Character Name and Glyph Sample		Unicode	Windows U.S. Keyboard	Macintosh U.S. Keyboard
quotedblbase	„	201E	Alt+0132	Shift+Option+w
quotedblright	"	201D	Alt+0148	Shift+Option+[
guillemotright	»	00BB	Alt+0187	Shift+Option+\
ellipsis	…	2026	Alt+0133	Option+;
perthousand	‰	2030	Alt+0137	Shift+Option+r
questiondown	¿	00BF	Alt+0191	Shift+Option+/
grave	`	0060	`	` (or Shift+Option+`
acute	´	00B4	Alt+0180	Shift+Option+e
circumflex	ˆ	02C6	Alt+0136	Shift+Option+i
tilde	˜	02DC	Alt+0152	Shift+Option+n
macron	¯	00AF	Alt+0175	Shift+Option+,
breve	˘	02D8	Char. Map, Spacing Mod. Letters	Shift+Option+.
dotaccent	˙	02D9	Char. Map, Spacing Mod. Letters	Option+h
dieresis	¨	00A8	Alt+0168	Shift+Option+u
ring	°	02DA	Char. Map, Spacing Mod. Letters	Option+k
cedilla	¸	00B8	Alt+0184	Shift+Option+z
hungarumlaut	˝	02DD	Char. Map, Spacing Mod. Letters	Shift+Option+g
ogonek	˛	02DB	Char. Map, Spacing Mod. Letters	Shift+Option+x
caron	ˇ	02C7	Char. Map, Spacing Mod. Letters	Shift+Option+t
emdash	—	2014	Alt+0151	Shift+Option+-
AE	Æ	00C6	Alt+0198	Shift+Option+'
ordfeminine	ª	00AA	Alt+0170	Option+9
Lslash	Ł	0141	Char. Map, Latin	Char. Palette
Oslash	Ø	00D8	Alt+0216	Shift+Option+o
OE	Œ	0152	Alt+0140	Shift+Option+q
ordmasculine	º	00BA	Alt+0186	Option+0
ae	æ	00E6	Alt+0230	Option+'
dotlessi	ı	0131	Char. Map, Latin	Shift+Option+b
lslash	ł	0142	Char. Map, Latin	Char. Palette
oslash	ø	00F8	Alt+0248	Option+o
oe	œ	0153	Alt+0156	Option+q
germandbls	ß	00DF	Alt+0223	Option+s

Adobe Western 2 Character Set

Character Name and Glyph Sample		Unicode	Windows U.S. Keyboard	Macintosh U.S. Keyboard
logicalnot	¬	00AC	Alt+0172	Option+l
uni00B5	µ	00B5	Alt+0181	Option+m
trademark	™	2122	Alt+0153	Option+2
Eth	Ð	00D0	Alt+0208	Char. Palette
onehalf	½	00BD	Alt+0189	Char. Palette
plusminus	±	00B1	Alt+0177	Shift+Option+=
Thorn	Þ	00DE	Alt+0222	Char. Palette
onequarter	¼	00BC	Alt+0188	Char. Palette
divide	÷	00F7	Alt+0247	Option+/
brokenbar	¦	00A6	Alt+0166	Char. Palette
degree	°	00B0	Alt+0176	Shift+Option+8
thorn	þ	00FE	Alt+0254	Char. Palette
threequarters	¾	00BE	Alt+0190	Char. Palette
registered	®	00AE	Alt+0174	Option+r
minus	−	2212	Char. Map, Math. Operators	Char. Palette
eth	ð	00F0	Alt+0240	Char. Palette
multiply	×	00D7	Alt+0215	Char. Palette
copyright	©	00A9	Alt+0169	Option+g
Aacute	Á	00C1	Alt+0193	(Option+e)+(Shift+a)
Acircumflex	Â	00C2	Alt+0194	(Option+i)+(Shift+a)
Adieresis	Ä	00C4	Alt+0196	(Option+u)+(Shift+a)
Agrave	À	00C0	Alt+0192	(Option+`)+(Shift+a)
Aring	Å	00C5	Alt+0197	Shift+Option+a
Atilde	Ã	00C3	Alt+0195	(Option+n)+(Shift+a)
Ccedilla	Ç	00C7	Alt+0199	Shift+Option+c
Eacute	É	00C9	Alt+0201	(Option+e)+(Shift+e)
Ecircumflex	Ê	00CA	Alt+0202	(Option+i)+(Shift+e)
Edieresis	Ë	00CB	Alt+0203	(Option+u)+(Shift+e)
Egrave	È	00C8	Alt+0200	(Option+`)+(Shift+e)
Iacute	Í	00CD	Alt+0205	(Option+e)+(Shift+i)
Icircumflex	Î	00CE	Alt+0206	(Option+i)+(Shift+i)
Idieresis	Ï	00CF	Alt+0207	(Option+u)+(Shift+i)
Igrave	Ì	00CC	Alt+0204	(Option+`)+(Shift+i)
Ntilde	Ñ	00D1	Alt+0209	(Option+n)+(Shift+n)
Oacute	Ó	00D3	Alt+0211	(Option+e)+(Shift+o)
Ocircumflex	Ô	00D4	Alt+0212	(Option+i)+(Shift+o)
Odieresis	Ö	00D6	Alt+0214	(Option+u)+(Shift+o)
Ograve	Ò	00D2	Alt+0210	(Option+`)+(Shift+o)

Character Name and Glyph Sample		Unicode	Windows U.S. Keyboard	Macintosh U.S. Keyboard
Otilde	Õ	00D5	Alt+0213	(Option+n)+(Shift+o)
Scaron	Š	0160	Alt+0138	Char. Palette
Uacute	Ú	00DA	Alt+0218	(Option+e)+(Shift+u)
Ucircumflex	Û	00DB	Alt+0219	(Option+i)+(Shift+u)
Udieresis	Ü	00DC	Alt+0220	(Option+u)+(Shift+u)
Ugrave	Ù	00D9	Alt+0217	(Option+`)+(Shift+u)
Yacute	Ý	00DD	Alt+0221	Char. Palette
Ydieresis	Ÿ	0178	Alt+0159	(Option+u)+(Shift+y)
Zcaron	Ž	017D	Alt+0142	Char. Palette
aacute	á	00E1	Alt+0225	(Option+e)+a
acircumflex	â	00E2	Alt+0226	(Option+i)+a
adieresis	ä	00E4	Alt+0228	(Option+u)+a
agrave	à	00E0	Alt+0224	(Option+`)+a
aring	å	00E5	Alt+0229	Option+a
atilde	ã	00E3	Alt+0227	(Option+n)+a
ccedilla	ç	00E7	Alt+0231	Option+c
eacute	é	00E9	Alt+0233	(Option+e)+e
ecircumflex	ê	00EA	Alt+0234	(Option+i)+e
edieresis	ë	00EB	Alt+0235	(Option+u)+e
egrave	è	00E8	Alt+0232	(Option+`)+e
iacute	í	00ED	Alt+0237	(Option+e)+i
icircumflex	î	00EE	Alt+0238	(Option+i)+i
idieresis	ï	00EF	Alt+0239	(Option+u)+i
igrave	ì	00EC	Alt+0236	(Option+`)+i
ntilde	ñ	00F1	Alt+0241	(Option+n)+n
oacute	ó	00F3	Alt+0243	(Option+e)+o
ocircumflex	ô	00F4	Alt+0244	(Option+i)+o
odieresis	ö	00F6	Alt+0246	(Option+u)+o
ograve	ò	00F2	Alt+0242	(Option+`)+o
otilde	õ	00F5	Alt+0245	(Option+n)+o
scaron	š	0161	Alt+0154	Char. Palette
uacute	ú	00FA	Alt+0250	(Option+e)+u
ucircumflex	û	00FB	Alt+0251	(Option+i)+u
udieresis	ü	00FC	Alt+0252	(Option+u)+u
ugrave	ù	00F9	Alt+0249	(Option+`)+u
yacute	ý	00FD	Alt+0253	Char. Palette
ydieresis	ÿ	00FF	Alt+0255	(Option+u)+y
zcaron	ž	017E	Alt+0158	Char. Palette

Character Name and Glyph Sample		Unicode	Windows U.S. Keyboard	Macintosh U.S. Keyboard
f_i	fi	FB01	Char. Map, Latin	Shift+Option+5
f_l	fl	FB02	Char. Map, Latin	Shift+Option+6
one.superior	¹	00B9	Alt+0185	Char. Palette
two.superior	²	00B2	Alt+0178	Char. Palette
three.superior	³	00B3	Alt+0179	Char. Palette
uni2126	Ω	2126	Char. Map, Letterlike Symbols	Option+z
pi	π	03C0	Char. Map, Greek	Option+p
Euro	€	20AC	Alt+0128	Shift+Option+2
afii61289	ℓ	2113	Char. Map, Letterlike Symbols	Char. Palette
estimated	℮	212E	Char. Map, Letterlike Symbols	Char. Palette
partialdiff	∂	2202	Char. Map, Math. Operators	Option+d
uni2206	Δ	2206	Char. Map, Math. Operators	Option+j
product	∏	220F	Char. Map, Math. Operators	Shift+Option+p
summation	Σ	2211	Char. Map, Math. Operators	Option+w
radical	√	221A	Char. Map, Math. Operators	Option+v
infinity	∞	221E	Char. Map, Math. Operators	Option+5
integral	∫	222B	Char. Map, Math. Operators	Option+b
approxequal	≈	2248	Char. Map, Math. Operators	Option+x
notequal	≠	2260	Char. Map, Math. Operators	Option+=
lessequal	≤	2264	Char. Map, Math. Operators	Option+,
greaterequal	≥	2265	Char. Map, Math. Operators	Option+.
lozenge	◊	25CA	Char. Map, Block Elem. & Geo.	Shift+Option+v

The above keyboard descriptions are based on the U.S. English keyboard. All characters in the Adobe Western 2 character set can be entered into any Adobe application with a "Glyph Palette," such as Adobe InDesign.

Windows For Windows, the (Alt key+number) combination is typed by holding down the Alt key while typing the number using the number keys found on the numeric keypad (it does not work with the number keys on the top horizontal row of the main keyboard). For Windows laptop computer users, a virtual numeric keypad can usually be activated by turning on the "num lock" key and using the following keys (7, 8, 9, U, I, O, J, K, L, M).

On Windows, the (Alt key+number) combination does not access every character in Adobe Western 2. However on Windows 2000 and XP, the additional characters can still be found and entered into a document through the "Character Map" utility found under Windows' Start menu Programs Accessories System Tools Character Map. After launching the Character Map utility, choose "Unicode Subrange" under the "Group by:" pop-up window. For example, under the "Greek" sub-range, the pi (π) glyph can be found.

In Microsoft Word, another method to enter glyphs is to type in a character's 4-digit hexadecimal Unicode value followed by the 2 keys: (Alt+x).

Mac OS For Macintosh, when a character's keyboard entry is listed above in the form of "(Option+e)+(Shift+a)," this indicates the need to: while holding the Option key down, press the "e" key, release both keys, press and keep holding down the Shift key, press the "a" key, then release both keys. The resulting "Aacute" (Á) character will be entered into the document.

Not all Adobe Western 2 characters can be entered through standard Macintosh keyboard key combinations. However, they can be accessed through Mac OS X's "Character Palette." The Character Palette is not turned on by default. To turn it on, select the System Preferences -> International -> Input Menu tab and click on "Character Palette." The Character Palette icon will then appear towards the top right of the active application's menu bar. Click on the icon's menu and select "Show Character Palette." Click on the "Unicode Table" tab and scroll to find the Unicode hexadecimal value corresponding to the desired glyph. Once the glyph is found, click on it and then click on the "Insert" button. The glyph should now be entered into an open editable document. (Note: it may be necessary to first change the currently selected font in your application to match the font that you intend to use for the inserted character.)

www.adobe.com/type